A VOYAGE TO TERRA AUSTRALIS

BY MATTHEW FLINDERS

VOLUME 2

IN THE ATLAS.

Plate.

I. General Chart of TERRA AUSTRALIS and the neighbouring lands, from latitude 7° to 44½° south, and longitude 102° to 165° east.

II. Particular chart of the South Coast, from Cape Leeuwin to the Archipelago of the Recherche.

III. Ditto from the Archipelago of the Recherche to past the head of the great Australian Bight.

IV. Ditto from the head of the great Australian Bight to past Encounter Bay.

V. Ditto from near Encounter Bay to Cape Otway at the west entrance of Bass' Strait.

VI. Ditto from Cape Otway, past Cape Howe, to Barmouth Creek.

VII. Particular chart of Van Diemen's Land.

(Detail from Plate VII.)

VIII. Particular chart of the East Coast, from Barmouth Creek to past Cape Hawke.

IX. Ditto from near Cape Hawke to past Glass-house Bay.

X. Ditto from Glass-house Bay to Broad Sound.

XI. Ditto from Broad Sound to Cape Grafton.

XII. Ditto from Cape Grafton to the Isle of Direction.

XIII. Particular chart of the East Coast from the I. of Direction to Cape York, and of the North Coast from thence to Pera Head; including Torres Strait and parts of New Guinea.

XIV. A particular chart of the North Coast, from Torres' Strait to Point Dale and the Wessel's Islands, including the whole of the Gulph of Carpentaria.

XV. The north-west side of the Gulph of Carpentaria, on a large scale.

XVI. Particular chart of Timor and some neighbouring islands.

XVII. Fourteen views of headlands, etc. on the south coast of Terra Australis.

XVIII. Thirteen views on the east and north coasts, and one of Samow Strait.

(Detail from Plate XVIII.)

AND

Ten plates of selected plants from different parts of Terra Australis.

(Detail from Plate 10.)

BOOK II.

TRANSACTIONS DURING THE CIRCUMNAVIGATION OF TERRA AUSTRALIS, FROM THE TIME OF LEAVING PORT JACKSON TO THE RETURN TO THAT PORT.

CHAPTER I.

Departure from Port Jackson, with the Lady Nelson.
Examination of various parts of the East Coast, from thence to Sandy Cape.
Break-sea Spit.
Anchorage in Hervey's Bay, where the Lady Nelson joins after a separation.
Some account of the inhabitants.
Variations of the compass.
Run to Bustard Bay.
Port Curtis discovered, and examined.
Some account of the surrounding country.
Arrival in Keppel Bay, and examination of its branches,
one of which leads into Port Curtis.
Some account of the natives, and of the country round Keppel Bay.
Astronomical and nautical observations.

[EAST COAST. TOWARDS HERVEY'S BAY.]
THURSDAY 22 JULY 1802

Lieutenant John Murray, commander of the brig Lady Nelson, having received orders to put himself under my command, I gave him a small code of signals, and directed him, in case of separation, to repair to Hervey's Bay; which he was to enter by a passage said to have been found by the south-sea whalers, between Sandy Cape and Break-sea Spit. In the morning of July 22, we sailed out of Port Jackson together; and the breeze being fair and fresh, ran rapidly to the northward, keeping at a little distance from the coast. (Atlas, Plate VIII.)

At eleven o'clock, the south head of Broken Bay bore W. by N. three leagues; and Mr. Westall then made a sketch of the entrance, with that of the Hawkesbury River, which falls into it (Atlas, Plate XVIII, View 2). The colonists have called this place Broken Bay, but it is not what was so named by captain Cook; for he says it lies in latitude 33° 42' (Hawkesworth III. 103), whereas the southernmost point of entrance is not further than 33° 34' south. There is, in captain Cook's latitude, a very small opening, and the hills behind it answer to his description of "some broken land that seemed to form a bay," when seen at four leagues, the distance he was off; but in reality, there is nothing more than a shallow lagoon in that place. In consequence of this difference in position, Cape Three-points has been sought three or four leagues to the north of Broken Bay; whereas it is the north head of the entrance into the bay itself which was so named, and it corresponds both in situation and appearance.

At noon, the south-eastern bluff of Cape Three-points bore S. 64° W., seven or eight miles, and was found to lie in 33° 32½' south and 151° 23½' east. In steering northward along the coast, at from six to two miles distance, we passed two rocky islets lying under the high shore; and at sunset, Coal Island, in the entrance of Port Hunter, bore N. 9° W., five or six miles. This port was discovered in 1797 by the late captain John Shortland, and lies in 32° 56' south, longitude 151° 43' east.

We passed Port Stephens a little before midnight; and the breeze being fresh at W. by S., the Lady Nelson was left astern, and we lay to for an hour next morning [FRIDAY 23 JULY 1802], to wait her coming up. The land was then scarcely visible, but a north course brought us in with the Three Brothers (Atlas Plate IX.); and at four in the afternoon, they bore from S. 56° to 65° W., the nearest land being a low, but steep point, distant four or five miles in the first direction. The Three Brothers lie from one to five miles behind the shore, at the eastern extremity of a range of high land, coming out of the interior country. The northernmost hill is the broadest, most elevated, and nearest to the water side; and being visible fifty miles from a ship's deck, is an excellent landmark for vessels passing along the coast: its latitude is 31° 43' south, and longitude 152° 45' east.

To the northward of the Three Brothers there is four leagues of low, and mostly sandy shore; and after passing it, we came up with a projection, whose top is composed of small, irregular-shaped hummocks, the northernmost of them being a rocky lump of a sugar-loaf form; further on, the land falls back into a shallow bight, with rocks in it standing above water. When abreast of the projection, which was called *Tacking Point*, the night was closing in, and we stood off shore, intending to make the same part next morning; for some of this coast had been passed in the dark by captain Cook, and might therefore contain openings.

SATURDAY 24 JULY 1802

At daybreak of the 24th, Tacking Point was distant three miles, and the breeze fresh at S. W. by W. with fine weather. Our little consort being out of sight, we stood an hour to the southward; and not seeing her in that direction, bore away along the coast until noon, when our situation was as under:

Latitude observed 30° 58¼' Longitude by time-keepers 153 6½ Northern Brother, dist. 48 miles, bore S. 23 W. Smoky Cape, distant 3 or 4 miles, N. 41° to 30 W. Northern extreme of the land, N. 5 W.

The coast from Tacking Point to Smoky Cape is generally low and sandy; but its uniformity is broken at intervals by rocky points, which first appear like islands. Behind them the land is low, but quickly rises to hills of a moderate height; and these being well covered with wood, the country had a pleasant appearance. Smoky Cape was found to answer the description given of it by captain Cook; its centre lies in 30° 55' south, and 153° 4' east. The three hummocks upon it stand on so many projecting parts; and at half a mile from the southernmost lie two rocks, and a third two miles further south, which were not before noticed. On the north side of Smoky Cape, the coast falls back four or five miles to the westward, forming a bight in the low land, where there may probably be a shallow inlet; it afterwards resumed a northern direction, and consisted as before of sandy beaches and stony points.

Our consort was not yet in sight; but we kept on until five in the evening, when the nearest land was two miles off, and the northern hummock on Smoky Cape bore S. 4° W. nine leagues. I had before seen the coast further northward, as far as 29° 20'; and having therefore no inducement to lose a night's run for its examination, we steered onward, passing without side of the Solitary Isles. At three in the morning [SUNDAY 25 JULY 1802], hove to until day-light; and at eight o'clock made the south head of a bay discovered in the Norfolk (Introd. Vol I, "In latitude 29° 43', we discovered a small opening like a river, with an islet lying in the entrance; and at sunset, entered a larger, to which I gave the name of SHOAL BAY, an appellation which it but too well merited."), and named *Shoal Bay*. One of the marks for finding this small place is a peaked hummock on the low land, thirteen miles distant; and it was now set over the south head of the bay at S. 20° W. In steering northward close along the coast, we passed two small reefs, and the water shoaled to 10 fathoms; they lie two miles off the land, and there did not seem to be any safe passage within them. Our latitude at noon was 29° 4', and longitude by time keepers 153° 31'; the shore was three miles off but until we came up with Cape Byron at five in the evening, there was no projection worthy of being particularly noticed. From Shoal Bay to Cape Byron is fifty miles, where the coast, with the exception of two or three rocky heads, is mostly low and sandy; and the soundings, at from two to four miles off, vary between 10 and 32 fathoms, on a sandy bottom. A few miles back the land rises to hills of moderate elevation, which were poorly covered with wood in the southern part, but towards the cape had a more fertile appearance.

Cape Byron is a small steep head, projecting about two miles from the low land, and in coming along the coast makes like an island; its latitude is 28° 38', and longitude 153° 37', or 7' east of the situation assigned to it by captain Cook. There are three rocks on its north side; and in the direction of N. 57° W., eight or nine leagues from it, is the peaked top of a mass of mountains, named by its discoverer *Mount Warning*, whose elevation is about 3300 feet, and exceeds that of Mount Dromedary, or any other land I have seen upon this East Coast. To Mr. Westall's sketch of this remarkable peak (Atlas, Plate XVIII. View 3.) it may be added, that the surrounding hills were well covered with wood, whose foliage announced a soil more fertile than usual so near the sea side.

The sun was near setting at the time Cape Byron bore west, three or four miles; and the coast from thence to Point Look-out having been seen by captain Cook, we steered off in order to avoid falling in with the reefs of Point Danger in the night. At eleven, hauled more in for the land; and at eight next day [MONDAY 26 JULY 1802], Mount Warning was set at S. 25° W., twenty leagues. On coming in with Point Look-out, I took observations for the latitude and longitude, which fixed it in 27° 27' south, and 153° 31' east. The latitude is the same as it had been made in the Norfolk, (Introd. Vol. I), but is 19' south, and 3' west of the situation given in captain Cook's chart. The bearings of the land at noon were,

Point Look-out, distant 3 leagues,   S. 9° W. Moreton entrance to Glass-house Bay, S. 55 W. Cape Moreton, distant six leagues,   N. 18 W.

A strange vessel seen to the southward, had induced me to carry little sail all the morning; it was now perceived not to be the Lady Nelson, but probably one of the two whalers known to be fishing off the coast; we therefore made sail for Cape Moreton, and came up with it at four o'clock. I was much surprised to see a small, but dangerous reef lying between four and five miles off this cape to the north-east, which had not been noticed in the Norfolk; in entering Glass-house Bay I had then hauled close round Cape Moreton at dusk in the evening, and in coming out had passed too far westward to observe it. The longitude of Cape Moreton was now fixed by the time keepers at 153° 26½' east, differing only 1½' from the lunar observations before taken in the Norfolk; when its latitude had been settled at 27° 0½' south.

(Atlas, Plate X.)
TUESDAY 27 JULY 1802
After passing the dangerous reef, we steered northward until three in the morning; and then hove to until daylight, for the purpose of examining the land about Double-island Point and Wide Bay, which did not appear to have been well distinguished by captain Cook. At seven o'clock the point bore N. 2° W., six leagues, and the shore abreast, a beach with

3

sandy hills behind it, was distant six miles. Between the S. 63. W. and a low bluff head bearing S. 32° W., was a bight in the coast where the sand hills seemed to terminate; for the back land further south was high and rocky with small peaks on the top, similar to the ridge behind the Glass Houses, of which it is probably a continuation.

At half past nine we hauled close round Double-island Point, within a rock lying between one and two miles to the N. N. E., having 7 fathoms for the least water. The point answered captain Cook's description: it is a steep head, at the extremity of a neck of land which runs out two miles from the main, and lies in 25° 56' south, and 153° 13' east. On the north side of the point the coast falls back to the westward, and presents a steep shore of white sand; but in curving round Wide Bay the sandy land becomes very low, and a small opening was seen in it, leading to a piece of water like a lagoon; but the shoals which lie off the entrance render it difficult of access, if indeed there be a passage for any thing larger than boats. Had the Lady Nelson been with me, I should have attempted to get her into the lagoon, having previously entertained a conjecture that the head of Hervey's Bay might communicate with Wide Bay; but the apprehension that lieutenant Murray would arrive at the first rendezvous, and proceed to the next before we could join him, deterred me from attempting it with the Investigator or with boats.

Upon the north side of the opening there was a number of Indians, fifty as reported, looking at the ship, and near Double-island Point ten others had been seen, implying a more numerous population than is usual to the southward. I inferred from hence, that the piece of water at the head of Wide Bay was extensive and shallow; for in such places the natives draw much subsistence from the fish which there abound, and are more easily caught than in deep water. So far as could be seen from the mast head at three or four miles off, the water extended about five miles westward, to the feet of some hills covered with small wood. Its extent north and south could not be distinguished, and it seemed probable that one, and perhaps two streams fall into it; for there were many large medusas floating at the entrance, such as are usually found near the mouths of rivers in this country.

We passed the shoals of Wide Bay in from 12 to 5 fathoms water; and steered northward at the distance of six, and from that to two miles off the shore, until dark. Captain Cook describes this part of the coast as moderately high and very barren; there being great patches of moveable sand many acres in extent, through which appeared in some places the green tops of trees half buried, and in others the naked trunks of such as the sand had destroyed. We sailed some miles nearer to it than the Endeavour had done, and saw extensive, bare patches in many parts; but nothing to indicate the sands being moveable; and in general, there were shrubs, bushes, and some trees scattered over the hills in front of the sea. Nothing however can well be imagined more barren than this peninsula; but the smokes which arose from many parts, corroborated the remark made upon the population about Wide Bay; and bespoke that fresh water was not scarce in this sandy country.

Our course at night was directed by the fires on the shore, and the wind being moderate from the south-westward, it was continued until ten o'clock; after which we stood off and on till daylight [WEDNESDAY 28 JULY 1802], and then had Indian Head bearing S. 54° W. one mile and a half. This head was so named by captain Cook, from the great number of Indians assembled there in 1770. Mr. Westall's sketch of it (Atlas, Plate XVIII, View 4.), taken as we steered close along the shore for Sandy Cape, will show that the same sterility prevailed here as in the southern part of the peninsula; and it continued to the northern extremity.

At eleven o'clock we reached Sandy Cape, and the master was sent ahead to sound in a small passage through Break-sea Spit. The ship followed under easy sail, until we got into 3 fathoms; and the master not making the signal for any deeper water, I tacked and called the boat on board. The channel appeared to go quite through the Spit, into Hervey's Bay; but as there were, in many parts, not more than 2 fathoms, it can be passed only by small vessels. At noon,

Sandy Cape, distant a miles, bore S. 64° to 80° W. Indian Head, distant 7 leagues, S. 12 E.

Our observations fixed Sandy Cape in 24° 42' south, and 153°' 16' east, being 3' north, and 7' east of the position assigned to it by captain Cook.

[EAST COAST. HERVEY'S BAY.]

At one o'clock we steered northward, close to the edge of Break-sea Spit, searching for a passage through it into Hervey's Bay. There were many small winding channels amongst the breakers, and a larger being perceived at three, the boat was sent to make an examination; in the mean time, the wind having shifted to north-west and become very light, we dropped the stream anchor two miles from the Spit, in 11 fathoms, fine grey sand. The channel where the boat was sounding, and out of which a tide came of more than one mile an hour, bore W. by N.½ N., and Sandy Cape S. 24° to 41° W., about three leagues.

Soon after sunset the master returned, and reported the channel to be nearly a mile and a half wide, and that it went quite through to the bay; but it did not generally contain more than fourteen feet water, and was therefore impassable for the Investigator. The bottom of this, and of the former small channel, as also the shoaler banks of the Spit, were of coral, mixed with coral sand.

THURSDAY 29 JULY 1802

At three in the morning, on a breeze springing up at S. W. by S., we stretched south-eastward; and a vessel having been observed over night off Indian Head, this tack was prolonged till seven o'clock; when seeing nothing of her, we stood back for the Spit, and coasted close along its east side as before, in from 10 to 5 fathoms water. At forty minutes after noon we passed over the tail of the Spit, in latitude 24° 24'; the water then deepening suddenly from 6 and 7, to 22 fathoms, and the white patches on Sandy Cape bearing S. 8° E. In standing N. W. by W. we crossed a bank in 11 fathoms, and on tacking, passed another part of it with only 5; the water upon it was not discoloured, nor had it been observed either by captain Cook, or by me in the Norfolk: it lies about 6 miles W. N. W. from the end of Break-sea Spit.

The first rendezvous appointed for lieutenant Murray, was the anchorage near Sandy Cape; but the wind being unfavourable, we did not reach it till four on the following afternoon [FRIDAY 30 JULY 1802]; at which time the anchor was dropped in 7 fathoms, sandy bottom, with the outer extremity of the cape bearing S. 79° E., and the nearest part distant two miles. A vessel was seen on the outside of the Spit, which proved to be the Lady Nelson; and the master being sent with a boat to assist her through the passage, she anchored near us at sunset, and lieutenant Murray came on board. The account he gave of his separation, and the delay in arriving at the rendezvous, convinced me both of the Lady Nelson being an indifferent vessel, and of the truth of an observation before made upon the currents: that they run much stronger to the southward at the distance of six, and from that to twenty leagues off the coast, than they do close in with the shore. Mr. Murray not being much accustomed to make free with the land, had kept it barely within sight, and had been much retarded.

In order to give the botanists an opportunity of examining the productions of Sandy Cape, I determined to remain here a day; and some natives being seen upon the beach, a boat was sent to commence an acquaintance with them; they however retired, and suffered Mr. Brown to botanise without disturbance. Next morning [SATURDAY 31 July 1802] the brig anchored within a quarter of a mile of the shore, to cover our landing parties; and the armed boats being moored as grapnels, out of the reach of the natives, we separated into three divisions. The naturalist's party, consisting of six persons, walked along the shore towards the upper part of the bay; Mr. Murray and his people went to cut wood for fuel; and the party with me, also of six persons, including my native friend *Bongaree*, went towards the extremity of Sandy Cape. Several Indians with branches of trees in their hands, were there collected; and whilst they retreated themselves, were waving to us to go back. Bongaree stripped off his clothes and laid aside his spear, as inducements for them to wait for him; but finding they did not understand his language, the poor fellow, in the simplicity of his heart, addressed them in broken English, hoping to succeed better. At length they suffered him to come up, and by degrees our whole party joined; and after receiving some presents, twenty of them returned with us to the boats, and were feasted upon the blubber of two porpoises, which had been brought on shore purposely for them. At two o'clock the naturalists returned, bringing some of the scoop nets used by the natives in catching fish; and we then quitted our new friends, after presenting them with hatchets and other testimonials of our satisfaction.

These people go entirely naked, and otherwise much resemble the inhabitants of Port Jackson in personal appearance; but they were more fleshy, perhaps from being able to obtain a better supply of food with the scoop nets, which are not known on the southern parts of the coast. I noticed in most of them a hard tumour on the outer knuckle of the wrist, which, if we understood them aright, was caused by the stretcher of the scoop coming in contact with this part in the act of throwing the net. Our native did not understand a word of their language, nor did they seem to know the use of his *womerah* or throwing stick; for one of them being invited to imitate Bongaree, who lanced a spear with it very dexterously and to a great distance, he, in the most awkward manner, threw both womerah and spear together. Nothing like a canoe was seen amongst these people; but they must have some means of passing over the water to short distances, since I found, in 1799, that Curlew Islet, near the head of this bay, had been visited.

A species of *pandanus* before found at Glass-house and Shoal Bays, grows in abundance upon Sandy Cape; and notwithstanding the extreme sterility of the soil, the sand hills were mostly covered with bushes, and the vallies contained trees of the *casuarina* and *eucalyptus*. There was fresh water in a pool near the shore, and as a ship may lie within half a mile, both wood and water might be procured here without great difficulty; but I doubt if the water would not altogether fail in the dry season.

A tolerably regular tide set past the ship, N. N. E. and S. S. W., nearly one mile an hour; and it appeared by the shore to be high water *about eight hours after* the moon's passage, and the common rise to be between six and seven feet.

No mention has been made of the variation of the compass since leaving Port Jackson, A gradual diminution seems to take place from Twofold Bay, near the southern extremity of this coast, to Sandy Cape; as will appear from the following observations.

Lat. 37° 4' Azim., one compass, on shore,   9° 29' E.   33 52 do ,   do
 , do ,   8 51   31 36   do ,   do , head north,   9 8   30 32
do , three comp.,   do   ,   8 42   26 10   do , one comp., head N. by W.   8° 40', corr. 8 7   25 0 Ampl.,   do , head N. W. by N. 9 39 , corr. 8 9   24 43   do ,
do , head S. E. ½ S. 6 33 , corr 8 14

The coast lies nearly north, and except Sandy Cape, appears to be mostly of free stone, which I have not found to produce any effect upon the needle; and what is remarkable, on comparing my observations with those of captain Cook, it appeared that little or no change had taken place in the variation, during thirty-two years; for wherever our observations were taken with the ships heads in the same direction, there the same variation was obtained to a few minutes.

Within Break-sea Spit, an amplitude gave the variation when corrected, 7° 25' east; and one taken at the anchorage near Sandy Cape, but uncorrected, the direction of the ship's head being unknown, 7° 57' east. There is little doubt that on bringing the land to the eastward of the ship, the variation was diminished at least half a degree: the stone of Sandy Cape is granitic.

SUNDAY 1 AUGUST 1802

In the morning of August 1, the wind was from the southward, and we steered across Hervey's Bay, towards a sloping hummock on the west side, where my examination in the Norfolk had terminated. The soundings increased from 7, gradually to 18 fathoms, and afterwards decreased till half past four in the afternoon; when the sloping hummock bore S. 2° E. eight miles, and we had no more than 3½ fathoms near some dry banks and breakers, which extend out three miles from two shallow inlets in the coast. At dusk the anchor was let go in 6½ fathoms, mud and sand; the shallow inlets to the south being distant 6 miles, and the sloping hummock bearing S. 17° E. In captain Cook's chart, the width of Hervey's Bay is fifty-nine miles, which had appeared to me too great when here in the Norfolk; and I now made the distance, from the north-west extremity of Sandy Cape to a low point running out from the hummock, to be forty three miles by the *time keepers*. Such errors as this are almost unavoidable without the aid of these instruments, when sailing either along a coast which lies nearly on the same parallel, or where no land is in sight to correct the longitude by bearings. From Port Jackson to Sandy Cape, captain Cook's positions had been found to differ from mine, not more than from 10' east to 7' west; which must be considered a great degree of accuracy, considering the expeditious manner in which he sailed along the coast, and that there were no time keepers on board the Endeavour; but from Sandy Cape northward, where the direction of the coast has a good deal of westing in it, greater differences began to show themselves.

[EAST COAST. NEAR BUSTARD BAY.]

There was a little tide running past the ship in the first part of the night from N. N. W., which appeared to be the flood setting into Hervey's Bay. At daybreak [MONDAY 2 AUGUST 1802] we pursued our course along the shore, at the distance of four or five miles, in soundings between 5 and 9 fathoms. The coast was low, but not sandy; and behind it was a range of hills extending north-westward, and like the flat country, was not ill clothed with wood. There was no remarkable projection till we came to the south head of Bustard Bay; and the night being then at hand, we ran in and anchored on a sandy bottom, in 4½ fathoms, nearly in the same spot where the Endeavour had lain thirty-two years before.

The rocky south head of Bustard Bay, from the survey between the preceding and following noons, should lie in 24° 9' south, and the time keepers placed it in 151° 52' east; or 5' south and 10' east of captain Cook's situation; nor did the form of the Bay correspond to his chart.* The variation observed a few miles from the anchorage, was 8° 20' east, with the ship's head N. W. by N., or 6° 52' reduced to the meridian; nearly as had been found in the morning, when it was 6° 56' corrected. This is a full degree less than it was on the east side of Sandy Cape, and captain Cook's observations show a still greater diminution.

[* The latitude 24° 4' was observed on board the Endeavour, at anchor here; by whom is uncertain, but it was not by captain Cook or Mr. Green. In the *Astronomical Observations* of the voyage, p. 134, Mr. Wales, in deducing the position of Bustard Bay, takes no notice of this observation, and omits the latitude.]

TUESDAY 3 AUGUST 1802

At daylight we proceeded along the coast; but the wind being very light, were no more than abreast of the north head of Bustard Bay at noon; and the ship being drifted by the tide toward some rocks lying off the head, a boat went to sound amongst them for a passage; in the mean time an air sprung up at north; and having got the ship's head to the eastward, we stretched off from the rocks. This north head lies in latitude 24° 0', as laid down by captain Cook, and bears from the south head N. 44° W., twelve miles; it is moderately high, and behind it is a mass of hummocky, barren hills, which extend far to the westward. A reef lies out as far as two miles from the north head; but within the outer rock above water our boat had 14 fathoms, and there was room for a ship to pass.

Not being able to weather the reef before dark, we worked to windward during the night; bearing down frequently to the Lady Nelson, to prevent separation. At daylight [WEDNESDAY 4 AUGUST 1802], the wind had shifted gradually round, from north to the south-westward; and at noon the north head of Bustard, Bay was brought to bear S. 16° E., four leagues, our latitude being then 23° 48', and longitude 151° 40'. A low island was seen from the mast head, bearing north at the supposed distance of six leagues, of which captain Cook does not make any mention;* and the furthest visible part of the main land was a conspicuous hill, named *Mount Larcom*, in compliment to captain Larcom of the navy. It bore W. ½° N., ten or eleven leagues; but the coast line between it and the north head of Bustard Bay, seemed to be much broken.

[* A cluster of low islands, about fifteen leagues from the coast, was seen in the following year by Mr. Bunker, commander of the Albion, south whaler. He described the cluster to be of considerable extent, and as lying in latitude 23¾°, and longitude about 152½°; or nearly a degree to the eastward of the low isle above mentioned. It is probably to these islands, whose existence captain Cook suspected, that the great flights of boobies he saw in Hervey's Bay retire at night.]

In the afternoon, a breeze from the north-westward enabled us to stretch in for the land; and we anchored soon after sunset in 10 fathoms, brown sand, five or six miles from a projection which received the name of *Gatcombe Head*; and to the southward of it there was a rather deep bight in the coast. The bearings of the land, taken a few minutes before anchoring, were as under.

North head of Bustard Bay, dist. 5 leagues, S. 56° E. Gatcombe Head,
S. 86 W. Mount Larcom, N. 80 W. Northern extreme of the coast,
N. 46 W.

The chain of hills which rises near Bustard Bay, was seen to stretch westward a few miles behind the shore, till it was lost at the back of Mount Larcom. These hills were not destitute of wood, but they had a barren appearance; and the coast was more rocky than sandy. At this anchorage, the flood tide came from the north-by-east, and the ebb set east, half a mile per hour.

[EAST COAST. PORT CURTIS.]
THURSDAY 5 AUGUST 1802

At daylight of the 5th, we closed in with the shore, steering north-westward; and at nine o'clock a small opening was discovered, and water seen over the low front land. The Lady Nelson was ordered to look for anchorage; and at eleven we came to, in 4 fathoms brown sand, one mile from the east point of the opening; and the following bearings were then taken:

Southern extreme of the coast, over the east point, S. 36° E. Rocky islet in the middle of the opening, dist. 1½ mile, S. 28 W. Mount Larcom,
S. 75 W. Hummock at the northern extreme (C. Capricorn), N. 18 W.

The opening was not so much as a mile in width, but from the extent of water within, it was conjectured to have a communication with the bight on the south side of Gatcombe Head; and this being an object worthy of examination, the sails were furled and the boats hoisted out. The naturalist and his companions landed at the west side of the entrance, where some Indians had assembled to look at the ship; but they retired on the approach of our gentlemen, and afterwards taking the advantage of a hillock, began to throw stones at the party; nor would they desist until two or three muskets were fired over their heads, when they disappeared. There were seven bark canoes lying on the shore, and near them hung upon a tree some parts of a turtle; and scoop nets, such as those of Hervey's Bay, were also seen.

I proceeded up the opening in a boat, and lieutenant Murray got under way to follow with the brig; but the tide ran up so rapidly, over a bottom which was rocky and very irregular in depth, that he anchored almost immediately, and came to the middle islet where I was taking angles. We then went over to the west shore, and ascended a hill called in the chart, *Hill View*, from whence it was evident, that this water did certainly communicate with the bight round Gatcombe Head, and by an opening much more considerable than that in which the vessels were anchored; the port was also seen to extend far to the westward, and I was induced to form a regular plan for its examination. The northern entrance being too full of rocks and shoals for the Lady Nelson to pass, although drawing no more than six feet when the keels were hoisted up, Mr. Murray was desired to go round to the southern opening; and about sunset he got under way.

FRIDAY 6 AUGUST 1802

Early in the morning I went off in the whale boat, with two days provisions, and made nearly a straight course up the port, for a low point on the south shore called *South-trees Point*. The water was very shallow, with many rocks and dry banks, until the southern entrance was fairly open, when the depth varied between 7 and 3 fathoms; but there was from 6 to 8 close to the low point. This forms the inner part of the southern entrance, and Gatcombe Head, the outer part, lies from it S. 64° E. about four miles; from the head southward, however, the width of the channel is much less, being contracted by banks which extend out from the opposite shore.

Seeing nothing of the brig, I proceeded in the examination, steering westward for a small island four or five miles up the port. This is the southernmost of six islets, lying behind the point of Hill View, and from one of two hillocks upon it, another set of bearings was taken. The depth of water thus far, had varied from 8 fathoms, to six feet upon a middle shoal; after which it deepened to 3, 4, and 7 fathoms, and there was 10 close to the southern islet. The Lady Nelson made her appearance off Gatcombe Head about noon; but not waiting for her, I went to a point on the northern shore, near two miles higher up, where the water was so deep that a ship might make fast to the rocks and trees: the soundings were very irregular from the southern islet, but the least depth was 5 fathoms.

The port was here contracted to one mile in width; but it opened out higher up, and taking a more northern direction, assumed the form of a river. In steering across to the western shore, I carried from 8 to 4, and afterwards from 6 to 2 fathoms; when turning northward for two islets covered with mangroves, the depth increased again to 7 fathoms. We tried to land upon a third islet, it being then sunset; but a surrounding bank of soft mud making the islet inaccessible, we rowed on upwards, and landed with difficulty on the west shore before it became quite dark. The breadth of the stream here was about a mile; and the greatest depth 6 fathoms at low water.

SATURDAY 7 AUGUST 1802

In the morning, a small opening was observed in the opposite, eastern shore; but reserving this for examination in returning, I proceeded upwards with a fair wind, five miles further, when the greatest depth any where to be found was 3 fathoms. The stream then divided into two arms; the largest, about one mile in breadth, continuing its direction to the N. W. by N., and apparently ending a little further up; the other running westward, but the greater part of both occupied by shallow water and mud banks. Upon the point of separation, which is insulated at high water, there were some low, reddish cliffs, the second observed on the west shore; and from thence I set Mount Larcom at S. 15° 15' W., distant seven or eight miles.

This station was nine miles above the steep point, where the port is first contracted, and the steep point is ten from Gatcombe Head; and conceiving it could answer no essentially useful purpose to pursue the examination where a ship could not go, I returned to the small opening in the eastern shore, opposite to where we had passed the night. There was 4 fathoms in the entrance of this little branch; but it presently became shallow, and I landed to ascend a hill which had but little wood at the top. The sea was visible from thence; and the ship at the northern entrance of the port was set at N. 89½° E, and Mount Larcom S. 59½° W. The small, mangrove islets below this branch, were passed on the east side in our way down, there being a narrow channel with from 3 to 5 fathoms in it, close past two trees standing alone in the water; and at sunset we got on board the brig, lying at anchor off South-trees Point.

Lieutenant Murray had found some difficulty in getting into the southern entrance, from a shoal which lay to the S. E. by E., one mile and a half from Gatcombe Head. He passed on the north side of the shoal, and brought deep water as far as South-trees Point; but in steering onward, in mid-channel, had met with other banks, and was obliged to anchor. I desired Mr. Murray to ascertain as he went out, whether there were any channel on the south side of the shoal near Gatcombe Head; and quitting the brig next morning [SUNDAY 8 AUGUST 1802], I landed on the larger island to the south of the point of Hill View, to take angles; and soon after nine o'clock, reached the ship.

During my absence, the botanical gentlemen had been on shore every day, lieutenant Flinders had made astronomical observations, and boats had been employed, though unsuccessfully, in fishing. No Indians had been seen on the east side of the port, and I therefore gave a part of the ship's company leave this afternoon, to land there and divert themselves. At eight in the evening a gun was heard in the offing; and by the guidance of our light, the Lady Nelson returned to her anchorage four hours afterward. Mr. Murray had struck upon a reef, having kept too near the shore in the apprehension of missing the anchorage in the dark; but his vessel did not appear to have sustained any other damage than the main sliding keel being carried away.

As much time having been employed in the examination of this port as the various objects I had in view could permit, we prepared to quit it on the following morning. This part of the East Coast had been passed in the night by captain Cook; so that both the openings escaped his notice, and the discovery of the port fell to our lot. In honour of admiral Sir Roger Curtis, who had commanded at the Cape of Good Hope and been so attentive to our wants, I gave to it the name of PORT CURTIS; and the island which protects it from the sea, and in fact forms the port, was called *Facing Island*. It is a slip of rather low land, eight miles in length, and from two to half a mile in breadth, having Gatcombe Head for its southern extremity.

The northern entrance to Port Curtis is accessible only to boats; but ships of any size may enter the port by the southern opening. Mr. Murray did not find any passage on the south side of the shoal near Gatcombe Head, but could not say that none existed; he thought the deep channel to be not more than a mile wide; but at half a mile from the head there was from 6 to 10 fathoms, and the channel from thence leads fair up the port to beyond South-trees Point; I suspected, however, from the account given by Mr. Murray, that there might be a second shoal, lying not so much as a mile from the head, and one is marked in the plan accordingly, that ships may be induced to greater caution. There is good anchorage just within Gatcombe Head; and at a small beach there, behind a rock, is a rill of fresh water, and wood is easily to be procured.

I cannot venture to give any other sailing directions for going up this port, than to run cautiously, with a boat ahead and the plan upon the binnacle. Both the bottom and shoals are usually a mixture of sand, with mud or clay; but in the northern entrance, and off some of the upper points and islands where the tides run strong, the ground is in general rocky.

The country round Port Curtis is overspread with grass, and produces the *eucalyptus* and other trees common to this coast; yet the soil is either sandy or covered with loose stones, and generally incapable of cultivation. Much of the shores and the low islands are overspread with mangroves, of three different species; but that which sends down roots, or rather supporters from the branches, and interweaves so closely as to be almost impenetrable, was the most common. This species, the *Rhizophora Mangle* of Linnaeus, is also the most abundant in the East and West Indies; but is not found at Port Jackson, nor upon the south coast of this country.

Granite, streaked red and black, and cracked in all directions, appeared to be the common stone in the upper parts of the port; but a stratified argillaceous stone was not unfrequent; and upon the larger island, lying off the point of Hill View, there was a softish, white earth, which I took to be calcareous until it was tried with acids, and did not produce any effervescence.

Traces of inhabitants were found upon all the shores where we landed, but the natives kept out of sight after the little skirmish on the first day of our arrival; they subsist partly on turtle, and possess bark canoes and scoop nets. We saw three turtle lying on the water, but were not so fortunate as to procure any. Fish seemed to be plentiful, and some were speared by Bongaree, who was a constant attendant in my boat; and yet our efforts with the seine were altogether unsuccessful. The shores abound with oysters, amongst which, in the upper parts of the port, was the kind producing pearls; but being small and discoloured, they are of no value. The attempts made near the ship with the dredge, to procure larger oysters from the deep water, were without success.

I saw no quadrupeds in the woods, and almost no birds; but there were some pelicans, gulls, and curlews about the shores and flats. Fresh water was found in small pools on both sides of the northern entrance, and at the point of Hill View I met with some in holes; but that which best merits the attention of a ship, is the rill found by Mr. Murray at the back of the small beach within Gatcombe Head.

The *latitude* of our anchorage at the northern entrance, from four meridian altitudes of the sun, is 23° 44' 16" south.

Six sets of distances of the sun west of the moon, taken by lieutenant Flinders, would make the *longitude* 151° 21' 22" east; the two time keepers gave 151° 20' 10"; and fifty sets of distances, reduced from Broad Sound by the survey, which I consider to be the best authority, place the anchorage in 151° 20' 15" east.

These being reduced by the survey to the southern entrance, place Gatcombe Head in latitude 23° 52½° S. longitude 151° 24' E.

No *variations* were observed at the anchorage; but two amplitudes off Gatcombe Head gave 11° 11', and azimuths with three compasses, 10° 50' east, the ship's head being W. S. W. and W. N. W. These being reduced to the meridian, will give the true variation to be 8° 40' east.

This is an increase of near 2° from Bustard Bay; and seems attributable to the attraction of the granitic land which lay to the westward, and drew the south end of the needle that way.

The rise of *tide* at the place where I slept near the head of the port, was no more than four feet; but upon the rocky islet in the northern entrance, there were marks of its having risen the double of that quantity. The time of high water was not well ascertained, but it will be between eight and nine hours after the moon's passage over and under the meridian.

MONDAY 9 AUGUST 1902

On getting under way at daylight of the 9th, to prosecute the examination of the coast, the anchor came up with an arm broken off, in consequence of a flaw extending two-thirds through the iron. The negligence with which this anchor had been made, might in some cases have caused the loss of the ship.

[EAST COAST. KEPPEL BAY.]

In following the low and rather sandy shore, northward to Cape Capricorn, we passed within a rocky islet and another composed of rock and sand, four miles south-east of the cape, the soundings being there from 8 to 9 fathoms; and at ten o'clock hauled round for Cape Keppel, which lies from Cape Capricorn N. 80° W., ten miles. The shore is low, with some small inlets in it, and sand banks with shoal water run off more than two miles; at six miles out there is a hummocky island and four rocks, one of which was at first taken for a ship. We passed within these, as captain Cook had before done; and at half past two in the afternoon anchored in Keppel Bay, in 6 fathoms soft bottom, three-quarters of a mile from a head on the east side of the entrance.

My object in stopping at this bay was to explore two openings marked in it by captain Cook, which it was possible might be the entrances of rivers leading into the interior. So soon as the ship was secured, a boat was sent to haul the seine, and I landed with a party of the gentlemen to inspect the bay from an eminence called *Sea Hill*. There were four places where the water penetrated into the land, but none of these openings were large; that on the west side, in which were two islands, was the most considerable, and the hills near it were sufficiently elevated to afford an extensive view; whereas in most other parts, the shores were low and covered with mangroves. These considerations induced me to begin the proposed examination by the western arm; and early next morning [TUESDAY 10 AUGUST 1802] I embarked in the Lady Nelson, intending to employ her and my whale boat in exploring the bay and inlets, whilst the botanists made their excursions in the neighbourhood of the ship.

The depth in steering for the western arm was from 6 to 9 fathoms, for about one mile, when it diminished quickly to 2, upon a shoal which seemed to run up the bay; the water afterwards deepened to 5 and 7 fathoms, but meeting with a second shoal, the brig was obliged to anchor. I then went on in my boat for the nearest of the two islands, passing over the banks and crossing the narrow, deep channels marked in the plan. The two islands are mostly very low, and the shores so muddy and covered with mangroves, that a landing on the northern and highest of them could be effected only at the west end; but a hillock there enabled me to take an useful set of bearings, including Mount Larcom, which is visible from all parts of this bay, as it is from Port Curtis.

In the afternoon I proceeded up the western arm, having from 3 to 8 fathoms close along the northern shore; and about four miles up, where the width was diminished to one mile, found a landing place, a rare convenience here, and ascended a hill from whence there was a good view. At five or six leagues to the south, and extending thence north-westward, was a continuation of the same chain of hills which rises near Bustard Bay and passes behind Mount Larcom; but at the back of Keppel Bay it forms a more connected ridge, and is rocky, steep, and barren. Within this ridge the land is low, and intersected by various streams, some falling into the western arm at ten or twelve miles above the entrance, and others into the south-west and south arms of the bay. The borders of the western arm, and of its upper branches so far as could be perceived, were over-run with mangroves; whence it seemed probable the water was salt, and that no landing was practicable, higher than this station; the sun also was near setting when my bearings from *West-arm Hill* were completed; and I therefore gave up the intention of proceeding further, and returned to the northern island in the entrance, to pass the night.

It was high water here at seven in the evening, and the tide fell nine and a half feet; but the morning's tide rose to six and a half only [WEDNESDAY 11 AUGUST 1802]. In rowing out between the two islands, I had from 8 to 3 fathoms; but shoal water in crossing from thence to the entrance of the south-west arm, where again there was 5 to 8 fathoms. A strong wind from the south-eastward did not permit me to go up this arm, and the extensive flats made it impossible to land upon the south side of the bay; and finding that nothing more could be done at this time, I returned to the ship.

The numerous shoals in Keppel Bay rendering the services of the Lady Nelson in a great measure useless to the examination, I directed lieutenant Murray to run out to the hummocky island lying to the north-east from Cape Keppel, and endeavour to take us some turtle; for there were no signs of inhabitants upon it, and turtle seemed to be plentiful in this neighbourhood. He was also to ascend the hills, and take bearings of any island or other object visible in the offing; and after making such remarks as circumstances might allow, to return not later than the third evening.

THURSDAY 12 AUGUST 1802

Next afternoon, I went, accompanied by the naturalist, to examine the eastern arm of the bay, which is divided into two branches. Pursuing the easternmost and largest, with soundings from 6 to 3 fathoms, we came to several mangrove islands, about four miles up, where the stream changed its direction from S. S. E. to E. S. E., and the deepest water was 2 fathoms. A little further on we landed for the night, cutting a path through the mangroves to a higher part of the northern shore; but the swarms of musketoes and sand flies made sleeping impossible to all except one of the boat's crew, who was so enviably constituted, that these insects either did not attack him, or could not penetrate his skin. It was high water here at nine o'clock; and the tide afterwards fell between ten and twelve feet.

FRIDAY 13 AUGUST 1802

In the morning, I set Broad Mount in Keppel Bay at N. 61° 20' W. and Mount Larcom S. 8° 20' E; and we then steered onward in six to eight feet water, amongst various little islands of mud and mangroves; the whole width of the stream being still more than half a mile, nearly the same as at the entrance. Three miles above the sleeping place the water began to increase in breadth, and was 2 fathoms deep; and advancing further, it took a direction more southward, and to our very agreeable surprise, brought us to the head of Port Curtis; forming thus a channel of communication from Keppel Bay, and cutting off Cape Capricorn with a piece of land twenty-five miles in length, from the continent.

I landed on the eastern shore, nearly opposite to the reddish cliffs which had been my uppermost station from Port Curtis, and set

Broad Mount in Keppel Bay at N. 60° 45' W. Mount Larcom,   S. 16 15 W.

Having found one communication, we rowed up the western branch near the reddish cliffs, hoping to get back to Keppel Bay by a second new passage; but after going two miles, with a diminishing depth from 4 fathoms to three feet, we were stopped by mangroves, and obliged to return to the main stream.

The tide was half ebbed when we came to the shallowest part of the communicating channel; and it was with much difficulty that the boat could be got over. A space here of about two miles in length, appears to be dry, or very nearly so, at low water; but it is possible that some small channel may exist amongst the mangroves, of sufficient depth for a boat to pass at all times of tide.

We reached the entrance of the eastern arm from Keppel Bay, with the last of the ebb; and took the flood to go up the southern branch. The depth of water was generally 3 fathoms, on the eastern side, and the width nearly half a mile. This continued three miles up, when a division took place; in the smallest, which ran southward, we got one mile, and up the other, leading south-westward, two miles; when both were found to terminate in shallows amongst the mangroves. It was then dusk; and there being no possibility of landing, the boat was made fast to a mangrove bush till high water, and with the returning ebb, we got on board the ship at eleven o'clock.

The Lady Nelson had returned from the hummocky island, without taking any turtle. No good anchorage was found, nor was there either wood or water upon the island, worth the attention of a ship. Mr. Murray ascended the highest of the hummocks with a compass, but did not see any lands in the offing further out than the Keppel Isles.

SATURDAY 14 AUGUST 1802

I left the ship again in the morning, and went up the southern arm to a little hill on its western shore; hoping to gain from thence a better knowledge of the various streams which intersect the low land on the south side of the bay. This arm is one mile in width, and the depth in it from 3 to 6 fathoms; the shores are flat, as in other parts, and covered with mangroves; but at high water a landing was effected under the *South Hill*, without much trouble. The sides of this little eminence are steep, and were so thickly covered with trees and shrubs, bound together and intertwisted with strong vines, that our attempts to reach the top were fruitless. It would perhaps have been easier to climb up the trees, and scramble from one to another upon the vines, than to have penetrated through the intricate net work in the darkness underneath.

Disappointed in my principal object, and unable to do any thing in the boat, which could not then approach the shore within two hundred yards, I sought to walk upwards, and ascertain the communication between the south and south-west arms; but after much fatigue amongst the mangroves and muddy swamps, very little more information could be gained. The small fish which leaps on land upon two strong breast fins, and was first seen by captain Cook on the shores of Thirsty Sound, was very common in the swamps round the South Hill. There were also numbers of a small kind of red crab, having one of its claws uncommonly large, being, indeed, nearly as big as the body; and this it keeps erected and open, so long as there is any expectation of disturbance. It was curious to see a file of these pugnacious little animals raise their claws at our approach, and open their pincers ready for an attack; and afterwards, finding there was no molestation, shoulder their arms and march on.

At nine in the evening, the tide brought the boat under the hill, and allowed us to return to the ship. All the examination of Keppel Bay which our time could allow, was now done; but a day being required for laying down the plan of the different arms, I offered a boat on Sunday [15 AUGUST 1802] morning to the botanists, to visit the South Hill, which afforded a variety of plants; but they found little that had not before fallen under their observation. A part of the ship's company was allowed to go on shore abreast of the ship, for no Indians had hitherto been seen there; but towards the evening, about twenty were observed in company with a party of the sailors. They had been met with near Cape Keppel, and at first menaced our people with their spears; but finding them inclined to be friendly, laid aside their arms, and accompanied the sailors to the ship in a good-natured manner. A master's mate and a seaman were, however, missing, and nothing was heard of them all night.

MONDAY 16 AUGUST 1802

At daylight, two guns were fired and an officer was sent up the small inlet under Sea Hill; whilst I took a boat round to Cape Keppel, in the double view of searching for the absentees and obtaining a set of bearings from the top of the cape. This station afforded me a better view of the Keppel Isles than any former one; and to the northward of them were two high peaks on the main land, nearly as far distant as Cape Manifold.

Amongst the number of bearings taken, those most essential to the connection of the survey were as under.

Cape Capricorn, outer hummock, S. 79° 30' E. Mount Larcom, S. 6 10 E. The ship at anchor, S. 59 50 W. Highest peak near Cape Manifold, N. 25 10 W. Keppel Isles, outermost, called first lump, N. 0 45 E. Hummocky Island, N. 54° 35' to 61 40 E.

On my return to the ship, the master's mate and seaman were on board. The officer had very incautiously strayed away from his party, after natives had been seen; and at sunset, when he should have been at the beach, he and the man he had taken with him were entangled in a muddy swamp amongst mangroves, several miles distant; in which uncomfortable situation, and persecuted by clouds of musketoes, they passed the night. Next morning they got out of the swamp; but fell in with about twenty-five Indians, who surrounded and took them to a fire place. A couple of ducks were broiled; and after the wanderers had satisfied their hunger, and undergone a personal examination, they were conducted back to the ship in safety. Some of the gentlemen went to meet the natives with presents, and an interview took place, highly satisfactory to both parties; the Indians then returned to the woods, and our people were brought on board.

TUESDAY 17 AUGUST 1802

The anchor was weighed at daylight of the 17th, but the wind and tide being unfavourable, it took the whole day to get into the offing; at dusk we came to, in 9 fathoms, mud and sand, having the centre of the hummocky island bearing S. 72° E. two leagues. A sketch of the island and of Cape Keppel was taken by Mr. Westall (Atlas, Plate XVIII. View 5.) whilst beating out of the bay.

Keppel Bay was discovered and named by captain Cook, who sailed past it in 1770. A ship going in will be much deceived by the colour of the water; for the shores of the bay being soft and muddy, the water running out by the deep channels with the latter part of the ebb, is thick; whilst the more shallow parts, over which the tide does not then set, are covered with sea water, which is clear. Not only are the shores for the most part muddy, but a large portion of the bay itself is occupied by shoals of mud and sand. The deep water is in the channels made by the tides, setting in and out of the different arms; and the best information I can give of them, will be found by referring to the plan. The broadest of these channels is about two miles wide, on the east side of the bay; and our anchorage there near Sea Hill, just within the entrance, seems to be the best for a ship purposing to make but a short stay. Wood is easily procured; and fresh water was found in small ponds and swamps, at a little distance behind the beach. This is also the best, if not the sole place in the bay for hauling the seine; and a fresh meal of good fish was there several times procured for all the ship's company.

The country round Keppel Bay mostly consists either of stony hills, or of very low land covered with salt swamps and mangroves. Almost all the borders of the bay, and of the several arms into which it branches, are of this latter description; so that there are few places where it was not necessary to wade some distance in soft mud, and afterwards to cut through a barrier of mangroves, before reaching the solid land.

Mention has been made of the ridge of hills by which the low land on the south side of the bay is bounded. The upper parts of it are steep and rocky, and may be a thousand, or perhaps fifteen hundred feet high, but the lower sloping sides are covered with wood; Mount Larcom and the hills within the ridge, are clothed with trees nearly to the top; yet the aspect of the whole is sterile. The high land near the western arm, though stony and shallow in soil, is covered with grass, and trees of moderate growth; but the best part of the country was that near Cape Keppel; hill and valley are there well proportioned, the grass is of a better kind and more abundant, the trees are thinly scattered, and there is very little underwood. The lowest parts are not mangrove swamps, as elsewhere, but pleasant looking vallies, at the bottom of which are ponds of fresh water frequented by flocks of ducks. Cattle would find here a tolerable abundance of nutritive food, though the soil may perhaps be no where sufficiently deep and good to afford a productive return to the husbandman.

After the mangrove, the most common trees round Keppel Bay are different kinds of *eucalyptus*, fit for the ordinary purposes of building. A species of *Cycas*, described by captain Cook (Hawkesworth, III. 220, 221) as a third kind of palm found by him on this coast, and bearing poisonous nuts, was not scarce in the neighbourhood of West-arm Hill. We found three kinds of stone here: a greyish slate, quartz and various granitic combinations, and a soft, whitish stone, saponaceous to the touch; the two first were often found intermixed, and the last generally, if not always lying above them. The quartz was of various colours, and sometimes pure; but never in a state of crystallisation.

Wherever we landed there had been Indians; but it was near the ship only, that any of them made their appearance. They were described by the gentlemen who saw them, as stout, muscular men, who seemed to understand bartering better than most, or perhaps any people we had hitherto seen in this country. Upon the outer bone of the wrist they had the same hard tumour as the people of Hervey's Bay, and the cause of it was attempted, ineffectually, to be explained to one of the gentlemen; but as cast nets were seen in the neighbourhood, there seems little doubt that the manner of throwing them produces the tumours. These people were not devoid of curiosity; but several things which might have been supposed most likely to excite it, passed without notice. Of their dispositions we had every reason to speak highly, from their conduct to our sailors; but particularly to the master's mate and seaman who had lost themselves, and were absolutely in their power. On the morning we quitted the bay, a large party was again seen, coming down to the usual place; which seemed to imply that our conduct and presents had conciliated their good will, and that they would be glad to have communication with another vessel.

It is scarcely necessary to say, that these people are almost black, and go entirely naked, since none of any other colour, or regularly wearing clothes, have been seen in any part of Terra Australis. About their fire places were usually scattered the shells of large crabs, the bones of turtle, and the remains of a parsnip-like root, apparently of fern; and once the bones of a porpoise were found; besides these, they doubtless procure fish, and wild ducks were seen in their possession. There are kangaroos in the woods, and several bustards were seen near Cape Keppel. The mud banks are frequented by curlews, gulls, and some lesser birds. Oysters of a small, crumply kind, are tolerably plentiful; they do not adhere to the rocks, but stick to each other in large masses on the banks; here are also pearl oysters, but not so abundantly as in Port Curtis.

The *latitude* of our anchorage, from the mean of three meridian altitudes to the north, was 23° 29' 34" south.

Longitude from twenty-four sets of distances of the sun and moon, the particulars of which are given in Table I. of Appendix No. I. to this volume, 151° 0' 28"; but from fifty other sets, reduced by the survey from Broad Sound, the better longitude of the anchorage is 150° 58' 20" east.

According to the time keepers the longitude would be 150° 57' 43"; and in an interval of six days, they were found to err no more than 5" of longitude on the Port-Jackson rates.

From three compasses on the binnacle, lieutenant Flinders observed the *variation* 6° 48', when the ship's head was north, and 5° 47' when it was south-south-east. This last being reduced to the meridian, the mean of both will be 6° 47' east, nearly the same as in Bustard Bay; but 2° less than was observed off Gatcombe Head. At the different stations round Keppel Bay whence bearings were taken, the variation differed from 5° 10' to 6° 30' east.

Whilst beating off the entrance, I had 7° 52' east variation, from azimuths with the surveying compass when the head was N. W., and from an amplitude, with the head N. by W., 6° 54'; the mean reduced to the meridian. will be for the outside of the bay 6° 16' east.

Captain Cook had 7° 24' near the same situation, from amplitudes and azimuths observed in 1770, with the Endeavour's head W. N. W.

The rise of *tide* in the entrance of Keppel Bay seems to vary at the neaps and springs, from nine to fourteen feet, and high water to take place *nine hours and a half* after the moon's passage over and under the meridian; but the morning's tide fell two or three feet short of that at night. The set past the ship was greatest at the last quarter of the flood and first of the ebb, when it ran two-and-half knots, and turned very suddenly. In the offing, the flood came from the eastward, at the rate of one mile per hour.

CHAPTER II.

The Keppel Isles, and coast to Cape Manifold.
A new port discovered and examined.
Harvey's Isles.
A new passage into Shoal-water Bay.
View from Mount Westall.
A boat lost.
The upper parts of Shoal-water Bay examined.
Some account of the country and inhabitants.
General remarks on the bay.
Astronomical and nautical observations.

[EAST COAST. FROM KEPPEL BAY.]
AUGUST 1802

The rocks and islands lying off Keppel Bay to the northward, are numerous and scattered without order; two of them are of greater magnitude than the rest, and captain Cook had attempted to pass between these and the main land, from which they are distant about five miles; but shoal water obliged him to desist. When we got under way in the morning of the 18th [WEDNESDAY 18 AUGUST 1802], our course was directed for the outside of these two islands, and we passed within a mile of them in 9, and from that to 13 fathoms water. They are five miles asunder, and the southernmost and largest is near twelve miles in circumference; its rocky hills are partly covered with grass and wood, and the gullies down the sides, as also the natives seen upon the island, implied that fresh water was to be had there.

[EAST COAST. CAPE MANIFOLD.]

At the back of the islands the main coast is low and sandy, with the exception of two or three rocky heads; but at a few miles inland there is a chain of hills, moderately elevated and not ill clothed with wood. These hills are a continuation of the same which I had ascended on the west side of Keppel Bay, and extend as far as the two peaks behind Cape Manifold.

After passing the Keppel Isles we steered for a small opening in the coast, seven or eight miles to the north-west, and the Lady Nelson was directed to lead in; but on her making the signal for 3 fathoms, and the inlet appearing to be a sandy cove fit only for boats, we kept on northward, between one and two miles from the shore. At five o'clock, the south-east breeze died away, and a descent of the mercury announcing either little wind for the night or a breeze off the land, a kedge anchor was dropped in 8 fathoms, sandy bottom. The bearings then taken were,

Keppel Isles, the first lump, S. 45° E. C. Manifold, east end of the island near it, N. 9 E. Peaked islet in the offing, N. 28½ E. Flat islet, distant four or five leagues, N. 43 E.

The two last are called the Brothers., in captain Cook's chart; though described in the voyage as being, one "low and flat, and the other high and round." A perforation in the higher islet admits the light entirely through it, and is distinguishable when it bears nearly south-east.

THURSDAY 19 AUGUST 1802

At seven next morning, having then a light air from the land with foggy weather, we steered northward along the coast; and at noon were in latitude 22° 47¾', and two rocks near the shore bore S. 54° W. two or three miles. From that time until evening, we worked to windward against a breeze from the north-east, which afterwards veered to N. N. W.; and at nine o'clock, a small anchor was dropped in 14 fathoms, two miles from the shore. The Lady Nelson had fallen to leeward; and made no answer to our signals during the night.

FRIDAY 20 AUGUST 1802

At daylight, supposing the brig had passed us by means of a shift of wind to W. N. W., we proceeded along the coast to the island lying off Cape Manifold. This island, with some of the northern hills, had been sketched by Mr. Westall (Atlas, Plate XVIII. View 6.) on the preceding evening; it is slightly covered with vegetation, and lies in latitude 22° 42', and longitude 150° 50'. The cape is formed of several rocky heads and intermediate beaches; and the hills behind, from which the cape was named, rise one over the other to the two peaks set from Cape Keppel, and appeared to be rocky and barren. The easternmost, and somewhat the highest peak, is about four miles from the shore, and lies S. 49° W. from the east end of the island whose situation is above given.

The wind was from the northward at noon, and we were then making a stretch for the land, which was distant four or five miles.

Latitude, observed to the north, 34° 36½' C. Manifold, east end of the island, S. 1 W. C. Manifold, the highest peak, S. 30½ W. Small isle (Entrance I.) at the northern extreme, N. 29 W. Peaked islet in the offing, distant 7 miles, S. 61 E.

From Cape Manifold the coast falls back to a sandy beach, six miles long, and near it are some scattered rocks. The land is there very low; but at the north end of the beach is a hilly projection, from which we tacked at one o'clock, in 12 fathoms; being then within a mile of two rocks, and two miles from the main land. The brig was seen to the south-eastward, and we made a long stretch off, to give her an opportunity of joining, and at two in the morning [SATURDAY 21 AUGUST 1802] lay by for her; but the wind veering to south-west at five, we stretched in for the land, and approached some rocky islets, part of the Harvey's Isles of captain Cook, of which, and of the main coast as far as Island Head, Mr. Westall made a sketch (Atlas, Plate XVIII. View 7). At half past nine, when we tacked from Harvey's Isles, I was surprised to see trees upon them resembling the pines of Norfolk Island; none such having been before noticed upon this coast, nor to my knowledge, upon any coast of Terra Australis. Pines were also distinguished upon a more southern islet, four miles off, the same which had been the northern extreme at the preceding noon; and behind it was a deep bight in the land where there seemed to be shelter. The breeze had then shifted to south, and the Lady Nelson being to windward, the signal was made for her to look for anchorage; but the brig being very leewardly, we passed her and stood into the bight by an opening between the islets of one mile wide and from 10 to 7 fathoms in depth. On the soundings decreasing to 5, we tacked and came to an anchor near the pine island in the entrance, in 7 fathoms coarse sand, exposed between N. 75° and S. 23° E, and the wind was then at south-east; but having a fair passage by which we could run out to the northward., in case of necessity, I did not apprehend any danger to the vessels.

[EAST COAST. PORT BOWEN.]

Instead of a bight in the coast, we found this to be a port of some extent; which had not only escaped the observation of captain Cook, but from the shift of wind, was very near being missed by us also. I named it PORT BOWEN, in compliment to captain James Bowen of the navy; and to the hilly projection on the south side of the entrance (see the sketch), I gave the appellation of Cape Clinton, after colonel Clinton of the 85th, who commanded the land, as captain Bowen did the sea forces at Madeira, when we stopped at that island

A boat was despatched with the scientific gentlemen to the north side, where the hills rise abruptly and have a romantic appearance; another went to the same place to haul the seine at a small beach in front of a gully between the hills, where there was a prospect of obtaining fresh water; and a third boat was sent to *Entrance Island* with the carpenters to cut pine logs for various purposes, but principally to make a main sliding keel for the Lady Nelson. Our little consort sailed indifferently at the best; but since the main keel had been carried away at Facing Island, it was as unsafe to trust her on a lee shore, even in moderate weather. On landing at Entrance Island, to take angles and inspect the form of the port, I saw an arm extending behind Cape Clinton to the southward, which had the appearance of a river; a still broader arm ran westward, until it was lost behind the land; and between Entrance Island and Cape Clinton was a space three miles wide, where nothing appeared to obstruct the free passage of a ship into both arms. Finding the port to be worthy of examination, and learning that the seine had been successful and that good water was to be procured, I left orders with lieutenant Fowler to employ the people in getting off pine logs and watering the ship; and early next morning [SUNDAY 22 AUGUST 1802], set off in my whale boat upon an excursion round the port.

From the ship to the inner part of Cape Clinton the soundings were from 5 to 8 fathoms, on a sandy bottom; but close to the innermost point there was no ground at 10 fathoms. From thence I steered up the western arm, passing to the south of a central rock lying a mile out; and got with difficulty to the projection named *West-water Head*. The arm terminated a little further on; but to the northward, over the land, I saw a long shallow bay at the back of Island Head, and beyond it was the sea. This western arm being full of sandy shoals, and of no utility, if at all accessible to ships, I observed the latitude and took angles, and then returned to the inner part of Cape Clinton. In rowing to the southward, close along the inside of the cape, we had from 3 to 9 fathoms water; but it was too late in the evening to make an examination of the southern arm, and I therefore ascended a hill near the shore, to inspect it. This was called *East-water Hill*, and I saw from its top, that the southern arm extended S. 16° W. about seven miles, to the foot of the hills behind Cape Manifold, where it terminated in shallows and mangroves. Close under Eastwater Hill there was a small branch running eastward, nearly insulating Cape Clinton; but neither this branch nor the main arm seemed to be deep enough to admit a ship much higher than the cape; and in consequence, I gave up the further examination, and returned on board at seven o'clock.

Amongst the useful bearings for the survey, taken at Eastwater Hill, were the following:

Entrance Island, centre,   N. 9° 45' E. Peaked Islet in the offing,   S. 58 45 E. Cape Manifold, east end of the island,   S. 29 40 E. Cape Manifold, highest of the two peaks, S. 3 20 W.

By means of this last bearing, the longitude of Port Bowen was connected with Keppel Bay and Port Curtis, independently of the time keepers.

A fresh wind from the south-eastward had blown all day, and raised so much surf on the north side of the port, that our watering there was much impeded; a midshipman and party of men remained on shore with casks all night, and it was not until next evening [MONDAY 23 AUGUST 1802] that the holds were completed and pine logs got on board. The water was very good; it drained down the gully to a little beach between two projecting beads which have rocky islets lying off them. The gully is on the west side of the northern entrance, and will easily be known, since we sent there on first coming to an anchor, in the expectation of finding water, but Mr. Westall's sketch will obviate any difficulty (Atlas, Plate XVIII. View 9).

There were pine trees in the watering gully and on the neighbouring hills; but the best, and also the most convenient, were those upon Entrance Island, some of them being fit to make top masts for ships. The branches are very brittle; but the carpenter thought the trunks to be tough, and superior to the Norway pine, both for spars and planks: turpentine exudes from between the wood and the bark, in considerable quantities.

View of Port Bowen, from behind the Watering Gully.

For a ship wanting to take in water and pine logs, the most convenient place is under Entrance Island, where we lay in the Investigator; indeed fresh water was not found in any other place; but this anchorage is not tenable against a strong south-east wind. At the entrance of the southern arm, just within Cape Clinton, a ship may lie at all times in perfect safety; and might either be laid on shore or be hove down, there being 3 fathoms close to the rocks, at each end of the beach; it is moreover probable, that fresh water might be there found, or be procured by digging at the foot of the hills. In the southern arm the bottom is muddy; but it is of sand in other parts of the port.

Of the country round Port Bowen not much can be said in praise; it is in general either sandy or stony, and unfit for cultivation; nevertheless, besides pines, there are trees, principally *eucalyptus*, of moderate size, and the vallies of Cape Clinton are overspread with a tolerably good grass. No inhabitants were seen, but in every part where I landed, fires had been made, and the woods of Cape Clinton were then burning; the natives had also been upon Entrance Island, which implied them to have canoes, although none were seen. There are kangaroos in the woods; hawks, and the bald-headed mocking bird of Port Jackson are common; and ducks, sea-pies, and gulls frequent the shoals at low water. Fish were more abundant here than in any port before visited; those taken in the seine at the watering beach were principally mullet, but sharks and flying fish were numerous.

The *latitude* of the north-west end of Entrance Island, from an observation taken by lieutenant Flinders in an artificial horizon, is 22° 28' 28" south.

Longitude from twelve sets of lunar distances by the same officer, 150° 47' 54"; and by the time keepers, 150° 45' 36"; but from the fifty sets which fix Broad Sound, and the reduction from thence by survey, the more correct situation will be 150° 45' 0" east.

Dip of the south end of the needle, 50° 20'.

Variation from azimuths with the theodolite, 7° 40' east; but on the top of the island, where my bearings were taken, the variation appeared to be 8° 30' east; and 8° in other parts of the port.

The time of high water, as near as it could be ascertained, was *ten hours after* the moon's passage over and under the meridian, being half an hour later than in Keppel Bay; and the tide rises more than nine feet, but how much was not known; it is however to be presumed, from what was observed to the south and to the north of Port Bowen, that the spring tides do not rise less than fifteen feet.

TUESDAY 24 AUGUST 1802

At daylight of the 24th, we steered out of Port Bowen by the northern passage, as we had gone in. The wind was from the westward; but so light, that when the ebb tide made from the north-west at ten o'clock, it was necessary to drop the kedge anchor for a time. In the evening we came to, in 10 fathoms fine grey sand, one mile and a half from the main; being sheltered between N. E. by E. and E. by S. by the same cluster of small isles upon which the pine trees had been first seen. In the morning [WEDNESDAY 25 AUGUST 1802] we worked onward along the coast, against a breeze at north-west, till ten o'clock; when the tide being unfavourable, an anchor was dropped in 15 fathoms, sand and shells, near three islets, of which the middlemost and highest bore S. 29° E., one mile: these were also a part, and the most northern of Harvey's Isles.

A boat was lowered down, and I landed with the botanical gentlemen on the middle islet; where we found grass and a few shrubs, and also ants, grasshoppers, and lizards. Upon the rocks were oysters of the small, crumply kind, which seemed to indicate that the sea here is not violently agitated; and in the water we saw several large turtle, but were not able to harpoon any of them. Several of the Northumberland Isles were in sight from the top of the islet, and the following observations were taken.

Latitude, observed in artificial horizon, 22° 20' 42" Longitude, deduced from survey, 150 42 Peaked Islet in the offing bore   S. 35 35 E. Island Head, distant 3 miles,   S. 82 45 W. Cape Townshend, the rock near it,   N. 57 45 W. Northumberland Isle, the 4th, a peak, N. 43 30 W.

When the tide slacked in the afternoon we stretched over towards Island Head, and saw a canoe with two Indians, who made for the shore near a place where the woods were on fire. At dusk we anchored in 18 fathoms, soft mud, in a bight between Island Head and Cape Townshend, at the bottom of which was an opening one mile wide, where captain Cook had suspected an entrance into Shoalwater Bay. The Lady Nelson had fallen to leeward, as usual; and not being come up in the morning [THURSDAY 26 AUGUST 1802], the master was sent ahead of the ship in a boat, and we steered for the opening with a strong flood tide in our favour. From 22 fathoms, the water shoaled to 12, and suddenly to 3, on a rocky bottom, just as we reached the entrance. A kedge anchor was dropped immediately; but seeing that the opening went through, and that the master had deep water further in, it was weighed again, and we backed and filled the sails, drifting up with the tide so long as it continued to run. At nine o'clock the anchor was let go in 6 fathoms, sand and shells, one mile within the entrance, the points of which bore N. 34° and S. 89° E.; but the extent of deep water was barely sufficient for the ship to swing at a whole cable.

[EAST COAST. STRONG-TIDE PASSAGE.]

(Atlas, Plate XI.)

Lieutenant Flinders landed on the north side of the entrance, and observed the latitude 22° 17' 53', from an artificial horizon; and a boat was sent to haul the seine upon a beach on the eastern shore, where fish to give half the ship's company a meal was procured. We had no prospect of advancing up the passage until the turn of tide, at three in the afternoon; and I therefore landed with a party of the gentlemen, and ascended the highest of the hills on the eastern side. From the top of it we could see over the land into Port Bowen; and some water was visible further distant at the back of it, which seemed to communicate with Shoal-water Bay. Of the passage where the ship was lying, there was an excellent view; and I saw not only that Cape Townshend was on a distinct island, but also that it was separated from a piece of land to the west, which captain Cook's chart had left doubtful. Wishing to follow the apparent intention of the discoverer, to do honour to the noble family of Townshend, I have extended the name of the cape to the larger island, and distinguish the western piece by the name of *Leicester Island*. Besides these, there were many smaller isles scattered in the entrance of Shoal-water Bay; and the southernmost of them, named *Aken's Island* after the master of the ship, lies in a bight of the western shore. Out at sea there were more of the Northumberland Islands, further westward than those before seen, the largest being not less distant than fifteen leagues; Pier Head, on the west side of Thirsty Sound, was also visible; and in the opposite direction was the highest of the two peaks behind Cape Manifold, the bearing of which connected this station with Port Curtis and Keppel Bay. The view was, indeed, most extensive from this hill; and in compliment to the landscape painter, who made a drawing from thence of Shoal-water Bay and the islands, I named it Mount Westall.* The bearings most essential to the connection of the survey, were these;

Pier Head, the northern extreme,   N. 62° 40' W. Aken's Island in Shoal-water Bay,   N. 86 55 W. Pine Mount, on its west side,   S. 80 40 W. Double Mount, S. 56 35 W. Cape Manifold., highest peak behind it,   S. 20 10 E. West-water Head in Port Bowen,   S. 30 25 E. Northern Harvey's Isles, last station,   N. 81 20 E. Cape Townshend, north-east extreme,   N. 20 25 W. Northumberland Isles, the 4th, a peak, N. 26 25 W.

[* A painting was made of this view, and is now in the Admiralty; but it has not been engraved for the voyage.]

Mount Westall and the surrounding hills are stony, and of steep ascent; pines grow in the gullies, and some fresh water was found there, standing in holes. The lower hills are covered with grass and trees, as is also the low land, though the soil be shallow and sandy; the wood is mostly *eucalyptus*. No natives were seen during our walk, and only one kangaroo.

At dusk in the evening, when we returned on board, I found the Lady Nelson at anchor near us, and two boats absent from the ship. In hauling them up to be hoisted in, the cutter had been upset from the rapidity of the tides, which ran above four knots, the man in her was thrown out, and the boat went adrift. The man was taken up by the Lady Nelson; but the boatswain, who with two men in a small gig had gone after the cutter, was not heard of till next morning [FRIDAY 27 AUGUST 1802], when he returned without any intelligence of his object, having been bewildered in the dark by the rapid tides in a strange place, and in danger of losing himself.

[EAST COAST. SHOAL-WATER BAY.]

On weighing the kedge anchor to go further up the passage, it came up broken near the crown, having in all probability hooked a rock. The Lady Nelson went one mile ahead, a boat was kept sounding close to the ship, and in this manner we drifted up with the flood tide, till half past eight; when another kedge anchor was dropped in 7 fathoms, a short mile from the land on each side, and two from the inner end of the opening. Lieutenant Fowler was immediately sent away in the whale boat, to search for the lost cutter; and in the mean time we weighed with the afternoon's flood, to get through the passage. On approaching a low, triangular island on the eastern shore, the depth diminished quick, and an anchor was let go; but in swinging to it, the ship caught upon a bank of sand and shells where there was no more than twelve feet water. In half an hour the tide floated her off; and the whale boat having returned, but without any information of the cutter, it was kept ahead; and before dark we anchored in 5 fathoms, at the entrance of Shoalwater Bay.

The opening through which we had come was named *Strong-tide Passage*. It is six miles long, and from one to two broad; but half the width is taken up by shoals and rocks, which extend out from each shore and sometimes lie near the mid-channel; and the rapid tides scarcely leave to a ship the choice of her course. The bottom is rocky in the outer entrance, but in the upper part seems more generally to consist of sand and shells. By the swinging of the ship, it was high water *ten hours after* the moon's passage, and the rise was thirteen feet by the lead; but at the top of the springs it is probably two or three feet greater; and the rate at which the tides then run, will not be less than five miles an hour. It will be perceived, that I do not recommend any ship to enter Shoal-water Bay by this passage.

SATURDAY 28 AUGUST 1802

In the morning, I went in the whale boat to the westward, both to search for the lost cutter and to advance the survey. In crossing the inner end of Strong-tide Passage, my soundings were 5, 4, 3, 2½, 2, 3 fathoms, to a rock near the south end of Townshend Island, whence it appeared that the deepest water was close to the Shoals on the eastern side. After searching along the shore of Townshend Island., and amongst the rocky islets near it, I crossed the western channel over to the south end of Leicester Island; where a set of bearings was taken, and the latitude observed to be 22° 18' 17" from an artificial horizon. This channel is about one mile wide, and I proceeded up it until a passage out to sea was clearly distinguishable; but although there be from 4 to 7 fathoms with a soft bottom, the deep part is too narrow for a stranger to pass with a ship. I returned on board in the evening, without having discovered any traces of the lost cutter or seen any thing worthy of particular notice; unless it were three of the large bats, called flying foxes at Port Jackson: when on the wing and at a distance, these animals might be taken for crows.

SUNDAY 29 AUGUST 1802

On the following morning, we got up the anchor and steered further into Shoal-water Bay. The land on the western side appeared to be high; and as the botanists were likely to find more employment there, during the time of my proposed expedition to the head of the bay, than they could promise themselves at any other place, I was desirous of leaving the ship on that side, in a situation convenient for them. After running three miles to the westward, mostly in 3 fathoms, we anchored in 6, till four o'clock, and then again weighed. The soundings became very irregular; and at five, seeing a shoal which extended up and down the middle of the bay, we tacked from it and came to, in 5 fathoms soft bottom, it being then low water.

Mount Westall bore   N. 86° E. Leicester Island, the south end,   N. 9
W. Pine Mount,   S. 78 W.

The western land was still six or seven miles distant, but there was no prospect of getting nearer, without taking time to make a previous examination of the shoal; and I therefore embarked early next morning [MONDAY 30 AUGUST 1802] on board the brig, and proceeded towards the head of the Bay.

Steering south-eastward, in a slanting course up the bay from the middle shoal, we had from 5 to 8 fathoms; and passed a shallow opening in the eastern low shore, four miles above Strong-tide Passage. Three miles higher up there was another opening, near two miles in width; and the wind being then light and foul, I quitted the brig and proceeded three miles up in my boat, when the arm was found to be divided into two branches. Pursuing that which led eastward in a line for Port Bowen, and was three-quarters of a mile wide, I carried a diminishing depth, from 6 fathoms to six feet, above two miles further; and the branch then terminated at the foot of a ridge of hills. I wished much to ascend this ridge, believing that Westwater Head in Port Bowen, lay close at the back; but the shore was so defended by mud flats and interwoven mangroves, that it was impossible to land.

The other branch of the eastern arm led south-eastward, and was a mile wide, with a depth of 6 fathoms as far as two miles above the division; it then separated into three, but the entrances were shallow and the borders every where muddy and covered with mangroves. I therefore returned to the brig which had anchored at the entrance of the branch; and in the night, we dropped out of the eastern arm with the tide, to be ready for going up the bay with the morning's flood.

TUESDAY 31 AUGUST 1802

On the 31st, in steering for the middle of the bay, the brig grounded upon a spit which runs out from the south point of entrance to the eastern arm, and I believe extends so far down the bay as to join the middle shoal near the ship. The bottom was muddy, and the rising tide soon floated her; but our progress being slow, I went onward in the boat and got into a channel of a mile wide, with regular soundings from 6 to 4 fathoms.

Abreast of the eastern arm, the width of the bay had diminished to about four miles; and in advancing upwards, I found it to go on contracting until, at four miles above the arm, the shores were less than one mile asunder, and the head of the bay assumed the form of a river, though the water remained quite salt. The depth here was from 4 to 6 fathoms; and the east side of the contracted part being a little elevated, I was able to land and take a set of angles to fix its position. The width and depth continued nearly the same two miles higher up, to a woody islet in the middle of the channel; where the latitude 22° 37' 6" was observed from an artificial horizon, and more bearings taken.

A ship may get up as high as this islet, for the channel is no where less than half a mile wide, nor the depth in it under 3 fathoms; but there the stream divides into several branches, which appeared to terminate amongst the mangroves, similar to the branches of the eastern arm. The largest runs S. S. E; and I could see three or four miles up it, near to the foot of the hills behind Cape Manifold, where it probably ends, as did the southern arm of Port Bowen.

The islet had been visited by Indians, and several trees upon it were notched, similar to what is done by the people of Port Jackson when they ascend in pursuit of opossums. Upon the main, to the west of the islet, where I walked a mile inland, fire Places and other signs of inhabitants were numerous, and still more so were those of the kangaroo; yet neither that animal nor an Indian was seen. Around the extinguished fires were scattered the bones of turtle, and the shells of crabs, periwinkles, and oysters of the small kind; and in the low grounds I observed many holes, made apparently by the natives in digging for fern roots. An iguana of between two and three feet long, which lay upon the branch of a high tree watching for its prey, was the sole animal killed; but the mud banks are frequented at low water by sea pies of both kinds, curlews, and small cranes.

The soil was stiff, shallow, and often stony; the vegetation consisted of two or three species of *eucalyptus* and the *casuarina*, not thickly set nor large--of several kinds of shrubs, amongst which a small grass-tree was abundant--and of grass, with which the rest of the soil was thinly overspread.

After making my observations, I rejoined the Lady Nelson two miles below the woody islet; but the wind blowing fresh up the bay, and the brig being leewardly, went on and with some difficulty landed on the west side, opposite to the entrance of the eastern arm. This part is stony; but equally low with the rest of the shores, and is probably an island at high water. A confined set of bearings was taken here; and the sun being then nearly down and the brig at anchor, I went on board for the night. Next afternoon [WEDNESDAY 1 SEPTEMBER 1802], when the ebb tide enabled the vessel to make progress against the strong north-west wind, we beat down in a channel of between one and two miles wide, with soundings from 2 to 8 fathoms; but they were not regular, for the depth was less in some parts of the middle than at the sides of the channel. The wind moderated in the evening; and being then within three miles of the ship, I quitted the brig, and got on board at sunset.

One object of my research in this expedition had been the lost cutter, and orders had been left with lieutenant Fowler to send again into Strong-tide Passage upon the same errand, but all was without success.

During my absence, the naturalist and other gentlemen had gone over in the launch to the west side of the bay, where they had an interview with sixteen natives; their appearance was described as being much inferior to the inhabitants of Keppel and Hervey's Bays, but they were peaceable, and seemed to be very hungry. They had bark canoes which, though not so well formed, were better secured at the ends than those of Port Jackson; and in them were spears neatly pointed with pieces of quartz, for striking turtle. The number of bones lying about their fire places bespoke turtle to be their principal food; and with the addition of shell fish, and perhaps fern roots, it is probably their sole support.

The same muddy flats which rendered landing so difficult in the upper parts of the bay, run off to some distance from the shore under *Double Mount*; and the land is low for two or three miles back. The hills then rise, ridge over ridge to a considerable elevation; and at the top are several hummocks, of which two, higher than the rest, obtained for this high land its present name. So far as the gentlemen were able to ascend, the hills were found to be tolerably well covered with pines and other trees; and the soil of the vallies was better than in those near Mount Westall on the opposite side of the bay.

THURSDAY 2 SEPTEMBER 1802

Early on the 2nd the brig rejoined; and the wind being at S. by E., we steered across towards Pine Mount, passing over the shoal in sixteen feet. In crossing the middle channel, our soundings increased to 9, and then diminished to less than 3 fathoms upon a second shoal, the width of the channel here being not quite three miles. On the west side of the second shoal is another channel, nearly as wide as the former; and the greatest depth in it, reduced to low water as usual, was 8 fathoms. The water shoaled again suddenly on approaching the west side of the bay, and obliged us to veer round off; we then steered to pass within Aken's Island, intending to anchor in the West Bight behind it; but the depth not being sufficient for the ship at low water, we came to in 4 fathoms, muddy bottom, one mile from the shore and two from Aken's Island, the east end of which bore N. 27° W.

Pine Mount is a single round hill with a high peaked top, standing about two miles inland from the West Bight; and to obtain a set of bearings from it which should cross those from Mount Westall, had induced me to anchor here; but finding my health too much impaired by fatigue to accomplish a laborious walk, I sent the launch next morning [FRIDAY 3 SEPTEMBER 1802] with the scientific gentlemen, and as an easier task, landed upon Aken's Island and took angles from the little eminence at its north-east end.

At every port or bay we entered, more especially after passing Cape Capricorn, my first object on landing was to examine the refuse thrown up by the sea. The French navigator, La Pérouse, whose unfortunate situation, if in existence, was always present to my mind, had been wrecked, as it was thought, somewhere in the neighbourhood of New Caledonia; and if so, the remnants of his ships were likely to be brought upon this coast by the trade winds, and might indicate the situation of the reef or island which had proved fatal to him. With such an indication, I was led to believe in the possibility of finding the place; and though the hope of restoring La Pérouse or any of his companions to their country and friends could not, after so many years, be rationally entertained, yet to gain some certain knowledge of their fate would do away the pain of suspense; and it might not be too late to retrieve some documents of their discoveries.

Upon the south-east side of Aken's Island, there was thrown up a confused mass of different substances; including a quantity of pumice stone, several kinds of coral, five or six species of shells, skeletons of fish and sea snakes, the fruit of the pandanus, and a piece of cocoa-nut shell without bernacles or any thing to indicate that it had been long in the water; but there were no marks of shipwreck. A seine was hauled upon the small beaches at the south end of the island, and brought on shore a good quantity of mullet, and of a fish resembling a cavally; also a kind of horse mackerel, small fish of the herring kind, and once a sword fish of between four and five feet long. The projection of the snout, or sword of this animal, a foot and a half in length, was fringed with strong, sharp teeth; and he threw it from side to side in such a furious way, that it was difficult to manage him even on shore.

A boat was sent in the evening to the foot of Pine Mount, for the naturalist and his party, but returned without any tidings of them; and it was noon next day [SATURDAY 4 SEPTEMBER 1802] before they got on board. They had reached the top of the mount, but were disappointed in the view by the pines and underwood. In returning to the boat, a chase after a kangaroo had led one of the gentlemen out of his reckoning; and this, with the labour of bringing down their prize, had prevented them from reaching the water side that night. Pine Mount is stony, but covered with large trees of the kind denoted by its epithet; the country between it and the water side is grassy, bears timber trees, and is of a tolerably good soil, such as might be cultivated. There are small creeks of salt water in the low land; and in one of them a fish was shot which furnished the party with a dinner.

Pine Mount is composed of the *greenstone* of the German mineralogists; but in some other parts of the neighbourhood the stone seems to be different, and contains small veins of quartz, pieces of which are also scattered over the surface. At Aken's Island there was some variety. The most common kind was a slate, containing in some places veins of quartz, in a state nearly approaching to crystallization, and in others some metallic substance, probably iron. The basis of most other parts of the island was *greenstone*; but in the eastern cliffs there was a soft, whitish earth; and on the north-west side of the island, a part of the shore consisted of water-worn grains and small lumps of quartz, of coral, pumice stone, and other substances jumbled together, and concreted into a solid mass.

Speaking in general terms of Shoal-water Bay, I do not conceive it to offer any advantages to ships which may not be had upon almost any other part of the coast; except that the tides rise higher, and in the winter season fish are more plentiful than further to the south. No fresh water was found, unless at a distance from the shore, and then only in small quantities. Pine trees are plentiful; but they grow upon the stony hills at a distance from the water side, and cannot be procured with any thing like the facility offered by Port Bowen. The chart contains the best information I am able to give of the channels leading up the bay, and of the shoals between them; but it may be added, that no alarm need be excited by a ship getting aground, for these banks are too soft to do injury. The shelving flats from the shores are also soft; and with the mangroves, which spread themselves from high water at the neaps, up in the country to the furthest reach of the spring tides, in some places for miles, render landing impossible in the upper parts of the bay, except at some few spots already noticed.

Were an English settlement to be made in Shoal-water Bay, the better soil round Pine Mount and the less difficulty in landing there, would cause that neighbourhood to be preferred. There is not a sufficient depth at low water, for ships to go into the West Bight, by the south side of Aken's Island, and the north side was no otherwise sounded than in passing; but there is little doubt that the depth on the north side is adequate to admit ships, and that some parts of the bight will afford anchorage and good shelter.

The tides do not run strong in Shoal-water Bay, the rate seldom exceeding one knot; but they stir up the soft mud at the bottom, and make the water thick, as in Keppel Bay. I am not able to speak very accurately of the rise in the tide; but it may be reckoned at twelve or fourteen feet at the neaps, and from seventeen to eighteen at the springs. High water takes place about *ten hours and a half after* the moon's passage; but on the east side of the bay, the flood runs up a full hour later.

The *latitude* of the north-east end of Aken's Island, from an observation in the artificial horizon, is 22° 21' 35" south.

Longitude from twelve sets of distances of the sun and moon, taken by lieutenant Flinders, and reduced to the same place, 150° 18' 45"; but from the survey, and the position afterwards fixed in Broad Sound, it is preferably 150° 15' 0" east.

Variation from azimuths taken with a theodolite at the same place, 9° 48'; but the bearings on the top of the eminence showed it to be 9° 0'. The variation on shore, on the *west* side of the bay, may therefore be taken at 9° 24' east.

Upon Mount Westall on the east side, and at the south end of Leicester Island, it was from the bearings 8° 50'. Upon the small islet at the head of the bay, 9° 25'.

At our anchorage on the west side of the bay, Mr. Flinders took azimuths when the ship's head was S. E. by E., which gave 6° 31' by one compass; before he had done, the ship swung to the flood tide with her head W. N. W., and two other compasses then gave 11° 27' and 11° 4': the mean corrected to the meridian, will be 8° 46' east.

At an anchorage towards the east side of the bay, the same officer observed the variation with two compasses, when the head was east, to be 4° 49', or corrected, 7° 21' east.

The difference in Strong-tide Passage, where the land was one mile to the south-south-east on one side, and the same to the west on the other, was still more remarkable; for when the head was N. E. by N., an amplitude gave me 9° 10', or corrected, 10° 34' east.

There might have been an error in any of the ship observations of half a degree; but I am persuaded that the attraction of the land, sometimes to the east and sometimes west, as the ship was near one or the other side of the bay, was the great cause of the difference in the corrected results; and it will presently be seen, that the effect on a neighbouring part of the coast was much more considerable.

CHAPTER III.

Departure from Shoal-water Bay, and anchorage in Thirsty Sound.
Magnetical observations.
Boat excursion to the nearest Northumberland Islands.
Remarks on Thirsty Sound.
Observations at West Hill, Broad Sound.
Anchorage near Upper Head.
Expedition to the head of Broad Sound: another round Long Island.
Remarks on Broad Sound, and the surrounding country.
Advantages for a colony.
Astronomical observations, and remarks on the high tides.

[EAST COAST. THIRSTY SOUND.]
SATURDAY 4 SEPTEMBER 1802

At noon September 4, when the botanical gentlemen returned from their excursion to Pine Mount, we made sail out of Shoal-water Bay with a breeze from the eastward. In steering north-west amongst the small islands, the soundings were between 9 and 14 fathoms; and nearly the same afterwards, in keeping at three or four miles from the coast. I intended to go into Thirsty Sound; but not reaching it before dark, the anchor was dropped in 8 fathoms, sandy bottom, when the top of Pier Head bore west, three miles. In the morning [SUNDAY 5 SEPTEMBER 1802] we ran into the Sound, and anchored in 6 fathoms, with the points of entrance bearing N. 16° and S. 67° E., one mile. The carpenters had for some time been employed in making a sliding keel for the Lady Nelson, from the pine logs cut in Port Bowen; and being now finished, it was sent on board.

The botanists landed upon the east shore, preferring the main land for their pursuits; and the launch was sent to haul the seine on that side, at a beach a little way up the Sound. I went to the top of Pier Head and took bearings of the Northumberland Islands, as also of the points and hills of the coast to the east and west; the most essential of them to the connexion of the survey, were as under:

Mount Westall, station on the top, S. 63° 20' E. Aken's Island, station on the N. E. end, S. 43 10 E. Pine Mount, S. 25 5 E. Long Island, the north point, distant 8 miles, N. 65 5 W. Peaked Hill, west side of Broad Sound, N. 61 25 W. Northumberland I., a peak, marked h, N. 22 25 W. Northumberland I., No. 3 peak (of Percy Isles), N. 20 10 E.

Captain Cook observed, when taking bearings upon the top of Pier Head, "that the needle differed very considerably in its position, even to thirty degrees, in some places more, in others less; and once he found it differ from itself no less than two points in the distance of fourteen feet." (Hawkesworth, III, 126); from whence he concluded there was iron ore in the hills. I determined, in consequence, to make more particular observations, both with the theodolite and dipping needle; and shall briefly state the results obtained on this, and on the following day.

Azimuths were taken, and the bearing of Mount Westall, distant thirty-four miles, was set at S. 63° 28' E. (true), whilst the theodolite remained in the same place; and from a comparison between this bearing and those of the same object at different parts of the head, the variations were deduced. The dip was observed with both ends of the needle, and the face of the instrument changed each time.

At the highest top of Pier Head, Var. 3° 25' E. Dip 53° 20' S. West, three yards from it, 6 10 S. E. three yards, 10 5 S. S. E., ten yards, 8 6 52 19 North, four, 6 55 N. E., twenty, 6 50 50 35 N. N. E., one-sixth mile, at the water side, 7 6 50 28 S. E., one-third mile, at ditto, 8 2 50 50

There are here no differences equal to those found by captain Cook; but it is to be observed, that he used a ship's azimuth compass, probably not raised further from the ground than to be placed on a stone, whereas my theodolite stood upon legs, more than four feet high. The dipping needle was raised about two feet; and by its greater inclination at the top of the hill, shows the principal attraction to have been not far from thence. The least dip, 50° 28', taken at the shore on the north side of the head, was doubtless the least affected; but it appears to have been half a degree too much, for at Port Bowen, twenty-two miles further south, it was no more than 50° 20'. An amplitude taken on board the ship in the Sound by lieutenant Flinders, when the head was S. S. W., gave variation 8° 39', or corrected to the meridian, 7° 40' east. As Pier Head lay almost exactly in the meridian, from the ship, its magnetism would not alter the direction of the needle; and I therefore consider 7° 40' to be very nearly the true variation, when unaffected by local causes: in Port Bowen, it varied from 7° 40' to 8° 30' east.

Notwithstanding this very sensible effect upon the needle, both horizontally and vertically, I did not find, any more than captain Cook, that a piece of the stone applied to the theodolite drew the needle at all out of its direction; nevertheless I am induced to think, that the attraction was rather dispersed throughout the mass of stone composing Pier Head, than that any mine of iron ore exists in it. The stone is a porphyry of a dark, blueish colour.

MONDAY 6 SEPTEMBER 1802

On the 6th, at noon, when the observations were finished and I had proposed to quit Thirsty Sound, the wind and tide were both against us. To employ the rest of the day usefully, I went over in the whale boat, accompanied by the landscape painter, to the 6th, 7th, and 8th Northumberland Islands, which, with many low islets and rocks near them, form a cluster three or four leagues to the north-east of the Sound. Orders were left with lieutenant Fowler to get the ship under way as early as possible on the following morning, and come out to meet us.

Nearly mid-way between Pier Head and the cluster, lie some rocks surrounded with breakers; and until they were passed the depth was from 6 to 8 fathoms, and 11 afterwards. We rowed to a beach at the north-west end of the 7th island, proposing there to pass the night, and hoped to turn some turtle; but proofs of natives having lately visited, or being perhaps then on the island, damped our prospects, and still more did the absence of turtle tracks; yet under each tree near the shore were the remains of a turtle feast.

TUESDAY 7 SEPTEMBER 1802

In the morning I ascended the highest hill on the 7th island, and took bearings; but the hazy weather which had come on with a strong wind at E. S. E., confined them within a circle of three leagues. This island is somewhat more than a mile in length, and was covered with grass, but almost destitute of wood; the rock is a greenish, speckled stone, with veins of quartz finely inserted, and is something between granite and porphyry. The 6th island is the largest of this little cluster, being two and a half miles long; and it was well covered with wood. We rowed over to it with some difficulty on account of the wind, but could not sound in the channel; it appeared to be deep, its least width three-quarters of a mile, and in fine weather a ship might anchor there and procure pines fit for top masts, at several places in the group. Water was found under the hills on the 6th island; but not in sufficient quantities for the purpose of a ship.

I looked anxiously, but in vain, for lieutenant Fowler to come out of Thirsty Sound; for the wind blew so strong that it was uncertain whether the boat could fetch over, or that it was even safe to attempt it; our provisions, besides, were nearly exhausted, and nothing more substantial than oysters could be procured. Pressed by necessity, we set off under close-reefed sails; and the boat performing admirably, fetched the low neck to leeward of Pier Head, whence another boat took us to the ship; and at high water in the evening, the whale boat floated over the neck and followed.

When Mr. Fowler had weighed in the morning, according to my directions, the ship had driven so near the shore before the stream anchor was at the bows, that he let go the small bower; but the cable parted, and obliged him to drop the best bower, being then in 3 fathoms water with the wind blowing strong into the sound. By means of a warp to the brig, the best bower was shifted into 4 fathoms; and when I got on board, the stream and small bower anchors had just been recovered. The weather tide made at nine in the evening, and we ran into 7 fathoms in the channel; and at daylight stood out of the sound, with the brig in company, having then a moderate breeze at south-east.

Of Thirsty Sound as a harbour, very little can be said in praise; the north-east and east winds throw in a good deal of sea, and there is not room for more than three or four ships, without running up into the narrow part; and what the depth may be there I did not examine, but saw that there were shoals. The entrance of the sound may be known by two round hills, one on each side, lying nearly north and south, one mile and a half from each other: the northernmost is Pier Head. The surrounding country is clothed with grass and wood; but on the Long-Island side the grass is coarse, the trees are thinly scattered, and the soil is every where too stony for the cultivation of grain.

There were many traces of natives, though none recent. Judging from what was seen round the fire places, turtle would seem to be their principal food; and indeed several turtle were seen in the water, but we had not dexterity enough to take any of them. In fishing with the seine, at a small beach two miles up the sound, we always had tolerably good success; but no fresh water accessible to boats could be found in the neighbourhood.

The *latitude* of Pier Head, from an observation made at the top in an artificial horizon, is 22° 6' 53" S.

Longitude from thirteen sets of distances of the sun west of the moon, observed by lieutenant Flinders, 149° 47' 50"; but by the survey and the fixed position in Broad Sound, with which the time-keepers agreed, it will be more correctly 150° 0' 10" E.

Captain Cook specifies the situation of Thirsty Sound to be in latitude 22° 10', longitude 149° 42' (Hawkesworth, III, 128); but in the chart published by Mr. Dalrymple, it is 22° 7' and 149° 36', which agrees nearer with the deductions of Mr. Wales (*Astron. Obs.* p. 135). In either case it appears, that my longitude was getting more eastward from captain Cook as we advanced further along the coast.

WEDNESDAY 8 SEPTEMBER 1802

The tides in Thirsty Sound were neaped at this time, and the rise, judging by the lead line, was from ten to twelve feet; but captain Cook says, "at spring tides the water does not rise less than sixteen or eighteen feet," which I have no doubt is correct. It ceases at *ten hours and three quarters after* the moon passes over and under the meridian.

On quitting Thirsty Sound we steered north-westward, to pass round a chain of rocks extending six miles out from Pier Head, and behind which there was a bight in Long Island, with some appearance of an opening. It was my intention to examine Broad Sound up to the furthest navigable part, and we hauled up between the north point of Long Island and a cluster of small isles lying three miles to the north-west; but finding the water too shallow, and that it would be more advantageous to begin the examination on the west side, I desired Mr. Murray to lead round the *North-point Isles* and across the sound. A small reef lies between four and five miles N. E. by E. from the largest and easternmost of these isles; it is covered at half tide, and therefore dangerous, but we had 7 to 8 fathoms at less than a mile distance, on the inside.

At noon, the depth was 8 fathoms, the largest North-point Isle, which is nearly separated into two, was distant four miles, and our situation was as under:

Latitude observed to the north, 21° 56' 17" Pier Head top, bore S. 38 E. Northumberland Island, peak marked 'h', N. 15 W. North-point I., westernmost, highest part, S. 56 W. North-point I., largest, S. 37 to 16 W.

In steering W. by N., rippling water was seen ahead at one o'clock. and the depth diminishing to 4 fathoms, we hauled a little to the southward and then resumed our course. This rippling seems to have been on a part of the same shoal near which captain Cook anchored in 3 fathoms; for it lies five miles from the North-point Isles, and as he says, "half way between them and three small islands which lie directly without them."

[EAST COAST. BROAD SOUND.]

Our course for the west side of Broad Sound passed close to some low, flat isles, lying to the south-east of the peaked West Hill set from Pier Head. At dusk I sought to anchor behind the hill, for it had the appearance of being separated from the main land; but the water being too shallow, we hauled off upon a wind. At ten o'clock, however, the breeze having become light and the sea gone down, an anchor was dropped in 5 fathoms, sandy bottom; whence the top of West Hill bore N. 68° W. three miles. A flood tide was found running from the N. N. E., one mile and a quarter per hour.

THURSDAY 9 SEPTEMBER 1802

In the morning I landed with the botanical gentlemen, and wished to ascend the top of the hill; but the brush wood was too thick to be penetrable. Upon a projecting head on the north-east side, I took a part, and about half way up the hill on the south-east side, the remainder of a set of bearings, which included many of the Northumberland Isles not before seen, and other of the Flat Isles within Broad Sound. The furthest visible part of the main land towards Cape Palmerston, was distant about five leagues, and behind it was a hill to which, from its form, I gave the name of *Mount Funnel*; the shore both to the north and south was low, and the Flat Isles to the southward of the ship were mostly over-run with mangroves. I did not go round West Hill, and could not see whether it were connected with the main land, or not; but if joined, it must be by a very low isthmus. The bearings at this station, most essential to the connection of the survey, were these:

Main coast, the extremes, N. 1° and S. 10° 45' E. Pier Head, the top, S. 61 25 E. Northumberland Isles, peak marked 'h', N. 61 45 E. Northumberland Isles, high northmost marked 'i', dist. 11 L. N. 19 15 E.

The stone of the hill had in it specks of quartz or feldtspath, and was not much unlike that of Pier Head; but it had a more basaltic appearance. A piece of it applied to the theodolite, drew the needle two degrees out of its direction, and yet the bearings did not show any great difference from the true variation; for an amplitude taken on board the ship by Mr. Flinders, when the head was N. N. E, gave 6° 18', or corrected to the meridian, 7° 17' east, and the variation on the eastern side of the hill was 8° 15', according to the back bearing of Pier Head.

From an observation of the sun's upper and lower limbs in an artificial horizon, the latitude was 21° 50' 18", and the ship bore from thence S. 68° E. two miles and a half; the latitude of the ship should therefore have been 21° 51' 14"; but a meridian altitude observed to the north by lieutenant Flinders, gave 21° 49' 54"; and I believe that altitudes from the sea horizon can never be depended on nearer than to one minute, on account of the variability of the horizontal refraction. From this cause it was that, when possible, we commonly observed the latitude on board the ship both to the north and south, taking the sun's altitude one way and his supplement the other, and the mean of the two results was considered to be true; separately, they often differed 1', 2', and even 3', and sometimes they agreed. The observation to the north most commonly gave the least south latitude, but not always, nor was there any regular coincidence between the results and the heights of the barometer or thermometer; though in general, the more hazy the weather, the greater were the differences. At this time, the wind was light from the eastward and weather hazy; the thermometer stood at 72°, and barometer at 30.15 inches.

At two o'clock we got under way to go up Broad Sound, it being then near low water. After steering south-east one mile, the depth rapidly diminished and we tacked; but the ship was set upon a bank of sand, where she hung five minutes and then swung off. I afterwards steered nearer to the shore, in deeper water; and at dusk the anchor was dropped in 5 fathoms, sandy bottom, between the Flat Isles and the main, West Hill bearing N. 35° W. three leagues; the master sounded towards the coast, which was five miles off, and found the deepest water to be on that side. In the morning [FRIDAY 10 SEPTEMBER 1802] the wind had shifted to south, and we beat up in a channel formed by the Flat Isles and the shoals attached to them, on one side, and the shelving banks from the main coast, on the other. We had the assistance of a strong flood tide till eleven o'clock; at which time the anchor was let go, one mile from the north end of the 4th Flat Island.

I landed immediately, with the botanists; and at the south-east end of the island, which is a little elevated, took bearings and the meridian altitude of both limbs of the sun from an artificial horizon. The latitude deduced was 22° 8' 33"; and the ship bearing N. 19° 30' W., two miles, it should have been for her, 22° 6' 40"; but lieutenant Flinders' observation to the north gave 22° 5' 19", or 1' 21" less, nearly as on the preceding day; and it was ascertained that the difference arose neither from the eye nor the instrument. Amongst the bearings were,

West Hill, the top,   N. 16° 40' W. Northumberland Isles. the peak marked 'h',   N. 25 15 E. Long Island, extreme of the north point,   N. 73 35 E. Upper Head, on the west shore up Broad Sound, S. 39 55 E.

The 4th Flat Isle is about one mile long, and there is a smaller lying off its south-east end; they are a little elevated, and bear grass and small trees; but the shores are covered with mangroves, and surrounded with extensive flats of mud and sand. The main coast, from which they lie two or three miles, is also low, with mangroves and shelving mud banks; but there is a deep channel between, of a mile in width. In the evening, when the flood made, we steered into this channel with a light sea-breeze; but not having time to clear it before dark, the anchor was dropped in 4 fathoms at six o'clock.

My attention was attracted this evening by the vast extent of mud left dry on each side of the channel, and I ordered particular attention to be paid to the tides during the night. At eleven o'clock, when the flood had ceased running, the depth was sounded and the lead line measured, and the same at half past five in the morning [SATURDAY 11 SEPTEMBER 1802] when it was low water; the difference was no less than thirty-two feet, and it wanted a day of being full moon; so that the springs may reach two or three feet higher. The flood set S. by E., but its greatest rate did not exceed one mile and three quarters an hour.

At daylight the wind was south-east, directly against us. We backed and filled, drifting up with the flood between the shoals on each side, and having the Lady Nelson and a boat ahead; but on approaching the end of the channel, our passage into the sound was blocked up by a bank running across, upon which there was not water enough for the ship by a fathom, and we therefore anchored. At nine the tide had risen a fathom. and we passed over into the open sound; the depth immediately increasing to 4 and 7 fathoms, reduced to low water. So long as the flood continued running we worked up the sound; and when it ceased, anchored three miles from a shallow opening in the low western shore, the second which had been observed. We again proceeded upwards with the evening's tide until dusk; and at nine next morning [SUNDAY 12 SEPTEMBER 1802] passed a fifth opening, and anchored abreast of the hilly projection on its east side, which I have named *Upper Head*, in 4 fathoms, soft bottom, two-thirds of a mile from the shore. This was the first place on the main where there was any prospect of being able to land; for the western shore, thus far up, was equally low, and as much over-run with mangroves and defended by muddy flats, as the shores of Keppel Bay.

It being my intention to explore the head of Broad Sound with the brig and whale boat, a situation where tents could be fixed and an easy communication held with the ship during my absence, was the object now sought; and I immediately went with a party of the gentlemen, to ascertain how far Upper Head was calculated for our purpose. We landed at half flood, without difficulty; and on ascending the hill, obtained a view of the Sound which exceeded my expectations. Amongst the many bearings taken, were the following fixed points in the survey.

Pine Mount, of Shoal-water Bay,   S. 84° 38' E. Pier Head, the western part,   N. 36   7 E. West hill, the top,   N. 28   5 W. Flat Isles, the 4th, station there, N. 39 53 W.

The breadth of the Sound, from Upper Head over to the inner end of Long Island, appeared to be three leagues, but it contracted upwards, and assumed the same river-like form as Shoalwater Bay; and it was to be feared, from the mangrove shores and muddiness of the water, that it would terminate in the same manner. No shoals could be then distinguished; but towards low water in the evening I again ascended the hill, and saw to my regret, that the upper parts were mostly occupied with banks of mud and sand, many of which were dry, and extended downward past the inner entrance of Thirsty Sound. Amongst the banks were various channels; but that of about two miles wide where the ship lay, was by far the most considerable. The small fifth opening, close on the west side of Upper Head, ran some miles in the low land towards the foot of a ridge of hills, lying three or four leagues at the back of the shore; but the greater part of this inlet was also taken up by mud banks, and the borders covered with mangroves. There was no fresh water at Upper Head, nor did I see any prospect of obtaining wherewith to complete the holds of the two vessels before leaving the coast; unless it were at a place a little higher up on the same side, to which the appearance of another opening between two hills, induced me to move the ship.

MONDAY 13 SEPTEMBER 1802

Next morning, when the flood made, we drifted upwards, with the Lady Nelson and a boat sounding ahead. After advancing three miles the brig suddenly took the ground, and we dropped a stream anchor; but in swinging to it, the ship was caught upon a bank of quick sand in eleven feet; and the tide running strong upon the broad side, it made her heel in a manner to excite alarm. The sails were immediately clewed down, and the top-gallant yards struck; and it appearing that the stream anchor allowed the ship to drive further up the bank as the tide rose, the best bower was let go, and then she righted and swung to the tide. The Lady Nelson also got off safe; but a part of the after sliding keel was carried away.

I went in a boat to examine the place which had presented the appearance of an opening; but it proved to be only a bending in the shore, and the mud banks and mangroves did not admit of landing; we therefore went back with the returning ebb to Upper Head, and moored the ship nearly in our first situation; where there was something more than 3 fathoms all round, at low water.

TUESDAY 14 SEPTEMBER 1802

On the following morning, the time keepers and other instruments were sent on shore under the charge of lieutenant Flinders, with two of the young gentlemen to assist him, and a guard of marines for the protection of the tents. It had appeared from the survey, that the time keepers were losing more than the Port-Jackson rates supposed; and before quitting this coast for the Gulph of Carpentaria, it was necessary to take fresh observations.

Mr. Flinders undertook as usual to perform this service, whilst I should be absent up the Sound; and lieutenant Fowler was directed to examine and air all the stores, and make the ship ready for sea against my return.

Having made these dispositions, I embarked in the Lady Nelson with the naturalist, taking my whale boat and surveying instruments. We had a strong flood tide; and after grounding on a bank, anchored eleven miles above the ship, in 3 fathoms, that being the greatest depth to be found. It was then high water; and the brig being expected to be left dry by the ebb, we prepared for it by mooring, to prevent all chance of settling on the anchor, and hove up the fore and after keels; the new main keel being swelled by the wet, could not be raised, and when it took the ground, the vessel turned about violently and dragged both the anchors, until the keel broke off, and then she lay easy.

At low water, the seamen went out upon the dry flat and found the best bower cable parted, and the anchor so far buried in the quicksand, that it could not be raised. At ten o'clock the flood tide came rolling in, and presently set the brig afloat; the anchor was then weighed with ease, by means of a hawser previously bent to it, and the vessel rode by the small bower, against a tide which ran at the strongest between four and five knots.

WEDNESDAY 15 SEPTEMBER 1802

The Lady Nelson again took the ground at six in the morning. On sounding over to the east shore, distant half a mile, I found a small channel leading upwards, with four or five feet more water in it than where the brig lay; the western shore was two miles distant over a silty flat, which was dry at low water and level as a race ground.

At eleven, the flood came in, six or eight inches perpendicular, with a roaring noise; and so soon as it had passed the brig, I set off with Mr. Brown and Mr. Lacy in the whale boat, to follow it up the small channel on the eastern shore; and having a fair wind we outran the tide and were sometimes obliged to wait its rising before we could proceed. At the end of six miles the small channel led across to the western side; and the rare opportunity of a landing place induced me to pitch our tent there for the night: two miles higher up, the whole breadth of the Sound was reduced to half a mile.

The country here was a stiff, clayey flat, covered with grass, and seemed to have been overflowed at spring tides; though the high water of this day did not reach it by five feet. Three or four miles to the southward there were some hills, whence I hoped to see the course of the stream up to its termination; and having time before dark, we set off. The grass of the plain was interspersed with a species of sensitive plant, whose leaves curled up in, and about our footsteps in such a manner, that the way we had come was for some time distinguishable. From the nearest of the small hills, I set the bearings of Double and Pine Mounts, our tent, and the brig at anchor, by which this station was fixed as in the chart; but in order to reconcile the bearings, I found it necessary to allow 12° of east variation.

Towards Double Mount and Shoal-water Bay, the country consisted of gently-rising hills and extensive plains, well covered with wood and apparently fertile. The stream at the head of Broad Sound could not be traced from hence more than three or four miles above the tent; but it may possibly run up much further to the south-eastward, though too small to be distinguished in the wood, or to be navigable for boats. To the south and westward there was a ridge of high land, which appeared to be a prolongation of the same whence the upper branches of Port Bowen and Shoal-water Bay take their rise, and by which the low land and small arms on the west side of Broad Sound are bounded. A similar ridge ran behind Port Curtis and Keppel Bay, and it is not improbable that the two are connected, and of the same substance; for at Port Curtis the basis stone of the country was a granite, and this small hill was the same. It has been more than once observed, that granite is amongst the substances which exert an influence upon the magnetic needle; and it is to the attraction of the ridge of mountains to the south and westward, that I attribute the great variation found in the bearings at this station.

We returned to the tent at sunset; and there passed a disagreeable night amongst musketoes, sand flies, and ants. At four in the morning [THURSDAY 16 SEPTEMBER 1802] the ebb had made, and we embarked in the boat; but the depth of water was so little that we could not proceed, and were obliged to re-land and wait for the following tide; not without apprehension of being left till the next springs came on. At two in the afternoon the flood came up rapidly, and in half an hour it was high water; we set off immediately, and after some trouble from the shoals, reached the brig at five o'clock. Mr. Murray got under way at three the next morning [FRIDAY 17 SEPTEMBER 1802] to beat down to Upper Head, the wind being from the northward; but the Lady Nelson getting aground, I went off with Mr. Brown in my boat, and reached the ship at seven o'clock, and in the evening, the brig arrived.

Lieutenant Fowler had gone through the most essential duties, and the ship was nearly ready for sea; but on landing at the tents I found that the time keepers had been let down, and the business of finding new rates for them was to be recommenced. This accident would require a week to be repaired; and being unwilling to remain so long inactive, I determined to leave Mr. Flinders at Upper Head, and take the ship over to the inner end of Thirsty Sound, where it appeared there was something to correct in captain Cook's chart.

SATURDAY 18 SEPTEMBER 1802

The Lady Nelson had lost two sheets of copper, and the trunks of the sliding keels required some reparation; I therefore desired lieutenant Murray to lay his vessel on shore and get these matters arranged, to cut wood for himself, and be ready to sail in a week for Torres' Strait; and his stock of water was completed out of the Investigator.

SUNDAY 19 SEPTEMBER 1802

On the 19th in the morning we unmoored the ship, and a little before low tide stretched over towards Thirsty Sound; but the numerous shoals to be encountered, and which cannot be concisely described otherwise than in a chart, caused much delay; and it was near noon of the day following [MONDAY 20 SEPTEMBER 1802] before we anchored at the south end of Long Island, in 3 fathoms, and about one mile from the low mangrove shore. At the south end of the island was a small hill, bearing S. 55° E. one mile and a half from the ship, where I landed with a party of the gentlemen; it forms the west point of the inner entrance to Thirsty Sound, as some low red cliffs, one mile and a half distant, do the east point; but a shoal, dry at low water, lies in the middle, and the channels on each side are not calculated for a ship. The small hill was found to be on a detached islet one mile long, the greater part of which is mud covered with mangroves; the hill is partly excavated by an arched way running through it, and the stone is of a mixed red and white colour, and of an ochry consistence. From the highest top, I set:

Upper Head, bearing S. 28° 22' W. Double Mount. S. 53 20 E. Pine Mount, S. 61 5 E.

These bearings place the inner end of Thirsty Sound in latitude 22° 16'; and curtail the distance of thirty miles from Pier Head in captain Cook's chart, to twelve miles and a half.

TUESDAY 21 SEPTEMBER 1802

On the 21st, the botanical gentlemen went over in the launch to the east side of Thirsty Sound, the main land having been always found more productive in the objects of their pursuit, than any island however large. I went to examine along the west side of Long Island; but had not proceeded two miles before an opening presented itself amongst the mangroves. It led to the eastward, and then separated into two branches; and in following that which trended north-east I came into Thirsty Sound, and landed five miles above the inner entrance, at an islet in mid-channel, which had been set from Pier Head and is laid down by captain Cook.

No less than five different pieces of land were found to be cut off from the south end of Long Island, by winding channels amongst the mangroves; and I now saw the prospect of a passage through the middle, leading out at the bight between the north point and Pier Head. A woody and rather elevated islet obscures the inner end of the opening, and seems to have prevented captain Cook's observing this separation when going up Thirsty Sound in his boat. I found in it a good bottom, with 3 to 5 fathoms water, and room for a ship to swing, or sail through as far as the outer opening to sea; but another island lies in the outlet, the bottom is rocky, and the regular depth at low water is not so much as 3 fathoms on either side.

Having taken a second set of angles, and passed out by the new opening, I steered northward along the east side of Long Island; but although the land be high and rather steep, there was seldom so much as 3 fathoms at a mile distance. I landed at the north end of the island, to ascertain better the forms and positions of the North-point Isles; and then, steering southward along the west side, entered a cove where the form of the surrounding land gave a hope of finding fresh water for the ship; but the borders were covered with mangroves, and we could not get sufficiently far up to know whether any part of the stream running through them were fresh. Another set of angles was taken from a hill on the south side of the cove; and the sun being then set, our tent was pitched for the night.

WEDNESDAY 22 SEPTEMBER 1802

Next morning I steered onward along the west side of Long Island, landing occasionally to examine the gullies made by the rains; but at this time they were all dry. As far to the south as Westside Islet, the shore is tolerably high and the water deep; and near to the inner end of the islet, where I landed to take angles, there was no bottom with 10 fathoms; but the shore from thence to the ship was low and covered with mangroves, and even the rocky points cannot be approached within half a mile, except by boats.

Not a single Indian was seen during this excursion round Long Island; nor from the length of the grass and appearance of their fire places, do I think they had been there for some months.

THURSDAY 23 SEPTEMBER 1802

Next day I made a further examination of the winding channels at the south end of Long Island; and also went to an inlet on the east side of Broad Sound, the entrance of which is so much obstructed by shoals, that it was difficult to find a sufficient depth, even for the boat. I landed with the naturalist at a low, cliffy head on the north side of the entrance; but not without wading a quarter of a mile in the mud. We saw from thence, that this inlet, though presenting the appearance of a respectable river when the tide was in, had no perceptible breadth at five miles within the land, that it was almost wholly dry at low water, and that the shores were covered with mangroves to a great extent; even the cliffy head where we stood, was surrounded with mangroves, and appeared to be insulated at spring tides.

FRIDAY 24 SEPTEMBER 1802

In the morning of the 24th, we got under way to return to Upper Head; and having the same difficulties to encounter amongst the shoals as before, did not reach our former anchorage until next day [SATURDAY 25 SEPTEMBER 1802]. On landing at the tents, I found, to my no less surprise than regret, that the time keepers had again been let down; and no more than one day's rates had been since obtained. Twenty-five sets of distances of the sun and moon had been taken to correspond with an equal number on the opposite side; and it appeared that lieutenant Flinders being intent upon these, had forgotten to wind up the time keepers on the 22nd at noon.

This fresh difficulty was very embarrassing. To go away for Torres' Strait and the Gulph of Carpentaria without good rates, was to cripple the accuracy of all our longitudes; and on the other hand, the expected approach of the contrary monsoon on the North Coast admitted of no longer delay in Broad Sound. On comparing the last day's rates with those of the four days previously obtained, the letting down did not appear to have produced any material alteration; and I therefore determined to combine the whole together, and to sail immediately.

SUNDAY 26 SEPTEMBER 1802

The following day was occupied in completing the holds with wood, taking on board our shore establishment, and preparing for sea; and next morning [MONDAY 27 SEPTEMBER 1802] we steered down Broad Sound, with the Lady Nelson in company, keeping near the western side to avoid the middle shoals. On a sea breeze coming in at north, we tacked towards the North-point Isles; and at sunset, the flood tide having then made, anchored in 8 fathoms, upon a bottom of sand and rock, the north-westernmost isle bearing N. 6° E., two leagues. In the morning we passed round the North-point Isles, with a breeze from the south-east; and thus quitted Broad Sound, steering off for the outermost and largest of the Northumberland Islands.

There remains little to be said upon the navigation of Broad Sound, more than what has been related of our courses in it, and what will be found in the chart. The western channel, between the Flat Isles and the main, is not to be recommended; but after steering up the middle of the Sound and passing these isles, the western shore should be kept nearest a-bord. A ship may then reach Upper Head without difficulty, and lie there in perfect safety from all winds, at two-thirds of a mile off; but cannot go higher up the sound without risk of grounding on the banks. From half flood to half ebb, landing is easy at Upper Head, and it is perhaps the sole place on the main possessing that advantage; every where else the shore is very low, fronted with mud banks, and covered, in some places miles deep, with interwoven mangroves, amongst which the tide flows at high water.

The stone of Upper Head, and apparently of all the hills in its neighbourhood, is granitic; whilst that of Long Island and West Hill approach nearer to porphyry. At the inner entrance of Thirsty Sound the points are mostly composed of an earth, which is not heavy, is sometimes red, but more frequently white, or mixed; and of a consistence not harder than ochre.

Long Island, though covered with grass and wood, is stony and incapable of ordinary cultivation. On the main land, the low parts between the mangroves and the hills seemed to be of a tolerably good soil; and according to the report of some of the gentlemen, who made an excursion at the back of Upper Head, the vallies there produce good grass and appeared fertile. There seems, indeed, to be a considerable extent of land about Broad Sound and on the peninsula between it and Shoal-water Bay, which, if not calculated to give a rich return to the cultivator of wheat, would support much cattle, and produce maize, sugar, and tobacco; and cotton and coffee would grow upon the more rocky sides of the hills, and probably even upon Long Island. Should it ever be in contemplation to make an establishment in New South Wales within the tropic, in aid of Port Jackson and the colonies to the southward, this neighbourhood would probably be chosen; and the great rise of tide presents advantages which might be some time turned to account in ship building. On the west side of the sound, near the Flat Isles, the rise at spring tides is not less than thirty, and perhaps reaches to thirty-five feet. At Upper Head it is from twenty at the neaps, to thirty or more at the springs; but the bottom rises so much towards the top of the sound, that the tide there never seems to exceed twelve feet. The time of high water is nearly *eleven hours after* the moon's passage over and under the meridian; though the flood runs up near an hour on the west side of the sound, after it is high water by the shore.

The places best calculated for the construction of docks, appear to be at the uppermost or 4th Flat Isles, where the shoals form a natural harbour, and at the entrance of the opening near Upper Head, in which is a small islet of sand and rock, not covered with mangroves nor surrounded with mud flats. The pines of Port Bowen, Shoal-water Bay, and the Northumberland Isles, would furnish the necessary spars and lighter planking; and there is no reason to think that the *eucalyptus*, which grows all over the country, should not be as fit for timbers, etc., as it is found to be further southward. No iron ore was seen in the neighbourhood; but were a colony established and the back ridge of mountains well examined, this and other metallic productions might be found. The attraction which the mountains seemed to have upon the needle, is in favour of this probability; but the iron work might be prepared at Port Jackson where the ore exists, and in whose vicinity there are plenty of coals.

Fresh water was scarce at this time, none being any where discovered near the sea side, except a small rill at the back of Upper Head, little more than adequate to the supply of the tents; it can however be scarcely doubted, that fresh water for domestic purposes would be found in most parts of the country; and there is a season of the year, most probably the height of summer, when rain falls abundantly, as was demonstrated by the torrent-worn marks down the sides of the hills.

Not a single native was seen, either on the shores of Thirsty, or Broad Sounds, during the whole time of our stay.

There are kangaroos in the woods, but not in numbers. The shoals all over the sound are frequented by flocks of ducks and curlews; and we saw in the upper part, some pelicans, an individual of a large kind of crane, and another of a white bird, in form resembling a curlew. Many turtle were seen in the water about Long Island, and from the bones scattered around the deserted fire places, this animal seemed to form the principal subsistence of the natives; but we had not the address to obtain any. Hump-backed whales frequent the entrance of the sound, and would present an object of interest to a colony. In fishing, we had little success with hook and line; and the nature of the shores did not admit of hauling the seine.

The climate here, being one degree within the tropic, was warm at this season, which may be considered as the spring and the driest time of the year. On board the ship, the height of the thermometer did not exceed 76°, with the warm winds from the northward, but at the tents it averaged at noon somewhat above 90°; and the musketoes and sand flies were very troublesome at all places near the mangroves. We did not see any snakes or other venemous reptiles or insects.

The *latitude* of Upper Head, from six meridian observations in the artificial horizon, is 22° 23' 24" S.

Longitude from fifty sets of distances of the sun and moon, given in Table II of the second Appendix to this Volume, 149° 46' 53" E.

The errors of the time keepers from mean Greenwich time, at noon there Sept. 26, and their mean rates of going during seven days, of which four were before and three after they had been let down the second time, were as under:

Earnshaw's No. 543 slow 2h 3' 37.23" and losing 9.62" per day. Earnshaw's No. 520 slow 3h 29' 15.57" and losing 21.41" per day.

These errors and rates were found by lieutenant Flinders, from equal altitudes taken with a sextant on a stand, and using an artificial horizon of quicksilver.

The longitudes given by the time keepers on Sept. 12 a.m. at Upper Head, with the Port-Jackson rates, were these:

No. 543, 149° 54' 27" east. No. 520, 149° 53' 47.5" east.

The mean is 7' 14" to the east of the lunars; but on using rates equally accelerated from those at Port Jackson to the above at Upper Head, and commencing the acceleration on Aug. 15, at Keppel Bay, where the time keepers were found to be keeping their former rates, the mean longitude will be 149° 48' 56.6", or 2' 3.6" from the lunar observations; which is therefore the presumable sum of their irregularities after August 15, or in 27.7 days.

In fixing the positions of places along the East Coast, I have made use of the time keepers from Port Jackson to Port Curtis, without any correction. From Port Curtis to Broad Sound, the coast and islands are laid down from theodolite bearings taken on shore, combined with the observed latitudes; and consequently the accuracy in longitude of the first portion depends upon that of Port Jackson and the time keepers, and of the last, upon Upper Head and the survey. These two unconnected longitudes meet at Port Curtis, and the difference between them is there no more than 5".

From observations with the theodolite upon the top of Upper Head, the *variation* was 8° 37' east; but on moving the instrument ten yards to the south-west, it was 45' less. At two other stations on the west side of the sound, it was 8° 15', and 8° 0'; and on board the ship 7° 17' and 7° 46', corrected. On the east side of the sound it differed at six stations on shore, from 8° to 6°; and on board the ship was 6° 44' corrected. As general results, therefore, but subject to many small deviations, the variation may be taken,

On the west side of Broad Sound at 8° 0' E. On the east side   7 0 At the head of the sound it was, at one station 12°, at another 10°; the mean,   11 0

The differences between the two sides of the sound, both on shore and on board, are nearly similar to what took place in Shoal-water Bay.

The rise of *tide* and time of high water have been mentioned; but it may be proper to say what I conceive to be the cause of the extraordinary rise in Broad Sound. From Cape Howe, at the southern extremity of the East Coast, to Port Curtis at the edge of the tropic, the time of high water falls between seven and nine hours after the moon's passage, and the rise does not exceed nine feet; but from thence to the northward, commencing with Keppel Bay, the time becomes later, and the rise augments, till, at Broad Sound, they reach eleven hours, and between thirty and thirty-five feet. The principal flood tide upon the coast is supposed to come from the south-east, and the ebb from the north, or north-west; but from the particular formation of Keppel and Shoal-water Bays, and of Broad Sound, whose entrances face the north, or north-west, this ebb tide sets into them, and accumulates the water for some time, becoming to them a flood. This will, in some degree, account for the later time and greater rise of the tide; and is conformable to what captain Cook says upon the same subject (Hawkesworth, III. 244); but I think there is still a super-adding cause. At the distance of about thirty leagues to the N. N. W. from Break-sea Spit, commences a vast mass of reefs, which lie from twenty to thirty leagues from the coast, and extend past Broad Sound. These reefs, being mostly dry at low water, will impede the free access of the tide; and the greater proportion of it will come in between Break-sea Spit and the reefs, and be late in reaching the remoter parts; and if we suppose the reefs to terminate to the north, or north-west of the Sound, or that a large opening in them there exist, another flood tide will come from the northward, and meet the former; and the accumulation of water from this meeting, will cause an extraordinary rise in Broad Sound and the neighbouring bays, in the same manner as the meeting of the tides in the English and Irish Channels causes a great rise upon the north coast of France and the west coast of England.

That an opening exists in the reefs will hereafter appear; and captain Cook's observations prove, that for more than a degree to the north-west of Broad Sound, the flood came from the northward. I found, when at anchor off Keppel Bay, and again off Island Head, that the flood there came from the east or south-east; but when lying three miles out from Pier Head, there was no set whatever; and I am disposed to think that it is at the entrance of Broad Sound, where the two floods meet each other.

CHAPTER IV.
The Percy Isles: anchorage at No. 2.
Boat excursions.
Remarks on the Percy Isles; with nautical observations.
Coral reefs: courses amongst them during eleven days search for a passage through, to sea.
Description of a reef.
Anchorage at an eastern Cumberland Isle.
The Lady Nelson sent back to Port Jackson.
Continuation of coral reefs; and courses amongst them during three other days.
Cape Gloucester.
An opening discovered, and the reefs quitted.
General remarks on the Great Barrier; with some instruction relative to the opening.
[EAST COAST. PERCY ISLES.]
TUESDAY 28 SEPTEMBER 1802
On quitting Broad Sound, we steered for the north-easternmost of the Northumberland Islands., which I intended to visit in the way to Torres' Strait. These are no otherwise marked by captain Cook, than as a single piece of land seen indistinctly, of three leagues in extent; but I had already descried from Mount Westall and Pier Head a cluster of islands, forming a distinct portion of this archipelago; and in honour of the noble house to which Northumberland gives the title of duke, I named them *Percy Isles*.

(Atlas, Plate XI.)
At noon, the observed latitude on both sides was 21° 51' 20"; the west end of the largest North-point Isle bore S. 18° W. three or four leagues, and the Percy Isles were coming in sight ahead. The weather was hazy; and the wind at E. S. E. preventing us from fetching No. 2, the largest isle, we tacked at five o'clock, when it bore S. 31° to 54° E, two or three leagues; No. 5, the north-westernmost of the cluster, bearing N. 24° W., two miles and a half. At dusk the anchor was dropped in 14 fathoms, sandy ground, two or three miles from some rocky islets which lie off the west side of No. 2. The flood tide at this anchorage came from the north-east, one mile per hour.

We got under way again in the morning [WEDNESDAY 29 SEPTEMBER 1802]; but the wind being light and unfavourable, and the tide adverse, I went off in the whale boat, accompanied by Messrs. Brown and Westall, to examine the passage between the rocky islets and No. 2, directing lieutenant Fowler to follow with the ship when the signal should be made. We first landed at the islets, where the same kind of pine as seen at Port Bowen and other places, was abundant; and leaving the two gentlemen there, I sounded the passage, which was a mile and a half wide, with a sandy bottom of 8 to 13 fathoms deep, and sheltered from all eastern winds. The signal was then made to the ship; and so soon as she was brought to anchor, I went to examine a little cove, or basin, into which the height of the surrounding hills gave expectation of finding a run of fresh water. The entrance is little more than wide enough for the oars of a rowing boat, the basin, within side, is mostly dry at low water, and the borders are over-run with the tiresome mangrove; but when the tide is in, it is one of the prettiest little places imaginable. In searching round the skirts, between the mangroves and feet of the hills, a torrent-worn gully was found with several holes of water; and one in particular, near the edge of the mangroves, where, by cutting a rolling way for the casks, the holds of the two vessels might be filled; and at a beach without side of the entrance to the basin, several hauls of the seine were made with good success.

THURSDAY 30 SEPTEMBER 1802

Early next morning, lieutenant Fowler landed with a party of men prepared to cut through the mangroves; but fresh water was discovered to ooze out from amongst them, much below high-water mark; and by digging in the sand at half ebb, our casks might be filled more easily, and with better water than in the gully. Whilst this duty was going on, the carpenters were sent to cut fire wood and pine logs upon the rocky islets, the botanical gentlemen followed their pursuits where it best pleased them, and my time was occupied in surveying. From a hill near the head of the basin, I took bearings of all the objects to the south and westward; amongst which, the five following were the most important to the connexion of the survey.

Mount Westall on the main (not distinct),   S. 23° 5' E. Northumberland Islands, the 4th, a peak,   S. 18 20 E. Northumberland Islands, the 7th, station on the hill,   S. 19 30 W. Northumberland Islands, a peaked I. marked 'h', S. 89° 55' to N. 87 35 W. Northumberland Islands, high northmost, marked 'i',   N. 57 0 W.

The circle was completed in the afternoon, from a higher part of the island near the north point; and the weather being tolerably clear, nearly the whole of the Northumberland Islands were comprehended in the bearings from one or the other station. Two distant pieces of land in the N. W. by N., marked *k* and *k1*, situate near the eastern Cumberland Islands of captain Cook, were also distinguished; but to the north-east, where I expected to see a continuation of the reefs discovered by captain Campbell of the brig Deptford, in 1797, neither reef nor island was visible.

SATURDAY 2 OCTOBER 1802

On the 2nd of October, Mr. Brown accompanied me to No. 1, the southernmost of the Percy Isles, which is near five miles long, and the second of the group in magnitude. Fresh water was found in ponds near the shore, and there were clusters of pine trees; but in general, this island is inferior to No. 2, both in soil and productions. Of the two peaked hills upon it, the south-easternmost is highest; but being craggy and difficult to be ascended, my bearings were taken from the western hill. In returning to the ship in the evening, we passed between No. 6 and the east side of No. 2, and round the north end of the latter island, in order to see the form of its coasts: the water was deep, and there appeared to be no hidden dangers.

SUNDAY 3 OCTOBER 1802

On the 3rd, Mr. Bauer, the natural-history painter, went with me to the northern Percy Isles, upon each of which is a hill somewhat peaked; but that on No. 3 is much the most so, and the highest; and being thickly covered with pine trees, is called *Pine Peak*: it lies in 21° 31½' south and 150° 14½' east. My principal object was to take angles for the survey; and not being able to ascend Pine Peak, from its great acclivity, we went onward to the two smaller islands No. 4; and from the top of the easternmost, a third Cumberland Island, marked *k2*, was distinguished, and the following amongst many other bearings, were taken.

Percy Isle No. 3, Pine Peak, distant 2½ miles,   S 2° 5' W. The ship, at anchor under No. 2,   S. 10 48 W. Northumberland I., the 7th, station,   S. 14 0 W. Northumberland I., the peak marked 'h',   S. 67 35 W. Northumberland I., the high, northmost, marked 'i', N. 73 10 W. Cumberland I., marked 'k', centre,   N. 36 0 W. Cumberland I., marked 'k2', centre,   N. 42 50 W.

There is no shelter amongst the northern Percy Isles against east winds; but ships may pass between them, taking care to avoid a rock which lies one mile northward from the Pine Peak, and is dry at low water. Nothing was seen on these islands to merit more particular notice; and their forms and situations will be best learned from the chart.

On returning to the ship at nine in the evening, I found lieutenant Fowler had quitted the shore with his tents and people, the holds were completed with water, and both vessels ready for sea.

No. 2, the largest of the Percy Isles, is about thirteen miles in circumference; and in its greatest elevation perhaps a thousand feet. The stone is mostly of two kinds. A concreted mass of different substances, held together by a hard, dark-coloured cement, was the most abundant; I did not see either coral or pumice-stone in the composition, but it otherwise much resembled that of Aken's Island in Shoal-water Bay, and still more a stratum seen at the north-west part of Long Island: it was found at the tops of the highest hills, as well as in the lower parts. The second kind of stone is light, close-grained, and easily splits, but not in layers; it is of a yellowish colour, and probably argillaceous.

The surface of the island is either sandy or stony, or both, with a small proportion of vegetable soil intermixed. It is generally covered with grass and wood; and some of the vallies round the basin might be made to produce vegetables, especially one in which there was a small run, and several holes of fresh water. The principal wood is the *eucalyptus*, or gum tree, but it is not large; small cabbage palms grow in the gullies, and also a species of fig tree, which bears its fruit on the stem, instead of the ends of the branches; and pines are scattered in the most rocky places.

No inhabitants were seen upon any of the islands, but there were deserted fire places upon all. The Indians probably come over from the main land at certain times, to take turtle, in which they must be much more dexterous than we were; for although many turtle were seen in the water, and we watched the beaches at night, not one was caught. There are no kangaroos upon the Percy Isles; nor did we see any useful birds. The large bats or vampyres, common to this country, and called flying-foxes at Port Jackson, were often found hanging by the claws, with their heads downward, under the shady tops of the palm trees; and one solitary eel of a good size, was caught on clearing out the hole where our water casks had been first intended to be filled.

Pines, fresh water, and fish will be some inducement to visit the Percy Isles; as perhaps may be the hump-backed whales, of which a considerable number was seen in the vicinity. The best and most convenient anchorage, and indeed the only one to be recommended, is that where the Investigator lay, directly off the basin; in mid-channel between No. 2 and the western pine islets. It is sheltered at fourteen points to the eastward, and three towards the west; and there being a clear passage out, both to the north and south, no danger is to be apprehended: the bottom, however, does not hold very well.

A wet dock might be made of the basin without other trouble or expense than a little deepening of the narrow entrance, and throwing a pair of gates across; and were the mud to be cleared out, the basin would contain fifteen or twenty sail of merchant ships with great ease.

The flood *tide* came from the north and the ebb from the south, past the anchorage; but on the outside, they run south-west and north-east. It is not extraordinary that the rise and fall by the shore did not exactly coincide with the swinging of the ship; but that the time of high water should differ three hours, and the rise twenty feet from Broad Sound, is remarkable. According to Mr. Fowler's observations in the basin, it was high water there *eight hours after* the moon's passage; and the rise at the neaps and springs appeared to be from eight to twelve feet.

Three meridian observations to the north, taken by lieutenant Flinders, gave the *latitude* of our anchorage, 21° 39' 31" S.

Longitude, according to the position of Upper Head and the survey from thence, 150° 12' E.

Variation of the needle, observed on the low south-west point of No. 2, 8° 28' E.

Three compasses on board the ship at anchor, gave 5° 34' when the head was east, or corrected to the meridian, 8° 4' E.

Upon the different elevated places whence bearings were taken, the variation differed from 7° 30' to 9° 30' east.

MONDAY 4 OCTOBER 1802

Early in the morning of the 4th, we got under way, with the Lady Nelson in company, to proceed on our voyage to Torres' Strait and the Gulph of Carpentaria. The wind was at E. by N., and we kept close up to weather the northern Percy Isles; for I had a desire to fall in with the reefs laid down by Mr. Campbell, three-quarters of a degree to the eastward, in latitude 21½°; and to ascertain their termination to the north-westward.

[EAST COAST. BARRIER REEFS.]

The tide prevented us from weathering the islands till three in the afternoon; we then passed between No. 4 and some rocks lying two miles to the north-east, with 33 fathoms water. During the night we tacked every two hours, working to the eastward, in from 30 to 36 fathoms; and at daylight [TUESDAY 5 OCTOBER 1802], my station on the eastern isle No. 4 bore N. 89° W., four leagues. Nothing was seen in the offing, but in stretching to the N. N. E, reefs were discovered from the mast head a little before noon; and after the observation for the latitude was taken, I set one bearing East to E. by S., two leagues, and another N. 14° W. to 29° E., four or five miles. Our situation was in 21° 15 2/3' south, and longitude from the bearing of the Pine Peak, 150° 34' east.

These reefs were not exactly those seen by Mr. Campbell; but they are probably not more than five or six leagues to the north-westward of them, and form part of the same *barrier* to the coast. In standing on between the two reefs above set, others, or parts of the same, came in sight ahead; upon which I shortened sail to the three top sails, desired the Lady Nelson to take the lead, and bore away north-westward along the inner side of the northern reef. In an hour we had passed its west end; but another reef came in sight, and for a time obliged us to steer W. by S. At four o'clock we ran northward again, following the direction of the reef on its lee side; and at six anchored in 27 fathoms, coarse sand, in the following situation:

Latitude observed from the moon.,   21° 4' S. Longitude from bearings, 150 19 E. Nearest part of the reef, dist. 2½ miles,   E. ½ S. A smaller reef, distant 3 miles, N. W. ½ N. Percy Isles, Pine Peak of No. 3,   S. 9 0 W. Cumberland Island marked 'k', W. 6 0 N.

The reefs were not dry in any part, with the exception of some small black lumps, which at a distance resembled the round heads of negroes; the sea broke upon the edges, but within side the water was smooth, and of a light green colour. A further description of these dangers is unnecessary, since their forms and relative positions, so far as they could be ascertained, will be best learned from the chart.

Until midnight, five hours after the moon had passed the meridian, a tide came from S. by E., half a mile per hour. The ship then tended to the N. E. by E.; and this tide, whose rate was one mile, appearing to be the flood, led me to suppose there might be an open sea in that direction. In the morning [WEDNESDAY 6 OCTOBER 1802], I sent a boat to lieutenant Murray with instructions for his guidance in case of separation; and appointed him Murray's Islands in Torres' Strait, discovered by captain Edwards in 1791, for the first rendezvous; cautioning him to be strictly on his guard against the treachery of the natives.

We weighed at seven o'clock, and steered N. N. E., close to the wind; at ten, reefs came in sight, extending from W. by N., to N. by E. ½ E., which we weathered one mile, having 35 fathoms water. Our situation at noon was in latitude 20° 45' 40", from observations to the north and south, and the longitude by time keeper 150° 28'; the east end of the great reef to leeward bore S. W. ½ W. two miles, and it extended in patches to N. 16° W., where, at the distance of two leagues, was either a dry white sand or high breakers but which could not be discerned from the reflection of the sun. Nothing was seen to the north-east, and we now lay up in that direction; but at one o'clock there was a small reef bearing N. ½ E.; and at three, a larger one extended from N. by W. ½ W. to E. N. E., and on the outside of it were such high breakers, that nothing less than the unobstructed waves of the ocean could produce them. We stood on for this reef, until four; and being then one mile off, tacked to the southward, having 33 fathoms, nearly the same depth as before.

The larbord tack was continued to six o'clock, at which time we anchored in 32 fathoms, white sand, shells, and pieces of coral, having neither reef nor danger of any kind in sight; but the smoothness of the water left no doubt of many lying to windward. From the high breakers seen in the afternoon, however, hopes were entertained of soon clearing the reefs; for by this time I was weary of them, not only from the danger to which the vessels were thereby exposed, but from fear of the contrary monsoon setting in upon the North Coast, before we should get into the Gulph of Carpentaria.

At this anchorage, the tide came from between S. W. by S. and W. by S., till midnight; and at two in the morning [THURSDAY 7 OCTOBER 1802] the ship rode north, and afterwards N. E. by E., to the flood; which seemed to imply two openings in the reefs, and one of them near the high breakers. The depth of water changed from 35 to 32 fathoms, in the night; but a part of the difference might arise from irregularities in the bottom.

We got under way at daybreak, and stretched south-east to gain the wind; at nine, a reef was passed on each beam; and at noon, when we tacked to the northward in 20° 58' south and 150° 48' east, there were five others, distant from two to five miles, bearing from S. 20° W., round by the east and north to N. 25° W.; but apparently with passages between most of them. Upon these reefs were more of the dry, black lumps, called negro heads, than had been seen before; but they were so much alike as to be of no use in distinguishing one reef from another; and at high water, nearly the whole were covered.

In the afternoon, a very light wind at north-east left no prospect of weathering the reef before dark, upon which the high breakers had been seen; we therefore tacked to the E. S. E., and anchored at sunset in 84 fathoms, fine white sand, not far from our noon's situation; a reef, partly dry, was then distant one mile and a half, and bore E. ½ S. to S. E. The flood tide here ran something more than one mile an hour, and came from between north and north-west, the ship tending to it at one in the morning.

FRIDAY 8 OCTOBER 1802

At seven, when the flood had done running, the two vessels were lying up E. N. E., with a light breeze from the northward; but a rippling which extended a mile from the reef, caused us to tack until a boat was sent to sound upon it; for the Lady Nelson was so leewardly, that much time was lost in waiting for her. At ten we passed through the rippling, in from 14 to 34 fathoms; and at noon were in latitude 20° 55', and longitude 150° 55' by time keeper. We seemed at this time to be surrounded with reefs; but it was ascertained by the whale boat, that many of these appearances were caused by the shadows of clouds and the ripplings and eddies of tide, and that the true coral banks were those only which had either green water or negro heads upon them. Of these, however, there was a formidable mass, all round ahead, with but one small channel through them; and this I was resolved to attempt, in the hope of its carrying us out to windward of the high breakers.

At two o'clock, the eastern reef, which was a mile distant to leeward and nearly dry, was seen to terminate, whilst the northern reefs extended out of sight to the north-east; the opening between them was a mile and a half wide, and full of ripplings; but having the whale boat ahead, we bore away E. S. E., to go through the least agitated part. Having little wind, and a flood tide making against us, the boat was called back to tow, and the brig directed to take its station by means of her sweeps. Our soundings were irregular in the narrow part, between 24 and 9 fathoms, on rocky ground; but after getting through, we had from 30 to 32, the usual depth in the open places. At sunset, the stream anchor was dropped on a bottom of coral sand and shells; the reefs then in sight extending from about E. S. E., round by the north to N. W., where was the great northern bank. Whether there were any passage through them, could not be discerned; but the breakers on many of the outer parts proved the open sea to be not far distant, and that the waves ran high; whilst within side, the water was as tranquil as in harbour.

The ship rode north-west, till between eight and nine o'clock, when it appeared to be high water, and the depth was 35 fathoms; at 9h 34' the moon passed the meridian, and we were then riding S. by W., to a tide which ran at the strongest one and a quarter mile per hour. Between three and four in the morning [SATURDAY 9 OCTOBER 1802] this tide had done, the depth was 31 fathoms, and the ship afterwards rode N. N. E. till daylight. The first of the flood therefore came from the N. N. E. and the latter part from N. W.; it was high water at *one hour before* the moon's passage, and the rise at least three fathoms, or eighteen feet. This time of high water coincides with that of Broad Sound; but it is remarkable, that at the Percy Isles, lying between them, it should be three hours earlier. The rise in Broad Sound was five fathoms, and three, or more, amongst the reefs; whereas at the Percy Isles, there was nothing on the shore to indicate a higher tide than two fathoms.

In the morning we steered E. N. E., with a light air from the southward; the brig was ahead, and at half past nine, made the signal for immediate danger; upon which the stream anchor was dropped in 16 fathoms. The tide ran one mile and a half to the E. N. E, and this leading me to expect some opening in that direction, I sent the master to sound past the brig; and on his finding deeper water we followed, drifting with the tide. At eleven he made the signal for being on a shoal, and we came to, in 35 fathoms, broken coral and sand; being surrounded by reefs, except to the westward from whence we had come. On the outside were high breakers, not more than three or four miles distant; these terminated at E. by S., and between them and other reefs further on, there seemed a possibility of finding an outlet; but no access to it could be had, except by a winding circuit amongst the great mass of banks to the southward, which it was not advisable to make upon such an uncertainty. I therefore determined to remain at the present anchorage till low water, when the reefs would be dry, and the channels between them, if any such there were, would be visible: and should nothing better then present itself, to steer north-westward, as close within the line of the high breakers as possible, until an opening should be found.

The latitude observed to the north and south, at this fifth anchorage amongst the reefs, was 20° 53' 15"; longitude by time keeper, 151° 5' east. In the afternoon, I went upon the reef with a party of the gentlemen; and the water being very clear round the edges, a new creation, as it was to us, but imitative of the old, was there presented to our view. We had wheat sheaves, mushrooms, stags horns, cabbage leaves, and a variety of other forms, glowing under water with vivid tints of every shade betwixt green, purple, brown, and white; equalling in beauty and excelling in grandeur the most favourite *parterre* of the curious florist. These were different species of coral and fungus, growing, as it were, out of the solid rock, and each had its peculiar form and shade of colouring; but whilst contemplating the richness of the scene, we could not long forget with what destruction it was pregnant.

Different corals in a dead state, concreted into a solid mass of a dull-white colour, composed the stone of the reef. The negro heads were lumps which stood higher than the rest; and being generally dry, were blackened by the weather; but even in these, the forms of the different corals, and some shells were distinguishable. The edges of the reef, but particularly on the outside where the sea broke, were the highest parts; within, there were pools and holes containing live corals, sponges, and sea eggs and cucumbers;* and many enormous cockles (*chama gigas*) were scattered upon different parts of the reef. At low water, this cockle seems most commonly to lie half open; but frequently closes with much noise; and the water within the shells then spouts up in a stream, three or four feet high: it was from this noise and the spouting of the water, that we discovered them, for in other respects they were scarcely to be distinguished from the coral rock. A number of these cockles were taken on board the ship, and stewed in the coppers; but they were too rank to be agreeable food, and were eaten by few. One of them weighed 47½ lbs. as taken up, and contained 3lbs. 2 oz. of meat; but this size is much inferior to what was found by captains Cook and Bligh, upon the reefs of the coast further northward, or to several in the British Museum; and I have since seen single shells more than four times the weight of the above shells and fish taken together.

[* What we called sea cucumbers, from their shape, appears to have been the *bêche de mer*, or *trepang*; of which the Chinese make a soup, much esteemed in that country for its supposed invigorating qualities.]

There were various small channels amongst the reefs, some of which led to the outer breakers, and through these the tide was rushing in when we returned to the ship; but I could not any where see an opening sufficiently wide for the vessels. Low water took place at a quarter past three, which corresponded with the time of high water observed at the preceding anchorage.

It was too late in the day to begin following the line of the high breakers to the north-westward; but we lifted the anchor to remove further from the eastern reef, which was dry within a mile of the ship. The wind was light at south-east; and in steering westward, with a boat sounding ahead, we got into one of the narrow streams of tide which carried us rapidly to the south-west; nor could the boat assist us across, so much was it twisted about by the whirlpools. At six o'clock, being well clear of the stream, an anchor was dropped upon coral sand, in 30 fathoms; at ten, when the ship swung to the ebb, the depth was 33 fathoms, and 28 at low water; as, however, we had two-thirds of a cable out, some of the difference probably arose from the irregularity of the bottom.

SUNDAY 10 OCTOBER 1802

At daylight we steered N. N. W.; but reefs were presently seen all round in that direction, and the course was altered for the small passage through which we had come on the 8th. Such, however, was the change in the appearance of the reefs, that no passage could then be discovered; and fearing to be mistaken, I dared not venture through, but took a more southern channel, where before no passage had appeared to exist. At nine o'clock, having sandy ground in 32 fathoms, and it being very difficult to distinguish the shoals at high water, the anchor was dropped in latitude 20° 56½' south and longitude 150° 54½' east. Between one and two in the afternoon, we steered W. N. W. and N. W.; and meeting with a small dry reef at four, hauled up northward, following the line of the great northern reefs upon which the high breakers had been seen. At half past five we came to, in 26 fathoms sand and shells, having reefs from S. by E., round by the east and north, to W. by S.; but there were openings at N. N. W. ½ W. and N. E. by E., and we had the pleasure to see high breakers, five or six miles distant in the latter direction. The latitude here, from an observation of the moon, was 20° 49½', and longitude 150° 48' by time keeper.

MONDAY 11 OCTOBER 1802

Next morning, the brig and whale boat went ahead, and we steered north, after them; the eastern opening was choaked up with small reefs, and we had scarcely entered that to the west when Mr. Murray made the signal for danger, and hauled the wind to the southward. We did the same, round two inner shoals; and finding the bottom irregular, and more shallow than usual, dropped the stream anchor in 27 fathoms. The Lady Nelson was carried rapidly to the south-west, seemingly without being sensible of it, and I therefore made the signal of recall; but although favoured by a fresh breeze, she did not get up against the tide till past nine o'clock. We rode a great strain on the stream cable, and the ship taking a sudden sheer, it parted at the clinch and we lost the anchor; a bower was immediately let go; but the bottom being rocky, I feared to remain during the lee tide, and in a short time ordered it to be weighed. Mr. Murray had lost a kedge anchor, and was then riding by a bower; and when the signal was made to weigh, he answered it by that of inability. The tide was, indeed, running past the brig at a fearful rate, and I feared it would pass over her bows; for she lay in one of the narrow streams which came gushing through the small openings in the outer reef. So soon as our anchor was purchased, a boat's crew was sent to her assistance; and just before noon she got under sail.

We beat up till one o'clock, towards the anchorage of the preceding evening; but the reefs being deeply covered, they could not be distinguished one from the other; and having found a good bottom, in 35 fathoms, we came to, and made signal for the brig to do the same. Lieutenant Murray informed me that his anchor had come up with a palm broken off; and having only one bower left, he applied to me for another. Our anchor had swiveled in the stock; and the work required to it, with getting the last stream anchor out of the hold, and sending Mr. Murray two grapnels, which were all that our own losses could allow of being spared, occupied us till the evening. At low water, two reefs were seen, bearing N. 18° to 41° E., a third S. 72° E., and a fourth S. 74° W.; their distances being from two to four or five miles.

The loss of anchors we had this day sustained, deterred me from any more attempting the small passages through the Barrier Reef; in these, the tide runs with extraordinary violence, and the bottom is coral rock; and whether with, or without wind, no situation can be more dangerous. My anxious desire to get out to sea, and reach the North Coast before the unfavourable monsoon should set in, had led me to persevere amongst these intricate passages beyond what prudence could approve; for had the wind come to blow strong, no anchors, in such deep water and upon loose sand, could have held the ship; a rocky bottom cut the cables; and to have been under sail in the night was certain destruction. I therefore formed the determination, in our future search for a passage out, to avoid all narrow channels, and run along, within side the larger reefs, until a good and safe opening should present itself. This plan, which was dictated by a common regard to safety, might carry us far to the north-west, and delay our arrival in the Gulph of Carpentaria; yet I hoped not; for captain Cook had found the flood tide to come from south-east after passing the Cumberland Islands, whereas before, it ran from the northward; a circumstance which seemed to indicate a termination of the reefs, or a great opening in them., to the north or north-west of those islands.

TUESDAY 12 OCTOBER 1802

In the morning., we got under way and steered N. N. W.; but anchored again on finding the flood tide too strong to be stemmed with a light breeze. Our latitude at this tenth anchorage amongst the reefs, was 20° 53' 10", from observations to the north and south, and longitude by time keeper 150° 42' east. At one o'clock our course was resumed, and continued till sunset in clear water; when we came to, in 32 fathoms sand and shells, not far to the south of where the first high breakers had been seen, in the afternoon of the 6th. A dry reef bore N.½ E., distant two and a half, and another E. ½ S. one-and-half miles; and from the mast head others were seen at the back of them, extending from N. W. by N. to near S. E. by E.

WEDNESDAY 13 OCTOBER 1802

On going upon deck next morning at daybreak, to get the ship under way, I found her situation different to that wherein we had anchored in the evening. The wind had been light, and as usual in such cases, the cable was shortened in; and it appeared from the bearings, and from the soundings marked every hour on the log board, that between four and five in the morning, the anchor had been lifted by the tide, or dragged, two miles north-east amongst the reefs, from 33 into 28 fathoms; where it had again caught. This change of place had not been perceived; and it was difficult, from the circumstance having occurred at the relief of the watch, to discover with whom the culpable inattention lay; but it might have been attended with fatal consequences.

Having weighed the anchor, we steered westward with the brig and whale boat ahead, until past ten; when the eastern breeze died away and the stream anchor was dropped in 30 fathoms, fine white sand. The reefs were then covered. and a dry bank, bearing N. W. by W. five or six miles, was the sole object above water; and towards noon it was covered also. Between this bank and the great reef and breakers, was a space which seemed to be open; but it was not sufficiently large, nor did the tide run with that regularity and strength, to induce a belief that, if there were a passage, it could be such as I desired for the vessels. We therefore again steered westward, on a breeze rising at N. W., until reefs were seen extending southward from the dry bank, and we bore away along their eastern side. At sunset, the anchor was dropped in 36 fathoms, near to our situation on the 6th at noon; the dry reefs bearing from S. 20° to N. 21° W., distant from one to three miles.

THURSDAY 14 OCTOBER 1802

At daylight the breeze was still from the north-westward, and our course was pursued to the south and south-west, close round the inner end of the reefs, till they trended west and we could no longer keep in with them. The Pine Peak of the northern Percy Isles, and several of the Cumberland Islands were then in sight; and at noon our situation and bearings were as under.

Latitude observed to the north and south,   21° 2' S. Longitude by time keeper, 150 11 E. Pine Peak,   S. 6 30 E. Northumberland I., marked 'i', S. 60 40 W. Cumberland I., marked 'k',   N. 89° to N. 85 30 W. Cumberland I., six others,   S. 75 to N. 54 30 W.

The nearest of these isles was little better than a sand bank surrounded with rocks, and was distant two leagues in the direction of N. 54° W. We tacked ship at one, and at four o'clock; and anchored at dusk, in 27 fathoms fine sand, about five miles to the N. N. W. of our noon's situation.

FRIDAY 15 OCTOBER 1802

The wind was at S. by E. in the morning, and we steered northward after the brig, in order to fall in with the reefs and prosecute our search for an opening; in an hour they were visible, and we passed along their west side at the distance of a mile. Before nine o'clock the brig made signal for having only 17 fathoms, other reefs were discovered in the north-west, and the course was altered to pass within them. At eleven we rounded their west end; and at noon were in latitude 20° 38' 58", and from the bearing of the Cumberland Isle *k*, in longitude 150° 1' east. We were now obliged to steer westward again, having reefs at the distance of two miles, from N. E. by E., to N. W. by W.; and seeing that they extended onward, and the breeze was fresh, I hauled up for the Cumberland Island marked *l*, the largest yet seen, with the intention of anchoring there for the night. The tide carried us too far to leeward, but we fetched a lesser island, *l2*, seven miles to the north; and came to, in 17 fathoms grey sand, one mile from a beach on its north-west side, and half a mile from the reef which surrounds the island.

SATURDAY 16 OCTOBER 1802

Early in the morning I landed with a party of the gentlemen, and scrambled through a thick brush and over lumps of rock, to the highest part near the north end of the island. Hazy weather much contracted my view; but several new Cumberland Islands were visible, making up the number to fifteen, of which the greater part had not been seen by captain Cook. Amongst the bearings taken with a theodolite, were those of *k* and *k2*, which had been set from No. 4 of the Percy Isles.

k, the extremes, bore   S. 48° 30' to 46° 40' E. k2,   S. 36 50 to 33 40 E. Ship at anchor, dist. one mile,   N. 64 0 W.

From these bearings and the several latitudes, I ascertained the difference of longitude made from Upper Head to the ship, to be 12' 37" west.

This little island *l2* is of a triangular shape, and each side of it is a mile long; it is surrounded by a coral reef which, as usual, presented a beautiful piece of marine scenery. The stone which forms the basis of the island, and is scattered loosely over the surface, is a kind of porphyry; a small piece of it, applied to the theodolite, did not affect the needle, although, on moving the instrument a few yards southward, the east variation was increased 2° 23'. Not much vegetable earth was contained amongst the stones on the surface, yet the island was thickly covered with trees and brush wood, whose foliage was not devoid of luxuriance. Pines grow here, but they were more abundant, and seemingly larger, upon some other of the islands, particularly on *l3*, to the westward. There did not appear to be any fixed inhabitants; but proofs of the island having been visited some months before, were numerous; and upon the larger island *l*, there was a smoke. The time of high water coincided with the swinging of the ship, and took place one hour before the moon's passage, as it had done amongst the barrier reefs; from ten to fifteen feet seemed to be the rise by the shore, and the flood came from the northward.

We returned on board the ship at noon; but I deferred getting under way till next morning, on account of the wind blowing fresh, and some business to be executed which could not be attended to whilst among the reefs. This gave an opportunity of making further observations by the time keepers, from which it appeared that they gave only 8' 36.3" of longitude west from Upper Head, with the rates there found; whereas by the survey, we had made 12' 37". The time keeper No. 520, taken alone, gave 11' 35.8"; and when the correction, afterwards found necessary in the Gulph of Carpentaria, is applied, the difference becomes 12' 41", almost exactly as by survey. The previous positions of the ship amongst the reefs, and wherever I had not any bearings of fixed points, have therefore been deduced from this time keeper.

The *latitude* of the anchorage, from observations to the north and south., was 20° 45' 28" S.

Longitude from a chain of bearings, connected with the fixed station in Broad Sound, 149° 34' 12" E.

Variation of the theodolite, observed on the north-west beach of *l2*, 7° 39' east; but it differed on the north head of the island, from 7° to 9° 23' east, in the space of a few yards.

The variation amongst the Barrier Reefs has not been mentioned; but five azimuths and amplitudes were taken between the 6th, p.m. and the 15th a.m. When corrected to the meridian, the extremes were 7° 53' and 7° 11'; and the mean, in latitude 20° 44', longitude 150° 32', will be 7° 30' east.

SUNDAY 17 OCTOBER 1802

At daylight on the 17th, the breeze was moderate at E. by N., with fine weather; and in steering northward, close to the wind, we passed three miles to leeward of a dry bank of rocks and sand. Several of the Cumberland Islands were in sight at noon, when our situation and the most essential bearings were as under.

Latitude, observed to the north and south, 20° 23' 56" Longitude from bearings, 149 33¼ Island l2, station on the north end, S. 5 E. Other isles, large and small, from thence to N. 67½ W. Pentecost I. (of capt. Cook), resembling a tower, S. 89 W.

No reefs were in sight, nor in steering N. N. E. and N. E. by N., could any be distinguished from the mast head all the afternoon. At half past five we tacked and bore down to the brig; and then anchored in 31 fathoms, speckled sand and small stones, and sent a boat to lieutenant Murray with orders.

Our latitude here, by an observation of the moon, was 20° 10' south; and now hoping we should not meet with any more interruption from the reefs, I resolved to send the brig back to Port Jackson. The Lady Nelson sailed so ill, and had become so leewardly since the loss of the main, and part of the after keel, that she not only caused us delay, but ran great risk of being lost; and instead of saving the crew of the Investigator, in case of accident, which was one of the principal objects of her attendance, it was too probable we might be called upon to render her that assistance. A good vessel of the same size I should have considered the greatest acquisition in Torres' Strait and the Gulph of Carpentaria; but circumstanced as was the Lady Nelson, and in want of anchors and cables which could not be spared without endangering our own safety, she was become, and would be more so every day, a burthen rather than an assistant to me. Lieutenant Murray was not much acquainted with the kind of service in which we were engaged; but the zeal he had shown to make himself and his vessel of use to the voyage, made me sorry to deprive him of the advantage of continuing with us; and increased my regret at the necessity of parting from our little consort.

The stores and provisions already supplied to the brig, were returned; and Mr. Murray spared us his old launch, to replace, in some sort, the cutter we had lost in Strong-tide Passage. *Nanbarre*, one of the two natives, having expressed a wish to go back to Port Jackson, was sent to the Lady Nelson in the morning [MONDAY 18 OCTOBER 1802], with two seamen exchanged for the same number of that vessel's crew; and Mr. Denis Lacy, who had been lent, returned back to the Investigator. I wrote to His Excellency governor King, an account of our proceedings and discoveries upon the East Coast; and requested a new boat might be built against our return to Port Jackson, and that the brig should be repaired and equipped ready to accompany me in the following year.

At nine o'clock we got under way, and showed our colours to bid farewell to the Lady Nelson; she steered southward for the Cumberland Islands, whilst our course was directed north-east, close to the wind. The brig was not out of sight when more reefs were discovered, extending from east to N. N. W.; and in pursuance of my plan to avoid small openings, we bore away to run along their inner side. At noon, the latitude was 19° 58' 20", and longitude by time keeper, 149° 37' east. Reefs extended from E. ½ N. to S. ½ E., at the distance of one to three miles; and there were separate patches somewhat further, bearing W. by N. ½ N. and N. N. E. Between the first and last bearing was an opening of a good appearance, and we hauled up for it; but the water having shoaled to 12 fathoms, though no breakers were seen ahead, we kept away again; and from that time till evening, passed a variety of reefs, hauling up between them to look into the openings, and bearing away when repulsed. None of these banks were dry, nor was there much breaking water upon them; which made it probable that they were far within the outer line of the barrier.

The breeze was fresh at south-east, and by sunset we had run eleven leagues upon various courses to the north-westward, with soundings from 14 to 33 fathoms; the bottom being rocky in the shallow, and sandy in the deeper parts. We were steering north-west, at the rate of six knots, when new reefs were discovered, from ahead to abaft the larbord beam; upon which we clapped upon a wind to the southward, and just weathered them, passing through rippling water in 30 fathoms. Upon this occasion I felt very happy that the Lady Nelson was gone, for in all probability she could not have escaped this danger. Being now dark, it was too hazardous to stand on; and therefore, on finding a bottom of grey sand in 34 fathoms, we came to with the best bower, veered to a whole cable, and sent down the topgallant yards. The latitude here, from a meridian altitude of the moon, was 19° 48 1/3', and the longitude 149° 13½'; there was a small drain of ebb tide from the S. by W., until eleven o'clock, but no run was perceptible afterwards.

TUESDAY 19 OCTOBER 1802

In the morning, we saw the reef from N. ½ E. to W. ½ N., not further distant than two miles, and the northernmost of captain Cook's Cumberland Islands bore S. 56° W., about eight leagues. The wind was at E. S. E, blowing fresh; and our course was pursued along the south side of the reef till nine o'clock; when it terminated, and we steered northward twelve miles, with no soundings at 30 fathoms. Another reef was then seen, bearing from N. ½ E. to W. N. W., and obliged us to steer westward again.

The latitude at noon was 19° 35' 15", and longitude by time keeper 148° 47½'; four reefs then extended from E. by S. to N. W. by W., at the distance of two to five miles; the northern Cumberland Island bore S. 9° E, and the outer of two hills which I judged to be upon Cape Gloucester, S. 39½° W. This bearing, and captain Cook's latitude of the cape, would make its longitude to be 148° 26½', or 15½' east of what that great navigator lays it down; and it is to be observed, that from the time of passing Sandy Cape, my longitude had gradually become more eastward as we advanced along the coast. It has before been said, that captain Cook had no time keeper in his first voyage; nor did he possess many of our advantages in fixing the positions of places; it cannot therefore be thought presumptuous, that I should consider the Investigator's longitude to be preferable.

We ran from noon, five leagues W. ¾ N. along the south side of the reefs; and seeing their termination at two o'clock, steered N. N. W., Holborne Isle then bearing S. 53° W., about four leagues. At half past four we had a small reef two or three miles to the W. S. W., and a larger four miles to the N. E.; and behind this last was one more extensive, with high breakers on the outside, reaching from N. E. by N. to E.½ S. I hauled up with the intention of anchoring under the lee of these reefs, till morning; but not finding sufficient shelter against the sea, we tacked and stretched southward for the clear water between the reefs and the land. At sunset, the variation from amplitude was 5° 39' east; Holborne Isle bore S. by W. from the mast head, and no breakers were in sight. This tack was prolonged, under treble-reefed top sails, till ten o'clock; when a light was seen bearing S. by E. ½ E., probably upon the isle, and we stood to the northward.

The wind blew fresh from the eastward all night, and raised a short swell which tried the ship more than any thing we had encountered from the time of leaving Port Jackson; and I was sorry to find, brought on her former leakiness, to the amount of five inches of water per hour. We tacked to the south, soon after mid-night, and to the northward at three in the morning [WEDNESDAY 20 OCTOBER 1802]. Holborne Isle was seen bearing S. 6° W., four or five leagues, at daylight; and at seven we passed between three small reefs, of which the easternmost had been set at W. S. W. on the preceding afternoon. In half an hour, when the latitude from the moon was 19° 14', and longitude by time keeper 148° 21½', distant high breakers were seen to the north and eastward; the nearest small reef bore S. W. ½ W., two miles, and a much larger one extended from N. ½ E. to W. by N. The passage between these two being three miles wide, we bore away through it; and in following the south side of the great reef, left another, five or six miles long, on the larbord hand, the passage being equally wide with the former, and the least depth 21 fathoms. Soon after ten o'clock, we steered northward, round the west end of the great reef.

At noon, the latitude from observations to the north and south was 19° 8' 15", and longitude by time keeper, 147° 59' east. No land was in sight, and the high breakers were lost in the eastern quarter; but we had detached reefs in the N. E., the N. E. by N., and W. N. W., distant from two to five miles. Towards the north there was six points of clear water, and I steered onward till near three o'clock; when, besides two new reefs already passed, one on each side, we had five others: two in the E. by N. at the distances of one and five miles. one E. S. E. four miles, another N. W. by W. six miles, and a fifth N. W. by N. three miles. Whether to steer onward amongst these, and trust to finding shelter for the night, or to run south-westward towards the land, and get within all the reefs before night came on, was an important, but difficult point to decide. The reefs in sight were small, and could not afford shelter against the sea which was breaking high upon them; but these breakers excited a hope that we might, even then, be near an opening in the barrier; and although caution inclined to steering back towards the land, this prospect of an outlet determined me to proceed, at least until four o'clock, at the chance of finding either larger reefs for shelter, or a clear sea. We were successful. At four, the depth was 43 fathoms, and no reefs in sight; and at six, a heavy swell from the eastward and a depth of 66 fathoms were strong assurances that we had at length gained the open sea.

The topsails were then treble reefed, and we hauled to the wind, which blew strong at E. S. E., with squally weather. At eight, hove to and sounded: no ground with 75 fathoms; and at twelve, none with 115. But the wind unfortunately headed two points; and the probability of meeting unknown reefs being thereby much increased, I tacked to the southward at one in the morning [THURSDAY 21 OCTOBER 1802]; preferring, if we must of necessity be again driven amongst them, to come in where we knew of an opening, rather than where their formation was totally unknown.

At four, tacked ship to the northward, and sounded with 100 fathoms, no bottom. At daylight, no reefs could be seen from the mast head, the wind had moderated its strength, and we made all possible sail to the N. by E.; keeping two points free, to make the ship go through the water. We now considered ourselves entirely clear of the reefs; but at noon high breakers were seen extending from West to N. N. W., at the distance of six or seven miles, and we hauled up a point more to the eastward. Our latitude was 17° 54', longitude 148° 37', and at the depth of 100 fathoms there was no ground; the variation observed in the morning, with three azimuth compasses, was 6° 8' east, corrected to the meridian. Another reef was discovered at two o'clock, lying nearly three leagues to the northward of the former; but although there were many boobies, and tropic and man-of-war birds about, no more dangers had been descried at dusk; nor did we see any more until approaching Torres' Strait.

I shall conclude this chapter with some general remarks on the reefs, which form so extraordinary a barrier to this part of New South Wales; and amongst which we sought fourteen days, and sailed more than five hundred miles, before a passage could be found through them, out to sea.

The easternmost parts of the barrier seen in the Investigator, lie nearly in 21° south and 151° 10' east; but there can be no doubt that they are connected with the reefs lying to the southward, discovered in 1797 by captain Campbell of the brig Deptford; and probably also with those further distant, which captain Swain of the Eliza fell in with in the following year. If so, the Barrier Reefs will commence as far south-eastward as the latitude 22° 50' and longitude about 152° 40', and possibly still further; Break-sea Spit is a coral reef, and a connexion under water, between it and the barrier, seems not improbable. The opening by which we passed out, is in 18° 52', and 148° 2'; so that, did the Barrier Reefs terminate here, their extent would be near 350 miles in a straight line; and in all this space, there seems to be no large opening. Mr. Swain did, indeed, get out at the latitude 22°; but it was by a long, and very tortuous channel.

Of what extent our opening may be, is uncertain; but since captain Cook had smooth water in running to the west and northward to Cape Tribulation, where he first saw the reefs, it should seem to be not very great; certainly, as I think, not exceeding twenty, and perhaps not five leagues. I therefore assume it as a great probability, that with the exception of this, and perhaps several small openings, our Barrier Reefs are connected with the Labyrinth of captain Cook; and that they reach to Torres' Strait and to New Guinea, in 9° south; or through 14° of latitude and 9° of longitude; which is not to be equalled in any other known part of the world.

The breadth of the barrier seems to be about fifteen leagues in its southern part, but diminishes to the northward; for at the Northumberland Islands it is twelve, and near our opening the breadth is not more than seven or eight leagues. The reefs seen in latitude 17¾°, after we got through, being forty leagues from the coast, I consider to be distinct banks out at sea; as I do those discovered by Mons. de Bougainville in 15½°, which lie still further off. So far northward as I explored the Barrier Reefs, they are unconnected with the land; and continue so to latitude 16°; for, as before said, captain Cook saw none until he had passed Cape Tribulation.

An arm of the sea is inclosed between the barrier and the coast, which is at first twenty-five or thirty leagues wide; but is contracted to twenty, abreast of Broad Sound, and to nine leagues at Cape Gloucester; from whence it seems to go on diminishing, till, a little beyond Cape Tribulation, reefs are found close to the shore. Numerous islands lie scattered in this inclosed space; but so far as we are acquainted, there are no other coral banks in it than those by which some of the islands are surrounded; so that being sheltered from the deep waves of the ocean, it is particularly well adapted to the purposes of a coasting trade. The reader will be struck with the analogy which this arm of the sea presents to one in nearly the same latitude of the northern hemisphere. The Gulph of Florida is formed by the coast of America on the west, and by a great mass of islands and shoals on the east; which shoals are also of coral.

On the outside of the barrier, the sea appears to be generally unfathomable; but within, and amongst the reefs, there are soundings every where. Nor is the depth very unequal, where the bottom is sandy; but like the breadth of the reefs and the arm they inclose, it diminishes as we advance northward, from 60 to 48, to 35, and to 30 fathoms near our opening; and to 20 at Cape Tribulation. The further to leeward, the shallower the water, seems to be a law amongst coral reefs.

There is some variation in the tide in different parts of the barrier, but the most general rise is about two fathoms; abreast of the Northumberland Islands, however, where the flood from the south-east seems to meet that from the northward, it is three fathoms, and perhaps more. The time of high water there, and also at the eastern Cumberland Islands, is *eleven hours after* the moon's passage; but it probably accelerates north-westward, to the opening, and then retards further on: at Endeavour River, captain Cook found it to be high water an hour and a half earlier than is above given.

It has been said, that the width of the opening by which we got out to sea, is uncertain; it is undoubtedly four, and possibly more leagues, but there are many small, unconnected banks in it. To a ship desiring access to any part of the coast, south of Endeavour River, I should certainly recommend her to enter the inclosed sea by the way of Break-sea Spit, if able to choose her own route; but the question is, whether a ship driven by stress of weather, or by accident, to seek the coast, might steer for the opening with a fair prospect of passing through in safety? I certainly think she might; with the precaution of not attempting the passage late in the day. The marks to be given for it, are, the latitude 18° 52', longitude 148° 2', variation 6° east with the ship's head north or south, and the soundings. When right off the opening, bottom will be found at from 70 to 40 fathoms before any reefs come in sight; whereas, if breakers be seen and no soundings can be obtained, it may be certainly concluded that the ship is not in the fair way for this opening, and probably, that no large opening exists in that part of the barrier. On getting soundings and afterwards making the reefs near the situation above given, a ship should push through the first opening of two miles wide that presents itself, and steer south-westward amongst the inner reefs for the land; and it will not be many hours, perhaps minutes, before she will find smooth water and anchoring ground. The commander who proposes to make the experiment, must not, however, be one who throws his ship's head round in a hurry, so soon as breakers are announced from aloft; if he do not feel his nerves strong enough to thread the needle, as it is called, amongst the reefs, whilst he directs the steerage from the mast head, I would strongly recommend him not to approach this part of New South Wales.

CHAPTER V.

Passage from the Barrier Reefs to Torres' Strait.
Reefs named Eastern Fields.
Pandora's Entrance to the Strait.
Anchorage at Murray's Islands.
Communication with the inhabitants.
Half-way Island.
Notions on the formation of coral islands in general.
Prince of Wales's Islands, with remarks on them.
Wallis' Isles.

Entrance into the Gulph of Carpentaria.
Review of the passage through Torres' Strait.
[EAST COAST. TOWARDS TORRES' STRAIT.]
THURSDAY 21 OCTOBER 1802

The last reefs were out of sight in the evening of Oct. 21, and our course was continued for Torres' Strait; but the barrier was yet at too little distance, not to cause apprehension of straggling reefs; and I thought it too hazardous to run in the night, during this passage.

At noon of the 22d [FRIDAY 22 OCTOBER 1802], our latitude was 16° 39', longitude 148° 43', and there was no bottom at 150 fathoms (Atlas, Plate XII.); nor was any thing unusual to be seen, unless it were tropic and man-of-war birds, and gannets. The *Bâture de Diane* of Mons. de Bougainville should lie about thirty-eight leagues to the N. E. by E., and his western reefs about twenty-eight leagues to the N. N. W. ½ W., of this situation; and to them, or perhaps some nearer banks, the birds might probably belong.* A piece of land is marked to the south-west of the first reefs, but its existence is very doubtful; for all that M. de Bougainville says of it (II, 163) is, that "some even thought they saw low land to the south-west of the breakers."

[* Bougainville's longitude of the north end of Aurora Island, one of his *Archipel de Grandes Cyclades* (the New Hebrides of Cook), differed 54' of longitude to the east of captain Cook's position; and it seems very probable that it was as much too great when the above dangers were discovered. Admitting this to be the case, the situations extracted from his voyage (II, 161, 164) will be as under: Bâture de Diane 15° 41' south 150° 25' east of Greenwich. Reef   15 34½   148 6 Second reef,   15 17   147 57]

SATURDAY 23 OCTOBER 1802

Next day at noon, we were in 15° 12' south, and 149° 2' east; the current had set half a knot to the N. N. W., and many of the former kinds of birds, as also boobies and petrels, were seen. Hitherto we had kept up nearly to the wind, in order to gain an offing from the coast and Barrier Reefs; but next morning [SUNDAY 24 OCTOBER 1802] the course was directed N. W. At noon, latitude 13° 47', longitude 148° 39': many boobies seen, and some petrels and tropic birds. On the 25th [MONDAY 25 OCTOBER 1802], a shag flew round the ship, and a large flock of petrels was seen: latitude at noon, 12° 55', longitude 147° 23', and the current setting more than a mile an hour to the west (Atlas, Plate XIII.). At eight in the evening, when we hauled to the wind, there was no bottom at 130 fathoms.

WEDNESDAY 27 OCTOBER 1802

In the morning of the 27th, a small land bird, resembling a linnet, was seen; at noon we were in 10° 28' south and 146° 7' east, and the current had set W. N. W., three quarters of a mile an hour, since the 25th. The wind, which had been at south-east, then shifted suddenly to north, and blew fresh with squally weather; but at midnight it veered to south-east again. These changes were accompanied with thunder, lightning and rain; indications, as I feared, of the approaching north-west monsoon. We lay to, during a part of the night; and at day-break [THURSDAY 28 OCTOBER 1802] bore away again upon our north western course. At eight o'clock, breakers were seen extending from S. W. by W. to N. by E., distant from two to six miles; there was a small gap in them, bearing N. by W.½ W., but we hauled up north-east, to windward of the whole, and made more sail. I ventured to bear away at ten; and at noon our latitude was 9° 51' 36", and longitude 145° 45½' by time keeper. No reefs were then in sight; but in steering west, we passed through a rippling of tide or current, and a single breaker was seen from the mast head, at three o'clock, bearing S. W. four or five miles.

These reefs lie nearly a degree to the eastward of those first seen by the captains Edwards and Bligh, when entering Torres' Strait; for the north-eastern extreme lies in 10° 2' south, and 145° 45' east. From this position, the eastern line of the breakers extended ten or twelve miles to the S. S. W., and the single breaker afterwards seen, lies about six leagues to the W. N. W.; but how far they may be connected, or what the extent of the reefs may be to the south-west, could not be seen. In the belief that this was the first discovery of these coral banks, I called them the *Eastern Fields*, intending thereby to designate their position with respect to the other reefs of Torres' Strait.

Our latitude at noon was exactly that of the opening by which captain Edwards of the Pandora had entered the Strait in 1791; and which I call the *Pandora's Entrance*. This opening appeared to be preferable to that further northward, by which captain Bligh and Mr. Bampton had got within the reefs; more especially as it led directly for Murray's Islands, where, if possible, I intended to anchor. Our course was therefore steered west; and seeing no more reefs, it was continued until eight in the evening, at which time we hauled to the wind, having no bottom at 105 fathoms.

FRIDAY 29 OCTOBER 1802

At daylight, after sounding ineffectually with 100 fathoms, we bore away on our western course. Two reefs were seen at six o'clock; the one bearing N. by W.½ W. three, and the other W. by N. ½ N. four miles. They seemed to be small, and unconnected; but in all probability were parts of those which form the north side of the Pandora's Entrance, and which captain Bligh, who saw them more to the northward, named collectively, Portlock's Reef. The situation of the southernmost part, deduced from the preceding and following noons, will be 9° 48' south, and 144° 45' east.

[EAST COAST. TORRES' STRAIT.]

After passing these reefs, our course was west, by compass; and nothing further was descried till eleven o'clock; breakers then came in sight ahead, and we hauled up north-east, till noon; when the observed latitude from both sides was 9° 36' 55", longitude 144° 13', and the depth 50 fathoms on a bottom of fine, white sand. The reef was distant one mile and a half in the nearest part, and three miles at the extremes, which bore N. 15° E. and S. 60° W.; a sand bank or key upon it bore W. ¾ S., and is probably dry at all times, for it was then near high water.

Finding by the latitude that we had been set considerably to the north, and were out of the parallel of Murray's Islands, I tacked to the S. S. W.; and at two o'clock, the largest island was seen bearing S. 38° W. about five leagues. Soon afterward, a reef came in sight to the south-east, extending in patches toward the islands; and presently another was distinguished to the westward, from the mast head, which took nearly a parallel direction, the passage between them being about four miles wide. We steered along the lee side of the eastern reef, at the distance of a mile, with soundings from 29 to 24 fathoms, coral sand, until four o'clock; the reef then trended more southward, and we edged away for the islands, of which Mr. Westall sketched the appearance (Atlas Plate XVIII. View 10). At half past five, the largest island bore S. 36° E. to 28° W., one mile and a half; and there being more reefs coming in sight to the westward, the anchor was immediately let go in 20 fathoms, coarse sand and shells. The north and east sides of the island are surrounded by a reef, which may probably include the two smaller isles on its southwest side; but it is totally unconnected with the reefs to the north-east. These appear to be a northern continuation of the vast bank, on the outside of which the Pandora sailed as far as 11½° south, and in the chart of captain Edwards' track, published by Mr. Dalrymple, it is marked as surrounding the islands; whereas it is at least four miles distant from the reef which probably does surround them.

A number of poles standing up in various places, more especially between the islands, appeared at a distance like the masts of canoes, and made me apprehend that the inhabitants of the Strait had collected a fleet here; but on approaching nearer, the poles were found to be upon the reefs, and were probably set up for some purpose connected with fishing. We had scarcely anchored when between forty and fifty Indians came off, in three canoes. They would not come along-side of the ship, but lay off at a little distance, holding up cocoa nuts, joints of bamboo filled with water, plantains, bows and arrows, and vociferating *tooree! tooree!* and *mammoosee!* A barter soon commenced, and was carried on in this manner: a hatchet, or other piece of iron (tooree) being held up, they offered a bunch of green plantains, a bow and quiver of arrows, or what they judged would be received in exchange; signs of acceptance being made, the Indian leaped overboard with his barter, and handed it to a man who went down the side to him; and receiving his hatchet, swam back to the canoe. Some delivered their articles without any distrust of the exchange, but this was not always the case. Their eagerness to get tooree was great, and at first, any thing of that same metal was received; but afterwards, if a nail were held up to an Indian, he shook his head, striking the edge of his right hand upon the left arm, in the attitude of chopping; and he was well enough understood.

View of Murray's Islands, with the natives offering to barter.
At sunset, two of the canoes returned to Murray's Island, paddling to windward with more velocity than one of our boats could have rowed; the third set a narrow, upright sail, between two masts in the fore part of the canoe, and steered north-westward, as I judged, for the Darnley's Island of captain Bligh.

I did not forget that the inhabitants of these islands had made an attack upon the Providence and Assistant in 1792 (Vol I, Introduction*); nor that Mr. Bampton had some people cut off at Darnley's Island in 1793 (Vol I, Introduction**). The marines were therefore kept under arms, the guns clear, and matches lighted; and officers were stationed to watch every motion, one to each canoe, so long as they remained near the ship. Bows and arrows were contained in all the canoes; but no intention of hostility was manifested by the Indians, unless those who steered for Darnley's Island might be supposed to go for assistance.

[* "On the 5th, boats were again sent to sound the passage. Several large sailing canoes were seen; and the cutter making the signal for assistance, the pinnace was sent to her, well manned and armed. On the return of the boats in the afternoon, it appeared, that, of four canoes which used their efforts to get up to the cutter, one succeeded. . . ."]

[** "After having gone entirely round the island, and seen nothing of the object of his research, Mr. Dell returned to the first cove; where a great concourse of natives, armed with bows, arrows, clubs, and lances, were assembled at the outskirt of the wood. . . ."]

[SATURDAY 30 OCTOBER 1802]
We did not get under way in the morning, until the sun was high enough for altitudes to be taken for the time keepers. Soon after daylight, the natives were with us again, in seven canoes; some of them came under the stern, and fifteen or twenty of the people ascended on board, bringing in their hands pearl-oyster shells and necklaces of cowries; with which, and some bows and arrows, they obtained more of the precious *tooree*. Wishing to secure the friendship and confidence of these islanders to such vessels as might hereafter pass through Torres' Strait, and not being able to distinguish any chief amongst them, I selected the oldest man, and presented him with a hand-saw, a hammer and nails, and some other trifles; of all which we attempted to show him the use, but I believe without success; for the poor old man became frightened, on finding himself to be so particularly noticed.

At this time we began to heave short for weighing, and made signs to the Indians to go down into their canoes, which they seemed unwilling to comprehend; but on the seamen going aloft to loose the sails, they went hastily down the stern ladder and ship's sides, and shoved off; and before the anchor was up they paddled back to the shore, without our good understanding having suffered any interruption.

The colour of these Indians is a dark chocolate; they are active, muscular men, about the middle size, and their countenances expressive of a quick apprehension. Their features and hair appeared to be similar to those of the natives of New South Wales, and they also go quite naked; but some of them had ornaments of shell work, and of plaited hair or fibres of bark, about their waists, necks, and ancles. Our friend Bongaree could not understand any thing of their language, nor did they pay much attention to him; he seemed, indeed, to feel his own inferiority, and made but a poor figure amongst them. The arms of these people have been described in the voyage of captain Bligh (Vol I, Introduction*); as also the canoes., of which the annexed plate, from a drawing by Mr. Westall, gives a correct representation. The two masts, when not wanted, are laid along the gunwales; when set up, they stand abreast of each other in the fore part of the canoe, and seemed to be secured by one set of shrouds, with a stay from one mast head to the other. The sail is extended between them; but when going with a side wind, the lee mast is brought aft by a back stay, and the sail then stands obliquely. In other words, they brace up by setting in the head of the lee mast, and perhaps the foot also; and can then lie within seven points of the wind, and possibly nearer. This was their mode, so far as a distant view would admit of judging; but how these long canoes keep to the wind, and make such way as they do, without any after sail, I am at a loss to know.

[* "Their arms were bows, arrows, and clubs, which they bartered for every kind of iron work with eagerness; but appeared to set little value on any thing else. The bows are made of split bamboo; and so strong, that no man in the ship could bend one of them. The string is a broad slip of cane, fixed to one end of the bow; and fitted with a noose, to go over the other end, when strung. The arrow is a cane of about four feet long, into which a pointed piece of the hard, heavy, *casuarina* wood, is firmly and neatly fitted; and some of them were barbed. Their clubs are made of the *casuarina*, and are powerful weapons. The hand part is indented, and has a small knob, by which the firmness of the grasp is much assisted; and the heavy end is usually carved with some device: One had the form of a parrot's head, with a ruff round the neck; and was not ill done."]

Murray's largest island is nearly two miles long, by something more than one in breadth; it is rather high land, and the hill at its western end may be seen from a ship's deck at the distance of eight or nine leagues, in a clear day. The two smaller isles seemed to be single hills, rising abruptly from the sea, and to be scarcely accessible; nor did we see upon them any fires, or other marks of inhabitants. On the shores of the large island were many huts, surrounded by palisades, apparently of bamboo; cocoa-nut trees were abundant, both on the low grounds and the sides of the hills, and plantains, with some other fruits, had been brought to us. There were many Indians sitting in groups upon the shore, and the seven canoes which came off to the ship in the morning, contained from ten to twenty men each, or together, about a hundred. If we suppose these hundred men to have been one half of what belonged to the islands, and to the two hundred men add as many women and three hundred children, the population of Murray's Isles will amount to seven hundred; of which nearly the whole must belong to the larger island.

The *latitude* of the highest hill, deduced from that of the ship at the following noon, is 9° 54' south, and *longitude* by the time keeper corrected, 144° 2' east; being 3' north, and 20' east of its position by captain Edwards. A regular tide of about one knot an hour set E. by S. and W. by N., past the ship; and by her swinging, it was high water at half an hour after midnight, or about *ten hours and a half after* the moon had passed over the meridian. The bottom seemed to be loose at our anchorage; but were these islands examined, it is probable that better ground and shelter would be found on their western sides. I distinguished from the mast head the north end of a reef, three miles distant to the W. N. W.; but could not see whether it joined the reef surrounding the large island. At N. N. W. ¾ W. four miles, was the south-west end of another reef; and when we got under way at half past eight in the morning, our course was directed between the two.

Ripplings of a suspicious appearance caused the whale boat to be kept ahead for some time; but finding no ground upon them with 30 fathoms, and the breeze becoming fresh, the boat was called on board. At 9h 40' the following bearings were taken:

    Darnley's Island, highest part,   N. 39° W. Murray's Islands, the largest, S. 58° to 40 E. Murray's Islands, two smaller, nearly touching, S. 36 to 27 E. Rippling off the N. end of a reef, dist. ½ mile,   S. W. ½ W. East end of a reef, distant 1½ miles, N. 6 E.

Mr. Westall's second view of Murray's Isles was taken from this position. (Atlas Pl. XVIII. View 11.)

Knowing the difficulties experienced by captain Bligh and Mr. Bampton in the northern part of the strait, I kept as much up to the southward, for Cape York, as the direction of the reefs would admit. On the windward side, we had a long chain of them extending W. S. W. to a great distance; but its breadth was not great, as the blue water was seen beyond it, from the mast head. On the north side there was no regular chain, and but one reef of much extent; small patches were indeed announced every now and then, from aloft, but these did not cause us much impediment; the greatest was from two right in our track; but being a mile apart, we passed between them at eleven o'clock.

[NORTH COAST. TORRES' STRAIT.]

Until noon, we had no soundings with from 25 to 30 fathoms of line, but then found broken coral and shells at the latter depth; the great reefs to windward were two or three miles distant, stretching south-west, and our situation and bearings were as under:

Latitude observed, 9° 53½' S. Longitude from time keeper, 143 42 E. Murray's Isles, the largest, highest part, S. 88½ E. Murray's Isles, the westernmost, highest part, S. 81½ E. Darnley's I., highest part, obscure, N. 10 E. A small, low isle, To the westward. Nearest reef, distant two miles, S. 67° to N. 43 W.

Having a fresh breeze at S. E. by E, we ran at the rate of six knots, following the chain of reefs lying to windward. On the other side, there were still very few reefs; but several low isles were distinguished, similar to that seen at noon; these were small, but seemingly well covered with wood, and appertain, as I judge, to the group called by Mr. Bampton, Cornwallis' Range. At half past two, we passed between reefs one mile and a half asunder, having no ground at 25 fathoms; and then the chain which had been followed from Murray's Isles, either terminated or took a more southern direction. Another small, woody isle was then in sight, nearly in our track, at four it bore N. 67° W., two-and-half miles; and not seeing any other island ahead to afford shelter for the night, we bore away round the south end of its reef, and came to an anchor in 17 fathoms, coral sand.

Cent. of the island, dist. 1¼ miles, bore, S. 83° E. The surrounding reef, N. 78° to S. 12 E. A woody isle, westmost of five seen this p. m., N. 9 W. A dry sand, set from the mast head, S. W.¾ S.

A boat was lowered down, and I went on shore with the botanical gentlemen, to look about the island. It is little better than a bank of sand, upon a basis of coral rock; yet it was covered with shrubs and trees so thickly, that in many places they were impenetrable. The north-western part is entirely sand, but there grew upon it numbers of *pandanus* trees, similar to those of the east coast of New South Wales; and around many of them was placed a circle of shells of the *chama gigas*, or gigantic cockle, the intention of which excited my curiosity.

It appeared that this little island was visited occasionally by the Indians, who obtained from it the fruit of the pandanus, and probably turtle, for the marks of them were seen; and the reef furnishes them with cockles, which are of a superior size here to those we had found upon the reefs of the East Coast. There being no water upon the island, they seem to have hit upon the following expedient to obtain it: Long slips of bark are tied round the smooth stems of the pandanus, and the loose ends are led into the shells of the cockle, placed underneath. By these slips, the rain which runs down the branches and stem of the tree, is conducted into the shells, and fills them at every considerable shower; and as each shell will contain two or three pints, forty or fifty thus placed under different trees will supply a good number of men. A pair of these cockle shells, bleached in the sun, weighed a hundred and one pounds; but still they were much inferior in size to some I have since seen.

The fruit of the pandanus, as it is used by these Indians and by the natives of Terra Australis, affords very little nourishment. They suck the bottom part of the drupes, or separated nuts, as we do the leaves of the artichoke; but the quantity of pulp thus obtained, is very small, and to my taste, too astringent to be agreeable. In the third volume of the Asiatic Researches, the fruit of the pandanus is described as furnishing, under the name of *Mellori*, an important article of food to the inhabitants of the Nicobar Islands; and in Mauritius, one of these species is planted for its long and fibrous leaves, of which sacks, mats, and bags for coffee and cotton are in a made.

This little island, or rather the surrounding reef, which is three or four miles long, affords shelter from the south-east winds; and being at a moderate day's run from Murray's Isles, it forms a convenient anchorage for the night to a ship passing through Torres' Strait: I named it *Half-way Island*. It is scarcely more than a mile in circumference, but appears to be increasing both in elevation and extent. At no very distant period of time, it was one of those banks produced by the washing up of sand and broken coral, of which most reefs afford instances, and those of Torres' Strait a great many. These banks are in different stages of progress: some, like this, are become islands, but not yet habitable; some are above high-water mark, but destitute of vegetation; whilst others are overflowed with every returning tide.

It seems to me, that when the animalcules which form the corals at the bottom of the ocean, cease to live, their structures adhere to each other, by virtue either of the glutinous remains within, or of some property in salt water; and the interstices being gradually filled up with sand and broken pieces of coral washed by the sea, which also adhere, a mass of rock is at length formed. Future races of these animalcules erect their habitations upon the rising bank, and die in their turn to increase, but principally to elevate, this monument of their wonderful labours. The care taken to work perpendicularly in the early stages, would mark a surprising instinct in these diminutive creatures. Their wall of coral, for the most part in situations where the winds are constant, being arrived at the surface, affords a shelter, to leeward of which their infant colonies may be safely sent forth; and to this their instinctive foresight it seems to be owing, that the windward side of a reef exposed to the open sea, is generally, if not always the highest part, and rises almost perpendicular, sometimes from the depth of 200, and perhaps many more fathoms. To be constantly covered with water, seems necessary to the existence of the animalcules, for they do not work, except in holes upon the reef, beyond low-water mark; but the coral sand and other broken remnants thrown up by the sea, adhere to the rock, and form a solid mass with it, as high as the common tides reach. That elevation surpassed, the future remnants, being rarely covered, lose their adhesive property; and remaining in a loose state, form what is usually called a *key*, upon the top of the reef. The new bank is not long in being visited by sea birds; salt plants take root upon it, and a soil begins to be formed; a cocoa nut, or the drupe of a pandanus is thrown on shore; land birds visit it and deposit the seeds of shrubs and trees; every high tide, and still more every gale, adds something to the bank; the form of an island is gradually assumed; and last of all comes man to take possession.

Half-way Island is well advanced in the above progressive state; having been many years, probably some ages, above the reach of the highest spring tides, or the wash of the surf in the heaviest gales. I distinguished, however, in the rock which forms its basis, the sand, coral, and shells formerly thrown up, in a more or less perfect state of cohesion; small pieces of wood, pumice stone, and other extraneous bodies which chance had mixed with the calcareous substances when the cohesion began, were inclosed in the rock; and in some cases were still separable from it without much force. The upper part of the island is a mixture of the same substances in a loose state, with a little vegetable soil; and is covered with the *casuarina* and a variety of other trees and shrubs, which give food to paroquets, pigeons, and some other birds; to whose ancestors it is probable, the island was originally indebted for this vegetation.

The latitude of Half-way Island, deduced from that of the preceding and following noons, is 10° 8' south, and longitude by time keeper corrected, 143° 18' east. From the time of anchoring, to nine at night, there was a set past the ship to the north-east, of half a knot; it ceased for three hours, then recommencing at a slower rate, ran to the same point. Thus far in the strait, the current had been found to run at the rate of fourteen miles a day to the westward; and the above set might have been an eddy under the lee of the reef, for it seemed too irregular to be a tide.

[SUNDAY 31 OCTOBER 1802]

At daylight in the morning the south-east trade blew fresh with squally weather. We steered south-westward, passing at seven o'clock between two dry sands, three or four miles apart, with a depth of 15 fathoms; at eight, another dry bank was left two miles to the southward, and a small, low island set at N. by W., two or three leagues. From this time, and running at the rate of seven knots, nothing was seen until ten; a dry sand then bore N. 78° W., two miles and a half, and two more low isles were seen to the northward; the soundings had become regular, between 10 and 9 fathoms, and the bottom was of mixed sand and shells, fit for anchorage. Our latitude at noon was 10° 26' 45", and longitude 142° 39½'; and we had high land bearing S. 3° E. ten or twelve miles, which I supposed might be the easternmost of the York Isles, although captain Cook's longitude of it was 38' more westward. The weather being hazy, no other land was seen, nor any reefs; but at one o'clock, I set these bearings:

York Isle, high flat top,   S. 35° E. A more northern, double isle,   S. 84 W. A high peaked hill (Mt. Ernest of Bligh), N. 16 W.

[NORTH COAST. PRINCE OF WALES' ISLANDS.]
At two o'clock, when we passed on the north side of the double isle, it was seen to be surrounded with a coral reef, and there were rocks on its west and south sides. We then hauled tip S. W. by S. for some rocky islets lying, as I supposed, off Cape York; but finding no shelter there, bore away round the north end of an island, of which Mr. Westall took a view (Atlas, Plate XVIII. View 12), and anchored in 7 fathoms, gravel and shells, one mile and a half from the land, and two or three cables length from a shoal to the southward, which became dry at low water. Our latitude here was 10° 30' from bearings, and longitude by time-keeper 142(? illegible in book) 18½' east; but I was altogether at a loss to know what islands these were, under which we had anchored. Supposing the flat-topped island to have been the easternmost York Isle, the land we had in sight to the southward should have been Cape York; but no such isles as those around us were laid down by captain Cook, to the north of that cape. On consulting the sketch made by captain Bligh in the Bounty's launch (Voyage to the South Seas, p. 220), it appeared that the first land was not the easternmost isle, but one much nearer to Cape York; and that our anchorage was under the southern group of the Prince of Wales' Islands, the longitude of which, by captain Cook, is 1° 12' west of what I make it.* The north-eastern isle of this group, under which we more immediately lay, is that named Wednesday Island by captain Bligh; to the other isles he gave no name; but the one westward of the ship seems to have been the Hammond's Island of captain Edwards, when passing here with the Pandora's boats. So soon as the weather cleared a little, the subjoined bearings were taken.

[* Mr. Wales deduces from captain Cook's observations in the Endeavour, that the error of his chart here, is 35' west (*Astron. Observations*, p. 131).]

Wednesday I., distant 1½ to 3 miles,   S. 89° E. to 21° W. Hammond's Isle, dist. 4 or 5 miles,   S. 52 W. to 71 W. Hawkesbury I. (of Edwards), highest part,   N. 52 W. Mount Augustus (of Bligh),   N. 2 W. A small isle, distant three leagues, N. 24 E. Mount Ernest, peak,   N. 36 E. Double Isle, passed at 2 p.m., N. 70½ E. Breakers on a reef, distant 3½ miles,   N. 64 to 30 W.

[MONDAY 1 NOVEMBER 1802]
This evening and all the next day, the wind blew so strong that it was impossible to land; nor did I think it prudent to quit the anchorage, though anxious to commence the survey of the Gulph of Carpentaria. Upon Hammond's Island some fires were seen; but Wednesday Island showed no signs of being inhabited, unless some whitish, conical figures like sentry boxes, were huts; there were bushes and small trees scattered over both islands, but their general appearance was rocky and barren.

The tide here ran nine hours to the westward, at the strongest two-and-half knots; and three hours north-eastward, but scarcely perceptible; which deviation from the regular order was probably caused by the current setting westward. So far as the soundings taken every hour could ascertain the rise, it was at least two fathoms, and high water took place *four or five hours after* the moon's passage over and under the meridian, and was completed by the three hours tide. According to this, it would be high water here, and low water at Murray's Islands at the same time, which would present a remarkable analogy between this strait and that of Bass to the southward; this however is certain, that the tide set E. by S. one knot and a quarter, at Murray's Islands, at four in the morning; and that two days afterward, at Wednesday Island, it set from one-and-half to two-and-half knots W. by S., from one till seven in the morning. I will not venture to say that the latter part of the flood comes from southwest at the Prince of Wales' Islands, though appearances bespoke it; because captain Cook, who had better opportunity for observation, found it setting from the east, in Endeavour's Strait. He also gives the time of high water at one or two hours after the moon, which comes nearer to what I observed at Murray's Islands.

From azimuths with the surveying compass when the head was S. E. by E., the variation was 3° 32', or corrected to the meridian, 4° 52' east.

TUESDAY 2 NOVEMBER 1802
In the morning of Nov. 2, the wind being more moderate and at E. S. E., we steered between Hammond's Island and the north-western reef, with soundings from 6 to 9 fathoms. Another island appeared beyond Hammond's, to the south-west, which, as it had

no name, I called *Good's Island*, after Mr. Good, the botanical gardener; and we hauled up for it, passing a rock and a small reef between the two. On seeing an extensive shoal ahead, which would have carried us off the land to go round it, we anchored in 7 fathoms, dead coral and shells, with the north end of Hammond's Island bearing N. 64° E., four or five miles. The botanical gentlemen landed on Good's Island; and in the afternoon I took these bearings amongst others, from a hill near its south-west end.

The ship, distant 1¼ miles,   N. 58° 0' W. Wallis' Isles, over the Shoal Cape of Bligh,   S. 23 5 W. Booby Isle, centre,   S. 80 0 W. Northern isles, the westernmost visible, N. 28° 10' to 24 5 W. Hawkesbury Island, N. 9 15 to 4 0 W. North-west reef, its apparent termination,   N. 38 50 W.

The shoal which stopped our progress did not run off from Shoal Cape, as captain Bligh had supposed, but from a smaller and nearer island, two miles from my station. Within the large island, of which Shoal Cape forms the north-western point, I saw water like an inclosed port, probably the Wolf's Bay of captain Edwards; and it seemed possible that the land may be there divided; but the best information I can give of the forms and extent of all these islands, will be seen in the particular chart.

It was now ascertained, that the figures resembling sentry boxes were ant hills, of eight or more feet high; Pelsert found similar hills on the West Coast, and says they might have been taken for the houses of Indians, as in fact we did take them at a distant view. They were also seen by Dampier on the North-west Coast, who mistook them in the same way; but says he found them to be so many rocks, probably from not making the examination with his usual care. The insects which inhabit, and I suppose erect these structures, are small, reddish, with black heads, and seemed to be a sluggish and feeble race. We found the common black flies excessively numerous here; and almost as troublesome as Dampier describes them to be on the North-west Coast.

Good's Island is between one and two miles long, and resembles the rest of the cluster in being hilly, woody, and rocky, with small beaches on the leeward side. The stone is granitic and brittle; but there is also porphyry, and in one place I found streaks of verdegrease, as if the cliffs above had contained copper ore. A log of wood, resembling the cedar of Port Jackson, was thrown up on the beach, but none of the trees were seen; those scattered over the island, though of various kinds, were small and fit for little else than the fire. A species of silk-cotton plant was plentiful; the fibres in the pod are strong, and have a fine gloss, and might perhaps be advantageously employed in manufacture.

From two supplements of the sun's meridian altitude to the north, the *latitude* of our anchorage would be 10° 34' 12"; but the supplements observed on the 31st having given 1' 14" too far south, the correct latitude is taken to be 10° 32' 58". The *longitude* from nine sets of distances of the sun west of the moon, was 142° 23'; but by the corrected time keeper, which I prefer, it was 142° 10½' east. To compare this longitude with that of captain Cook, it must be reduced to some point distinctly laid down by him, and I take Booby Island, which was in sight. According to that navigator, Booby Isle is in 140° 38' east (Hawkesworth, III, 214); whereas I made it to lie in 141° 57', or 1° 19' further east, a difference which certainly appears very extraordinary; but it is still more so, that the island should be laid down 63' of longitude to the west of the high, flat-topped York Isle, instead Of 43' or 44'. To show that the longitude by my time keeper was not much, if any thing too great, I have to observe, that in captain Bligh's manuscript chart of 1792, Mount Augustus is laid down from his time keepers in 142° 14'; and the mean of his lunar observations, taken eight days before and six days afterward, was 16' *more east*. My time keeper now placed Mount Augustus in 142° 18', or only 4' more east than captain Bligh's chart, consequently in 12' less than by his lunar observations; by which quantity it was also less than the nine sets of distances now taken by lieutenant Flinders.

No run of tide was perceptible at the anchorage, from eight in the morning to two p.m.; but it then set westward, and continued so to do until four next morning, and was then running one knot and a half. The time of high water appeared by the soundings, to be nearly as they gave it at Wednesday Island.

WEDNESDAY 3 NOVEMBER 1802

In the morning of the 3rd, the wind was moderate at E. S. E., and we made sail to get in with the main land to the south of the Prince of Wales' Islands. In hauling round the dry part of the shoal, we fell into 3 fathoms, and were obliged to steer round off; nor was it until after many attempts, and running four or five miles further to the south-westward, that the shoal would allow us to steer a southern course. At 8h 45', being then in 5 fathoms,

    Booby Isle bore,   N. 56° W. Cape Cornwall,   S. 58 E. Station on Good's Island, dist. 11 miles N. 54½ E.

From hence we carried 6 to 7 fathoms until past ten, and afterwards irregular soundings between 3 and 9 fathoms, to noon; the latitude from a supplement to the north, with the same correction as applied on the 2nd, was then 10° 50' 44", and the bearings of the land were these;

    Station on Good's Island,   N. 29½° E. Cape Cornwall, N. 68 E. Wallis' Isles, the highest, distant 2½ miles,   N. 84 E. Wallis' Isles, a lower and broader, dist. 3 or 4 miles, S. 71° to 64 E. Main land, low sandy point, dist. 8 miles,   S. 43 E. Main land, furthest extreme near a smoke,   S. 77 E.

Between Cape Cornwall and the low main land above set, is the opening called in the old Dutch chart, Speult's River; but which captain Cook, who sailed through it, named Endeavour's Strait. Wallis' Isles are small, low, and rocky, and the northernmost seemed destitute of vegetation; they are surrounded with sandy shoals, which appeared to connect with the main land and leave no ship passage between them. On the north side of the isles there are several banks at the outlet of Endeavour's Strait; and the passage this way into the Indian Ocean is thereby rendered much inferior to that between Wednesday Island and the north-west reef, in which there are no difficulties.

[NORTH COAST. GULPH OF CARPENTARIA.]

We passed Wallis' Isles, steering southward to get in with the main coast; but the shoals forced us to run seven or eight miles to the west, out of sight of land, before regular soundings could be obtained and a southern course steered into the Gulph of Carpentaria. At dusk, the anchor was dropped in 8 fathoms, soft mud, in latitude 11° 5', as observed from the moon to the north and south, and longitude 141° 51' by time keeper. The variation from amplitude at sunset, was 2° 33', with the ship's head S. S. E., or 3° 10' east when reduced to the meridian; which is 1° 42' less than was obtained from azimuths under Wednesday Island.

I now considered all the difficulties of Torres' Strait to be surmounted, since we had got a fair entry into the Gulph of Carpentaria; and to have accomplished this, before the north-west monsoon had made any strong indications, was a source of much satisfaction, after the unexpected delay amongst the Barrier Reefs on the East Coast. It was this apprehension of the north-west monsoon that prevented me from making any further examination of the Strait, than what could be done in passing through it; but even this was not without its advantage to navigation, since it demonstrated that this most direct passage, from the southern Pacific, or Great Ocean to the Indian Seas, may be accomplished *in three days*. It may be remembered, that the reefs on the north side of the Pandora's Entrance were passed at six in the morning of Oct. 29; and that, after lying two nights at anchor, we reached the Prince of Wales's Islands at three in the afternoon of the 31st; and nothing then prevented us from passing Booby Isle, had I wished it, and clearing Torres' Strait before dusk. Our route was almost wholly to seek, and another ship which shall have that route laid down to her, may surely accomplish the passage in the same time; it must however be acknowledged, that this navigation is not without difficulties and dangers; but I had great hope of obviating many of them, and even of finding a more direct passage by the south of Murray's Islands in the following year, when I should have the assistance of the Lady Nelson in making a survey of the Strait.

CHAPTER VI.

Examination of the coast on the east side of the Gulph of Carpentaria.
Landing at Coen River.
Head of the Gulph.
Anchorage at Sweers' Island.
Interview with Indians at Horse-shoe Island.

Investigator's Road.
The ship found to be in a state of decay.
General remarks on the islands at the Head of the Gulph, and their inhabitants.
Astronomical and nautical observations.

[NORTH COAST. GULPH OF CARPENTARIA.]

THURSDAY 4 NOVEMBER 1802

In the morning of Nov. 4, the wind was at south-east, and we steered southward, close to it, with soundings from 8 to 11 fathoms. Several land birds of the size of a pigeon, but more slender, came off to the ship; when taken they fought desperately, being armed for war with a strong claw upon each wing. This bird had been seen at Port Philip on the South Coast, and belongs to the genus *Tringa*, being very nearly allied to the *Tringa Goensis*. At noon, the latitude was 11° 24½', longitude 141° 46½'; and at three, a sea breeze which set in from south-west, enabled us to steer in for the coast of Carpentaria on the east side of the Gulph; and it came in sight from the mast head soon afterwards. At five, the nearest part was six or eight miles distant, and the extremes bore N. E. to S. S. E.; the depth of water was 10 fathoms, which decreased to 7½ at dusk, when we anchored on a bottom of gravel and shells; the shore being then distant four miles, and the extremes bearing N. 38° to S. 8° E. It was sandy and low, like that on the south side of Endeavour's Strait, with which it is no doubt connected; although, in a space of five or six leagues, our distance was too great for the land to be seen; behind the shore it was indifferently covered with shrubs and small trees, but totally destitute of any thing like a hill: fires bespoke it to be inhabited. There was no set of tide past the ship in the night, but the depth of water diminished from 7½ to 6¼ fathoms.

FRIDAY 5 NOVEMBER 1802

When we got under way in the morning to proceed along shore, the wind was light, off the land, and soon after nine it fell calm; a drain of tide setting to the north-east, induced me to drop a stream anchor, four or five miles from a part of the beach where some natives were collected round a fire. At eleven the sea breeze came in from W. by N., with dark cloudy weather, and we steered onward, passing a small opening at one o'clock, four or five miles south of the natives. A much larger opening came in sight at two, into which I hoped to get the ship; but the water was so shallow at five or six miles off, that we were obliged to tack; and after making a second ineffectual attempt, it became dusk, and we anchored in 6½ fathoms, fine dark sand, the centre of the opening bearing S. 37° E. three leagues.

The coast was low, as before, but the trees upon it were taller. The largest opening is about two miles wide, leading in south-east; but turning afterwards more east, and apparently contracting its width. Near the south-west point of the entrance, which projects a little from the general line of the shore, was a clump of trees, higher than usual, presenting the first mark I had yet found for bearings. The latitude of this opening is 11° 55', and agrees nearly with that of Batavia River in the old Dutch chart; but the shoal which runs six miles out, seemed to render it inaccessible to a ship.

SATURDAY 6 NOVEMBER 1802

In the morning we had a breeze off the land; and the fear of the north-west monsoon preventing me from taking time to beat up, we passed Batavia River at the distance of six miles, with soundings from 5 to 8 fathoms. Several flocks of ducks were seen coming from the westward, where they had probably been to pass the night upon some island not inhabited. Our latitude at noon, from double altitudes, was 11° 56', and longitude by time keeper 141° 50'; the clump of trees near the entrance of Batavia River bore E. 1° S., the furthest extreme of the land, S. 11° W., and the nearest part was distant four miles.

The land wind continued to blow all day, but permitted us to lie along the shore. On its falling calm toward sunset, we anchored in 10 fathoms, soft mud, three or four miles from the coast; the extremes bearing N. 49° E. and S. 2° W. A light air came off the land at four in the morning [SUNDAY 7 NOVEMBER 1802], and at daylight we again steered southward; but in two hours the wind died off, and an anchor was dropped in 9 fathoms. There was a small opening at E. 5° S., about three miles; and the botanical gentlemen being desirous of seeing the productions of this part of the country, the whale boat was lowered down, and we went to examine the inlet.

On approaching the entrance, a canoe, or something like one, passed and repassed from the north to the south side, the rower using both hands to the paddle like the natives of Murray's Islands. We had a good deal of difficulty to get in, on account of the shoals; the channel amongst them being narrow and winding, and not more than nine to twelve feet deep. On the north side was a party of natives, and Bongaree went on shore to them, naked and unarmed; but although provided with spears, they retreated from him, and all our endeavours to bring about an interview were unsuccessful. It was not safe for the gentlemen to botanise in presence of these suspicious people; and therefore we rowed a mile higher up, to a green looking point on the same side, and landed about noon. The depth thus far, was 2 fathoms; and I could see two-and-half miles further up the inlet to the E. S. E., where it turned more southward, round a woody point; and from the strength of the tide, probably extended some miles into the country.

Whilst the botanists where making their examination and I walked along the shore to shoot some birds, several voices were heard in the wood, as of people advancing towards us; and there being too much opportunity here to creep on secretly, we assembled and retired into the boat, to wait their approach. A sea breeze had then set in; and the Indians not appearing, we rowed back to the first place, where the country was open; and the gentlemen botanised whilst centinels kept watch on the sandy hillocks.

In the upper parts of the port the country was well covered with wood, mostly *eucalyptus*; but near the entrance it was little better than bare sand, with some scattered trees of the *casuarina* and *pandanus*: a stone of imperfectly concreted coral sand and shells formed the basis. Foot marks of the kangaroo were imprinted on the sand, and a dog was seen; drupes of the pandanus, which had been sucked, lay in every direction, and small cockle shells were scattered on the beaches. I sought in vain for the canoe which had landed here, nor did I find any huts of the natives.

Before quitting the shore, a hatchet was made fast to the branch of a tree, and set up conspicuously near the water side. We had scarcely shoved off, when the party of Indians, sixteen in number, made their appearance and called to us; but when the boat's head was turned toward them, they ran away. On the south side of the entrance were four other natives, who also ran at our approach; we therefore set up another hatchet for them on the beach, and returned back to the ship.

These people were all naked; and in colour, as in every thing else, seemed to have a perfect resemblance to the inhabitants of the east and south coasts of Terra Australis. In Torres' Strait bows and arrows are the offensive weapons; but here we saw spears only: each man had several in his hand, and something which was supposed to be a throwing stick.

This small opening appears to be the *Coen River* of the Dutch chart; but the entrance is too small and shallow to admit any thing larger than boats: its latitude is 12° 13' south, and longitude 141° 47' east; and the variation of the compass, observed with the ship's head in the magnetic meridian, was 4° 36' east. The tide was running from south-west, at ten in in the morning, and on entering the inlet it was found to be setting in with considerable strength; at two in the afternoon the flood was still running; and admitting that it would be high water an hour afterwards, as seemed probable, the time would be *five hours and a half after* the moon passed the lower meridian; or an hour later than it had *appeared* to be at the Prince of Wales' Islands.

Lieutenant Fowler had got the ship under way, on the sea breeze setting in, and stood off and on the entrance to Coen River, until our return at three o'clock. We then steered south-westward along the shore; and soon after sunset, anchored in 10 fathoms, nearly four miles from the land, which extended from N. 38° to S. 6° E. and was still low and woody, and fronted with a sandy beach.

A breeze came off the land at night, as usual, and the weather was dark and squally. Early in the morning [MONDAY 8 NOVEMBER 1802] we steered along the coast, with good soundings between 10 and 9 fathoms, muddy bottom. A sandy point with two hillocks on it, which had been the extreme of the preceding evening, was passed at ten o'clock; and seeing a large bight round it, we tacked to work up. At noon, the point bore from N. 44° E., one mile and a half, to the southern extreme at east, three miles. This point is one of the very few remarkable projections to be found on this low coast, but it is not noticed in the Dutch chart; there is little doubt, however, that it was seen in 1606, in the yacht Duyfhen, the first vessel which discovered any part of Carpentaria; and that the remembrance may not be lost, I gave the name of the vessel to the point. Our observations placed the south extreme of *Duyfhen Point* in 12° 35' south, and 141° 42' east; and the variation from amplitude, with the ships head W. N. W., was 5° 24', or reduced to the meridian, 3° 43' east.

On the sea breeze setting in at two o'clock, we steered into the bight until past five; when having no more than 2½ fathoms, we tacked and stretched out. The bight extends eleven or twelve miles back from the line of the coast, and there are three small openings in it; but the shore being very low, and in many places over-run with mangroves, and the water shallow four or five miles off, these openings are probably no more than drains out of salt swamps or lagoons. The bearings when we tacked in 2½ fathoms, were,

Duyfhen Point, south extreme, dist. 6 or 7 miles, N. 63° W. Small opening behind it, distant 5 or 6 miles,　N. 23 W. A second opening, distant four miles,　　N. 64 E. A third, distant three miles,　　S. 78 E.

At eight in the evening, having reached out of the bight, and a breeze coming off the land, we steered southward until half past ten; and then anchored in 8 fathoms, muddy bottom. In the morning [TUESDAY 9 NOVEMBER 1802], I set the west extreme of Duyfhen Point at N. 9° E.; and the furthest land in the opposite direction, at S. 9° E. This land forms the south side of the large bight; and besides projecting beyond the coast line, and being a little higher than usual, is remarkable for having some reddish cliffs in it, and deep water near the shore. It is not noticed in the Dutch chart; but I called it *Pera Head*, to preserve the name of the second vessel which, in 1623, sailed along this coast.

(Atlas, Plate XIV.)

Pera Head was passed at the distance of one mile and a half, at noon, with 9 fathoms water; and the most projecting part of the cliffs found to be in 12° 58½' south, and 141° 40' east. The sea breeze had then set in, and we steered southward till past four o'clock; when a decrease in the soundings to 3 fathoms, obliged us to tack at a league from the land; and the wind being at S. W., we worked along shore till ten in the evening, and then anchored in 6 fathoms, oozy bottom. At daylight [WEDNESDAY 10 NOVEMBER 1802], the land was seen to be five miles distant, equally low and sandy as before; and a small opening in it, perhaps not accessible to boats, bore S. 79° E. On getting under way again, we closed in with the shore and steered along it at the distance of two or three miles, in soundings from 3 to 7 fathoms until noon; our latitude was then 13° 42' 35", longitude 141° 32', being nearly the position of *Cape Keer-Weer*, at which the yacht Duyfhen gave up her examination. I could see nothing like a cape here; but the southern extreme of the land, seen from the mast head, projects a little; and from respect to antiquity, the Dutch name is there preserved.

At four o'clock we passed the southern extremity of Cape Keer-Weer, round which the coast falls back somewhat; the water then became more shallow, and did not admit of being safely approached nearer than four miles. An opening is laid down here in the Dutch chart, called Vereenigde River, which certainly has no existence. All this afternoon the sea breeze was fresh and favourable; and by eight o'clock, when we anchored in 5 fathoms, the distance run from noon exceeded forty miles. A fire was seen on the land about four miles off, and some smokes had been passed in the day; so that the country should seem to be at least as well peopled in this part of Carpentaria as further northward. The coast was, if possible, still lower than before; not a single hill had yet been seen; and the tops of the trees on the highest land, had scarcely exceeded the height of the ship's mast head.

THURSDAY 11 NOVEMBER 1802

The land wind came from N. N. E.; and in the morning our course was pursued along the shore at the usual distance. At eight o'clock the depth decreased to 2½ fathoms, and obliged us to steer off, though five miles from the land; and when fair soundings were obtained, the tops of the trees only were visible from the deck. At noon we had closed in again, the shore being distant five or six miles, and the depth 6 fathoms on a gravelly bottom; our latitude was 14° 51' 5", longitude 141° 33', the extremes seen from the deck bore N. 29° to S. 66° E., and a smoke was seen rising at S. 28° E. The sea breeze came in from the south-westward; but the trending of the coast being nearly S. S. E., we lay along it until past four o'clock, and then tacked off, in 3 fathoms; the nearest part of the land being distant two or three miles, and the extremes bearing N. 3° and S. 7° W. At eight in the evening the breeze died away, and a stream anchor was dropped in 5 fathoms, mud and shells, five or six miles off shore; where the latitude from an observation of the moon was 15° 5' south.

FRIDAY 12 NOVEMBER 1802

At sunrise, next morning, the ship was steering southward with a land wind at east; and at seven o'clock we passed an opening near which several natives were collected. The entrance seemed to be a full mile in width; but a spit from the south side runs so far across, that there is probably no access to it, unless for rowing boats: its latitude is 15° 12' south, corresponding with a bight in the Dutch chart to the south of the second *Water Plaets*; and the variation, with the ship's head in the meridian, was 4° 43' east. Our course southward was continued at two or three miles from the shore, in 3 to 4 fathoms; but at eleven o'clock, the sea breeze having then set in, the depth diminished suddenly to 2 fathoms; and in tacking, the ship stirred up the mud.

The latitude at noon was 15° 25' 20", and longitude 141° 32'; at one o'clock we steered S. S. W., with the whale boat ahead, and carried from 4 to 6 fathoms until seven in the evening, when the stream anchor was dropped about four miles from the shore, in 5 fathoms, muddy bottom. This depth had diminished at daylight [SATURDAY 13 NOVEMBER 1802] to 3¾ fathoms, after a tide had been setting nine hours to the N. by E.; and for the first time upon this coast it had run with some strength, the rate being one mile an hour.

We were again under way soon after five o'clock; and at six, being then four miles from the land, and steering S. S. W., a lagoon was seen from the mast head, over the front beach. It has doubtless some communication with the sea, either by a constant, or a temporary opening, but none such could be perceived. The latitude 15° 53' corresponds with that of *Nassau River* in the old chart; and from the examples already had of the Dutch rivers here, it seems probable that this lagoon was meant. A few miles further south, the shoal water obliged me to run westward, out of sight of land from the deck; and even at the mast head, the tops of the trees were only partially distinguished; yet the depth was no more than from 4 to 6 fathoms. At noon, when our latitude was 16° 24' 29" and longitude 141° 14½', trees were visible from the deck at N. 70° E., and from thence to S. 50° E; the nearest part, whence a smoke arose, being distant seven or eight miles, and the depth of water 4 fathoms. The slight projection here is probably one of those marked in the old chart on each side of Staten River; but where that river can be found I know not.

The nearest approach made to the land in the afternoon, was five or six miles, with 3 fathoms water; at dusk we anchored in 6 fathoms, mud, at six or seven miles from the shore, having been forced off a little by the sea breeze veering southward. A tide here ran gently to the S. S. W., till near ten o'clock, and then set northward till daylight [SUNDAY 14 NOVEMBER 1802]; at which time the water had fallen nine feet by the lead line. We got under way with a land wind from the north-east, which afterwards veered to north-west, and steered a course nearly due south; which, as the coast then trended south-westward, brought us in with it. At noon, the latitude was 17° 3' 15", longitude 141° 0'; a projecting part bore N. 59° E. three or four miles, and the depth was 3½ fathoms. There appeared to be a small opening on the south side of this little projection, which corresponds in latitude to *Van Diemen's River* in the old chart; but across the entrance was an extensive flat, nearly dry, and would probably prevent even boats from getting in. If this place had any title to be called a river in 1644, the coast must have undergone a great alteration since that time.

In the afternoon our course along shore was more westward; and this, with the increasing shallowness of the water, made me apprehend that the Gulph would be found to terminate nearly as represented in the old charts, and disappoint the hopes formed of a strait or passage leading out at some other part of Terra Australis. At four o'clock, after running more than an hour in 3½ fathoms, or less than 3 at low water, our distance from the shore was five miles; and a small opening then bore S. 14° E, which seems to be the *Caron River*, marked at the south-east extremity of the Gulph in the Dutch chart; but whatever it might have been in Tasman's time, no navigator would now think of attempting to enter it with a ship: the latitude is 17° 26', and longitude 140° 52' east. From four till seven our course was

W. by S., close to the wind, the depth being mostly 3 fathoms, and the land barely within sight from the mast head. We then stood off; and the water being smooth, anchored on muddy ground, in 4½ fathoms, which became 3½ at low water. The flood tide here set S. S. W., till midnight; and the ebb N. by E., till we got under way in the morning.

MONDAY 15 NOVEMBER 1802

On the 15th, we ran before a north-east wind towards the furthest land seen from the mast head. The soundings were 3½, 3, and soon after seven o'clock, 2½ fathoms; which made it necessary to steer further off, though the land was distant six or eight miles, and scarcely visible from the deck. We kept in 3 fathoms, steering various westward courses, until noon; when the latitude was 17' 30' 9", and longitude 140° 23'. The land was distant seven or eight miles to the southward, and the furthest part distinguished from the mast head was at S. by W. ½ W.; it was low and sandy as ever, and with less wood upon it than any part before seen. A sea breeze at N. N. W. scarcely permitted us to lie along the shore in the afternoon; but the ground being soft, and soundings regular, though shallow, we kept on until five o'clock; and then tacked in 2½ fathoms, having reached within three miles of the land. At eight o'clock, the anchor was let go in 4 fathoms, on a bottom of mud and shells.

The coast to which we approached nearest this evening, was sandy and very barren; but there were some natives collected upon the hillocks, to look at the ship; so that even here, and at the end of the dry season, fresh water may be had. These people were black and naked, and made many wild gestures. Between this part and the land set at S. by W. ½ W. at noon, there was a bight falling back as far as the latitude 17° 42', or perhaps further, which appeared to be the southern extremity of the Gulph of Carpentaria; for the coast from thence took a direction to the northward of west. Shoals extended a great way out from the bight; and were almost dry to a considerable distance.

TUESDAY 16 NOVEMBER 1802

In the morning our route was pursued along the shore, at the distance of six to nine or ten miles; the course being N. W., close to a N. N. E. wind, and the soundings remarkably regular, between 3 and 3½ fathoms. Two leagues from the place where the natives had been seen, was a projecting part where the country again became woody; but the coast there, and onward, was as low as before. At noon, the observed latitude was 17° 21' 15", and the longitude by time keeper 139° 54' east; the furthest continuation of the land seen from the mast head, bore W. ½ S., but there was a small lump bearing N. 35° W., towards which we kept up as much as possible. At two o'clock the wind headed, and on coming into 2½ fathoms, we tacked; being then five miles from the low southern land, and three or four leagues from the northern hill, which bore N. 18° W. Not much was gained in working to windward from that time till dusk; and the anchor was then dropped in 4½ fathoms, blue mud, no other land than the small hill being in sight.

There being no island marked in the Dutch chart so near to the head of the Gulph as this hill, made me conclude that it was upon the main land; and to hope that the space of four leagues, between it and the southern coast, was an opening of some importance. In the morning [WEDNESDAY 17 NOVEMBER 1802], a fresh land wind at south-east favoured our course, the water deepened to 10 fathoms, and at eight o'clock to no ground with 13, near the south end of a reef extending out from the hill. On coming into 5 fathoms behind the reef, the anchor was dropped on a muddy bottom, with the hill bearing N. 15° E., one mile and a quarter, and the dry extremity of the reef S. E. ½ E. The coast to the southward was scarcely visible from the mast head, but land was seen to extend westward from the hill, as far as nine or ten miles; and in order to gain a better knowledge of what this land might be, I went on shore, taking instruments with me to observe for the rates of the time keepers.

The hill proved to be a mass of calcareous rock, whose surface was cut and honeycombed as if it had been exposed to the washing of a surf. It was the highest land we had seen in Carpentaria, after having followed one hundred and seventy-five leagues of coast; nor was any land to be distinguished from the top of the hill which had an equal degree of elevation; yet it did not much exceed the height of the ship's mast head! The land round it proved to be an island of five miles long; separated from other land to the west by a channel of nearly two miles in width. The wide opening between this land and the low coast to the southward, I take to have been what is called Maatsuyker's River in the old chart; and that the island, which Tasman, or whoever made the examination, did not distinguish well from being too far off, is the projecting point marked on the west side of that river. Maatsuyker was one of the counsellors at Batavia, who signed Tasman's instructions in 1644; but as there is no river here, his name, as it stands applied in the old chart, cannot remain. I would have followed in the intention of doing him honour, by transferring his name to the island, but Maatsuyker's Isles already exist on the south coast of Van Diemen's Land; I therefore adopt the name of Sweers, another member of the same Batavia council; and call the island at the entrance of the supposed river, *Sweers' Island*. The hill obtained the name of *Inspection Hill*; and after taking bearings from it, I rowed into the channel which separates Sweers' Island from the western land; and finding the shelter to be good, the bottom soft, and soundings regular between 3 and 6 fathoms, the shores on each side were searched for fresh water, with a view to filling up the holds there and caulking the ship, before proceeding further in the examination of the Gulph: the search, however, was unsuccessful.

In Torres' Strait, when running with a fresh side wind, the ship had leaked to the amount of ten inches of water per hour. and in some hours the carpenters had reported as much as fourteen; but no anchorage, adapted to the purpose of caulking the bends, had presented itself until our arrival here. Before going on shore, I had left orders for the ship to be put on a careen, and the carpenters began upon the larbord side. In the course of their work two planks were found to be rotten, and the timber underneath was in no better state; it was therefore desirable to find a place where the holds could be completed with water, and the botanists and myself find useful employment for a few days, whilst the deficiencies were repairing. Such a place, it was reasonable to expect, the opening to the westward would afford; and the carpenters having patched up the bad part by the evening of the 18th [THURSDAY 18 NOVEMBER 1802], and another set of observations for the time keepers being obtained, we were then ready to proceed in the examination.

[NORTH COAST. WELLESLEY'S ISLANDS.]
FRIDAY 19 NOVEMBER 1802

Next morning at sunrise, we steered up the opening with a land wind at S. S. E.; and until ten o'clock, when we had reached the furthest part of the western land seen from Inspection Hill, the soundings were between 6 and 3 fathoms, reduced to low water. This land proved to be an island of ten or eleven miles long, and I have given it the name of Bentinck, in honour of the Right Hon. LORD WILLIAM BENTINCK; of whose obliging attention, when governor of Madras, I shall hereafter have to speak in praise. To the north-west of Bentinck's Island, several small isles came in sight; but a northern sea breeze having set in, we kept on our western course for the low main land, which trended here north-westward. At one o'clock the diminution of depth to 2½ fathoms, obliged us to tack; the main being four miles distant, and the eastern extreme of the nearest island bearing N. 3° W., two leagues: this was named *Allen's Isle*, after the practical miner of the expedition. In working to windward, the water was found to be shallow in almost every direction; and the deepest being at three or four miles from the south-west point of Bentinck's Island, the anchor was there dropped in 4½ fathoms, muddy bottom.

SATURDAY 20 NOVEMBER 1802

In the morning we steered towards Allen's Isle, with the whale boat ahead; and anchored one mile and a half from its south-east end, in 3½ fathoms, mud. Our latitude here was 17° 5', longitude 139° 26'; and azimuths taken with the surveying compass, when the head was N. by E., gave variation 2° 49', or 3° 15' east, corrected. I went on shore with the botanical gentlemen, in order to take bearings, and explore further up the opening.

Allen's Isle is between four and five miles in length, and though generally barren, there are bushes and small trees upon it, and some tolerable grass. It is altogether low land; but the south-east end is cliffy, and within two cables length of it there is 4 fathoms; no fresh water was found near the shore, nor any place where casks could be conveniently landed. After taking a set of bearings I left the gentlemen to follow their pursuits, and rowed north-westward, intending to go round the island; but an impassable reef extended so far out, that the project was given up; and after taking angles from one of the rocks, I went eastward to a smaller island two miles off, where several Indians where perceived. The water was too shallow for the boat to get near them; but we landed at a little distance, and walked after three men who were dragging six small rafts toward the extreme northern rocks, where three other natives were sitting.

These men not choosing to abandon their rafts, an interview was unavoidable, and they came on shore with their spears to wait our approach. One of us advanced towards them, unarmed; and signs being made to lay down their spears, which were understood to mean that they should sit down, they complied; and by degrees, a friendly intercourse was established. They accepted some red worsted caps and fillets, as also a hatchet and an adze, the use of which being explained, was immediately comprehended. In return, they gave us two very rude spears, and a *womerah*, or throwing stick, of nearly the same form as those used by the natives of Port Jackson.

The rafts consisted of several straight branches of mangrove, very much dried, and lashed together in two places with the largest ends one way, so as to form a broad part, and the smaller ends closing to a point. Near the broad end was a bunch of grass, where the man sits to paddle; but the raft, with his weight alone, must swim very deep; and indeed I should scarcely have supposed it could float a man at all. Upon one of the rafts was a short net, which, from the size of the meshes, was probably intended to catch turtle; upon another was a young shark; and these, with their paddles and spears, seemed to constitute the whole of their earthly riches.

Two of the three men were advanced in years, and from the resemblance of feature were probably brothers. With the exception of two chiefs at Taheity, these were the tallest Indians I had ever seen; the two brothers being from three to four inches higher than my coxswain, who measured five feet eleven. They were not remarkable for being either stout or slender; though like most of the Australians, their legs did not bear the European proportion to the size of their heads and bodies. The third native was not so tall as the other two; and he was, according to our notions, better proportioned. Their features did not much differ from those of their countrymen on the South and East Coasts; but they had each of them lost two front teeth from the upper jaw. Their hair was short, though not curly; and a fillet of net work, which the youngest man had wrapped round his head, was the sole ornament or clothing seen amongst them. The two old men appeared, to my surprise, to have undergone circumcision; but the posture of the youngest, who remained sitting down, did not allow of observation being made upon him.

After being five minutes with them, the old men proposed to go to our boat; and this being agreed to, we proceeded together, hand in hand. But they stopped half way, and retreating a little, the eldest made a short harangue which concluded with the word *jahree!* pronounced with emphasis: they then returned to the rafts, and dragged them towards their three companions who were sitting on the furthest rocks. These I judged to be women, and that the proposal of the men to go to our boat was a feint to get us further from them; it did not seem, however, that the women were so much afraid of us, as the men appeared to be on their account; for although we walked back, past the rafts, much nearer than before, they remained very quietly picking oysters. It was not my desire to annoy these poor people; and therefore, leaving them to their own way, we took an opposite direction to examine the island.

This low piece of land is between one and two miles long, and from its form received the name of *Horse-shoe Island*; there is very little soil mixed with the sand on its surface, and except the mangrove trees upon the shore, it bears nothing larger than bushes. We did not find any huts; but the dried grass spread round two or three neighbouring fire places, marked the last residence of the Indians. Near it were lying several large spiral shells, probably the vessels in which they had brought water from the main land; for none was found on the island, nor was there any appearance that it could be procured. Shells and bones of turtle, some of them fresh, were plentifully scattered around; upon the beach also there were turtle tracks, and several of these animals were seen in the water during the day; but it was not our fortune to take one of them.

In returning to the ship in the evening, I steered from Horse-shoe, to the south-east end of Allen's Isle, and sounded the channel between them; but had only once so much as 3 fathoms. There was consequently no fit passage this way for the ship, and the several low islets to the north-east, precluded the expectation of finding one any where to the west of

Bentinck's Island; I therefore judged it most advisable to return, and place the ship between Bentinck's and Sweers' Islands, until the necessary caulking was finished. Natives had been seen on both those islands; and this gave a hope that water might still be found to complete the holds previously to encountering the bad weather of the north-west monsoon, which I had been expecting to set in every day.

SUNDAY 21 NOVEMBER 1802

At daylight next morning the anchor was weighed; and having to work against foul winds, the breadth of the ship passage between Bentinck's Island and the southern main, was ascertained and sounded; and at dusk in the evening we anchored half a mile from the west sandy point of Sweers' Island, in 5 fathoms, small stones and shells. This anchorage between the two islands, though it may not be called a port, is yet almost equally well sheltered, and I named it *Investigator's Road*; it has the appearance of being exposed between N. N. W. and N. E. ½ N.; but the rocks from each shore occupy nearly one half of the space, and the water is too shallow in the remaining part to admit any surge to endanger a ship.

MONDAY 22 NOVEMBER 1802

Next day, a boat was sent to fish with the seine upon Sweers' Island, and an officer went to the opposite shore to dig for water; the botanists divided themselves into two parties, to visit both islands, and the carpenters began caulking the starbord side of the ship. I repeated the observations under Inspection Hill, for the rates of the time keepers; and being informed on my return, that the midshipman of the seining boat had discovered a small hole containing a little muddy water, with a shell lying near it, I had the place dug out, through the sand and a stratum of whitish clay, to the depth of ten or eleven feet. Under the clay we found a bottom of stone and gravel, and the water then flowed in clear, and tolerably fast. This was a great acquisition; more especially as the spring was not far from the beach at the west point of Sweers' Island, where the casks could be conveniently landed, and where we had had great success in fishing.

The gentlemen who visited Bentinck's Island, found a small lake of fresh water at no great distance from the sea side; and it appeared that the interior part of Sweers' Island, towards the northern end, was occupied by swamps. This comparative abundance of water upon such low islands, and at the end of the dry season, seemed very remarkable; it may perhaps be attributed to the clayey consistence of the stratum immediately under the sand, and to the gravelly rock upon which that stratum rests; the one preventing the evaporation of the rains, and the other obstructing their further infiltration.

TUESDAY 23 NOVEMBER 1802

Early next morning the ship was removed to within two cables length of the west point, nearer to the spring; and lieutenant Fowler was established on shore with a party of seamen and marines, taking tents, a seine, and other necessaries for watering the ship and supplying us with fish. The carpenters proceeded in their work of caulking; but as they advanced, report after report was brought to me of rotten places found in different parts of the ship--in the planks, bends, timbers, tree-nails, etc., until it became quite alarming [WEDNESDAY 24 NOVEMBER 1802]. I therefore directed the master and carpenter to make a regular examination into all such essential parts, as could be done without delaying the service; and to give me an official report thereon, with answers to certain queries put to them. After two days examination, their report was made in the following terms [FRIDAY 26 NOVEMBER 1802].

SIR,

In obedience to your directions we have taken with us the oldest carpenter's mate of the Investigator, and made as thorough an examination into the state of the ship as circumstances will permit, and which we find to be as under:

Out of ten top timbers on the larbord side, near the fore channel, four are sound, one partly rotten, and five entirely rotten.

We have seen but one timber on the larbord quarter, which is entirely rotten.

On the starbord bow, close to the stem, we have seen three timbers which are all rotten. Under the starbord fore chains we find one of the chain-plate bolts started, in consequence of the timber and inside plank being rotten; and also a preventer eyebolt, from the same cause.

On boring into the second futtock timbers from the main hold, close under the beams of the lower deck on the larbord side, we find one sound and two rotten; and on the other side, one sound and one rotten.

On boring into one of the second futtock timbers in the cockpit, on each side, we find it to be sound on the starbord, but on the other side rotten: the inside plank on both sides is rotten. On boring into one timber of a side in the after hold, we find them to be sound.

On boring into one timber of a side from the bread room, one is sound; but on the larbord side it is rotten.

The stem appears to be good; but the stemson is mostly decayed.

The lower breast hook is decayed within side.

The transoms, sleepers, stern post, and postson are all sound.

The ends of the beams we find to be universally in a decaying state.

The tree-nails are in general rotten.

From the specimens we have seen of the top-sides and bends, we expect that the insides of them are rotten, fore and aft; but that about one inch of the outside of the greater part is yet quite sound.

After the above report, and upon due consideration, we give the following answers to the four questions put to us.

1st. The ship having before made ten inches of water an hour, in a common fresh breeze, we judge from that, and what we have now seen, that a little labouring would employ two pumps; and that in a strong gale, with much sea running, the ship would hardly escape foundering; so that we think she is totally unfit to encounter much bad weather.

2nd. We have no doubt but that, if the ship should get on shore under any unfavourable circumstances, she would immediately go to pieces; but with a soft bottom and smooth water, she might touch for a short time without any worse consequences than to another ship, if she did not heel much; but altogether, we judge it to be much more dangerous for her to get aground in her present state, than if she were sound.

3rd. It is our opinion that the ship could not bear heaving down on any account; and that laying her on shore might so far strain her as to start the copper and butt ends, which would make her unable to swim without vast repair.

4th. Mr. Aken has known several ships of the same kind, and built at the same place as the Investigator; and has always found that when they began to rot they went on very fast. From the state to which the ship seems now to be advanced, it is our joint opinion, that in twelve months there will scarcely be a sound timber in her; but that if she remain in fine weather and happen no accident, she may run six months longer without much risk.

We are, Sir, To Matthew Flinders, Esq. your obedient servants, Commander of His Majesty's John Aken, master, sloop the Investigator. Russel Mart, carpenter.

I cannot express the surprise and sorrow which this statement gave me. According to it, a return to Port Jackson was almost immediately necessary; as well to secure the journals and charts of the examinations already made, as to preserve the lives of the ship's company; and my hopes of ascertaining completely the exterior form of this immense, and in many points interesting country, if not destroyed, would at least be deferred to an uncertain period. My leading object had hitherto been, to make so accurate an investigation of the shores of Terra Australis that no future voyage to this country should be necessary; and with this always in view, I had ever endeavoured to follow the land so closely, that the washing of the surf upon it should be visible, and no opening, nor any thing of interest escape notice. Such a degree of proximity is what navigators have usually thought neither necessary nor safe to pursue, nor was it always persevered in by us; sometimes because the direction of the wind or shallowness of the water made it impracticable, and at other times because the loss of the ship would have been the probable consequence of approaching so near to a lee shore. But when circumstances were favourable, such was the plan I pursued; and with the blessing of GOD, nothing of importance should have been left for future discoverers, upon any part of these extensive coasts; but with a ship incapable of encountering bad weather--which could not be repaired if sustaining injury from any of the numerous shoals or rocks upon the coast--which, if constant fine weather could be ensured and all accidents avoided, could not run more than six months--with such a ship, I knew not how to accomplish the task.

A passage to Port Jackson at this time, presented no common difficulties. In proceeding by the west, the unfavourable monsoon was likely to prove an obstacle not to be surmounted; and in returning by the east, stormy weather was to be expected in Torres' Strait, a place where the multiplied dangers caused such an addition to be peculiarly dreaded. These considerations, with a strong desire to finish, if possible, the examination of the Gulph of Carpentaria, fixed my resolution to proceed as before in the survey, during the continuance of the north-west monsoon; and when the fair wind should come, to proceed by the west to Port Jackson, if the ship should prove capable of a winter's passage along the South Coast, and if not, to make for the nearest port in the East Indies.

SUNDAY 28 NOVEMBER 1802

By the 28th, the watering and wooding of the ship were completed, the gunner had dried all his powder in the sun, and the tents and people were brought on board. All that the carpenters could do at the ship was to secure the hooding ends to the stem--shift some of the worst parts in the rotten planking--and caulk all the bends; and this they had finished. The wind being south-east on the morning of the 29th [MONDAY 29 NOVEMBER 1802], I attempted to quit the Investigator's Road by steering out to the northward; but this being found impracticable, from the shallowness of the water, we were obliged to beat out to the south; and so contrary did the wind remain, that not being able to weather the reef at the south-east end of Sweers' Island, we anchored within it on the evening of the 30th [TUESDAY 30 NOVEMBER 1802].

I shall now sum up into one view, the principal remarks made during our stay amongst these islands. The stone most commonly seen on the shores is an iron ore, in some places so strongly impregnated, that I conceive it would be a great acquisition to a colony fixed in the neighbourhood. Above this is a concreted mass of coral, shells, coral sand, and grains of iron ore, which sometimes appears at the surface, but is usually covered either with sand or vegetable earth, or a mixture of both. Such appeared most generally to be the consistence of all the islands; but there are many local varieties.

The soil, even in the best parts, is far behind fertility; but the small trees and bushes which grow there, and the grass in some of the less covered places, save the larger islands from the reproach of being absolutely sterile. The principal woods are *eucalyptus* and *casuarina*, of a size too small in general, to be fit for other purposes than the fire; the *pandanus* grows almost every where, but most abundantly in the sandy parts; and the botanists made out a long list of plants, several of which were quite new to them.

We saw neither quadruped nor reptile upon the islands. Birds were rather numerous the most useful of them were ducks of several species, and bustards and one of these last, shot by Mr. Bauer, weighed between ten and twelve pounds, and made us an excellent dinner. The flesh of this bird is distributed in a manner directly contrary to that of the domestic turkey, the white meat being upon the legs, and the black upon the breast. In the woody parts of the islands were seen crows and white cockatoos; as also cuckoo-pheasants, pigeons, and small birds peculiar to this part of the country. On the shores were pelicans, gulls, sea-pies, ox-birds, and sand-larks; but except the gulls, none of these tribes were numerous. The sea afforded a variety of fish; and in such abundance, that it was rare not to give a meal to all the ship's company from one or two hauls of the seine. Turtle abound amongst the islands; but it seemed to be a fatality that we could neither peg any from the boat, nor yet catch them on shore.

Indians were repeatedly seen upon both Bentinck's and Sweers' Islands; but they always avoided us, and sometimes disappeared in a manner which seemed extraordinary. It is probable that they hid themselves in caves dug in the ground; for we discovered in one instance a large hole, containing two apartments (so to call them), in each of which a man might lie down. Fire places under the shade of the trees, with dried grass spread around, were often met with; and these I apprehend to be their fine-weather, and the caves their foul-weather residences. The fern or some similar root, appears to form a part of their subsistence; for there were some places in the sand and in the dry swamps, where the ground had been so dug up with pointed sticks that it resembled the work of a herd of swine.

Whether these people reside constantly upon the islands, or come over at certain seasons from the main, was uncertain; canoes, they seemed to have none, but to make their voyages upon rafts similar to those seen at Horse-shoe Island, and of which some were found on the shore in other places. I had been taught by the Dutch accounts to expect that the inhabitants of Carpentaria were ferocious, and armed with bows and arrows as well as spears. I found them to be timid; and so desirous to avoid intercourse with strangers, that it was by surprise alone that our sole interview, that at Horse-shoe Island, was brought about; and certainly there was then nothing ferocious in their conduct. Of bows and arrows not the least indication was perceived, either at these islands or at Coen River; and the spears were too heavy and clumsily made, to be dangerous as offensive weapons: in the defensive, they might have some importance.

It is worthy of remark, that the three natives seen at Horse-shoe Island had lost the two upper front teeth; and Dampier, in speaking of the inhabitants of the Northwest Coast, says, "the two front teeth of the upper jaw are wanting in all of them, men and women, old and young." Nothing of the kind was observed in the natives of the islands in Torres' Strait, nor at Keppel, Hervey's, or Glass-house Bays, on the East Coast; yet at Port Jackson, further south, it is the custom for the boys, on arriving at the age of puberty, to have *one* of the upper front teeth knocked out, but no more; nor are the girls subjected to the same operation. At Twofold Bay, still further south, no such custom prevails, nor did I observe it at Port Phillip or King George's Sound, on the South Coast; but at Van Diemen's Land it seems to be used partially, for M. Labillardière says (p. 320 of the London translation), "we observed some, in whom one of the middle teeth of the upper jaw was wanting, and others in whom both were gone. We could not learn the object of this custom; but it is not general, for the greater part of the people had all their teeth." The rite of circumcision, which seemed to have been practised upon two of the three natives at Horse-shoe Island, and of which better proofs were found in other parts of the Gulph of Carpentaria, is, I believe, novel in the history of Terra Australis.

On Sweers' Island, seven human skulls and many bones were found lying together, near three extinguished fires; and a square piece of timber, seven feet long, which was of teak wood, and according to the judgment of the carpenter had been a quarter-deck carling of a ship, was thrown up on the western beach. On Bentinck's Island I saw the stumps of at least twenty trees, which had been felled with an axe, or some sharp instrument of iron; and not far from the same place were scattered the broken remains of an earthen jar. Putting these circumstances together, it seemed probable that some ship from the East Indies had been wrecked here, two or three years back--that part of the crew had been killed by the Indians--and that the others had gone away, perhaps to the main land, upon rafts constructed after the manner of the natives. This could be no more than conjecture; but it seemed to be so supported by the facts, that I felt anxious to trace the route of the unfortunate people, and to relieve them from the distress and danger to which they must be exposed.

The advantages to be obtained here by a ship are briefly these: shelter against all winds in the Investigator's Road, wood for fuel, fresh water, and a tolerable abundance of fish and turtle; for to anticipate a little on the voyage, there are islands lying within reach of a boat from the Road, where the turtle are not disturbed by the Indians. Should it ever enter into the plan of an expedition, to penetrate into the interior of Terra Australis from the head of the Gulph of Carpentaria, the Investigator's Road is particularly well adapted for a ship during the absence of the travellers: the season most favourable to their operations would be in May, June, and July; but not so for the vessel, as the crew would probably be unable to procure turtle at that time. For a similar expedition from the opposite part of the South Coast, September, October, and November would seem to be most proper.

From the time of first arriving, to that of quitting Sweers' Island, the range of the thermometer on board the ship was between 81° and 90°, and on shore it might be 5° to 10° higher in the day time; the weather was consequently warm; but being alleviated by almost constant breezes either from sea or land, it was seldom oppressive; and the insects were not very troublesome. The mercury in the barometer ranged between 30.06 and 29.70 It stood highest with the winds from the sea, between north-east and north-west; and lowest when they blew gently off the land, between south-east and south-west, but most so from the latter direction. On the South Coast the winds from these points had produced a contrary effect: the mercury there stood lowest when the northern winds blew, and highest when they came from the southward; they coincided, however, so far, in that the sea winds raised, and the land winds depressed the mercury, the same as was observed at Port Jackson on the East Coast.

The *latitude* of Inspection Hill, from several single and two double observations, was 17° 8' 15" S.

Longitude from forty-two sets of lunar distances taken by lieutenant Flinders, the particulars of which are given in Table III. of the Appendix No. I. to this volume, 139° 44' 52" E.

The rates of the time keepers were deduced from morning's altitudes, taken with a sextant and artificial horizon at the shore under Inspection Hill, from Nov. 16 to 29; and the mean rates during this period, with the errors from mean Greenwich time at noon there on the 30th, were as under:

Earnshaw's No. 543, slow 2h 16' 29.51" and losing 14.74" per day. Earnshaw's No. 520, slow 3h 52' 19.70" and losing 20.01" per day.

The longitude given by the time keepers, with the rates from Upper Head in Broad Sound, on our arrival Nov. 16, was by

No. 543, 140° 6' 35.2" east. No. 520, 139° 47' 42.2" east.

No. 520 therefore differed very little to the east of the lunar observations, and the first day's rate was almost exactly the same as that with which we had quitted Upper Head; whilst No. 543 differed greatly, both in longitude and rate. A similar discordance had been noticed at the Cumberland Island, marked *l2*, twenty days after leaving Upper Head; No. 520 then differed only 1' 1.2" from the survey, but No. 543 erred 7' 2.2" to the east. I have therefore been induced to prefer the longitude given by No. 520, to the mean of both time keepers; and accordingly, the positions of places before mentioned or laid down in the charts, between Upper Head and Sweers' Island, including Torres' Strait, are from this time keeper alone; with such small correction equally proportioned; as its error from the lunars, 2' 50.2" to the east in fifty-two days, made necessary.

No. 543 had undergone some revolution on the passage, but seemed at this time to be going steadily; whereas No. 520, which had kept its rate so well, now varied from 18.79" to 25.39", and ceased to be entitled to an equal degree of confidence.

Mean *dip* of the south end of the needle, observed upon the west point of Sweers' Island, 44° 27'.

Variation of the theodolite in the same place, 4° 7' E.

Variation of the surveying compass in the Road, 2° 28' with the ship's head E. N. E, and 4° 30' with the head northward; the mean corrected to the meridian, will be 4° 31' E.

In bearings taken on the east side of Bentinck's Island, the variation appeared to be a full degree greater than on the west side of Sweers' Island.

The *tides* in the Investigator's Road ran N. N. E. and S. S. W., as the channel lies, and their greatest rate at the springs, was one mile and a quarter per hour; they ran with regularity, but there was only one flood and one ebb in the day. The principal part of the flood came from N. N. E.; but according to lieutenant Fowler's remarks on shore, between the 23rd and 27th, it was high water three hours after the opposite tide had set in; or about *three hours and a quarter before* the moon came to the meridian. At the Prince of Wales' Islands, and at Coen River, it had also appeared that the tide from south-west made high water. The time here happened between 8½h and 11½h at night, from the 23rd to the 27th; but whether high water will always take place at night, as it did at King George's Sound on the South Coast, I cannot be certain. About twelve feet was the greatest rise, which I apprehend would be diminished to eight, at the neap tides.

CHAPTER VII.

Departure from Sweers' Island.
South side of C. Van Diemen examined.
Anchorage at Bountiful Island: turtle and sharks there.
Land of C. Van Diemen proved to be an island.

Examination of the main coast to Cape Vanderlin.
That cape found to be one of a group of islands.
Examination of the islands; their soil, etc.
Monument of the natives.
Traces of former visitors to these parts.
Astronomical and nautical observations.

[NORTH COAST. WELLESLEY'S ISLANDS.]
WEDNESDAY 1 DECEMBER 1802
(Atlas, Plate XIV.)

On the 1st of December we got under way, and passed the reef at the south-east end of Sweers' Island. I wished to run close along the north side of this, and of Bentinck's Island, and get in with the main land to the west; but the shoal water and dry banks lying off them presented so much impediment, that we steered north-westward for land which came in sight in that direction. At noon, the land was distant six or seven miles, and appeared to be the inner part of that great projection of the main, represented in the old chart under the name of *Cape Van Diemen*; but the rocky nature of the shore and unevenness of the surface were so different from the sandy uniformity of the continent, that I much doubted of its connexion. Our situation at this time, and the bearings taken were as under:

Latitude, observed to the north and south, 16° 48' 29" Land of Cape Van Diemen, N. 70° W. to 25 W. A piece apparently separated, N. 18 W. to 11 E. Bentinck's I., highest part at the north end, S. 15 E.

A smoke was rising in the direction of Horse-shoe Island, but no land was there visible.

We had a light breeze at E. by N., and steered westward along the rocky shore, at the distance of two or three miles, till five in the evening; when the breeze having shifted to S. W., we tacked and came to an anchor in 6 fathoms, mud and shells. The land was then distant three miles, and extended from N. 61° E. to a point with a clump of high trees on it, which appeared to be the south-west extremity of the northern land and bore N. 84° W. Whether the space between it and the main near Allen's Isle were the entrance of an inlet, or merely a separation of the two lands, could not be distinguished; but the tide set W. by S., into the opening, and there was a low island and many rocks in it. From an amplitude at this anchorage, the variation was 3° 16' east, corrected to the meridian, nearly the same as at Allen's Isle, five leagues to the south; and a full degree less than in the Investigator's Road.

THURSDAY 2 DECEMBER 1802

At five next morning we steered for the opening, with light, variable winds. On each side of the low island and rocks there seemed to be passages leading into a large spread of water, like the sea; and our course was directed for the northernmost, until the water shoaled to 2½ fathoms and we tacked to the southward. The south-west point of the northern land then bore N. 74° W. four miles, and the north end of Allen's Isle was seen from the mast head, bearing S. 3° W. five leagues; but that part of the opening between them, not occupied by the main land, seemed to be so choked with rocks that there was little prospect of a passage for the Investigator. This being the case, and the wind becoming unfavourable to the search, we steered back eastward, along the shore; and at eight in the evening, anchored near the furthest part yet seen in that direction, in 6½ fathoms sand and shells.

FRIDAY 3 DECEMBER 1802

At daylight, the piece of hilly land before judged to be an island, and which still appeared so, bore N. 86° to 28° W., two or three miles, with some nearer rocks lying in front; the northern land extended from behind it to N. 32° E., and we followed its course at the distance of five, and from that to two miles off shore. At noon we approached the eastern extremity, and saw a small island two leagues further out, one of three laid down in the old chart near Cape Van Diemen; it is thickly covered with wood, principally of that softish, white kind, whence it obtained the name of *Isle Pisonia*. Another and a larger island afterwards opened from the cape; but this could not be one of the three, for it lies so close, that Tasman, or whoever discovered these parts, would scarcely have observed the separation; and in fact, the other two isles presently came in sight to the southward, nearly in the situation assigned to them. The wind being unfavourable to doubling the cape, we bore

69

away for the two islands; and soon after four o'clock, anchored on the south-east side of the outermost, in 6½ fathoms, good holding ground.

Turtle tracks were distinguished on the beach as we rounded the north-east point, and afforded us the pleasurable anticipation of some fresh food. We had explored tropical coasts for several months, without reaping any one of the advantages usually attending it, and been frequently tantalized with the sight of turtle in the water, and of bones and shells round the fire places on shore; but we now hoped to have found a place where the Indians had not forestalled us, and to indemnify ourselves for so many disappointments.

In rowing to the Island, we carried 5 fathoms nearly close to the beach. Several turtle were swimming about, and some perceived above high-water mark, which we ran to secure, but found them dead, and rotten; they appeared to have fallen on their backs in climbing up a steep part of the beach, and not being able to right themselves, had miserably perished. I walked the greater part of the length of the island; and from the highest hillock set the eastern extreme of the island close to Cape Van Diemen, at N. 34¾° W., and Isle Pisonia from N. 22¾° to 19½° W.

During my absence from the boat, the impatient crew, not waiting for the turtle to come on shore, had been attacking them in the water; and had caught three large ones, and broken my harpoon. They had also been scratching out some of the holes, of which the upper part of the sandy beach was full; from one they filled a hat with turtles eggs, and from another took a swarm of young ones, not broader than a crown piece, which I found crawling in every part of the boat. It was then past sunset, and numbers of turtle were collected, waiting only for our departure to take the beach; I therefore hastened to the ship, and sent lieutenant Fowler with a party of men, to remain all night and turn them.

SATURDAY 4 DECEMBER 1802

Next morning, two boats went to bring off the officer and people with what had been caught; but their success had been so great, that it was necessary to hoist out the launch; and it took nearly the whole day to get on board what the decks and holds could contain, without impediment to the working of the ship. They were found by Mr. Brown to be nearly similar to, but not exactly the true green turtle, and he thought might be an undescribed species. We contrived to stow away forty-six, the least of them weighing 250 lbs, and the average about 300; besides which, many were re-turned on shore, and suffered to go away.

This *Bountiful Island*, for so I termed it, is near three miles long, and generally low and sandy; the highest parts are ridges of sand, overspread with a long, creeping, coarse grass, which binds the sand together, and preserves it from being blown away; grass of the common kind grows in the lower parts, and in one place there were some bushes and small trees. The basis consists partly of a streaked, ochrous earth, and in part of sand, concreted with particles of iron ore. Nothing bespoke this island to have been ever before visited, whence it is probable that the natives of the neighbouring lands do not possess canoes; for with them, the distance of four leagues from Cape Van Diemen would not have been too great to be passed, though too far in a tide's way for such rafts as I saw at Horse-shoe Island.

A kind of bustard, with a very strong bill, and not larger than a hen, was numerous at Bountiful Island; and appeared to subsist upon the young turtle. The effect of instinct is admirable in all cases, and was very striking in these little amphibious creatures. When scratched out from their holes, they no sooner saw the day light than they made for the water, and with speed, as if conscious that the bustards were watching them; when placed in a direction from the sea, which was done for experiment, they turned themselves and took the straightest course to the water side. But it is not only in the bustards, nor on land alone, that they have enemies to fear; tiger sharks were numerous. and so voracious, that seven were hooked along-side the ship, measuring from five to nine feet in length. These were ready to receive such of the little animals as escape their first enemies; and even one of the full grown turtle had lost a semi circular piece, equal to the tenth part of its bulk, which had been bitten out of its side; and what seemed more extraordinary, the shell had closed, and the place was healed up. Were it not for the immense destruction made of these animals in the different stages of their existence, and that food must in the end fail, their fecundity is such, that all the tropical seas and shores would scarcely afford room for them in a few years. The number of eggs found in the females, and there were few, if any males amongst the forty-six taken here, usually ran from four to seven hundred; and in one weighing 459 lbs, taken earlier in the following season, the number of eggs counted was 1940, as recorded in lieutenant Fowler's journal; but many were not bigger, some not so large as peas. They seem to lay from twenty to a hundred eggs at once, and this is done many times in the season; after which they go very little on shore. In Terra Australis, the season appears to commence in August, and to terminate in January or February.

The *latitude* of our anchorage, one mile from the south-east side of Bountiful Island, was 16° 41' south. Lieutenant Flinders observed six sets of lunar distances, which gave 139° 46' 18" east *longitude*; but the time keeper No. 543 made it 14½' east of Inspection Hill, or in 139° 59½'. The *variation* of the compass, from azimuth and amplitude observed with the ship's head in the magnetic meridian, was 3° 46' east; and at my station on shore, an amplitude with the theodolite gave 3° 47' east. From a little past ten in the morning to eleven at night, the *tide* ran half a mile an hour to the S. W., and N. E. during the remainder of the twenty-four hours; the first, which seemed to be the flood, was only three hours after the moon, above six hours earlier than in the Investigator's Road; but the time of high water by the shore might be very different: no greater rise than five feet was perceivable by the lead line.

SUNDAY 5 DECEMBER 1802

In the morning of the 5th, we quitted Bountiful Island to resume our examination at Cape Van Diemen; and the weather being rainy, with thunder and lightning, and the wind fresh at N. N. E., we passed round the smaller island, two miles to the southwest, before hauling to the northward. At ten o'clock, Cape Van Diemen was distant three miles, and we tacked to the east; and from that time till evening, continued to work up between the cape and a shoal lying two leagues from it to the E. S. E. This shoal is a narrow ridge of sand, over which we had passed in going to Bountiful Island; but there were now breakers upon a more southern part. It seems to be formed by different sets of tide amongst the islands, and to be steep to; for in passing over, the soundings had been 13, 4, 5, 7, 11 fathoms, almost as quick as the lead could be heaved. At dusk the wind had gone down, and the anchor was dropped in 6 fathoms, sand and shells, in the following situation.

C. Van Diemen, the S. E. extreme, dist. 3 miles,   S. 75° W. The island close to it, N. 57° to 21 W. Isle Pisonia, distant 3 miles,   N. 55 to 61 E. Bountiful I., station on the green hillock,   S. 40 E.

That part of Cape Van Diemen above set, is in latitude 16° 32' south, and longitude 139° 49½' east.

The tide here set N. N. E. and S. S. W., between the island close to the cape and Isle Pisonia; and at daylight [MONDAY 6 DECEMBER 1802] we steered for the middle of the opening. On seeing breakers ahead, the master was sent in the whale boat to sound, and we kept more westward, after him. There were natives upon the island nearest to the land, who seemed to wait in expectation of being visited; but our soundings diminishing to 3 fathoms, and the master having still less, we stood out and were followed by the boat. The wind was then at N. E.; and Isle Pisonia being brought to bear N. W. at nine o'clock, we tacked and weathered it nearly a mile, carrying from 9 to 13 fathoms water. Turtle tracks were very distinguishable upon the beach, but these prognostics, once so much desired, did not now interest us; however, on the wind becoming so light that we could not weather some breakers whilst the lee tide was running, the stream, anchor was dropped in 9 fathoms, and I went to the island with the botanical gentlemen.

More holes were scratched in the sand here by the turtle, than even upon the island last quitted; and several of the poor animals were lying dead on their backs. The isle is nothing more than a high sand bank upon a basis of coral rock, which has become thickly covered with wood, and much resembles several of the smaller isles in Torres' Strait. There was no trace of former visitors, though it is not more than four miles from the island where Indians had been seen in the morning; the tides probably run too strong in a narrow, four-fathom channel, close to Isle Pisonia, to be encountered by their rafts.

TUESDAY 7 DECEMBER 1802

Next morning, the wind was at N. E.; and after weathering a reef which runs out three miles from the island under Cape Van Diemen, we closed in with the land, and steered westward along it with soundings from 9 to 4 fathoms. A low head with white cliffs was passed at nine o'clock, and proved to be the northernmost point of this land; beyond it the coast extended W. by S., in a long sandy beach, and the country was better clothed with trees than on the south side. At noon we came abreast of a low woody point, with a shoal running off, where the coast took a south-west direction; and our situation and bearings were then as under:

Latitude, observed to the north., 16° 26' Longitude, from time keeper and bearings, 139 25 Cliffy north head of this land, N. 86 E. Woody shoal point, distant two miles, S. 35 E. Furthest southern extreme, S. 29 W. Islet from the mast head, distant 3 leagues, North.

From one o'clock till four, we steered S. S. W. past three other small cliffy projections; and I then saw the clump of high trees on the south-west point of this land, bearing S. 31° E. six miles, the same which had been set five days before from the inner side. Our course was continued, to get in with the main land; but in half an hour the depth had diminished to 2½ fathoms, and obliged us to haul out W. by N., close to the wind. The low main coast was then in sight from the mast head to the south-westward, and at dusk we anchored about three leagues off, in 5 fathoms, sandy bottom.

No doubt remained that the land of Cape Van Diemen was an island; for it had been circumnavigated, with the exception of about three leagues, which the rocks and shoal water made impracticable. Its extent is considerable, being thirty-five miles long, and the circumference near ninety, independently of the smaller sinuosities in the coast; I did not land upon any part, but the surface appeared to be more rocky than sandy; and judging from the bushes and trees with which it is mostly covered, there must be some portion, though perhaps a small one, of vegetable soil. In any other part of the world, this would be deemed low land; but here, where even the tops of the trees on the main scarcely exceed a ship's mast head in elevation, it must be called moderately high; for it may in some parts, reach three hundred feet. Several smokes and some natives were seen, and it is reasonable to suppose there are fixed inhabitants, but their number is probably small.

Had not the name of Van Diemen so often occurred in Terra Australis, as to make confusion, I should have extended it from the cape to the whole island; but such being the case, I have taken this opportunity of indulging my gratitude to a nobleman of high character and consideration; who, when governor-general of British India, humanely used his efforts to relieve me from an imprisonment which was super-added to a shipwreck in the sequel of the voyage. This large island is therefore distinguished by the name of *Isle Mornington*; and to the whole of the group, now discovered to exist at the head of the Gulph of Carpentaria, I have given the appellation of WELLESLEY'S ISLANDS.

WEDNESDAY 8 DECEMBER 1802

In the morning of the 8th, the wind was light from the southward, and unfavourable for closing in with the main land; but a water spout brought the wind up from north-east, and obliged us to double reef the top sails. At noon the squalls had mostly passed over, and the shore, which then extended from S. E. by S. to W. S. W., was distant five miles in the nearest part; our latitude being then 16° 42½' south, and longitude 138° 49' east. We continued to steer westward till five o'clock, at nearly the same distance from the land, and in soundings between 5 and 3 fathoms; the wind then drew forward, and the trending of the shore being W. N. W., we could barely lie along it. At seven, tacked for deeper water; and in half an hour anchored in 4 fathoms, sand and shells, the land being distant five or six miles, and the furthest extreme from the mast head bearing N. 70° W. A meridian altitude of the star *Achernar* gave the latitude 16° 39 2/3'; and from the sun's western amplitude the variation was 4° 10', with the ship's head N. W., or 2° 37' east, corrected to the meridian.

The main land, from Wellesley's Islands to this anchorage, is of the same description as that along which we had previously sailed a hundred and ninety leagues, being a very low, woody country, fronted by a sandy beach; there are some slight wavings in the shore, but so slight, that not any part of it could be set twice. This tedious uniformity began, however, to be somewhat broken; for a range of low hills was perceived at three or four leagues inland, and the sinuosities of the shore were becoming more distinguishable: two smokes were seen during the day.

THURSDAY 9 DECEMBER 1802
Our progress next morning was very little, until the sea breeze set in; and we were then obliged, from the more northern trending of the coast, to keep up to the wind. The soundings varied between 6 and 3 fathoms; and at five in the evening diminished rather suddenly to 2½, on a rocky bottom, two or three miles from the land. We then tacked, and worked to windward till dark, when the anchor was dropped in 4½ fathoms upon rocky ground covered with mud; but as there was little wind and no sea, the anchor held. The observed latitude here, from the moon, was 16° 28', and longitude by time keeper 138° 6½' east.

During the night, the wind came as usual off the land; and in the morning [FRIDAY 10 DECEMBER 1802] we lay up N. by W., nearly parallel to the then direction of the coast. At ten, the sea breeze set in at N. by W.; and from that time until evening we worked to windward, tacking from the shore when the depth diminished to 2½ fathoms, and stretching in again when it increased to 6; the distances from the land being in miles, as nearly as might be what the depth was in fathoms, a coincidence which had been observed in some parts on the east side of the Gulph. At sunset, a hillock upon a projecting point bore N. 73° W. four miles, and behind it was a small opening which answered in situation to the *River Van Alphen* of the old chart; our last tack was then made from the shore; and at dusk we anchored in 4 fathoms, coarse sand and gravel. Variation from amplitude, with the head W. by N., 4° 45', or corrected to the meridian, 2° 38' east, nearly as on the 8th.

[NORTH COAST. GULPH OF CARPENTARIA.]
SATURDAY 11 DECEMBER 1802
At daylight, we steered northward with a land wind; and when the sea breeze came, stretched W. S. W. towards the shore.
At noon,
Latitude observed,   16° 11½' Longitude by time keeper, 137 53 The extremes of the land bore S. 21° E. to 89 W. Nearest part, dist. 3 miles, S. 35 W. Small opening, supposed R. Van Alphen, S. 3 W.

This opening may be half a mile in width, but a dry sand runs across from the west side, and left no prospect of its being accessible to the ship; the shoal water, indeed, extended further out than usual, being caused, probably, by a deposit of sand from the inlet. The range of low hills, before mentioned as running behind the coast, was still perceived; but in front, the country was low as before, and somewhat less covered with wood.

The direction of the coast, which had been from north to north-west the day before, was now again W. N. W.; and after making a tack at noon, in 3 fathoms, and stretching off for an hour, we lay along it till near eight o'clock. At that time the depth diminished from 3½, suddenly to 2½ fathoms; and before the helm was put down the ship touched upon a rock, and hung abaft. By keeping the sails full she went off into 3 fathoms, but in five minutes hung upon another rock; and the water being more shallow further on, the head sails were now laid aback. On swinging off, I filled to stretch out by the way we had come; and after another slight touch of the keel we got into deep water, and anchored in 4 fathoms, on a bottom of blue mud. The bad state of the ship would have made our situation amongst these rocks very alarming, had we not cleared them so quickly; but the water was very smooth at this time, and it could not be perceived that any injury had been sustained.

Our distance here from the shore was three miles. It is very low and broken, with many dry rocks and banks lying near it; and in the space of seven or eight miles we had counted five small openings, and behind them some lagoons were perceived from the mast head. *The Abel Tasman's River* of the old chart is marked in about this situation; and however little these shallow openings and salt lagoons resemble a river, there is no other place to which the name could have been applied.

I was preparing to take altitudes of the star *Rigel*, to ascertain our longitude at this anchorage, when it was found that the time keepers had stopped, my assistant having forgotten to wind them up at noon. In the morning [SUNDAY 12 DECEMBER 1802] they were set forward, and altitudes of the sun taken to find their errors from the time under this meridian. The moon and planet Mars had been observed in the night, from which, and the noon's observation following, the latitude of the anchorage was ascertained to be 16° 7½';

and a projection on the west side of the R. Van Alphen, which had been the nearest shore at the preceding noon, was now set at S. 64½° E. From these *data* and from the log, I ascertained the difference of longitude, from half past ten in the morning of the 11th, when the last observations for the time keepers had been taken, to be 20' 18"; and that this anchorage was in 137° 37' 18" east. The errors from mean Greenwich time were thence obtained; and they were carried on as before, with the rates found at Sweers' Island, which it was to be presumed, had undergone no alteration from the letting down, since none had been caused by former accidents of the same kind. An amplitude taken when the ship's head was W. N. W., gave variation 3° 46', or 1° 47' east, corrected to the meridian; being nearly a degree less than on the east side of the River Van Alphen, when the land lay to the west of the ship.

Soon after seven o'clock the anchor was weighed; and the breeze being at N. W., we stretched off till noon, when the observed latitude from both sides was 16° 2' 11", and the land was nine or ten miles distant; but the only part visible from the deck was the range of low hills, two or three leagues behind the shore. We then tacked to the westward, and kept closing in with the coast until sunset; at which time the corrected variation was 1° 47' east, as on the preceding evening, and the following bearings were taken.

Eastern extreme of the shore   S. 31° E. Small opening, dist. 4 or 5 miles, S. 54 W. Western extreme of the main, a sandy head, N. 75 W.

Beyond the head, much higher land than any we had passed in the gulph was seen from aloft as far as N. W. by N. This I expected was the Cape Vanderlin of the old chart; and if so, there ought to be a large double bay between it and the sandy head; and in fact, no land was visible there in a space of two points.

Our course along the shore was prolonged till dusk, when we tacked in 3½ fathoms; and on getting 4½, came to an anchor upon fine sandy ground. In the morning [MONDAY 13 DECEMBER 1802], the wind was light from the south-westward, and little progress was made until the sea breeze set in. At noon, our situation was in

Latitude, observed to the north avid south,   15° 50' 31" Longitude by time keeper,   137 19½ West extreme of the sandy head, dist. 7 miles, S. 24 W. Land of Cape Vanderlin,   N. 28° to S. 88 W. Land of Cape Vanderlin, highest part,   N. 56 W. Land of Cape Vanderlin, sandy east point, dist. 6 miles, N. 47 W. Low islet off the south end.,   S. 77½ to S. 85 W.

Many rocks are scattered along the east side of this land; some of them are steep, and one, which we approached within a mile soon after one o'clock, resembled the crown of a hat. The whale boat was then sent towards the opening, and we bore away S. W. by S. after her; but the water shoaling fast, and looking worse ahead, we hauled out close to the wind, and worked northward; anchoring at dusk, two or three miles from the east point of the northern land, in 6 fathoms, coarse sand and shells.

The main coast on the south side of the opening had been seen extending W. N. W., two or three leagues from the sandy head; it was low as ever, and there was no appearance of the northern land, which was hilly and rocky, being connected with it; and I therefore called the separated piece *Vanderlin's Island*. Having no prospect of being able to get the ship up the opening, we proceeded northward next morning [TUESDAY 14 DECEMBER 1802], along the east side of the island; but the wind being directly contrary, it was sunset before the outermost of the scattered rocks could be weathered; soon afterward the anchor was dropped in 6 fathoms, one mile and a quarter from the north-east point, and something more from the outer rocks which bore S. 63° E. The north point of the island, which is the true Cape Vanderlin, bore N. 71° W., and was distant three or four miles: its utmost extremity lies in 15° 34½' south, and 137° 8½' east.

Some Indians had been seen tracking a canoe or raft, along the east side, and a body of thirty-five of them had been there collected, looking at the ship. This comparatively numerous population, and the prospect there was of this island proving more than usually interesting to the naturalists, made me desirous of finding a secure anchorage near it; and in the morning [WEDNESDAY 15 DECEMBER 1802] we landed at the north-east point, which is a peninsula joined to the island by a low sandy neck, and has three hummocks upon it, near the extremity. From the highest of these hummocks, I set two small islands in the offing, to the north-west, where two are laid down in the old chart; and saw more land to the west of Cape Vanderlin, apparently a large and distinct island. The water between them was extensive; and as it promised to afford good shelter, we returned on board after a short examination, in order to work the ship into it.

A hard, close-grained sand stone forms the basis of the north-east point of Vanderlin's Island; but the hummocks and the upper rocks are calcareous, similar to Inspection Hill at the head of the Gulph. The soil is very sandy, and poorly clothed with vegetation; though in the more central parts of the island the hills seemed to be moderately well covered with wood. There were foot marks of men, dogs, and kangaroos, and tracks of turtle near the shore; but none of the men, nor of the animals, were seen.

We got under way soon after ten o'clock with a breeze from the north-westward, and were obliged to make a long stretch to sea before Cape Vanderlin could be weathered. Towards evening we came in with a small reef, lying N. 40° E. two-and-half miles from the extremity of the cape; and this, with the lateness of the hour, making it hazardous to run into the new opening, we anchored at dusk, under the easternmost of the two small islands in the offing, in 6 fathoms, coral sand and rock. The white beach here seemed to be so favourable a situation for turtle, that an officer with a party of men was sent on shore to watch them; but he returned immediately, on finding the beach to be not sand, but pieces of coral bleached white by the sun, which bore no traces of turtle.

[NORTH COAST. PELLEW'S GROUP.]
THURSDAY 16 DECEMBER 1802

I landed early in the morning, with the botanical gentlemen, to take bearings; and amongst them set the craggy north end of the western island., which I call *Cape Pellew*, at S. 87° W., distant three or four miles. It lies in latitude 16° 30½', longitude 137° 2', and there is a rock lying half a mile off to the N. E.; indeed these two small isles and another rock may be considered as also lying off, and appertaining to it. The basis of the easternmost and largest isle was found to be the same close-grained sand stone as at Vanderlin's Island; but the surface consisted of loose pieces of coral, with a slight intermixture of vegetable soil, producing a few shrubs and small bushes: there were no traces either of men or turtle.

On our return to the ship, we steered for the opening between the Capes Vanderlin and Pellew; the wind was from the north-westward, and this being now the most settled quarter for it, we anchored under the western island, in 4½ fathoms soft bottom, half a mile from the shore; with the extremes bearing N. 25° E. one mile, and S. 23° W. two miles. An outer rocky islet near Cape Vanderlin bore N. 70° E., and a small island within half a mile of the ship covered five points in the south-eastern quarter; to the south there was very little land visible, but no sea was to be feared from that side; and the sole direction in which we were not sheltered, was between N. N. E. and E. N. E.

The botanical gentlemen landed abreast of the ship, and lieutenant Flinders went to commence a series of observations for the rates of the time keepers on the small isle, thence called *Observation Island*. My attention was attracted by a cove in the western shore, upon the borders of which, more abundantly than elsewhere, grew a small kind of cabbage palm, from whence it was called *Cabbage-tree Cove*. This presented the appearance of a complete little harbour; and supposing it to afford fresh water, was just such a place as I wished for the ship, during the time necessary for making an examination of the islands in my whale boat. I found the cove to run near two miles into the island, and there was a small rill at the head; but unfortunately, the depth at the entrance was insufficient for the ship, being no more than 2 fathoms, and in the upper part it was too shallow even for a boat.

View in Sir Edward Pellew's Group--Gulph of Carpentaria.
FRIDAY 17 DECEMBER 1802

In the morning, a party of men was sent to cut wood at the nearest shore; and there being a sort of beach, uncovered at low tide, the seine was hauled there with some success. A small drain of fresh water ran behind the mangroves at the back of the beach, and by cutting a rolling way to it, our empty casks, it was thought, might be filled; but I hoped to find a better place, and went away in the boat, as well with that object in view as to carry on the survey.

From the furthest part of the western island visible from the ship, I found the shore trending S. 73° W., to a point where there was an opening out to the westward, of a mile and a half wide and of considerable depth. About three leagues up the opening were two craggy islands; and beyond them was more extensive land, which proved to be an island also, and from its situation in this group was called *West Island*. The island whose north end is Cape Pellew, and whose southern extremity I had now reached, was called *North Island*; and the land opposite to me, which formed the south side of the opening and seemed to be extensive, is marked with the name of *Centre Island* in the chart. These lands are moderately high, and seemed to form several coves and small inlets, with promise of runs of fresh water; but the weather was too unfavourable to make much examination at this time, and after taking bearings from the south and south-east points of North Island, I returned on board.

SATURDAY 18 DECEMBER 1802

The wooding of the ship was carried on next day; and although the weather remained squally, with frequent heavy rain, some further bearings were obtained, and observations taken for the time keepers. In the morning of the 19th [SUNDAY 19 DECEMBER 1802], the weather cleared, and I took the ship over to Cape Vanderlin; both for the convenience of the survey, and to give the botanical gentlemen a better opportunity of examining that island, which appeared to be the most interesting, as it was the largest of the group. Besides three rocky islets, lying off the west side of the cape, there is a small island one mile to the south-west, and I sought to anchor behind it; but being prevented by a shoal which extends southward from the island, the anchor was dropped half a mile without side, in 4½ fathoms, muddy ground.

After the latitude had been observed, and bearings taken from the island, we crossed over in the boat to Cape Vanderlin. There was a depth of 4 to 7 fathoms between them, with a passage leading in from the north, and a ship would lie here in perfect safety during the south-east monsoon; but with the present north-west winds and squally weather, this otherwise good anchorage was not equal to the place we had quitted. The highest parts of Cape Vanderlin are hillocks of almost bare sand; on the isthmus behind it were many shrubs and bushes, and amongst the latter was found a wild nutmeg, in tolerable abundance. The fruit was small, and not ripe; but the mace and the nut had a hot, spicy taste.

There was no appearance of fresh water here, nor was the ship in a situation safe to remain all night; so soon, therefore, as my bearings were taken from the top of Cape Vanderlin, we returned on board, and steered for the opening between North and Centre Islands. At dusk, the anchor was dropped in 6 fathoms, muddy ground, a little within the opening; where we had land at different distances all round, with the exception of one point to the W. N. W.

TUESDAY 21 DECEMBER 1802

During the two days we remained here, I examined a shallow bay on the east side of Centre Island, and went to the westward as far as the Craggy Isles, taking bearings from various stations. Several rills of fresh water were found at the heads of little coves, but the depth was not sufficient for the ship to get near any of them; and therefore we returned to our first anchorage near Cabbage-tree Cove [WEDNESDAY 22 DECEMBER 1802], to cut through the mangroves and get the holds completed with water at the small run there. This duty I left to the care of the first lieutenant, and the rates of the time keepers to be continued by the second; and went away the same afternoon in my boat, upon an excursion of four days, accompanied by Mr. Westall, the landscape painter.

The soundings we had in steering for the west point of Vanderlin's Island and southward along the shore, will be best known from the particular plan of this group. Bearings were taken at two chosen stations; and we stopped in the evening, at the furthest of two small isles near the south-west side of the island, to pass the night without disturbance from the Indians. It then rained and blew hard, with thunder and lightning, and the soil being sandy and destitute of wood to break off the wind, it was with difficulty the tent could be secured; the islet had been visited, and we found the remains of more than one turtle feast. Amongst the bearings set from hence was a projecting part of the low main land, at S. 19½° W. six or seven miles, and it was the furthest visible.

THURSDAY 23 DECEMBER 1802

We had more moderate weather in the morning, and went on towards the south point of Vanderlin's Island; but stopped two or three miles short of it, at a station whence the south point and the low islet lying off were visible, as also was the sandy head set from the ship on the 12th and 13th; and from the bearings of these objects my survey round Vanderlin's Island became connected. A part of the sandy main coast was distant not more than four miles to the S. S. W., whence it extended as far as S. 62° W.; the water appeared to be too shallow for a ship to pass between it and the island.

A fresh wind from the north-west prevented me from going any further to leeward; and it was with much difficulty that we rowed back to the isle where we had passed the night. Strong squalls again came on towards evening, and the larger isle, lying a mile to the north-west, was chosen for our night's residence, on account of its affording some shelter; but the lightning was so violent and close to us, that I feared to place the tent near the trees, and was surprised in the morning, not to see half of them shivered to pieces: the rain fell in torrents, during a part of the night.

FRIDAY 24 DECEMBER 1802

Next morning the weather was better, but the wind still adverse to my project of going over to the south end of Centre Island; by noon, however, we reached a low islet half way across, where I observed the latitude 15° 42° 47", and took a set of bearings very useful to the survey; and we afterwards made an attempt to get over, and succeeded. A rocky hillock on the south-east point of Centre Island, was my next station; and from thence we proceeded westward along the south side, to a low islet near the south-west point, for the purpose of landing, the sun being then set; but the islet proving to be a mere mud bank covered with mangroves, we rowed onward to the large South-west Island, in very shallow water; and there passed a night which, happily for the fatigued boat's crew, turned out fine.

SATURDAY 25 DECEMBER 1802

I took azimuths and some bearings in the morning, and we then proceeded northward through a small passage between the Centre and South-west Islands; there was 5 fathoms in the very narrow part, but no deep water within; and without side, it was also very shoal for two or three miles. Near the north-west point of Centre Island lies an islet and two rocks, and from the cliffy north end of the islet another set of bearings was taken; after which we steered eastward, sounding along the north side of Centre Island. It was noon when we reached the north-east point, and I observed the latitude 15° 39' 35" upon the south-east end of a rocky islet there, and took more bearings from the top; and in the afternoon, we reached the ship.

Very little has been said upon the islands or their productions, or upon the various traces of native inhabitants and of former visitors found in this, and in former boat excursions; the observations on these heads being intended for the general and conclusive remarks upon this group. These are now to be given; for the wooding and watering were completed on the day after my return [SUNDAY 26 DECEMBER 1802], and the ship was then ready to proceed in the examination of the Gulph.

In the old Dutch chart, Cape Vanderlin is represented to be a great projection from the main land, and the outer ends of North and West Islands to be smaller points of it. There are two indents or bights marked between the points, which may correspond to the openings between the islands; but I find difficulty in pointing out which are the four small isles laid down to the west of Cape Vanderlin; neither does the line of the coast, which is nearly W. S. W. in the old chart, correspond with that of the outer ends of the islands, and yet there is enough of similitude in the whole to show the identity. Whether any change have taken place in these shores, and made islands of what were parts of the main land a century and a half before--or whether the Dutch discoverer made a distant and cursory examination, and brought conjecture to aid him in the construction of a chart, as was too much the practice of that time--it is perhaps not now possible to ascertain; but I conceive that the great alteration produced in the geography of these parts by our survey, gives authority to apply a name which, without prejudice to the original one, should mark the nation by which the survey was made; and in compliment to a distinguished officer of the British navy, whose earnest endeavours to relieve me from oppression in a subsequent part of the voyage demand my gratitude I have called this cluster of islands SIR EDWARD PELLEW'S GROUP.

The space occupied by these islands is thirty-four miles east and west, by twenty-two miles of latitude; and the five principal islands are from seven to seventeen miles in length. The stone which seems to form the basis of the group is a hard, close-grained sand stone, with a small admixture of quartz, and in one or two instances it was slightly impregnated with iron; calcareous, or coral rock was sometimes found at the upper parts, but the hard sand stone was more common. Where the surface is not bare rock, it consists of sand, with a greater or less proportion of vegetable soil, but in no case did I see any near approach to fertility; yet all the larger islands, and more especially the western side of Vanderlin's, are tolerably well covered with trees and bushes, and in some low places there is grass.

As in most other parts of Terra Australis, the common trees here are various species of the *eucalyptus*, mostly different from, and smaller than those of the East and South Coasts. The cabbage palm, a new genus named by Mr. Brown *Livistona inermis*, is abundant; but the cabbage is too small to be an interesting article of food to a ship's company; of the young leaves, drawn into slips and dried, the seamen made handsome light hats, excellent for warm weather. The nutmeg was found principally on Vanderlin's Island, growing upon a large spreading bush; but the fruit being unripe, no accurate judgment could be formed of its quality. Amongst the variety of other plants discovered by the naturalist, were two shrubs belonging to the genus *Santalum*, of which the sandel wood, used as a perfume in the East, is also one; but this affinity to so valuable a tree being not known at the time, from the description of the genus being imperfect, no examination was made of it with that object in view.

All the larger islands seem to possess the kangaroo; for though none were seen, their foot marks were perceptible in most of the sandy places where I landed: the species seemed to be small. In the woods were hawks, pigeons of two kinds, and some bustards; and on the shore were seen a pretty kind of duck and the usual sea fowl. Turtle tracks were observed on most of the beaches, but more especially on the smaller islands, where remains of turtle feasts were generally found.

There were traces of Indians on all the islands, both large and small, but the latter are visited only at times; these people seemed to be equally desirous of avoiding communication with strangers, as those of Wellesley's Islands, for we saw them only once at a distance, from the ship. Two canoes found on the shore of North Island were formed of slips of bark, like planks, sewed together, the edge of one slip overlaying another, as in our clincher-built boats; their breadth was about two feet, but they were too much broken for the length to be known. I cannot be certain that these canoes were the fabrication of the natives, for there were some things near them which appertained, without doubt, to another people, and their construction was much superior to that on any part of Terra Australis hitherto discovered; but their substance of bark spoke in the affirmative. The same degree of doubt was attached to a small monument found on the same island. Under a shed of bark were set up two cylindrical pieces of stone, about eighteen inches long; which seemed to have been taken from the shore, where they had been made smooth from rolling in the surf, and formed into a shape something like a nine pin. Round each of them were drawn two black circles, one towards each end; and between them were four oval black patches, at equal distances round the stone, made apparently with charcoal. The spaces between the oval marks were covered with white down and feathers, stuck on with the yolk of a turtle's egg, as I judged by the gluten and by the shell lying near the place. Of the intention in setting up these stones under a shed, no person could form a reasonable conjecture; the first idea was, that it had some relation to the dead, and we dug underneath to satisfy our curiosity; but nothing was found. This simple monument is represented in the annexed plate, with two of the ducks near it: the land in the back ground is Vanderlin's Island.

Indications of some foreign people having visited this group were almost as numerous, and as widely extended as those left by the natives. Besides pieces of earthen jars and trees cut with axes, we found remnants of bamboo lattice work, palm leaves sewed with cotton thread into the form of such hats as are worn by the Chinese, and the remains of blue cotton trousers, of the fashion called moormans. A wooden anchor of one fluke, and three boats rudders of violet wood were also found; but what puzzled me most was a collection of stones piled together in a line, resembling a low wall, with short lines running perpendicularly at the back, dividing the space behind into compartments. In each of these were the remains of a charcoal fire, and all the wood near at hand, had been cut down. Mr. Brown saw on another island a similar construction, with not less than thirty-six partitions, over which was laid a rude piece of frame work; and the neighbouring mangroves, to the extent of an acre and a half, had been cut down. It was evident that these people were Asiatics, but of what particular nation, or what their business here, could not be ascertained; I suspected them, however, to be Chinese, and that the nutmegs might possibly be their object. From the traces amongst Wellesley's Islands, they had been conjectured to be shipwrecked people; but that opinion did not now appear to be correct.

The barometer stood here from 29.96 to 29.62 inches, being highest with the winds at north-east, and lowest with those from the southward; in the heavy squalls of wind, rain, thunder, and lightning from the north-west, the mercury stood at a medium elevation. On board the ship, the average standard of the thermometer was nearly 85°. On shore it was hotter, yet the musketoes were not very troublesome; but the common black flies, from their extraordinary numbers and their impudence, were scarcely less annoying than musketoes; they get into the mouth and nose, and settle upon the face or any other part of the body, with as much unconcern as they would alight on a gum tree; nor are they driven away easily. This was the case on shore, and on board the ship whilst lying at anchor, and for a day or two afterwards; but the society of man wrought a change in the manners even of these little animals. They soon became more cautious, went off when a hand was lifted up, and in three or four days after quitting the land, behaved themselves orderly, like other flies; and though still numerous on board, they gave little molestation. Dampier found these insects equally troublesome on the North-west Coast; for he says (Vol. I. p. 464), speaking of the natives, "Their eye-lids are always half closed, to keep the flies out of their eyes; they being so troublesome here, that no fanning will keep them from coming to one's face; and without the assistance of both hands to keep them off, they will creep into one's nostrils, and mouth too, if the lips are not shut very close."

Sir Edward Pellew's Group, as will be seen by a reference to the plan, affords numerous anchorages against both the south-east and north-west monsoon; but unless it should be within the two small isles near the south-west side of Vanderlin's Island, where the depth was not well ascertained, there is not a single harbour, the different bays and coves being too shallow to admit a ship. Wood for fuel is easy to be procured; and water may be had in December, and probably as late as April or May, but I think not afterwards. The most accessible watering place we could find, was at the back of the mangroves near our principal anchorage, within the east point of North Island, where, with some trouble, our casks were filled; and at a beach there, left dry at low water, the seine was hauled with some success. At Vanderlin's Island there are many beaches fit for the seine; and indeed it seemed superior to the other islands as well for this, as for every other purpose, when a ship can lie there; it is also the most frequented by the Indians, and may probably have fixed inhabitants.

The *latitude* of Observation Island, from two meridian altitudes to the north and south, is 15° 36' 46" S.

Longitude from six sets of distances of the sun east of the moon, given in Table IV. of Appendix No. 1, 137° 6' 42"; but by the time keeper No. 543 corrected, it is preferably 137° 3' 15" E.

The rates of the time keepers were found from afternoon's altitudes in an artificial horizon, between the 16th and 26th; and the means, with their errors from mean Greenwich time, at noon there on the last day of observation, were as under:

Earnshaw's No. 543, slow 2h 29' 11.17" and losing 14.93" per day Earnshaw's No. 520, slow 4h 11' 37.59" and losing 28.25" per day

This rate of No. 543 is only 0.19" more than that found at Sweers' Island, and so far as the six sets of lunars may be relied on, the longitude by this time keeper was not far from the truth; the letting down on the passage therefore did not seem to have produced any change; but in No. 520, the rate is more than 8" greater, and the longitude was getting 1½' per day too much to the east, as well before as after it was let down. The coast from Sweers' to Observation Island is consequently laid down by No. 543, with the small accelerating correction arising from the 0.19" increase of rate in 16.4 days.

Variation of the theodolite, observed on the east side of South-west Island, 2° 22' east.

In the bearings taken at different parts within the group, the variation seemed to differ from 2° 30' to 1° 30'. The largest variations were on the east sides of the islands, and the smallest on the west sides; seeming to show an attraction of the land upon the south end of the needle. On board the ship, when coasting along the east side of Vanderlin's Island, and the whole group lay to the west, the variation appeared from the bearings to be as much as 4° east.

The best observation made on the *tide*, was on the 23rd, during my boat excursion to the south end of Vanderlin's Island. On that morning the moon passed over the meridian at sixteen minutes past ten, and the perpendicular movements of the tide were as follows. At seven o'clock, when I left the shore, the tide was falling; on landing at nine it was stationary, and appeared to be low water; at noon it rose fast, and at three was still rising, and continued so to do, but slowly, until seven in the evening, The tide then began to fall; but after subsiding one foot, it rose again until ten o'clock, and had then attained its greatest height. Low water took place therefore about an hour before, and high water at *eleven hours and a quarter after* the moon passed the meridian: the rise appeared to be from four to seven feet. At Wellesley's Islands high water had taken place an hour and a half earlier, which seems extraordinary, if, as it necessarily must, the flood come from the northward. I think it very probable, that the tide in both places will follow what was observed in King George's Sound on the South Coast; where high water, after becoming gradually later till midnight, happened on the following day before seven in the evening, and then later as before.

The break of three hours in the tide here, is somewhat remarkable: it was not observed amongst Wellesley's Islands, where the tide ran twelve hours each way; but was found to increase as we proceeded west and northward until it became six hours, and the tides assumed the usual course.

CHAPTER VIII.

Departure from Sir Edward Pellew's Group.
Coast from thence westward.
Cape Maria found to be an island.
Limmen's Bight. Coast northward to Cape Barrow: landing on it.
Circumnavigation of Groote Eylandt.
Specimens of native art at Chasm Island.
Anchorage in North-west Bay, Groote Eylandt;
with remarks and nautical observations.
Blue-mud Bay. Skirmish with the natives.
Cape Shield.
Mount Grindall.
Coast to Caledon Bay.
Occurrences in that bay, with remarks on the country and inhabitants.
Astronomical and nautical observations.

[NORTH COAST. GULPH OF CARPENTARIA.]
MONDAY 27 DECEMBER 1802
(Atlas, Plate XIV.)

At daylight of Dec. 27, we got under way from Pellew's Group; and passing between the small isles near Cape Pellew, stretched off to sea with a fresh breeze at W. N. W. At noon the cape bore S. 26° W. four leagues, and towards evening we weathered it, having 10 fathoms water at the distance of five miles; the soundings afterwards diminished gradually to 4½ fathoms, at two miles from West Island, where the anchor was dropped on a muddy bottom, for the night. Next morning [TUESDAY 28 DECEMBER 1802], the wind being still at north-west, we again stretched out to sea; and at noon, when the latitude was 15° 24', Cape Pellew bore S. 60° E. four leagues. We were then standing south-westward; and at three o'clock, West Isle bore from S. 74° E. to about South, the last extreme being hidden by an islet and rock distant two-and-half miles. The main coast was in sight to the south and westward, and we stood for it until six; the ship was then tacked to the north-east, in 3 fathoms, the shore being three miles off, and extending from behind West Island to N. 36° W. It was low, mostly sandy, and covered with wood behind the beaches; and except that some places on the shore were rocky, it altogether resembled the more eastern parts of the gulph. At dusk, the anchor was let go in 6 fathoms, mud and shells.

WEDNESDAY 29 DECEMBER 1802

A small reef was seen in the morning, two miles to the north-east of the ship, and about seven from the coast. We passed half a mile to windward of it with 3½ fathoms, and stretched off to sea until noon, with the usual north-western wind; the latitude was then 15° 7', longitude 135° 40', and we tacked towards the land, which was not in sight from the mast head. At six in the evening it was distant two leagues, and the extremes bore S. 26° E. to 74° W., the first being the same part which had been set at N. 36° W., the evening before. At seven, we tacked from the shore in 3½ fathoms, and on the water deepening to 4, anchored on coarse sandy ground. In working along the shore next day [THURSDAY 30 DECEMBER 1802], we met with a shoal of sand and rocks., as far as three leagues off the land; the outer part, upon which we had less than 2½ fathoms at noon, lying in 15° 13' south and 136° 16' east. After getting clear of this danger, we stretched off until dusk; and then anchored in 9 fathoms, grey sand, some back hills being visible in the S. W. by W., but no part of the low shore.

FRIDAY 31 DECEMBER 1802

We had the wind at W. by S. in the morning, and stood off until noon, nine or ten leagues from the coast; two small lumps of land were then seen, bearing S. 53° and 58° W., and at the mast head they were perceived to join, and apparently to form an island. On the wind veering to the south and eastward we steered for it, and before sunset got to an anchor in a small bay on its south side, in 4 fathoms; the extremes of the island bearing N. 81° E. one mile and a half, to S. 83° W. three miles. The main land was visible three or four leagues to the southward, and a projecting part of the back hills, which at first made like a head land, bore S. 3° W.

A similar error to that at the Capes Van Diemen and Vanderlin has been made here in the Dutch chart, this island being represented as a projection of the main land, and called Cape Maria. To the west of it is marked a large bay or bight, called Limmen's Bogt, where the coast turns north-eastward to a projecting cape without name, which has a shoal, forty miles in length, running out from it; and between this shoal and Cape Maria, is laid down a small island. In these particulars, the old chart was found to be correct as to the general matter of fact, but erroneous in the forms and positions.

SATURDAY 1 JANUARY 1803

Fires were seen at night, upon the island; and early in the morning I landed with the botanical gentlemen, to examine the productions and take bearings. My attention was attracted by something like a native's hut, which proved to be an ant hill composed of red earth, about eight feet high, and formed like a haycock; the inhabitants were the same feeble race of insect as before seen at the Prince of Wales' Islands, and the least pressure was sufficient to crush them. From the highest hill on the south side of the island, I set the furthest visible extremity of the main land to the eastward, near which is a low islet, at S. 21° 50' E.; from thence it extended past the projecting part of the hills to N. 80° W., where it was lost in Limmen's Bight; but re-appearing 16° further north, it was distinguishable to N. 33° W.

The length of the island is about seven miles, N. E. and S. W., by a variable breadth from one to four miles; and its northern extremity, to which I continue the name of *Cape Maria*, lies in 14° 50' south, and 135° 53½' east. A slaty rock seemed to form its basis; the surface is hilly, well covered with wood, and grass grows up from amongst the loose stones; and notwithstanding its barren soil, the appearance from the ship was green and pleasant. That men were upon the island was shown by the fires, and it was corroborated by the fresh prints of feet upon the sand; but they eluded our search, and we did not find either canoes or habitations.

On returning to the ship at nine o'clock, we stretched southward for the main coast, with the wind at west. When within five or six miles, the water shoaled to 3½ fathoms; and the ship being found to drift to leeward with the tide, a stream anchor was dropped. There seemed to be two tides here in the day, setting nearly east and west, but the rise and fall were so imperceptible by the lead, that it could not be known which was the flood.

The west wind died away at noon, and being succeeded by a sea breeze from the north-eastward, we steered for Limmen's Bight so long as it lasted; and then anchored in 4 fathoms, blue mud, with the island of Cape Maria bearing S. 56° to 86° E., ten or twelve miles. The main land was eight or nine miles off, and visible all round the Bight and as far as N. 6° W.; it was low and woody, and an extensive shelving flat seemed to render it inaccessible to a ship.

At seven in the evening, the land wind came off in a strong squall, with thunder, lightning, and rain; afterwards the weather cleared; and at day light [SUNDAY 2 JANUARY 1803] we followed the line of the coast to the northward. I wished to get as near to it as possible; but the water shoaling to 2½ fathoms when six or seven miles off, we ran out east, till it deepened to 4, and then steered north-eastward, parallel to the line of the shoal. A low rock came in sight to seaward, which I took to be the small island laid down to the north-east of Cape Maria, but it lies nearly north from it. At nine o'clock, when the main land was distant seven miles and the depth 6 fathoms,

The low rock, distant 4 miles, bore   S. 65½° E. Station hill near C. Maria, dist. 6 leagues, S. 7½ E. A sloping part of the main, higher than the rest, N. 50 W. Extreme from the mast head, North.

Our latitude at noon was 14° 26' 29", and longitude 135° 54½'; the main coast was seven miles off, and seen from the mast head as far as N. N. E. Three miles to the N. 80° E. there were two dry sands, and shoal water extended from them to the north and southward, further than could be distinguished. We had already no more than 3 fathoms; but a sea breeze having set in at E. by S., unfavourably for going without side of the sands, we kept on close to the wind, hoping to find a passage within them. The depth varied between 8 and 4 fathoms, till past five o'clock, when it diminished to 2½, the main coast being distant five or six miles, and the sands out of sight astern; we then tacked, and stretched E. S. E. into 4 fathoms, and anchored at dusk on a bottom of gravel. An observation of the moon gave the latitude here 14° 19'; and the variation from an amplitude, with the head E. by S., was 0° 43' east, or corrected to the meridian upon the principle often before mentioned, 2° 44' east for the true variation.

There is no doubt that the dry banks seen at noon, were meant to be represented in the Dutch chart by the great shoal to the north-east of Cape Maria; but their direction from the cape is there too far eastward; neither do they join to the main land, nor lie out from it more than one-quarter of the distance marked: several turtle were seen in the vicinity of the banks. The main coast in the northern part of Limmen's Bight is not altogether so low as at the head; but the shoal water extends equally far out, and even the southern head of the gulph is not more inaccessible to ships.

We had strong squalls of wind in the night, with rain, thunder, and lightning, and were obliged to drop a second anchor; the wind, however, remained in the north-east, and at daylight [MONDAY 3 JANUARY 1803] we stood for the edge of the shoal. At seven, tacked ship in 3 fathoms; and a breeze coming off the land soon afterward, we steered along the shore until noon, with a good depth of water. Several pieces of distant land, which seemed to be islands of greater elevation than usual, were then seen, from N. by E. to E. S. E.; the main coast was about five miles off, and the furthest part bore north from the mast head. Our latitude at this time was 14° 5', and longitude 136° 6' east.

In the afternoon, the soundings became irregular between 4 and 7 fathoms, and the whale boat was sent ahead; but a fresh wind setting in at N. E., the boat was called back, and in being veered astern, got filled with water, broke adrift, and the two men were thrown out. Another boat was lowered down to save them and I ran the ship to leeward and came to an anchor. The whale boat was picked up, as also one of the men; but the other, William Murray, captain of the fore top, being unable to swim, was unfortunately lost.

The weather remained squally, and wind unsettled during the night. In the morning [TUESDAY 4 JANUARY 1803] our course was continued to the northward, leaving extensive land, which I supposed to be the *Groote Eylandt* of the old charts, six or eight leagues on the starbord hand. Before commencing the investigation of that island, I wished to trace the main coast further on, and if possible, give the botanists an opportunity of examining its productions; for it was upon the main that they usually made the most interesting discoveries, and only once, since entering the Gulph of Carpentaria, had we been able to land there. At seven o'clock we edged in for the coast; and on coming into 3½ fathoms, dropped the anchor on a bottom of blue mud, within a mile of the shore. No part of Groote Eylandt was in sight; but an island of considerable extent and elevation, not noticed in the old chart, lay six or seven miles to the E. N. E.; and I have called it BICKERTON'S ISLAND, in compliment to admiral Sir Richard Bickerton. Between it and the main coast is an open space, from four to six or seven miles wide, through which, to all appearance from this side, a ship might safely pass.

Whilst the botanical gentlemen landed abreast of the ship, I took the whale boat to a woody islet, five miles off, close to Bickerton's Island, the soundings across the opening in going to it, being from 3 to 7 fathoms. A meridian observation to the north and south, placed the islet in latitude 13° 48' 30", and the points of the opening to the northward bore N. 18° E. and N. 2½° W.; this last was the furthest visible part of the main land; and proving afterwards to be a projecting cape, I named it *Cape Barrow*, after John Barrow, Esq., author of the interesting travels at the Cape of Good Hope. The islet is about half a mile long, and though many bushes and some trees grew upon it, is little more than a bed of sand. There were holes in the beach, made by turtle; and besides other proofs of the islet being sometimes visited by the Indians, I found four human skulls lying at the back of the shore.

From the woody islet I crossed over to the main land near the ship, and took another set of bearings for the survey. Upon the shore were pieces of bamboo, and other traces of the same foreign people of whom mention has frequently been made; and three small huts were found, so entirely covered with grass that no opening was left; but they were empty, and nothing was buried underneath. On the borders of a small fresh lake the botanists reaped a harvest of new plants, without molestation; indeed no natives were seen any where; but several skeletons were found, standing upright in the hollow stumps of trees; and the skulls and bones being smeared or painted, partly red and partly white, made a very strange appearance. Some kangaroos were perceived at a distance; and judging by their foot-marks on the sand, they were rather numerous. The country near the sea side is stony and barren; further back, it rises gently to a small elevation, and seemed to be moderately well covered with grass and wood.

WEDNESDAY 5 JANUARY 1803

In the morning of the 5th we got under way, and steered eastward for Groote Eylandt, which I now intended to circumnavigate. In passing the south side of Bickerton's Island, we observed in it a deep bight or bay which would afford shelter in the north-west monsoon., if there be depth sufficient for a ship; and the hills at the back being high and woody, there was a probability of its receiving a stream of fresh water. The country round the entrance of the bight, had the appearance of being sandy and sterile.

Between the nearest parts of Groote and Bickerton's Islands is a space of eight miles, which seemed to offer a perfectly safe passage, with soundings, if I may judge from what we had in crossing the south side, between 13 and 17 fathoms; nor can the rather high and woody isle, which lies almost exactly in the middle of the opening, be considered as presenting any obstacle. This isle, from its local position, would seem to be the central one of three laid down in the Dutch chart between Groote Eylandt and the main; but the latitude corresponds with the southernmost. I call it *Connexion Island*; because my survey round Groote Eylandt was connected by its means, and made in a great measure independent of the time keepers. The centre of Connexion Island, from observations at noon to the north and south, lies in 13° 50½' south; and the longitude, deduced at three o'clock when the extremes bore N. 20° W. to 11° E. four miles, would be 136° 27' from the best time keeper; but from the survey and lunar observations, 136° 24½' east should be more correct.

Our distance from the west side of Groote Eylandt at four o'clock, was not quite three miles, and we then bore away southward along the shore, in 8 to 6 fathoms water. This depth diminished gradually to 4 fathoms, and suddenly from that to 2½; on which we steered off into 7, and then resumed our southern course. Soon after sunset,

Bickerton's island, south point, bore N. 53° W. Connexion I., the west extreme., N. 11 W. Groote Eylandt, north-west extreme, N. 16 E. Groote Eylandt, central hill., N. 87 E. Groote Eylandt, a low projection, dist. 4 or 5 miles, S. 42 E.

In half an hour, the anchor was dropped in 11 fathoms, muddy bottom.

At the north-west end of Groote Eylandt is a bluff head, the termination that way of a range of woody hills from the interior, of which the highest is what was set under the name of Central Hill. On the west side of the island these hills do not come close to the water side, but leave a space of increasing breadth to the southward, where the land is low, sandy, and sterile; and even the hills, though mostly covered with wood, had little of fertility in their appearance: the shore is partly rock, and in part sandy beach.

THURSDAY 6 JANUARY 1803

We had the wind light and variable in the morning, and proceeded to the southward very slowly. The shore trended S. S. E., for some time; and then turning westward to the south-west cape, it formed a bight in the low land three or four miles back, in which there seemed to be much shoal water. There is a sandy hill upon the south-west cape, and a rock lies close to it; and at three or four miles off the soundings were exceedingly irregular, jumping from 7 to 5, and 4 to 11 fathoms, on a rocky bottom. This irregularity, and the meeting of two tides, one from the north and another from the east, caused great ripplings in the water; and with the light winds, retarded our progress round the cape. The extreme south-west point lies in latitude 14° 15' south, and from six sets of lunar distances with stars east and west, the longitude would be 136° 17' east; but according to the survey, 136° 25' is the better situation. An amplitude at sunset gave the variation 1° 9', with the ship's head S. E., or corrected to the meridian, 2° 36' east. We anchored at dusk in 13 fathoms, muddy bottom, five or six miles to the south of the cape.

[NORTH COAST. GROOTE EYLANDT.]
SATURDAY 8 JANUARY 1803

On the 7th and 8th, the winds hung between S. E. and N. N. E.; and the direction of the south side of Groote Eylandt being nearly east, it took us those two days and part of a third, to make the examination, though the extent be little more than twelve leagues. The land here is more sandy than on the west side, and the trees upon the hills are more thinly scattered and present a less agreeable foliage. No islands are laid down near the south side in the Dutch chart; but I counted eight scattered along it, of which the easternmost and largest is more than two miles long; and besides these, there are several rocks. The positions of these rocks and islets, with our courses and soundings amongst them, will be best seen in the chart.

SUNDAY 9 JANUARY 1803

In the afternoon of the 9th, we passed round the south-east rocky point of Groote Eylandt, which lies in 14° 17' south, and 137° 2½' east. The shore then trended northward, to a small cluster of rocks and islets three miles distant; and two miles further was another islet, behind which we anchored in 12 fathoms, coarse sand, in a sandy bight of the great island; but the bight being exposed to south-east winds, and containing much foul ground, the anchorage was far from being good.

MONDAY 10 JANUARY 1803

In the morning, we steered out on the north side of the islet, between it and a low point two miles off, with a boat ahead; our soundings being 9, 6, 4, 2½, 5, 8, and soon afterward 23 fathoms. The low point, which has several rocks near it, lies seven or eight miles northward from the south-east extremity of Groote Eylandt; from thence the shore trends westward about four leagues, and forms a large bight, mostly bounded by a sandy beach; but in the middle of it is a point with many rocks. On the west side of the bight, two or three miles back, are the same woody hills which seem to occupy all the middle of the island; and on this side they terminate to the north-east in a bluff. The depth of water at noon was 19 fathoms, and our situation and principal bearings were as under.

Latitude, observed to the north and south, 14° 5' 31" Longitude by time keeper and survey, 137 3 Groote Eylandt, low eastern point, dist. 4 miles, S. 1

W. Groote Eylandt, woody hills, the north-east bluff,   N. 64 W. Groote Eylandt, furthest visible extreme,   N. 6 W.

We were then steering across the bight before a south-east wind; but the depth of water becoming less, and the wind more dead on the shore, we hauled up N. by E. for the furthest land in sight. At three o'clock, a small opening was seen under the north-east bluff, but our distance of three leagues was too great to distinguish it accurately. Towards evening, when three miles from the shore, the sounding jumped from 9 to 4 fathoms, and we tacked to the south-east; and the night promising to be fine, anchored at dusk in 19 fathoms, mud and sand, with the north-east point of Groote Eylandt bearing N. 33° W., about seven miles (Atlas, Plate XV.); further out lay two small islands, and a hill upon the outermost was set at N. 10° W. The latitude of this anchorage was ascertained, from altitudes of two stars and the moon, to be 13° 53 1/3' south; and an amplitude with the ship's head N. E. by N., gave variation 2° 57', or 4° 4' east, corrected to the meridian.

TUESDAY 11 JANUARY 1803

We had the wind at N. W. in the morning, and steered close to it on the larbord tack, until noon; when the hill on the outer north-east island, bore S. 89½° W., nine or ten miles. The latitude of the hill is 13° 38¼', and from six sets of distances of stars east and west of the moon, its longitude would be 136° 36'; but from the survey and more numerous observations, it is 137° 0½' east.* After a calm the sea breeze came in, and our course was directed for the north-east point of Groote Eylandt; at sunset we approached a rocky islet three or four miles from the point, and anchored under it in 6½ fathoms, sandy ground, with the point bearing S. 5° E., and the furthest visible part, very low and sandy, S. 63° W. five or six miles. On the other side, the north-east islands extended from N. 32° E. to 39° W., with many small rocks scattered along them; the nearest of which, a split rock, was distant a short mile.

[* The apparent error of 24½' in the first longitude, is greater than should exist in the mean result of six sets of distances. There is an interval of three days in the observations of the moon at Greenwich with which these distances were compared; and it seems probable that a great part of the error might arise from that cause.]

WEDNESDAY 12 JANUARY 1803

In the morning we steered close to a N. N. W. wind, for the low sandy point, where the shore was found to trend southward; and five or six miles to the west there was other land, moderately high and in some places cliffy, which took nearly a parallel direction; and the bight between them ran so far up towards the north-east bluff of the woody hills, that a junction with the small opening seen on the outside appeared to be probable. A shelving spit extended out from the low point, and on opening the bight our soundings decreased from 6 to 2½ fathoms, which made it necessary to tack; and the wind being adverse to passing within the north-east islands, if indeed there be water enough for a ship, which seemed doubtful, we steered out by the way we had come in.

Having little wind, the isles were not passed till late in the evening, and from the same cause not much progress was made to the westward next day [THURSDAY 13 JANUARY 1803]; but the land was better distinguished than before, and many straggling rocks and two islets were seen to lie off the north end of Groote Eylandt. In the morning of the 14th [FRIDAY 14 JANUARY 1803] we weathered all these, and on the wind dying away, anchored in 11½ fathoms, blue mud; the outer *North-point Islet*, which lies in 13° 37' south and 136° 45' east, then bore E. 3° S. five miles, and the furthest extreme of a higher cliffy island, S. 38° W. three miles.

I went in a boat to this last island with the botanical gentlemen, intending to take bearings from the uppermost cliffs; but the many deep chasms by which the upper parts are intersected, made it impossible to reach the top in the short time we had to spare, and a few bearings from the eastern low point were all that could be obtained. This was called *Chasm Island*; it lies one mile and a half from a low point of Groote Eylandt, where the shore trends southward and seemed to form a bay, into which I proposed to conduct the ship.

We found upon Chasm Island a fruit which proved to be a new species of *eugenia*, of the size of an apple, whose acidity of taste was agreeable; there were also many large bushes covered with nutmegs, similar to those seen at Cape Vanderlin; and in some of the chasms the ground was covered with this fruit, without our being able, for some time, to know whence it came. Several trees shot up in these chasms, thirty or forty feet high, and on considering them attentively, these were found to be the trees whence the nutmegs had fallen; thus what was a spreading bush above, became, from the necessity of air and light, a tall, slender tree, and showed the admirable power in nature to accommodate itself to local circumstances. The fruit was small, and not of an agreeable flavour; nor is it probable that it can at all come in competition with the nutmeg of the Molucca Islands: it is the *Myristica insipida* of Brown's *Prodrom. Nov. Holl.* p. 400.

In the steep sides of the chasms were deep holes or caverns, undermining the cliffs; upon the walls of which I found rude drawings, made with charcoal and something like red paint upon the white ground of the rock. These drawings represented porpoises, turtle, kangaroos, and a human hand; and Mr. Westall, who went afterwards to see them, found the representation of a kangaroo, with a file of thirty-two persons following after it. The third person of the band was twice the height of the others, and held in his hand something resembling the *whaddie*, or wooden sword of the natives of Port Jackson; and was probably intended to represent a chief. They could not, as with us, indicate superiority by clothing or ornament, since they wear none of any kind; and therefore, with the addition of a weapon, similar to the ancients, they seem to have made superiority of person the principal emblem of superior power, of which, indeed, power is usually a consequence in the very early stages of society.

A sea breeze had sprung up from the eastward, and the ship was under way when we returned on board at three in the afternoon. At five we hauled round Chasm Island with 12 fathoms water, which diminished gradually as we proceeded up the bay, to 4½, where the anchor was dropped on a muddy bottom; the south-west end of Chasm Island then bore N. 16° E., three or four miles, and the cliffy end of a smaller isle on the west side of the entrance, N. 29° W. two miles and a half; and except between these two bearings, we were sheltered from all winds. The situation of this bay in Groote Eylandt, led me to give it the name of *North-west Bay*. It is formed on the east and south by that island; and on the west by a separate piece of land, five or six miles long, which, in honour of the noble possessor of Burley Park, in the county of Rutland, I named *Winchilsea Island*; and a small isle of greater elevation, lying a short mile to the east of the ship, was called *Finch's Island*.

SATURDAY 15 JANUARY 1803

Early next morning the botanists landed on Groote Eylandt, and I went to Finch's Island with the second lieutenant, to take bearings and astronomical observations. From the western head, I saw that the bay extended six or eight miles above the ship, to the southward, and that the southern outlet, beyond Winchilsea Island, was about one mile wide; but the whole seemed to be too shallow for any thing larger than boats. Amongst the bearings taken from this station, those most essential to the survey were,

Groote Eylandt, the woody north-west bluff,   S. 56° 46' W. A distant wedge-shaped rock, the N. E. bluff,   N. 59 55 W. Chasm I., the steep west end,   N. 3 51 E.

And from another station, half a mile to the E. S. E., I set Groote Eylandt, the central hill, at S. 14° 27' E.

This bearing and that of the north-west bluff, formed connecting links in the chain of longitude round the island.

SUNDAY 16 JANUARY 1803

Next day the botanists landed upon Winchilsea Island, and further astronomical observations were taken upon that of Finch; where also a part of the ship's company went to divert themselves, and to wash their linen; and in the evening, we prepared to quit North-west Bay.

A close-grained sand stone, nearly resembling that of Pellew's Group, seems to form the basis of Groote and the neighbouring islands; we found also coral, ironstone, and quartz. In many places, quartz in almost a crystallised state was sprinkled in grains through the sand stone, and in others, the sand stone itself was partly vitrified. Wherever we landed, the surface was so entirely composed of stone and sand, that the idea of any kind of cultivation could in no wise be assimilated with it; the hills at a little distance from the water side were, however, well covered with wood, and it is not improbable, that there may be vallies in the central parts of Groote Eylandt possessing some degree of fertility. The central hill, which is six or eight hundred feet in elevation, appeared to be not so much as three leagues from the head of North-west Bay, and I was desirous to have made an excursion to the top, to see the interior of the island; but the state of the ship being such as to press us forward with all practicable haste, it was not attempted; nor did I stop to examine particularly the head of the bay, since it appeared to be shallow, and of little interest to navigation.

The wood on Groote Eylandt was mostly composed of different species of *eucalyptus*; the trees were small, and might do for fire wood and very common purposes, but did not seem calculated for any superior use. Chasm Island was the sole place where the nutmeg was found, though in general, the gleanings of the botanists were tolerably fortunate. None of the native inhabitants were seen, nor any kangaroos or other quadrupeds; and birds seemed to be scarce. Small quantities of water, deposited in holes of the rocks by the late rains, were useful to the seamen for washing their clothes; but we did not find any from which a ship could be supplied, nor were there any beaches convenient for hauling the seine.

The *latitude* of Finch's Island, from a meridian observation to the north and south, is 14° 43' 31" S.

Longitude from six sets of distances of the sun east of the moon, taken by myself, 136° 38' 47", and from twelve sets by lieutenant Flinders (see Table V. of Appendix No. I), 136° 23' 38"; but there being no observations of the moon at Greenwich within two or three days, the longitude from survey and the position of Caledon Bay afterwards fixed, is preferred, and is 136° 36' 53" E.

Dip of the south end of the needle, 39° 22'.

Variation of the theodolite, 3° 6' east.

The variations of the surveying compass, from amplitudes taken near different parts of Groote Eylandt during the circumnavigation, were these:--

Near the main, opp. the S.W. Pt., head E. by S., 0° 43', cor. 2° 44' E. Near the south-west point,   S. E., 1 9 , cor. 2 36 Off the east side,   N. E. by N., 2 57 , cor. 4 4 Near the north-east isles,   N. W. by W., 3 33 , cor. 1 58 Off the north end, S. W. by W., 5 51 , cor. 4 14

Whether the small variation near the north-east isles arose from any peculiar attraction, or from some oversight in taking the amplitude, I cannot determine; if from the latter, it would appear that the variation is a degree and a half less on the south-west, than on the east and north sides of Groote Eylandt.

Scarcely any run of *tide* was perceptible in North-west Bay, nor did the rise appear to exceed four or five feet at any part of the island, though it runs with some strength off the projecting points. The irregularity in different places was such, that the time of high water could not be ascertained; but I think there is only one full tide in the day, and that the flood comes from the northward.

MONDAY 17 JANUARY 1803

Early on the 17th we worked out of the bay, and stretched off to sea with a W. N. W. wind; at noon the latitude was 13° 27' 10", and the furthest extreme of Chasm Island bore S. 26° W. After a calm in the afternoon, the sea breeze came in, and we steered south-westward till nine o'clock; when a bower anchor was let go in 14 fathoms, two or three miles from the north end of Winchilsea Island. In the morning [TUESDAY 18 JANUARY 1803] we lay up south-west, on the starbord tack, and weathered the island, leaving a rock one mile and a half on the other side. I wished, by a good bearing of Connexion Island, to join the survey completely round Groote Eylandt; and at nine o'clock it was set at S. 27½° to 47° W., two leagues. The wind then came ahead, and we tacked towards two small isles, where the anchor was dropped at ten, one mile and a half from their south side, in 16 fathoms, sand and shells. Our latitude here was 13° 43' 42" south, and the east side of Connexion Island bore S. 9½° W. six or seven miles; the difference of longitude from our situation on the 5th at three p.m., was hence ascertained to be it 1' 55" east, not differing 5" from what was given by No. 543, but No. 520 showed 6½' too much; the differences of longitude by the former time keeper alone have therefore been used round Groote Eylandt.

I went immediately, with the botanical gentlemen, to the northern and largest of the two sandy isles; and after observing the latitude 13° 42' 17" on the south-west point, ascended the highest hillock, which, from the clump of trees upon it, was called *Pandanus Hill*. Some of the trees being cut down, I had a tolerably extensive view of points and islands before passed; and saw more to the north-westward, behind Wedge Rock, all of which the Dutch chart represents as parts of the main land. One of these I have called *Burney's Island*, in compliment to captain James Burney of the navy, and another *Nicol's Island*, after His Majesty's bookseller, the publisher of this work. Beyond these was a more extensive land, which also proved to be an island; and its form having some resemblance to the whaddie or woodah, or wooden sword used by the natives of Port Jackson, it was named *Isle Woodah*. A low sandy island, lying four or five miles N. by. E. from my station, seems to be the northernmost of the three isles laid down between Groote Eylandt and the main; but it is placed, as are also the neighbouring lands, half a degree too far north: Connexion Island, taking it to be the southernmost of the three, is well fixed in latitude.

Amongst the many bearings taken at the top of Pandanus Hill, those which follow were the most important to the survey.

North-point Islet, outer extreme   N. 73° 15' E. Chasm Island,   N. 74° 15' to N. 78 25 E. Groote Eylandt, central hill,   S. 44 30 E. Groote Eylandt, north-west extreme,   S. 9 0 E. The ship distant 1¾ miles,   S. 7 45 E. Connexion Island,   S. 8 0 to S. 22 30 W. Bickerton's Island,   S. 43 40 to N. 75 45 W. Isle Woodah,   N. 60 30 to N. 38 15 W. Wedge Rock, steep north-east end,   N. 30 45 W. Nicol's I., steep east end,   N. 26 5 W.

There was very little wood upon the two sandy isles, nor did they furnish any thing new to the botanists; but they were partly covered with long grass amongst which harboured several bustards, and I called them *Bustard Isles*. The basis of the largest is nearly the same mixture of sand-stone and quartz, as at North-west Bay; broken coral and sand formed the beaches; and some fresh turtle tracks being there perceived, and the appearance of the weather being unfavourable, it induced me to remain at anchor all night; but only one turtle was procured.

WEDNESDAY 19 JANUARY 1803

In the morning we had a north-east wind, and after passing round a shoal which runs one or two miles from the south-west end of the Bustard Isles, hauled up to weather Bickerton's Island; but owing to a tide setting to leeward it was not accomplished before two in the afternoon. Soon after three we got to anchor one mile from the south side of Burney's Island, in 4½ fathoms, mud and shells; and I went on shore with the botanists.

This island is moderately high, rocky, and barren, yet thickly covered with the *eucalyptus* and *casuarina*. From the highest rock on the south-east side, I took bearings of the objects in sight; and amongst them set

Wedge Rock, the north extreme, at   N. 83° 50' E. Chasm Island, north extreme, S. 79 55 E. Pandanus Hill, the last station,   S. 53 5 E.

I afterwards got through the wood, intending to set the objects lying to the north and westward; but no clear place could be found for placing the theodolite. A small bay was observed on the north-west side of the island, which might be convenient for boats; and from the steep declivity of the land round it, there seemed a probability that fresh water might be procured at this season. The stone of this island is the same as that of the Bustard Isles; and the Indians had visited both. A set of azimuths, observed at the same station whence the bearings were taken, gave variation 2° 50' east; but on board the ship, with the head N. E. by E., Mr. Flinders observed 0° 23' east, with three compasses, which would be 2° 0' corrected; whence it should seem, that the stone of the island had some attraction on the south end of the needle.

[NORTH COAST. BLUE-MUD BAY.]

THURSDAY 20 JANUARY 1803

In the morning, we steered S. W. to take up the survey of the main coast at Cape Barrow, between which and Isle Woodah was an opening where no land was visible; but meeting with shoal water, and the wind being light, a stream anchor was dropped until the boat had time to sound. On her return, we steered for the north side of the opening, with a depth which increased from 4 fathoms to 17 off the south end of Woodah. A higher island, two or three miles long, then showed itself to the N. N. W.; and on the water shoaling to 3½ fathoms, the anchor was dropped at four in the afternoon, one mile and a half from its south side, on a bottom of blue mud. The main land was in sight to the westward, forming a large bay with Isle Woodah, and Bickerton's Island covered the entrance, so that the ship was in complete shelter.

On landing with the botanical gentlemen, I ascended a hummock at the east end of the island, where alone the view was not impeded by wood. Many of my former fixed points were visible from thence, and the main land was traced round to the northward, to a hill named *Mount Grindall*, near which was another round hill upon an island; and behind them the main extended eastward, nearly as far as over the middle of Isle Woodah. Amongst the numerous bearings taken from this eastern hummock, the following six were most essential to the survey.

Chasm Island, the centre,   S. 67° 46' E. Wedge Rock, steep north-east end, S. 59 47 E. Cape Barrow, the eastern extreme, S. 6 50 W. Mount Grindall,   N. 13 16 W. Round-hill Island, the top,   N. 8 5 W. Extreme of the main, over Woodah, N. 55 20 E.

FRIDAY 21 JANUARY 1803

A party of men was sent to cut wood on the following morning, and another to haul the seine; the botanists also landed, and I went to observe the latitude and take bearings from the west end of the island; every person was armed, for marks of feet had been perceived, so newly imprinted on the sand, that we expected to meet with Indians. After accomplishing my objects, I walked with a small party round the north-west end of the island; and then returned over the high land, through a most fatiguing brush wood, towards the wooders and the boat. On clearing the wood, four or five Indians were seen on a hill, half a mile to the left, and some of the wooding party advancing towards them. The sight of us seemed to give the natives an apprehension of being surrounded, for they immediately ran; but our proceeding quietly down to the boat, which I did in the hope that our people might bring on an interview, appeared to satisfy them. The scientific gentlemen accompanied me on board to dinner; and I learned from Mr. Westall, that whilst he was taking a sketch at the east end of the island, a canoe, with six men in it, came over from Woodah. He took little notice of them until, finding they saw him and landed not far off, he thought it prudent to retreat with his servant to the wooding party. The natives followed pretty smartly after him; and when they appeared on the brow of the hill, Mr. Whitewood, the master's mate, and some of his wooders went to meet them in a friendly manner. This was at the time that the appearance of my party caused them to run; but when we left the shore they had stopped, and our people were walking gently up the hill.

The natives had spears, but from the smallness of their number, and our men being armed, I did not apprehend any danger; we had, however, scarcely reached the ship, when the report of muskets was heard; and the people were making signals and carrying some one down to the boat, as if wounded or killed. I immediately despatched two armed boats to their assistance, under the direction of the master; with orders, if he met with the natives, to be friendly and give them presents, and by no means to pursue them into the wood. I suspected, indeed, that our people must have been the aggressors; but told the master, if the Indians had made a wanton attack, to bring off their canoe by way of punishment; intending myself to take such steps on the following day, as might be found expedient.

At five o'clock Mr. Whitewood was brought on board, with four spear wounds in his body. It appeared that the natives, in waiting to receive our men, kept their spears ready, as ours had their muskets. Mr. Whitewood, who was foremost, put out his hand to receive a spear which he supposed was offered; but the Indian, thinking perhaps that an attempt was made to take his arms, ran the spear into the breast of his supposed enemy. The officer snapped his firelock, but it missed, and he retreated to his men; and the Indians, encouraged by this, threw several spears after him, three of which took effect. Our people attempted to fire, and after some time two muskets went off, and the Indians fled; but not without taking away a hat which had been dropped. Thomas Morgan, a marine, having been some time exposed bare-headed to the sun, was struck with a *coup-de-soleil*; he was brought on board with Mr. Whitewood, and died in a state of frenzy, the same night.

So soon as the master had learned what had happened, he went round in the whale boat to the east end of the island, to secure the canoe; and forgetting the orders I had given him, sent Mr. Lacy with the wooders overland, to intercept the natives on that side. Their searches were for some time fruitless; but in the dusk of the evening three Indians were seen by the wooders, and before they could be intercepted had pushed off in the canoe. A sharp fire was commenced after them; and before they got out of reach, one fell and the others leaped out and dived away. A seaman who gave himself the credit of having shot the native, swam off to the canoe, and found him lying dead at the bottom, with a straw hat on his head which he recognised to be his own. Whilst displaying this in triumph, he upset the ticklish vessel, and the body sunk; but the canoe was towed to the shore, and the master returned with it at nine o'clock.

I was much concerned at what had happened, and greatly displeased with the master for having acted so contrary to my orders; but the mischief being unfortunately done, a boat was sent in the morning [SATURDAY 22 JANUARY 1803] to search for the dead body, the painter being desirous of it to make a drawing, and the naturalist and surgeon for anatomical purposes. The corpse was found lying at the water's edge, not lengthwise, as a body washed up, but with the head on shore and the feet touching the surf. The arms were crossed under the head, with the face downward, in the posture of a man who was just able to crawl out of the water and die; and I very much apprehend this to have been one of the two natives who had leaped out of the canoe, and were thought to have escaped. He was of the middle size, rather slender, had a prominent chest, small legs, and similar features to the inhabitants of other parts of this country; and he appeared to have been circumcised! A musket ball had passed through the shoulder blade, from behind; and penetrating upwards, had lodged in the neck.

The canoe was of bark, but not of one piece, as at Port Jackson; it consisted of two pieces, sewed together lengthwise, with the seam on one side; the two ends were also sewed up, and made tight with gum. Along each gunwale was lashed a small pole; and these were spanned together in five places, with creeping vine, to preserve the shape, and to strengthen the canoe. Its length was thirteen and a half, and the breadth two and a half feet; and it seemed capable of carrying six people, being larger than those generally used at Port Jackson.

It does not accord with the usually timid character of the natives of Terra Australis, to suppose the Indians came over from Isle Woodah for the purpose of making an attack; yet the circumstance of their being without women or children--their following so briskly after Mr. Westall--and advancing armed to the wooders, all imply that they rather sought than avoided a quarrel. I can account for this unusual conduct only by supposing, that they might have had differences with, and entertained no respectful opinion of the Asiatic visitors, of whom we had found so many traces, some almost in sight of this place.

The body of Thomas Morgan who died so unfortunately, was this day committed to the deep with the usual ceremony; and the island was named after him, *Morgan's Island*. The basis stone is partly argillaceous, and in part sand stone, with a mixture in some places of iron ore, but more frequently of quartz. A little soil is formed upon the slopes of the hills and in the vallies; and there, more especially at the east end of the island, it is covered with small trees and coarse grass, which the late rains had caused to look fresh and green; there were also some temporary drains of fresh water.

The *latitude* of the hummock at the east end of Morgan's Island, is 13° 27½', and *longitude* from the survey, 136° 9½'. Azimuths observed at the anchorage, with three compasses and the ship's head in the magnetic meridian, gave 2° 23' east *variation*, which corresponded very well with the bearings. The *tides* here are very inconsiderable, and there appeared to be only one flood and one ebb in the day; high water took place about midnight, when the moon was a little past the lower meridian; but whether it will always be so far behind the moon, may admit of a doubt.

A view of the main land to the westward, from Cape Barrow to Mount Grindall, had been obtained from the higher parts of Morgan's Island; but a probability still remaining that some river might fall into the bay, I proposed to coast round it with the ship. On a breeze springing up at E. S. E, early in the afternoon, we steered round the west end of the island, and hauled to the northward; but meeting almost immediately with shoal water, the course was altered for the south-west, and afterwards for the south part of the bay; and finding no where more than 3 fathoms, we tacked to the N. E. at dusk, and came to an anchor. The bottom here, and in most other parts of the bay, is a blue mud of so fine a quality, that I judge it might be useful in the manufactory of earthern ware; and I thence named this, *Blue-mud Bay*.

It was evident from the uniform shallowness of the water, that Blue-mud Bay did not receive any stream of consequence, either in its south or western part; and to the north, it seemed not to be accessible from this side. The main land rises very gradually from the water side into the country; and the wood upon it made a greater show of fertility than on any borders of the Gulph of Carpentaria we had before seen.

SUNDAY 23 JANUARY 1803

We got under way again at daylight; but the wind coming to blow strong from the eastward, with rain, thunder, and lightning, were not able to pass round the south end of Isle Woodah and get out of the bay, until the morning of the 25th [TUESDAY 25 JANUARY 1803]. Our soundings in working out diminished to 2½ fathoms, near the opening between Bickerton's Island and Cape Barrow; and it is probable that no ship passage exists there, although I had previously found as much as 7 fathoms in the southern part of the opening.

[NORTH COAST. GULPH OF CARPENTARIA.]

After clearing Blue-mud Bay, we worked to the north-eastward; and at eight in the evening, anchored under Nicol's Island in 5½ fathoms, muddy bottom, one mile from the shore, and two and a half from the low eastern point of Isle Woodah: two large rocks and much shoal water lie between the islands, and prevented me from seeking shelter there. In the morning [WEDNESDAY 26 JANUARY 1803] we stretched N. N. E., for the projecting part of the main land before set at N. 55° 20' E. from the eastern hummock of Morgan's Island; and to which I have given the name of CAPE SHIELD, in compliment to captain W. Shield, a commissioner of the navy. There is a small bay on its south-west side, and we anchored there in 4 fathoms, blue mud, with the outer points of the bay bearing S. 41° E. and N. 21° W., each distant one mile.

On landing with the botanists, I found the beach convenient for hauling the seine, and ordered one to be sent from the ship, which had tolerable success. The cape is low land, mostly covered with wood; and a sandy hillock, perceived from the mast head about one mile behind the beach, being the sole place whence a view was likely to be obtained, I went there with a theodolite. No part of the main coast to the eastward could be seen from thence beyond a low projection distant seven or eight miles, which I named *Point Arrowsmith*; to the west my view was obstructed by trees, but some points before set were visible, and more to the southward; and the following, amongst many useful bearings, were taken.

Chasm I., centre of the highest part,   S. 33° 15' E. Wedge Rock, centre, S. 5 55 W. Nicol's I., south-east point (over the south extreme of C. Shield, dist. 1½ miles), S. 26 30 W. Round-hill Island, the top,   S. 89 25 W. Point Arrowsmith, N. 62 20 E.

The sand hill whence these bearings were taken, stands close to the water on the east side of Cape Shield; and directly off it, at a mile and a half distance, lies a small island: upon the shore was found a carling of a ships deck, of teak wood, in a decayed state. On the land side of the hill was a small lake of fresh water, frequented by ducks, teal, and smaller aquatic birds, several of which were shot.

Cape Shield lies in latitude 13° 19¾' south, longitude by the survey 136° 23' east; it projects out six miles from the body of the land, and appears, when seen from the south, to be an island. Two cassowaries were seen upon it, and many tracks of men, dogs, and kangaroos. The wood is small, and the soil sandy; but the botanists made an ample collection of plants, some few of which made an addition to their former discoveries.

THURSDAY 27 JANUARY 1803

Next morning we steered westward, with a fair wind, to explore the main coast up to Mount Grindall, and see the northern part of Blue-mud Bay. At three leagues from Cape Shield, we passed a projecting point to which I gave the name of *Point Blane*, in compliment to Dr. (now Sir Gilbert) Blane, of the naval medical board. Five miles from it to the W. S. W., lies Round-hill Island, and after passing between them with 4 fathoms water, I sent the boat to sound between the island and Mount Grindall, purposing to anchor there; but the depth was too little for the ship. We then worked up to a large bight on the west side of Point Blane; and the water being shallow towards the head, anchored in 3 fathoms, muddy ground, with the extremity of the point bearing S. 41° E. two and a half miles.

An officer was sent on shore to search for fresh water and examine the beach with a view to hauling the seine, but had no success; the naturalist accompanied him, to botanise, and not coming down to the boat at dusk, the officer left a man with a fire on the beach, to wait his arrival. At ten o'clock a gun was fired, and the boat sent back; but nothing had been heard of the naturalist, or the seaman who carried his specimen boxes, and some apprehensions began to be entertained. Soon after daylight [FRIDAY 28 JANUARY 1803] we had the satisfaction to see Mr. Brown on the shore. It appeared that from one of those mistakes which so frequently occur in thick woods and dull weather, when without a compass, the east had been mistaken for west; and Mr. Brown reached the water side at dusk, but on the wrong side of the point. He thought it more prudent to remain there all night, than to re-enter the wood in the dark; and the report of the gun having given him the true direction, he had no difficulty in the morning. No natives were seen; but the howling of dogs was heard not far off.

Whilst the botanists continued to follow their pursuits upon Point Blane, I went over in the whale-boat to Mount Grindall, with the landscape painter; from whence, after cutting down some small trees at the top, my view extended over all the neighbouring islands, points, and bays. Blue-mud Bay was seen to reach further north than Mount Grindall, making it to be upon a long point, which I also named *Point Grindall*, from respect to the present vice-admiral of that name; further west, in the bay, was a stream running five or six miles into the land, terminating in a swamp, and with shoal banks and a low island at the entrance; all the northern part of the bay, indeed, seemed to be shallow, and to have no ship passage into it on the north side of Isle Woodah. The large bight between Points Grindall and Blane extended two leagues above the ship, but it did not appear to receive any stream of water; a still larger bight, between Point Blane and Cape Shield was also visible, though not so distinct as to speak of it particularly: the extremity of the cape bore S. 76° 15' E. An observation to the north and south, taken on the outermost rocks, places Mount Grindall in 13° 15½' south; and the longitude from survey is 136° 6 1/3' east. Mr. Westall's sketch in the Atlas, taken from the ship at anchor under Point Blane, will show the appearance of this mount and of the neighbouring land. (Atlas, Plate XVIII. View 13.)

The top of Mount Grindall consists of the same kind of sand stone, with particles of quartz in it, as seen at Groote Eylandt; but the rocks on the shore are granite, and one block made a brilliant appearance from the quantity of mica it contained. There is very little soil on the surrounding land, the surface being either sandy or stony; it was however mostly covered with grass and wood, and amongst the trees was a cluster of the new species of *eugenia*, from which the boat's crew filled their handkerchiefs with fruit, which they called apples. Two natives were distinguished upon Round-hill Island; but none at Point Grindall, nor any thing to show that they had been there recently: the foot-marks of dogs and kangaroos were both recent and numerous.

Strong squalls from the eastward, with rain, much impeded our return to the ship in the evening; and from a continuance of the same unfavourable weather, Point Blane could not be repassed until the afternoon of the 30th [SUNDAY 30 JANUARY 1803]. The wind was then S. E., and we worked to windward all night, between the main coast and Isle Woodah; and not being able to weather Cape Shield on the following day [MONDAY 31 JANUARY 1803], we ran to our former anchorage under it, and remained there for the night.

TUESDAY 1 FEBRUARY 1803

Next morning we stood out of the bay with light winds; and after being put into some danger by them, in passing the island near Cape Shield, a breeze sprung up at W. by S. and we proceeded in the examination of the main coast. The situation of the ship at noon, and the bearings of the land were as under:

Latitude, observed to the north and south,   13° 20' 16" Chasm I., centre of the high part,   S. 16 E. Cape Shield, the south extremity,   N. 86 W. Point Arrowsmith, dist. 6 miles,   N. 18 W. Furthest extreme visible from the deck.   N. 10 E.

Our course was then directed N. E. by N., parallel with the coast, until the wind veered round ahead and drove us off to the eastward; at six o'clock Point Arrowsmith bore W. 2° S., ten or eleven miles, and a round hummock, beyond the noon's extreme, was then seen at N. 2½° E. The coast here shows some projections on which are sandy hills, with shallow bights between them; the hills further back, especially behind Point Arrowsmith, are better covered with wood, but there was no appearance of fertility in the country, nor of shelter in the bights.

[NORTH COAST. CALEDON BAY.]

We worked to windward all night, with a north-western breeze; and in the morning [WEDNESDAY 2 FEBRUARY 1803] saw two islands, the outermost rather low and flat, nearly in the situation where three are marked in the Dutch chart. These are laid down at the entrance of an opening, of a river-like form; and there appeared to be a wide opening behind them, the entrance being round a projection upon which is the hummock set at N. 2½° E. in the evening: this projection I have named CAPE GREY, in compliment to the Hon. general Grey, lately commander of the forces at the Cape of Good Hope. Our situation and bearings at noon were,

Latitude, observed to the north and south,   13° 3' 41" Longitude from survey, 136 46½ Furthest southern extreme, from the deck,   S. 73 W. Cape Grey, the round hummock,   N. 56 W. Cape Grey, outermost rocks near it,   N. 41 W. Outer and rather flat isle, centre,   N. 3 W.

On the wind veering to north-east, we were enabled to weather the rocks near Cape Grey, but not more than a quarter of a mile; the depth in passing was 9 fathoms, and it continued between that and 11, two miles further up the bay, where, on its falling calm, an anchor was dropped. In the evening we ran further up, and at sunset anchored in 9 fathoms, mud and sand, near the innermost and largest of three islands which lie in the entrance. Around, and between these islands, were many islets and rocks, and others were seen to the north-eastward; the bay extended to the north-west, and was divided into two branches by a projection named *Point Middle*, the eastern branch being defended from the sea by a tongue of land, whose south point seemed to be connected by a reef of rocks with the inner island. This point I have called *Point Alexander*; and to a hill upon the furthest visible part of the coast to the northward, the appellation of *Mount Alexander* is given.

THURSDAY 3 FEBRUARY 1803

In the morning, there being no wind to move the ship, I sent the master up the bay with the whale boat, to search for fresh water and a secure anchorage; and on his making the signal to follow, a little before noon, we steered for Point Middle. A shoal was seen to extend from it, down the bay; and the depth having diminished to 4 fathoms, we hauled up into the eastern branch, and anchored under Point Alexander in 4½ fathoms, muddy bottom; our distance from the shore being one mile, and two cables length from a bank in front of it, upon which there was only six feet water. In this situation, the outer rocks near Cape Grey bore S 28° E., and the inner rocks from the island near Point Alexander., S. 35° E.; the intermediate angle of 7° being that at which alone we were open to the sea. Several natives were seen on the shore abreast of the ship, and lieutenant Fowler was sent to communicate with them, and to search for fresh water. They stayed to receive him, without showing that timidity so usual with the Australians; and after a friendly intercourse in which mutual presents were made, Mr. Fowler returned with the information that fresh water was plentiful.

FRIDAY 4 FEBRUARY 1803

Early next morning, having given directions for two tents, a seine, and a corporal's guard, to be sent on shore under the command of the first lieutenant, I landed with the botanical gentlemen; the natives running from their night residences to meet us. There were twelve middle-aged and young men, all of whom expressed much joy, especially at seeing *Bongaree*, our good-natured Indian from Port Jackson. On the arrival of two other boats, the natives retreated into the wood, except two, who assisted in hauling the seine; and the others came back by degrees, without arms as before, and received a portion of the fish. A situation was chosen for the tents, and confidence seeming to be established, I went into the wood, towards some sand hills, for the purpose of taking bearings; but whilst making the circuit of a salt swamp which lay in the way, the natives were heard running in the wood, and calling to each other. This happened twice, and at length a musket was fired; upon which I returned to the tents with all expedition.

When the botanical gentlemen had entered the wood with their attendants, the greater part of the natives followed them; and one took an opportunity of snatching a hatchet from the hand of a servant. The Indians then ran off, but seeing no pursuit, nor much notice taken, soon returned, and became more friendly than ever. Each of our party had a native with him, walking arm in arm, and Mr. Brown's servant had two, who paid him particular attention; so much so, that whilst one held him by the arm, the other snatched the musket off his shoulder, and they all again ran off; that is, all who remained, for several had previously withdrawn themselves. A musket was fired after the thief; but he had already got some distance, and it produced no other visible effect than that of making him run faster. The botanists then judged it imprudent to follow their pursuit, and returned to the tents.

Two hours passed before any thing more was heard of the natives; some were then seen in the wood, and an interview was obtained with two, who being made to understand that a hatchet would be given on the musket being returned, they went off to fetch it. In a little time it was actually brought, with the stock broken and ramrod gone, and the hatchet was paid; after which the natives came to the tents with confidence, and some would have remained all night, had they been permitted.

SATURDAY 5 FEBRUARY 1803

This afternoon and the following morning, I took bearings from two stations on Point Middle, and others from a sandy hummock on Point Alexander. The natives came early to the tents, and behaved themselves tranquilly until noon; when one of those who had been most kindly treated, ran off with a wooding axe, and from the thickness of the forest, eluded the pursuit made after him. The corporal and another marine, who had run after the Indian without their hats, received a *coup-de-soleil*, and were sent on board in a state nearly approaching to delirium; but they happily recovered.

Finding these people so determinately bent upon stealing every thing within their reach, I ordered lieutenant Fowler to watch an opportunity of seizing two of them; and after a while to release one, making him understand that the other would be carried away in the ship, if the stolen axe were not returned. In the evening, I went over with two of the gentlemen to the south side of the bay; for the purpose of taking a station upon a hill there named *Mount Caledon*, whose height exceeded that of any other near the water side.

We landed at dusk, at the foot of the mount; and ascended the top next morning [SUNDAY 6 FEBRUARY 1803] before the heat of the sun became excessive, passing in the way several streamlets which were coursing rapidly down to the sea. The view was fully equal to what had been anticipated, and extended to a projection half way to Point Arrowsmith on one side, and over all the islands in the entrance to Mount Alexander on the other. Out of thirty-nine bearings taken at this station, the following are selected as being most essential to the survey of the coast.

The tents, N. 2 ° 50' E. Point Alexander, the extremity, N. 60 0 E. Outer, and rather flat isle, N. 86° 15' to 88 22 E. Mount Alexander, the top N. 37 30 E. Cape Grey, the outer rocks near it, S. 65 5 E. A southern projection of the coast, S. 14 8 E.

We returned to the ship in the afternoon, and the natives had not then approached the tents since the theft of the axe; but next morning [MONDAY 7 FEBRUARY 1803] two of them advanced, bringing some small fruits; and on being invited to eat fish, they sat down and were immediately seized, some others who followed, running away on hearing their cries. In a little time the eldest and most intelligent of them was liberated; on his promising by signs to restore the axe, and being made to understand that his companion would be carried off, should he fail. We observed from the ship much running of the natives amongst the bushes, and peeping about the tents; and least they should attempt any mischief, a spring was put upon the cable, and a six-pounder, with grape shot, kept ready; but after one of the prisoners was released they seemed to have less anxiety, and several swam back across a salt creek, to their usual place of residence.

In the evening I landed at the tents; and taking the native, a youth of fourteen named *Woga*, into the boat, rowed to the place most frequented by the Indians, many of whom were seen behind the bushes. Two came forward, bringing a young girl in their arms; and by expressive signs they offered her to Bongaree, in order to entice him on shore, for the purpose, apparently, of seizing him by way of retaliation. We demanded the restoration of the axe, and our prisoner seemed to use all his powers to enforce it; but the constant answer was, that the thief *Yehangeree*, had been beaten and was gone away; and finding no axe likely to be brought, Woga was carried on board the ship, through a great deal of crying, entreating, threatening, and struggling on his part. He there ate heartily, laughed, sometimes cried, and noticed every thing; frequently expressing admiration at what he saw, and especially at the sheep, hogs, and cats. We had not seen any bows and arrows in the Gulph of Carpentaria, nor in any part of Terra Australis; but some of those from Murray's Islands being shown to Woga, he knew the use of them, and gave their names in his language; it may therefore be true, as Burgomaster Witsen relates, that they are used by the natives on the North-west Coast and in the Gulph; but when he describes the bows as being "of such a length, that one end rests on the ground when shooting," I cannot help suspecting some exaggeration in his informer.

TUESDAY 8 FEBRUARY 1803

After breakfast next morning, I took our prisoner to the tents. On approaching the shore, he was preparing to make a spring out of the boat, which made it necessary to bind him again, for he had been loosed on board the ship. He struggled much, calling upon Bongaree to assist him; but after a while, became quiet, and I left him bound to a tree, eating rice and fish.

A party of the gentlemen landed near the head of the bay, hoping to botanize without interruption; but a number of natives had collected there, two of whom advanced, and sought to entice them into the wood by explaining how many animals might be there shot. The gentlemen were aware of the treachery, and soon thought it advisable to return to the boat; upon which the natives closed in upon them, with poised spears and every appearance of intended mischief. The pointing of muskets stopped their forwardness for a moment; but they came on again, and a shot was fired at each of the two foremost, which put them to flight, and they were not seen afterwards; but the gentlemen thought it unsafe to proceed in their occupation, and returned to the ship. Neither of the two natives dropped; but the muskets being loaded with buck shot, it was supposed that one or both, must have been wounded.

The second evening of Woga's captivity came, and there was no appearance of the axe being restored; his detention, on the contrary, had caused some annoyance to us, and mischief to his countrymen; and if persevered in to the extent of carrying him away, might be an injury to those who should come after us, especially to captain Baudin, whom we daily expected to meet, according to what he had said at Port Jackson. Had the consequences affected ourselves alone, the time of our departure was so near that I should have been glad to have kept Woga; for he was a sprightly lad, whom our treatment would soon have reconciled, and in any future intercourse with his countrymen, as also in furnishing information upon many interesting points, he might have been of service; but for the above reason, and that it was not altogether just to do otherwise, I determined to release the poor prisoner though the axe should not be restored, and went to the tents for that purpose. Woga appeared to be a little melancholy in his bondage, but upon the whole, had not fared amiss, having been eating the greater part of the morning and afternoon. He begged hard to be released, promising, with tears in his eyes, to bring back the axe; and after giving him some clothing and presents, he was suffered to depart. As far as two hundred yards, he walked away leisurely; but then, looking firs behind him, took to his heels with all his might, leaving us no faith in the fulfilment of his pathetic promises.

At this time the holds were completed with water and wood, and on the following morning [WEDNESDAY 9 FEBRUARY 1803] the last observations for the time keepers were taken; after which the shore establishment was embarked, and we prepared for sea. The botanists made an excursion upon Point Middle, and pursued their researches without disturbance; and neither Woga nor any of his countrymen were seen during the whole day.

It has been said, that an opening of a river-like form is laid down in the Dutch chart, in the situation of this bay. No name is there given to it; and as I conceive our examination to confer the right of bestowing one, I have distinguished it by the title of CALEDON BAY, as a mark of respect to the worthy nobleman, lately governor of the Cape of Good Hope, after whom the mount on the south side was also named.

There is no other safe passage into the bay than that between the islands in the entrance and Cape Grey; which cape is remarkable for the round hummock on its extremity, and lies in latitude 13° 1' south, and longitude 136° 42' east. The western branch of the bay appeared to be shallow, and not well sheltered, so that I did not go up it to sound; but in the eastern branch, which is near three miles wide, there is from 4 to 3 fathoms on blue mud, up to within three-quarters of a mile of a rocky point at the head; and the rocks of Point Alexander may there be nearly, if not altogether brought to shut on with those of Cape Grey. Wood for fuel was plentiful every where, and there was no difficulty in procuring water from the ponds and holes in the low, sandy land near the shore of Point Alexander; but from May to December, I doubt whether they would not all be dried up, as well as the small streams which descended from Mount Caledon. Our success with the seine was very moderate, more sea slugs, or what we called sea cucumbers from their shape, being brought on shore than fish; these differed from what we had seen on the reefs of the East Coast, in being of a more firm consistence, and of a light brown or grey, instead of a black colour: when these slugs were pressed with the foot, they threw out a stream of water to some distance.

The country round Caledon Bay, especially at the heads of the two branches, is generally low land; Mount Caledon and the hills of the south side are of granite, and this stone is found in some other parts; but at Point Alexander the basis is a sand stone, more or less impregnated with iron, and at Point Middle it is almost iron ore. A piece of this last stone carried the needle of the theodolite entirely round; yet the bearings taken from thence did not show any difference from those at Mount Caledon, and from those upon Point Alexander, taken from a hillock of sea sand, they did not differ more than half a degree.

So far as our examination went the soil is poor, being either sandy or stony, with a small mixture in some places of vegetable earth; notwithstanding which both the grass and wood were luxuriant, owing to the abundance of rain which had lately fallen, and to the warmth of the climate: in the dry season, I should judge the country would be almost burnt up. The *casuarina* was plentiful in the sandy places, and the *eucalyptus* amongst the rocks, where it reached a tolerable size; the wild nutmeg was found upon Point Middle, and there alone; our apple, the new species of *eugenia*, grew on Point Alexander and elsewhere, and also a few other plants bearing small fruits of little use. Foot marks of the kangaroo were seen in different places, but none of the animals, nor indeed any quadruped; and birds seemed to be rare, both in the woods and on the shores.

The natives of Caledon Bay are the same race of men as those of Port Jackson and King George's Sound, places at nearly the two opposite extremities of Terra Australis;* in personal appearance they were behind some tribes we had seen, but the difference did not go beyond what a less abundant supply of food might produce. All those who came to the tents had lost the upper front tooth on the left side, whereas at Port Jackson it is the right tooth which is knocked out at the age of puberty; whether the women undergo the same operation, contrary to the usage at Port Jackson, we had no opportunity of knowing, having seen only one female, and that at a distance. This girl wore a small piece of bark, in guise of a fig leaf, which was the sole approximation to clothing seen among them. Above the elbow the men usually wore a bandage of net work, in which was stuck a short piece of strong grass, called *tomo*, and used as a tooth pick; but the most remarkable circumstance in their persons was, that the whole of them appeared to have undergone the Jewish and Mahometan rite of circumcision. The same thing was before noticed in a native of Isle Woodah, and in two at Wellesley's Islands; it would seem, therefore, to be general on the west side of the Gulph of Carpentaria; but with what view it may be done, or whence the custom were received, it is not in my power to state. No such practice was found on the

South or East Coasts, nor was it observed in the natives of the islands in Torres' Strait, who however, go naked as the Australians.

[* In Van Diemen's Land, according to captain Cook and succeeding visitors, and on the North-west Coast, according to Dampier, the inhabitants have woolly hair; in which particular they are different from the race above mentioned. Which of them may be aborigines can be only conjectured, until the interior of the new continent shall be explored.]

No other weapons than spears were seen amongst these people; but they were not unacquainted with bows and arrows. It is probable that they have bark canoes, though none were seen, for several trees were found stripped, as if for that purpose; yet when Bongaree made them a present of the canoe brought from Blue-mud Bay, they expressed very little pleasure at the gift, and did not seem to know how to repair it.

That this bay had before received the visits of some strangers, was evinced by the knowledge which the natives had of fire arms; they imitated the act of shooting when we first landed, and when a musket was fired at their request, were not much alarmed. A quantity of posts was lying near the water, which had been evidently cut with iron instruments; and when we inquired of the inhabitants concerning them, they imitated with their hands the motion of an axe cutting down a tree, and then stopping,
exclaimed *Poo!* Whence we understood that the people who cut the wood had fire arms. This was all that could be learned from the natives; but from the bamboos and partitions of frame work found here, similar to those at Pellew's Group, they were doubtless the same Asiatic nation, if not the same individuals, of whom so many traces had been seen all the way from the head of the gulph. The propensity shown by the natives to steal, especially our axes, so contrary to all I have known and heard of their countrymen, is not only a proof that they had been previously visited by people possessing iron implements, but from their audacity it would appear, that the effect of fire arms was either not very certain in the hands of the strangers, or had seldom been resorted to in the punishment of aggression; and from the circumstance of the Indians bringing us a few berries, as a recompense for the last stolen axe, it should seem that they had been accustomed to make very easy atonements for their thefts. I have some hope that those who may follow us will not be robbed, at least with so much effrontery; and at the same time, that the inhabitants of Caledon Bay will not avoid, but be desirous of further communication with Europeans.

I do not know that the language at any two parts of Terra Australis, however near, has been found to be entirely the same; for even at Botany Bay, Port Jackson, and Broken Bay, not only the dialect, but many words are radically different;* and this confirms one part of an observation, the truth of which seems to be generally admitted: that although similarity of language in two nations proves their origin to be the same, yet dissimilarity of language is no proof of the contrary position. The language of Caledon Bay may therefore be totally different to what is spoken on the East and South Coasts, and yet the inhabitants have one common origin; but I do not think that the language is absolutely and wholly different, though it certainly was no better understood by Bongaree than by ourselves. In three instances I found a similarity: the personal pronoun of Port Jackson, *gni-a* (I), was used here, and apparently in the same sense; when inquiry was made after the axe, the natives replied "*Yehangeree py*," making signs of beating; and *py* signifies to beat, in the Port-Jackson language; the third instance was of the lad Woga calling to Bongaree in the boat, which after he had done several times without being answered, he became angry, and exclaimed *Bongaree-gah!* in a vehement manner, as Bongaree himself would have done in a similar case. For the following list of words I am principally indebted to Mr. Brown, naturalist to the expedition; who remarked that the word here for eye was very nearly the same with that used, both at King George's Sound and Port Jackson, to express the same organ.

[* This multiplicity of tongues in the same country presents an extraordinary contrast with the *islands* in the Great Ocean, where, from the Sandwich Isles near the northern tropic, to the furthest extremity of New Zeeland in 47° south, the language is almost every where the same; and with so little difference of dialect, that the several inhabitants have not much difficulty to understand each other.]

[LIST OF ENGLISH WORDS AND THOSE USED BY THE PEOPLE AT CALEDON BAY TO EXPRESS THE SAME IDEA.--not included in ebook.]

In collecting the words some errors may possibly have been made, either from misunderstanding the natives or from their deceiving us intentionally; for after the trick put upon Mons. Labillardière at the Friendly Islands, in the words given him for the high numerals, they are always to be suspected.

During the week we remained in Caledon Bay, the following astronomical observations were taken.

Latitude from three observations to the north and south, taken in a boat astern of the ship and reduced to the tents on Point Alexander, 12° 47' 16" S.

Longitude from twelve sets of distances of stars east and west of the moon, taken on a stand by lieut. Flinders, and of which the individual results are given in Table VI. of the Appendix No. I, 136° 35' 47.5" E.

The rates of the time keepers were found from morning's altitudes of the sun in an artificial horizon, between Feb. 3 and 8; and the means, with the errors from mean Greenwich time at noon there on the 9th, were as under:

Earnshaw's No. 543, slow 2h 41' 0.91" and losing 16.53" per day. Earnshaw's No. 520, slow 2h 27' 19.55" and losing 30.83" per day.

No. 520 had been accidentally let down in Blue-mud Bay, whence its longitude is not now noticed; that given by No. 543 on Feb. 3, with the rate from Observation Island, was 136° 43' 3.5", or 7'16" greater than the lunars. Were a rate used, equally accelerated from that of Observation Island to what was found in Caledon Bay, the longitude would be 0' 55" less than the lunars; but during the twelve days occupied in circumnavigating Groote Eylandt, it was proved that this time keeper was keeping its former rate, and consequently the acceleration cannot here be admitted.

In constructing the chart of the coast and islands between Pellew's Group and Caledon Bay, a time keeper was required only in laying down the south and east sides of Groote Eylandt, and the main coast up to Cape Barrow; in all the remaining parts the longitude was preserved by a connected chain of bearings, mostly taken on shore. The time-keeper reckoning from Observation Island, and that by survey worked back from the fixed point in Caledon Bay, meet each other on Jan. 5 p.m. at Connexion Island; and the difference was there found to be 2' 41", which the time keeper gave more to the east. This may have arisen from Observation Island being laid down in a longitude too great by that quantity, or Caledon Bay too little, or from a small error in each; but the time keeper was not thought entitled to such perfect confidence, as to cause an alteration to be made in these stations. The difference of 2' 41" is therefore corrected by applying -16.3" of longitude per day to the time keeper, from Observation to Connexion Island; Groote Eylandt is laid down mostly from the time keeper, with the fixed correction -2' 41" all round; and from thence to Caledon Bay the chart is constructed from bearings and observed latitudes.

The mean *dip* of the south end of the needle, observed at the tents, was 36° 28'.

Variation of the theodolite, 2° 20' E.

On board the ship, at anchor off the south-west side of the inner island at the entrance, the variation from three compasses, with the head N. W. by W., was 2° 26'; by the surveying compass alone, 2° 46' east, and this, which I consider to be the best, would be, corrected, 1° 14' E.

At my different stations on shore, the variation seemed to be between 2° and 2° 20' east; except on the north-east end of the outer island in the entrance, where it appeared to be no more than 1° 30'.

The rise of *tide* in Caledon Bay was so small, that nothing certain could be determined on board, either upon the quantity or the time; but it appeared from the observations of lieutenant Fowler at the tents, that there were two tides in the day, the rise of which varied from 3 feet 10, to 4 feet 10 inches; and that the time of high water took place at *nine hours and a half after* the moon passed over and under the meridian.

On board the ship, the range of the thermometer was from 83° to 87°, nearly as it had been from first entering the Gulph of Carpentaria; and on shore it was probably 10° higher. Several of our people were ill of diarrhoeas at this time, accompanied with some fever, which was attributed by the surgeon to the heat and the moist state of the atmosphere; for since December, when the north-west monsoon began, not many days had passed without rain, and thunder squalls were frequent. Exposing the head uncovered to the sun, more especially if engaged in strong exercise, was proved to be very dangerous here; I lost one man in Blue-mud Bay from a want of due precaution in this particular, and at this place two others very narrowly escaped. Musketoes were numerous and exceedingly troublesome on shore, as also the black flies; but no venemous reptiles were seen in our limited excursions round Caledon Bay. The mercury in the barometer stood between 29.90 and 29.95 inches, in the rainy weather with strong winds from the eastward; but with fine weather and variable winds, more especially from the south and westward, it descended to 29.80 inches.

CHAPTER IX.
Departure from Caledon Bay.
Cape Arnhem.
Melville Bay.
Cape Wilberforce, and Bromby's Isles.
The English Company's Islands: meeting there with vessels from Macassar.
Arnhem Bay.
The Wessel's Islands.
Further examination of the North Coast postponed.
Arrival at Coepang Bay, in Timor.
Remarks and astronomical observations.

[NORTH COAST. GULPH OF CARPENTARIA.]
THURSDAY 10 FEBRUARY 1803
(Atlas, Plate XV.)

At daylight in the morning of Feb. 10, we sailed down Caledon Bay, and steered eastward along the south side of the islands lying in the entrance. In passing the outer island I landed with the botanical gentlemen, and took bearings from a small elevation on its north-east end, which materially assisted in fixing the positions of the northern islets, and extending the survey onward along the coast.

Cape Grey, the hummock on it, bore S. 27° 13' W. Mount Alexander, N. 11 45 W. Furthest extreme northward, N. 13 43 E.

This outer island is nearly a mile long, E. by N. and W. by S., and mostly destitute of wood; but one valley was thickly covered, and so interlaced with vines as to be impenetrable. The latitude observed to the north and south, at the sandy west point, was 12° 52' 59" south.

We re-joined the ship at one o'clock, and steered northward, without side of the islets and rocks which lie scattered along the shore as far as Mount Alexander. Amongst these are three near to each other, with hummocks upon them, which, as in many points of view they seem to make but one island, may probably have been meant by the northernmost of the three isles in the Dutch chart.

The wind had been from the southward, but on closing in with the coast at Mount Alexander it came from N. W. by N., and edged us off a little from the land. At sunset the shore was three or four miles distant, and

Mount Alexander bore S. 53° W. A hummock at the furthest extreme, N. 9 E.

We steered on till eight o'clock, and then anchored in 21 fathoms, blue mud. At daylight [FRIDAY 11 FEBRUARY 1803], the shore was found to be distant four or five miles; the furthest part then seen was near the eastern extremity of Arnhem's Land, and this having no name in the Dutch chart, is called CAPE ARNHEM.

Mount Alexander was set at S. 48° W. Two rocks under the shore, dist. 5 or 6 miles, N. 15 W. Cape Arnhem, rising land within the extremity, N. 11½ W.

From Mount Alexander to Cape Arnhem there is nine leagues of waving sandy coast; it affords only one small opening, which is on the south side of a cliffy point, with two islets lying off the entrance, and may probably afford shelter for boats.

At eight in the morning we passed Cape Arnhem, a smooth grassy projection which rises gently from the water's edge into the country, but is no where of much elevation; a broad rock lies near the south-eastern extremity, and its position was ascertained to be 12° 19' south, and 137° 1' east. Strong ripplings of a tide or current extended some distance off the cape, and in passing through them we had irregular soundings between 27 and 18 fathoms; beyond Cape Arnhem the shore trended N. W. by N., in rocky points and shallow bights, but the wind being from that direction, we could not follow it closely. The furthest land visible at noon was a flat-topped hill which I call *Mount Saunders*, and nearer to us was a higher and more woody hill, also flat-topped and steep at its north end, to which is given the name of *Mount Dundas*; their bearings, and our position at this time were as under:

Latitude observed, 12° 12½' Longitude from survey and time keeper, 137 2½ Mount Dundas, bluff north end, dist. 8 miles, S. 85 W. Mount Saunders, north end, N. 84½ W. Cape Arnhem, a rising within the extremity, S. 21 W.

We tacked to the westward in the afternoon, and an island came in sight, lying to the north of the two mounts, with several rocks and islets scattered on its north-east side. At sunset the wind died away, and a stream anchor was dropped in 16 fathoms sandy ground; our situation being five miles from the shore under Mount Dundas, and three from the nearest rocky islets to the north-west. The flood tide set gently to the westward, and induced me to suppose there might be a passage within the island and rocks, and in the morning [SATURDAY 12 FEBRUARY 1803] our endeavours were used to reach it; but the winds being light and mostly contrary, the evening came before we got through. An anchor was then dropped in 4 fathoms, coarse sand, one mile and a half from the sandy shore under Mount Saunders, and three miles from the south-west end of the island. The passage is more than two miles wide, and our soundings in working through it were between 4½ and 6 fathoms on a gravelly bottom; but afterwards we had little more in some places than 3 fathoms.

[NORTH COAST. MELVILLE BAY.]

Two natives, with a canoe, had been seen upon the island; and as our boat stood that way, sounding ahead of the ship, they waved and called to the people. The island is about five miles long, and between one and two in breadth; it is low, mostly destitute of wood, and the shores in general are sandy; and not being laid down in the Dutch chart, I distinguish it, with the islets and rocks to the north and north-east, by the name of *Melville Isles*: the south end which forms the passage, lies in 12° 8½' south, and 136° 52' east. In the opposite shore, between Mount Saunders and Dundas, is a sandy bight where ships would be sheltered from all winds except those at north-east, if the water be deep enough for them. The trees upon the hills showed a dark-green foliage; but the low land, especially under Mount Saunders, was sandy and barren, and so continued for seven miles westward, to a low point near a woody islet. Further on, the coast took a northern direction, and was seen from the mast head as far as N. N. W.; but no other part could be set from the deck than the highest of several eminences on the back land, named *Mount Bonner*, which proved to be an useful mark in the survey. The bearings taken at this anchorage were principally these:

Mount Dundas, bluff north end, S. 54° E. Woody islet, near a western sandy point, S. 62 W. Mount Bonner, N. 82 W. Melville Isles, the northernmost, N. 13 E. Melville Isles, the largest, N. 83° E. to East.

SUNDAY 13 FEBRUARY 1803

In the morning we steered westward, with a light air of wind at south and a flood tide in our favour; and having passed over some ripplings near the anchorage, our soundings became regular, increasing from 7 to 12 fathoms. On a breeze setting in at north-west, the course was directed towards a bight behind the woody islet; and a little before noon its appearance became so promising, that I steered into it before the wind. In passing the islet and sandy point we had from 10 to 7 fathoms, in an opening of four miles wide; and a bay of considerable extent then lay before us. In the middle of the bay were three rocks, and to the north-east of them a headland, beyond which the water extended eastward; we steered to pass between these till the depth diminished to 4 fathoms, when we tacked and let go the anchor in the north-eastern part of the bay, in 5 fathoms, muddy bottom; the sandy point at the entrance bore W. by N., one mile and a quarter, and the largest of some granitic rocks in front of the beach, N. by W. half a mile.

A boat was sent to haul the seine on the beach, and I went there with the botanical gentlemen. The depth was 5 fathoms close to the shore, even within the rocks; and the ship might have been placed there in perfect security, though the room was scarcely sufficient to allow of swinging at single anchor. I called the largest of the rocks which form the south-east side of this snug little place, *Harbour Rock*; and the sandy point at the entrance of the bay is named *Point Dundas*. After the seine had been hauled with good success, I walked to the extremity of the point; and from a hillock of sand a little way back, took a set of bearings to commence the survey, in which was included the bluff north end of Mount Saunders at N. 74° 55' E. Many foot-marks of men, dogs, and small kangaroos were observed on the beach., but neither natives nor quadrupeds were seen.

MONDAY 14 FEBRUARY 1803

Early next morning a party of men was sent to cut wood, and the botanical gentlemen landed on Point Dundas upon their pursuits; I went to examine the north-eastern part of the bay, where the water extended two miles above the ship; but the depth in it presently diminished to 2½ fathoms, and to 1 near the end. Beyond a low isthmus there, a piece of water was seen communicating with the south-eastern part of the bay, and making a peninsula of the high rocky land named *Drimmie Head*; at high water, indeed, it is an island, for the tide then flows over some parts of the isthmus. After taking two sets of bearings, I rowed southward along the shore of Drimmie Head; and from a hill near the south-west extremity obtained a good view of the bay, and saw the western coast as far northward as a cliffy cape which was named after *William Wilberforce*, Esq., the worthy representative of Yorkshire. The principal bearings from hence were,

Car. e Wilberforce, highest part, N. 25° 40' W. Mount Bonner, N. 51 55 W. Point Dundas, distant 2 miles, N. 52 30 W.

Leaving Drimmie Head, I steered over to the middlemost of the three rocks in the bay, with a depth of water from 3 to 6½ fathoms, on muddy ground. These rocks lie nearly due south from Point Dundas, and I proposed to observe the latitude on both sides from thence, whilst lieutenant Flinders did the same at the point, that a base line for the survey might be obtained from the difference; but the difficulty of finding a convenient position disappointed me, and no satisfactory base was obtained here; so that the extent of this bay in the chart is rather uncertain.

My course from the three rocks was directed S. S. E., for the south side of the bay; the distance was three miles, and the depth for half the way from 5 to 3 fathoms, but afterwards shoal. Upon some low cliffs there, partly composed of pipe clay, a few bearings were taken; and after walking a little way inland, to examine the country, I rowed back to a small island near the south extremity of Drimmie Head, with soundings mostly between 3 and 6½ fathoms; but there is no ship passage between it and the head. Having taken some additional bearings and looked over the islet, I returned on board in the evening; passing in the way near a rock, dry at half tide, but round which, at a ship's length, there is 2½ to 3 fathoms.

TUESDAY 15 FEBRUARY 1803

Some further bearings and observations were taken on the 15th, and my intention to sail on the following morning being frustrated by a fresh wind at north-west, with unsettled weather, Messieurs Brown and Bauer accompanied me [WEDNESDAY 16 FEBRUARY 1803] in a boat excursion to the eastern part of the bay. We first landed at the islet near Drimmie Head, that Mr. Brown might examine its mineralogy; and then steered three miles eastward for a low projection covered with mangroves, growing on rocks of strongly impregnated iron stone. Coasting along the mangrove shore from thence northward, and after landing at one other place, we came to the isthmus which connects Drimmie Head to the land of Point Dundas; and it being near high water, the boat was got over the isthmus by a small passage through the mangroves, and we reached the ship at one o'clock, where every thing was prepared for weighing the anchor.

This bay is unnoticed in the Dutch chart, and I name it MELVILLE BAY, in compliment to the Right Hon. Robert Saunders Dundas, viscount Melville, who, as first lord of the Admiralty, has continued that patronage to the voyage which it had experienced under some of his predecessors. It is the best harbour we found in the Gulph of Carpentaria; the entrance is from the N. N. W., four miles wide, and free from danger; and within side, the sole dangers not conspicuous, are a sandy spit running half a mile to the S. S. E. from Point

Dundas, and the *Half-tide Rock*. This lies half a mile from the north-west part of Drimmie Head, and bears (true as usual),

From the sandy hillock within Point Dundas, S. 48° 35' E. From Harbour Rock, S. 10 39 E.

Melville Bay every where affords good holding ground, the bottom being either mud or sand; and there is depth for a ship to run between the three rocks in the middle of the bay and Drimmie Head, and steer eastward until the head is brought to bear N. N. W., at the distance of one or two miles; but the most convenient anchorage is just within the entrance, between Point Dundas and Harbour Rock, where a ship may lie close to the sandy beach in from 3 to 5 fathoms. Even within the rock there is depth enough; and were moorings laid down, four or five sail might swing there in perfect security. We obtained here fire wood, and a tolerable supply of fish; and had water been wanted, it might have been obtained by digging at the foot of the small hills to the north-east of Harbour Rock, since a hole made there by the natives was found to contain good water.

The stone on the north side of Melville Bay is a granitic composition of quartz, mica, and coarse garnets; the garnets are large, and give the stone a plum-pudding-like appearance, and when polished, it would be beautiful: over the granite is a crust of calcareous rock in many places. On the south side of the bay the stone is argillaceous, but frequently mixed with ferruginous grains; and on the south-east side the rocks are of iron ore, of which a small piece drew the needle of my theodolite 8° from the meridian. The bearings taken here were found to have been 50° wrong; but too late to ascertain whether the error arose from the attraction of the shore, or from the needle having been placed at 310° by mistake, instead of 360°.

There did not appear to be any rich soil on the borders of the bay; but on the south and eastern sides the country was covered with an agreeable intermixture of grass and trees, and better adapted for cattle than any I have seen in so low a latitude. The soil, though not deep, would produce most things suited to the climate; for the heat and moisture do so much for vegetation, that very little earth seems necessary to its support. On the south side the trees are mostly different species of *eucalyptus*, growing tall and straight, though not large; whereas on the sandy parts of Point Dundas, a *casuarina*, of the same species as seen at Coen River and other parts of the gulph, was most abundant, and served us for fuel. A *santalum*, more nearly allied to the true sandel wood than any before seen in this country, was found on the borders of the bay.

No inhabitants were perceived, nor any fresh traces of them; but as dogs were seen twice, it is probable the natives were watching us at no great distance; they had visited all the places where I landed, and should therefore seem to possess canoes. Traces of the same strangers, of whom mention has been so often made, were found here; and amongst others were partitions of frame work and part of a large earthen jar. Kangaroos appeared to be rather numerous in the woods, brown doves and large white pigeons were tolerably plentiful, and a bird nearly black, of the size and appearance of a hen, was shot; there were also cockatoos, both black and white, and a beautiful species of paroquet not known at Port Jackson. The aquatic birds were blue and white cranes, sea-pies, and sand-larks. Besides fish, our seine usually brought on shore many of the grey slugs or sea cucumbers, but not so abundantly as in Caledon Bay.

We were not here pestered so much with the black flies as before; but the musketoes and sand flies were numerous and fierce. Most of the bushes contained nests made by a small green ant; and if the bush were disturbed, these resentful little animals came out in squadrons, and never ceased to pursue till the disturber was out of sight. In forcing our way amongst the underwood, we sometimes got our hair and clothes filled with them; and as their bite is very sharp, and their vengeance never satisfied, there was no other resource than stripping as expeditiously as possible.

The sun was at this time very near the zenith, which not only prevented the latitude from being observed in the artificial horizon, but rendered the observations from the sea horizon, to the north and south at the same noon, liable to inaccuracies; and in consequence, our positions in this neighbourhood may not be very correct.

The *latitude* of Point Dundas, from one double observation, was 12° 13' 50"; but from the bearing of Mount Saunders, it is taken to be 12° 13' 0" S.

Longitude by survey from Caledon Bay, being 1' greater than by time keepers,136° 41' 40" E.

Variation of the theodolite on Harbour Rock,1° 13' east.

And except in the doubtful instance of the iron-stone shore on the south-east side of the bay, the bearings in other parts did not differ more than 20' from it.

The greatest rise of *tide* here, according to the marks on shore, did not seem to have exceeded eight feet. High water took place nearly five hours before, and *seven hours after* the moon's passage over the meridian; which is nearly two hours and a half earlier than in Caledon Bay, as that is earlier than in Blue-mud Bay, further south in the gulph.

[NORTH COAST. GULPH OF CARPENTARIA.]
WEDNESDAY 16 FEBRUARY 1803

At two in the afternoon of the 16th, the wind being moderate at N. N. W., we worked out of Melville Bay; and anchored at dusk, five miles from the entrance in 13 fathoms, sand and mud. Next morning [THURSDAY 17 FEBRUARY 1803], in following the line of the western shore with a breeze off the land, we passed three rocks lying out from a point under Mount Bonner; and further on, six or seven miles short of Cape Wilberforce, there was a small shallow opening. From the north part of this cliffy cape, a chain of islands and rocks extends out three or four leagues to the E. N. E., which I call *Bromby's Isles*, after my worthy friend the Rev. John Bromby of Hull. One of these is cliffy, and two miles long; the rest are smaller, and the whole seemed to be connected by rocks under water; but between Cape Wilberforce and the nearest islet was a space three-quarters of a mile wide, towards which we worked up against a fresh wind at W. N. W. At noon, the two cliffy parts of the cape bore S. ¼ E. and W. ¼ N., from one to two miles; and the latter, which is the north extremity, was ascertained to lie in 11° 52' south, and 136° 33' east.

At this time the weather became squally with much rain; but after numberless tacks, made under double-reefed top sails and courses in the narrow passage, with soundings from 10 to 18 fathoms, we cleared it at two o'clock, and stretched southwestward as the main coast was found to trend; and thus was the examination of the Gulph of Carpentaria finished, after employing one hundred and five days in coasting along its shores and exploring its bays and islands. The extent of the Gulph in longitude, from Endeavour's Strait to Cape Wilberforce, is 5½° and in latitude 7°; and the circuit, excluding the numerous islands and the openings, is little less than four hundred leagues. It will be remarked that the form of it, given in the old charts, is not very erroneous, which proves it to have been the result of a real examination; but as no particulars were known of the discovery of the south and western parts, not even the name of the author, though opinion ascribed it with reason to Tasman, so the chart was considered as little better than a representation of fairy land, and did not obtain the credit which it was now proved to have merited. Henceforward, the Gulph of Carpentaria will take its station amongst the conspicuous parts of the globe in a decided character.

[NORTH COAST. ENGLISH COMPANY'S ISLANDS.]

After clearing the narrow passage between Cape Wilberforce and Bromby's Isles, we followed the main coast to the S. W.; having on the starbord hand some high and large islands, which closed in towards the coast ahead so as to make it doubtful whether there were any passage between them. Under the nearest island was perceived a canoe full of men; and in a sort of roadsted, at the south end of the same island, there were six vessels covered over like hulks, as if laid up for the bad season. Our conjectures were various as to who those people could be, and what their business here; but we had little doubt of their being the same, whose traces had been found so abundantly in the Gulph. I had inclined to the opinion that these traces had been left by Chinese, and the report of the natives in Caledon Bay that they had fire arms, strengthened the supposition; and combining this with the appearance of the vessels, I set them down for piratical Ladrones who secreted themselves here from pursuit, and issued out as the season permitted, or prey invited them. Impressed with this idea, we tacked to work up for the road; and our pendant and ensign being hoisted, each of them hung out a small white flag. On approaching, I sent lieutenant Flinders in an armed boat, to learn who they were; and soon afterward we came to an anchor in 12 fathoms, within musket shot; having a spring on the cable, and all hands at quarters.

Every motion in the whale boat, and in the vessel along-side which she was lying, was closely watched with our glasses, but all seemed to pass quietly; and on the return of lieutenant Flinders, we learned that they were prows from Macassar, and the six Malay commanders shortly afterwards came on board in a canoe. It happened fortunately that my cook was a Malay, and through his means I was able to communicate with them. The chief of the six prows was a short, elderly man, named *Pobassoo*; he said there were upon the coast, in different divisions, sixty prows, and that *Salloo* was the commander in chief. These people were Mahometans, and on looking into the launch, expressed great horror to see hogs there; nevertheless they had no objection to port wine, and even requested a bottle to carry away with them at sunset.

The weather continued squally all night, with frequent heavy rain, and the wind blew strong; but coming off the islands, the ship rode easily. In the morning [FRIDAY 18 FEBRUARY 1803], I went on board Pobassoo's vessel, with two of the gentlemen and my interpreter, to make further inquiries; and afterwards the six chiefs came to the Investigator, and several canoes were along-side for the purpose of barter. Before noon, five other prows steered into the road from the S. W., anchoring near the former six; and we had more people about the ship than I chose to admit on board, for each of them wore a short dagger or cress by his side. My people were under arms, and the guns were exercised and a shot fired at the request of the chiefs; in the evening they all retired quietly, but our guns were kept ready and half the people at quarters all night. The weather was very rainy; and towards morning [SATURDAY 19 FEBRUARY 1803], much noise was heard amongst the prows. At daylight they got under sail, and steered through the narrow passage between Cape Wilberforce and Bromby's Isles, by which we had come; and afterwards directed their course south-eastward into the Gulph of Carpentaria.

My desire to learn every thing concerning these people, and the strict look-out which it had been necessary to keep upon them, prevented me attending to any other business during their stay. According to Pobassoo, from whom my information was principally obtained, sixty prows belonging to the Rajah of Boni, and carrying one thousand men, had left Macassar with the north-west monsoon, two months before, upon an expedition to this coast; and the fleet was then lying in different places to the westward, five or six together, Pobasso's division being the foremost. These prows seemed to be about twenty-five tons, and to have twenty or twenty-five men in each; that of Pobassoo carried two small brass guns, obtained from the Dutch, but the others had only muskets; besides which, every Malay wears a cress or dagger, either secretly or openly. I inquired after bows and arrows, and the *ippo* poison, but they had none of them; and it was with difficulty they could understand what was meant by the *ippo*.

The object of their expedition was a certain marine animal, called *trepang*. Of this they gave me two dried specimens; and it proved to be the *beche-de-mer*, or sea cucumber which we had first seen on the reefs of the East Coast, and had afterwards hauled on shore so plentifully with the seine, especially in Caledon Bay. They get the *trepang* by diving, in from 3 to 8 fathoms water; and where it is abundant, a man will bring up eight or ten at a time. The mode of preserving it is this: the animal is split down one side, boiled, and pressed with a weight of stones; then stretched open by slips of bamboo, dried in the sun, and afterwards in smoke, when it is fit to be put away in bags, but requires frequent exposure to the sun. A thousand trepang make a *picol*, of about 125 Dutch pounds; and one hundred picols are a cargo for a prow. It is carried to Timor, and sold to the Chinese, who meet them there; and when all the prows are assembled, the fleet returns to Macassar. By Timor, seemed to be meant Timor-laoet; for when I inquired concerning the English, Dutch, and Portuguese there, Pobassoo knew nothing of them: he had heard of Coepang, a Dutch settlement, but said it was upon another island.

There are two kinds of trepang. The black, called *baatoo*, is sold to the Chinese for forty dollars the picol; the white, or grey, called *koro*, is worth no more than twenty. The *baatoo* seems to be what we found upon the coral reefs near the Northumberland Islands; and were a colony established in Broad Sound or Shoalwater Bay, it might perhaps derive considerable advantage from the trepang. In the Gulph of Carpentaria, we did not observe any other than the *koro*, or grey slug.

Pobassoo had made six or seven voyages from Macassar to this coast, within the preceding twenty years, and he was one of the first who came; but had never seen any ship here before. This road was the first rendezvous for his division, to take in water previously to going into the Gulph. One of their prows had been lost the year before, and much inquiry was made concerning the pieces of wreck we had seen; and a canoe's rudder being produced, it was recognised as having belonged to her. They sometimes had skirmishes with the native inhabitants of the coast; Pobassoo himself had been formerly speared in the knee, and a man had been slightly wounded since their arrival in this road: they cautioned us much to beware of the natives.*

[* A question suggests itself here: Could the natives of the west side of the Gulph of Carpentaria have learned the rite of circumcision from these Malay Mahometans? From the short period that the latter had frequented the coast, and the nature of the intercourse between the two people, it seems to me very little probable.]

They had no knowledge of any European settlement in this country; and on learning the name Port Jackson, the son of Pobassoo made a memorandum of it as thus, (foreign characters), writing from left to right. Until this time, that some nutmegs were shown to them, they did not know of their being produced here; nor had they ever met with cocoa nuts, bananas, or other edible fruits or vegetables; fish, and sometimes turtle, being all they procured. I inquired if they knew of any rivers or openings leading far inland, if they made charts of what they saw, or used any charts? To all which Pobassoo answered in the negative. There was a river at Timor, into which the ship could go; and he informed me of two turtle islands, one of them not far to the north-west of our situation in the road; the other would be seen from the mast head as we sailed along the shore.

I could find no other nautical instrument amongst them than a very small pocket compass, apparently of Dutch manufacture; by this their course is directed at sea, without the aid of any chart or astronomical observation. They carry a month's water, in joints of bamboo; and their food is rice, cocoa nuts, and dried fish, with a few fowls for the chiefs. The black *gummotoo* rope, of which we had found pieces at Sir Edward Pellew's Group, was in use on board the prows; and they said it was made from the same palm whence the sweet syrup, called *gulah*, is obtained.

My numberless questions were answered patiently, and with apparent sincerity; Pobassoo even stopped one day longer at my desire, than he had intended, for the north-west monsoon, he said, would not blow quite a month longer, and he was rather late. I rewarded his trouble and that of his companions with several presents, principally iron tools, which they seemed anxious to possess; and he begged of me an English jack, which he afterwards carried at the head of his squadron. He also expressed a desire for a letter, to show to any other ship he might meet; and I accordingly wrote him a note to captain Baudin, whom it seemed probable he might encounter in the Gulph, either going or returning.

So soon as the prows were gone, the botanical gentlemen and myself proceeded to make our examinations. The place where the ship was anchored, and which I call *Malay Road*, is formed by two islands: one to the S. W.. now named *Pobassoo's Island*, upon which was a stream of fresh water behind a beach; the other to the north, named *Cotton's Island*, after captain Cotton of the India directory. The opening between them is nearly half a mile wide; but the water being shallow, the road is well sheltered on the west side, and the opposite main coast lies not further off to the east than three miles; so that N. E. is the sole quarter whence much swell can come. I landed upon Cotton's Island; and ascending a high cliff at the south-east end, saw Mount Saunders and the northernmost Melville Isle over the land of Cape Wilberforce. Cotton's Island extends six or seven miles to the north. and beyond it, to the north-east, was another large island, which I called *Wigram's*, whose south-east part is also a high cliff. Further off were two small isles; and at a greater distance another, named *Truant Island*, from its lying away from the rest. Pobassoo's Island intercepted my view to the S. W.; but on moving back to a higher station, two other islands were seen over it, close to each other; to the furthest and largest I gave the name of *Inglis*, and to the nearer that of *Bosanquet*. In the west also, and not more than three miles distant, was an island of considerable size, which was distinguished by the name of *Astell*. The general trending of all these islands is nearly N. E. by E., parallel with the line of the main coast and of Bromby's Isles. In the Dutch chart, if they be marked at all, it is as main land, and without distinctive appellation; I have therefore applied names to each, mostly after gentlemen in the East-India directory; and in compliment to that respectable body of men, whose liberal attention to this voyage was useful to us and honourable to them, the whole cluster is named the ENGLISH COMPANY'S ISLANDS.

View of Malay Road, from Pobassoo's Island.

Amongst the bearings taken from the south-eastern cliff of Cotton's Island, the following were most essential to the survey.

Ship at anchor, distant 1¼ miles,   S. 41° 50' W. Mount Bonner,   S. 21 12 E. Mount Saunders, north end,   S. 47 52 E. Cape Wilberforce, N. W. cliff, N. 74 15 E. Bromby's Isles, the largest, N. 66° 39' to 69 39 E. Wigram's Island,   N. 41 45 to 15 40 E.   Moved S. 52½° W. one-third mile. Furthest part of the main land, S. 49 5 W. Inglis' Island, N. E. cliff,   S. 53 30 W. Bosanquet's I., N. W. extreme S. 69 5 W.

The Dutch chart contains an island of great extent, lying off this part of the North Coast; it has no name in Thevenot, but in some authors bears that of Wessel's or Wezel's Eylandt, probably from the vessel which discovered Arnhem's Land in 1636; and from the south end of Cotton's Island distant land was seen to the N. W, which I judged to be a part of it; but no bearings could be taken at this time, from the heavy clouds and rain by which it was obscured.

From the 19th to the 22nd, the weather was frequently rainy, with thunder and lightning; and the wind blew strong in squalls, generally between the north and west, and made it unsafe to move the ship. During these days, the botanical gentlemen over-ran the two islands which form Malay Road; and I made a boat excursion to Astell's, and another to the north end of Cotton's Island, to sound and take bearings for the survey. In the latter excursion [TUESDAY 22 FEBRUARY 1803], three black children were perceived on the north-east beach; and on walking that way we saw two bark huts, and an elderly man was sitting under a tree, near them. He smiled on finding himself discovered, and went behind a bush, when a confused noise was heard of women and children making off into the wood; the man also retreated up the hill, and our friendly signs were ineffectual to stop him. In one of the huts was a net bag, containing some pieces of gum, bone, and a broken spike nail; and against a neighbouring bush were standing three spears, one of which had a number of barbs, and had been wrought with some ingenuity. This I took away; but the rest of the arms, with the utensils and furniture of the huts, consisting of the aforesaid net bag and a shell to drink out of, were left as we found them, with the addition of a hatchet and pocket handkerchief.

Cotton's, Pobassoo's, and Astell's Islands, to which our examinations were limited, are moderately high, woody land; they slope down nearly to the water on their west sides, but on the east, and more especially the south-east, they present steep cliffs; and the same conformation seemed to prevail in the other islands. The stone of the upper parts is grit or sandstone, of a close texture; but the lower part of the cliffs is argillaceous and stratified, splitting in layers of different thicknesses, from that of a shilling to two or three feet; and the strata dip to the westward, about 15°. On breaking some pieces out of the cliffs, I found them curiously marked with the representation of flowers and trees, owing, as I am told, to manganese or iron ore inserting itself partially into the fissures. The layers are of a reddish colour, resembling flat tiles, and might, I conceive, be used as such, almost without any preparation; there are enough of them to cover a whole town, and the sand stone at the top of the cliffs is equally well calculated for building the walls of the houses.

The upper surfaces of these islands are barren; but in the vallies, down which ran streams of water at this time, there is a tolerable soil. One of these vallies, at the south end of Cotton's Island, might be made a delightful situation to a college of monks, who could bear the heat of the climate, and were impenetrable to the stings of musketoes. Here grew the wild nutmeg, in abundance, the fig which bears its fruit on the stem, two species of palm, and a tree whose bark is in common use in the East for making ropes; besides a variety of others, whose tops were overspread with creeping vines, forming a shade to the stream underneath. But this apparently delightful retreat afforded any thing rather than coolness and tranquillity: the heat was suffocating, and the musketoes admitted not of a moment's repose.

Upon Pobassoo's Island, near the stream of water at the back of the beach, Mr. Good, the gardener, planted four of the cocoa nuts procured from the Malays; and also some remnants of potatoes which were found in the ship.

The *latitude* of Malay Road, from two not very satisfactory observations, was 11° 53¾' S.

Longitude by the survey from Caledon Bay 136° 27' E.

From observations made on shore in the artificial horizon, the time-keeper No. 520 was differing from its Caledon-Bay rate, 15.4" of longitude per day, to the east, but No. 543 only 9.8"; and when the longitude of this last is corrected by the proportion afterwards found necessary, it will agree with the survey to less than half a mile.

No observations were taken for the *variation* of the compass, but I judge it to have been about 1° east, when not affected by any local attraction. Near the north-east end of Cotton's Island, and at the south-west point, the variation was 2° *more east* than upon the south-east head; as if the south end of the island attracted the north point, and the north end the south point of the needle.

On the day of the new moon, a particular observation was made upon the tide in Malay Road; and it was high water at ten minutes past eight in the morning, or nearly *eight hours and a quarter after* the moon had passed the lower meridian; and the rise was ten feet two inches. There were two tides in the day; but from the swinging of the ship in the road, it appeared that the last of the ebb, as well as the whole of the flood, came from the N. E.; an irregularity which might be caused by the shallow passage between the two islands.

WEDNESDAY 23 FEBRUARY 1803

The weather was still squally on the 23rd, but in the afternoon became finer; and at three o'clock we steered south-westward, between the islands and the main, with a flood-tide in our favour and the whale boat sounding ahead. All the points of the main coast, like the western sides of the islands, are low and rocky, and they are bordered with reef; but we had tolerably good soundings, from 20 to 7 fathoms, in passing along them at the distance of a mile. At dusk in the evening we came to, in 5 fathoms muddy ground, in a place much like Malay Road; it is formed by Inglis' and Bosanquet's Islands, and except in a space between them, of half a mile wide, we had land at various distances all round.

Inglis' Island forms here a pretty looking cove, in which is a woody islet. In the morning [THURSDAY 24 FEBRUARY 1803] I sounded the cove; and finding it to be shallow, went on, accompanied by the landscape painter, to take bearings from the steep north-east head of the island. From thence the main coast was visible four leagues further, extending in the same south-western direction; at the end of it was an island of considerable elevation, which I named *Mallison's Island*, and west of it another, with land running at the back. The bearings which most served to prolong the survey, were these:

Pobassoo's I., east cliff, in a line with Malay Road,   N. 55° 0' E.   Moved back S. 53° W. ¼ mile. Mallison's I., steep south-east head,   S. 38 25 W. Mallison's I., outer of two rocks on the north-west side, S. 48 47 W.

We had not brought any provision in the boat; but Inglis' Island appearing to terminate three or four miles further on, I hoped to make the circuit, and reach the ship to a late dinner. An Indian followed along the shore, inviting us by signs to land; but when the boat's head was turned that way, he retreated into the wood, and we had no time to follow, or to wait his pleasure to come down; for a good deal of delay had been caused by the tide, and the island was found to extend several miles further than was expected, to another steep head, from which I was desirous to obtain a set of bearings. At five o'clock, when we reached the head, it rained fast, which deterred me from attempting the steep ascent, and we pushed onward; but the island, instead of terminating here, extended four miles further in a west direction, to a low point, where sunset and the bad weather obliged us to stop for the night. No wood could be found to make a fire, nor had we any tent; and from the rain, the cold, and musketoes, and our want of dinner, the night passed uncomfortably.

FRIDAY 25 FEBRUARY 1803
At day-light, I took bearings from the low south-west point, whilst Bongaree speared a few fish.

Mallison's I., the high south-east head, bore   S. 11° 10' E. Mallison's I., west extreme S. 11 30 W. A probable island, dist. 5 miles,   S. 47° 50' W. to West.

The main coast was close at the back of, and perhaps joined the Probable Island; and to the south of it were other lands, apparently insulated, between which and Mallison's Island was an opening of four miles wide, which I marked for our next anchorage.

Bongaree was busily employed preparing his fish, when my bearings were concluded. The natives of Port Jackson have a prejudice against all fish of the ray kind, as well as against sharks; and whilst they devour with eager avidity the blubber of a whale or porpoise, a piece of skate would excite disgust. Our good natured Indian had been ridiculed by the sailors for this unaccountable whim, but he had not been cured; and it so happened, that the fish he had speared this morning were three small rays and a mullet. This last, being the most delicate, he presented to Mr. Westall and me, so soon as it was cooked; and then went to saunter by the water side, whilst the boats' crew should cook and eat the rays, although, having had nothing since the morning before, it may be supposed he did not want appetite. I noticed this in silence till the whole were prepared, and then had him called up to take his portion of the mullet; but it was with much difficulty that his modesty and forbearance could be overcome, for these qualities, so seldom expected in a savage, formed leading features in the character of my humble friend. But there was one of the sailors also, who preferred hunger to ray-eating! It might be supposed he had an eye to the mullet; but this was not the case. He had been seven or eight years with me, mostly in New South Wales, had learned many of the native habits, and even imbibed this ridiculous notion respecting rays and sharks; though he could not allege, as Bongaree did, that "they might be very good for white men, but would kill him." The mullet accordingly underwent a further division; and Mr. Westall and myself, having no prejudice against rays, made up our proportion of this scanty repast from one of them.

We rowed northward, round the west end of Inglis' Island, leaving a hummocky isle and a sandy islet to the left; but on coming to a low point with a small island near it, the rapidity of the flood tide was such, that we could not make head way, and were obliged to wait for high water. I took the opportunity to get another set of bearings, and then followed the example of the boat's crew, who, not finding oysters or any thing to eat, had fallen asleep on the beach to forget the want of food.

It was high water at eleven o'clock, and we then passed between the islet and sandy point, and across two rather deep bights in Inglis' Island; and leaving three rocks and as many small islands on the left hand, entered the passage to the west of the ship, and got on board at two in the afternoon.

This island is twelve miles long, by a varying breadth of one to three miles. Its cliffs and productions are much the same as those of Cotton's Island; but in the south-eastern part it is higher, and the size and foliage of the wood announced more fertility in the soil.

The construction of my chart, and taking bearings from the north end of Bosanquet's Island, occupied me the next day [SATURDAY 26 FEBRUARY 1803]; astronomical observations were also taken; and it appeared that the cliffy east end of Bosanquet's Island, a mile north of the anchorage, was in 11° 57 1/3' south, and 136° 19' east. According to the swinging of the ship in the evenings, the flood tide ceased to run at eight hours and a half after the moon passed the upper meridian, whereas in the mornings it ceased seven hours and a half after the moon passed below; whether the same difference took place in the times of high water by the shore, I cannot tell; but if the mean of the morning's and evening's tides be taken as the time of high water, it will follow *eight hours after* the moon, the same nearly as in Malay Road.

[NORTH COAST. ARNHEM BAY.]
SUNDAY 27 FEBRUARY 1803
In the morning of the 27th, we steered south-westward between Inglis' Island and the main, to explore the opening on the west side of Mallison's Island. The tide, which was in our favour, so stirred up the soft mud, that we did not perceive a shoal until from 4½, the

depth diminished to 2¼ fathoms, and the ship stuck fast. This was at less than a mile from the north-east head of Inglis' Island, yet the deepest water lay within; and towards noon, by carrying out a stream anchor, we got there into 10 fathoms, without having suffered any apparent injury. On the approach of low water next morning [MONDAY 28 FEBRUARY 1803], we resumed our course, keeping nearly midway between the main coast and the island, with soundings from 13 to 7 fathoms, muddy ground; the shores are above two miles asunder, but the reefs from each side occupy more than half of the open space. On clearing the south end of the passage, the boat ahead made signal for 4 fathoms, and we tacked, but afterwards followed till noon; heavy rain then came on, and the wind dying away, an anchor was dropped in 6 fathoms.

There was a rippling not far from the ship, and the master found it to be on a narrow shoal extending north and south, which seems to have been formed in the eddy of the tides. We got under way, on a breeze from N. W. bringing finer weather; and at two o'clock passed over the shoal with soundings twice in 3 fathoms, and afterwards in 5, 7, 10, 12, and 14. The bearings taken in 3 fathoms were,

Inglis' Island, north-east head,   N. 50° E. Inglis' Island, low south-west point, N. 15 W. Mallison's I., high south-east head,   S. 3 E.

At six o'clock we entered the opening, and steered south-eastward into a vast piece of water where the land could not be seen from the mast head; and the soundings were deep, though irregular, varying from 11 to 33 fathoms. At half past eight, being well within the opening, we tacked towards Mallison's Island, and came to an anchor in 15 fathoms, sand and shells.

TUESDAY 1 MARCH 1803

In the morning, our distance from the south side of the island was found to be something above a mile, and the extremes bore N. 64° W. to 39° E. In going to the shore with a party of the gentlemen I carried a good depth all the way, there being 5 fathoms within a few yards of a little beach where a stream of fresh water descended from the hills. A first view of the cliffs led me to think they contained coals; but this appearance arose from the colour of the slate, of which the lower parts are composed. The top of the island is of sand stone, similar to the English Company's Islands; and it seemed to be equally, or more barren than they, and to be destitute of any rich vallies.

My bearings were taken on the south-eastern head; but even from thence, the land was not visible to the southward beyond a low islet surrounded with shoals, and to the E. S. E. it was but faintly seen. The west side of the entrance was composed of broken land, like islands, extending out far to the northward; on the east, the space which separated Mallison's Island from the nearest part of the main seemed to be not more than half a mile broad, and was so filled with rocks as scarcely to admit the passage of a boat. This part of the main land is a projecting cape, low without side but forming a steep head within; and I have named it *Cape Newbald*. The most essential bearings were these:--

Inglis' I. station on the north-east head,   N. 39° 5' E. Inglis' I. west extreme, N. 15 18 W. Furthest western land visible,   N. 26 10 W. Probable Island, low north point,   N. 39 2 W. Low islet up the bay, dist. ten miles, S. 7° to 9 13 E.

These bearings and the observations place the south-east head of Mallison's Island in 12° 11¾' south, and 136° 8' east.

We returned on board at eleven, and then steered eastward along the south side of Cape Newbald; the flood tide, which set in that direction, having induced the hope of finding a river there. The wind was light and scant, so that we advanced principally by means of the tide; and finding it to run against us at five in the evening, anchored in 5 fathoms, mud and shells, eight or nine miles above the entrance of the bay, and one and a half from a rocky point on the Cape-Newbald side. We proceeded with the flood tide, next morning [WEDNESDAY 2 MARCH 1803], in a varying depth from 3 to 5 fathoms; and after advancing four or five miles, it was found impossible to go further without risk of getting aground, and we therefore came to an anchor. The land on the east side of the bay was distant three miles, and no other than a shallow opening in the north-east corner could be seen; a disappointment which left little to be expected in the southern parts of the bay, to which no set of tide had been perceived. In consequence, I gave up the intention of further prosecuting the examination in the ship, in favour of going round in my boat; and directed lieutenant Fowler, so soon as the botanical gentlemen should have explored the productions on the nearest part of Cape Newbald, to return with the ship to the entrance of the bay, and anchor near some low cliffs on the western side, where the botanists could again pursue their researches until my arrival.

Mr. Bauer the natural-history painter, himself a good botanist, expressed a wish to accompany me, and with Mr. Bell, the surgeon, we went off in the afternoon, steering S. S. E. for a small beach in the low, woody shore, five or six miles off. Squalls of wind with heavy rain prevented sounding in the first half of the way; but we then had nine feet, and nearly the same to the beach, where we landed at dusk. The wood was very thick here, the ground swampy, and the musketoes numerous and fierce; so that between them and our wet clothes we had very little rest.

THURSDAY 3 MARCH 1803

In the morning, after bearings had been taken from a projecting part of the ironstone shore, we steered four miles to the S. S. W., mostly in 2 fathoms, to some low cliffs of red earth; where Mr. Bauer examined the productions of the main land, whilst I took bearings from a small islet or bank of iron ore, lying near it.

The ship at anchor, dist. 8 or 9 miles, bore N. 1° 15' E. Mallison's I., south-western cliffs,   N. 50 25 W. Low islet in the bay, centre.,   S. 89 30 W.

Seeing that the shore took a western direction about five miles further on, we steered for the low islet; and at a mile from the land had 3, and afterwards 5 fathoms until approaching a long sandy spit, which extends out from the east end of the islet and was then dry. I landed upon it in time to observe the sun's meridian altitude, which gave 12° 22' 6" south, but a passing cloud deprived me of the supplement. The islet is little else than a bed of sand, though covered with bushes and small trees; there were upon it many marks of turtle and of turtle feasts; and finding the musketoes less numerous than on the main, we stopped to repose during the heat of the day.

In the afternoon, after taking bearings, we steered over to the south side of the bay, four miles off, with soundings from 7 at the deepest, to 3 fathoms at a mile from the iron-stone shore. The land is low and covered with wood, and the traces of kangaroo being numerous, the surgeon was induced to make a little excursion into the wood, whilst I took bearings and Mr. Bauer pursued his botanical researches. Mr. Bell found the country to be tolerably fertile, but had no success in his hunting; and at night we returned to the islet to sleep, hoping to procure some turtle; but no more than three came on shore, and one only was caught, the laying season appearing to be mostly past.

FRIDAY 4 MARCH 1803

At daylight we steered for a low rocky island, seven or eight miles to the W. N. W., where I took angles from the iron-stone rocks at its south end, and Mr. Bauer examined the vegetable productions. To the S. S. W., about five miles, was a woody point, on the east side of which no land was visible; and the depth of water in coming across from Low Islet having been as much as 10 fathoms, it left a suspicion that a river might fall into the south-west corner of the bay, and induced me to row over to the point. The soundings diminished from 5 to 3 fathoms; in which depth the boat being brought to a grapnel, I found the latitude to be 12° 20' 27", from observations to the north and south, and set Low Islet E. 7° S. by a pocket compass.

From thence to the point the water was shallow, and the open space proved to be a shoal bight, with very low land at the back. After I had taken bearings, to ascertain the position of the point and form this side of the bay, we returned northward, passing on the west side of the rocky island; and the ship having arrived at the appointed station, got on board at eight o'clock in the evening.

SATURDAY 5 MARCH 1803

On laying down the plan of this extensive bay, I was somewhat surprised to see the great similarity of its form to one marked near the same situation in the Dutch chart. It bears no name; but as not a doubt remains of Tasman, or perhaps some earlier navigator, having explored it, I have given it the appellation of the land in which it is situate, and call it ARNHEM BAY. So far as an extent of secure anchoring ground is concerned, it equals any harbour within my knowledge; there being more than a hundred square miles of space fit for the reception of ships, and the bottom seemed to be every where good. Of the inducements to visit Arnhem Bay, not much can be said. Wood is plentiful at all the shores, and the stream which ran down the hills at Mallison's Island would have supplied us conveniently with water, had it been wanted; but in three months afterwards it would probably be dried up. In the upper parts of the bay the shores are low, and over-run with mangroves in many places; but near the entrance they may be approached by a ship, and there are beaches for hauling the seine, where, however, we had not much success.

We saw no other stone on the low shores than iron ore, similar to that found in the upper part of Melville Bay, and on Point Middle in Caledon Bay; and it seems probable, that iron runs through the space of country comprehended between the heads of the three bays, although the exterior shores and the hills be either granitic, argillaceous, or of sand stone. The flat country where the iron ore is found, seems to afford a good soil, well-clothed with grass and wood, much superior to that where granite or sand stone prevails; this I judge from what was seen near the heads of the bays, for our excursions inland were necessarily very confined, and for myself, I did not quit the water side at Arnhem Bay, being disabled by scorbutic ulcers on my feet.

This country does not seem to be much peopled, though traces of men were found wherever we landed; in the woods were several species of birds, mostly of the parrot kind, and the marks of kangaroo were numerous, as at Melville Bay. These circumstances would be in favour of any colony which might be established in the neighbourhood; but should such a step come to be contemplated, it would be highly necessary, in the first place, to see what the country is in the dry season, from June to November; for it is to be apprehended that the vegetation may then be dried up, and the sources of fresh water almost entirely fail.

The middle of the entrance into Arnhem Bay is in latitude 12° 11' south, and longitude 136° 3' east. Azimuths taken on board the ship, when at anchor in the north-eastern part of the bay and the head E. by N., gave 0° 48' east variation, which corrected to the meridian, would be 2° 31' east; but the most allowed to the bearings on shore is 1° 40', and the least 1°, no greater difference being produced by the iron stone upon which some were taken. From general observation, the time of high water was nearly the same as in Malay Road, or about *eight hours after* the moon's passage, and the rise seemed to be six or eight feet.

Before noon of the 5th we quitted Arnhem Bay, and steered northward along the chain of islands extending out from the west side of the entrance. On approaching the north end of Probable Island the soundings diminished to 4 fathoms, and a short tack was made to the S. E.; and the flood tide becoming too strong to be stemmed with a light breeze, an anchor was dropped in 17 fathoms, sand and stones. A dry reef had been set from Mallison's Island, and should have lain about two miles S. E. from this anchorage; but it was not seen from the ship, being probably covered by the tide. There were two natives, with a canoe, under Probable Island, and some others were standing on the beach; but no attempt was made to approach the ship, nor did I send on shore to them.

SUNDAY 6 MARCH 1803

In the morning we had a moderate breeze at E. S. E., and pursued the line of the main coast and islands to the northward at the distance of three or four miles, with soundings from 10 to 17 fathoms. Both the coast and islands are in general so low and near to each other, that it was difficult to say whether some were not connected; at eleven, however, we approached two which certainly were islands, and there being a clear passage between the surrounding reefs of a mile and a half wide, we steered through it with 12 to 17 fathoms. The north-easternmost most, which I have named after captain *Cunningham* of the navy, is four or five miles in circumference, and of moderate elevation; and lies in 11° 47' south and 136° 6' east by the survey.

[NORTH COAST. WESSEL'S ISLANDS.]

A third chain of islands commences here, which, like Bromby's and the English Company's Islands, extend out north-eastward from the coast. I have frequently observed a great similarity both in the ground plans and elevations of hills, and of islands in the vicinity of each other; but do not recollect another instance of such a likeness in the arrangement of clusters of islands. This third chain is doubtless what is marked in the Dutch chart as one long island, and in some charts is called Wessel's Eylandt; which name I retain with a slight modification, calling them WESSEL'S ISLANDS. They had been seen from the north end of Cotton's Island to reach as far as thirty miles out from the main coast; but this is not more than half their extent, if the Dutch chart be at all correct.

At noon, when Cunningham's Island bore from S. 1° to 26° E., at the distance of two miles, the furthest visible part of Wessel's Islands bore N. 53° E.; it was not distant, for the weather was squally with rain, and both prevented us from seeing far and obscured the sun. To the westward, we had land at the distance of three or four miles; and from its north-east end, which is named *Point Dale*, three small isles with rocks extended out to the bearing of N. 16° E., which we could not weather without making a tack. At three they were passed; and at six in the evening the outer islet bore S. 14° E., four leagues, and the most western part of the land of Point Dale, S. 36° W.; but whether this last were an island or a part of the main, was still doubtful.

For the last several days the wind had inclined from the eastward, and at this time blew a steady breeze at E. by S., with fine weather; as if the north-west monsoon were passed, and the south-east trade had resumed its course. We had continued the survey of the coast for more than one-half of the six months which the master and carpenter had judged the ship might run without much risk, provided she remained in fine weather and no accident happened; and the remainder of the time being not much more than necessary for us to reach Port Jackson, I judged it imprudent to continue the investigation longer. In addition to the rottenness of the ship, the state of my own health and that of the ship's company were urgent to terminate the examination here; for nearly all had become debilitated from the heat and moisture of the climate--from being a good deal fatigued--and from the want of nourishing food. I was myself disabled by scorbutic sores from going to the mast head, or making any more expeditions in boats; and as the whole of the surveying department rested upon me, our further stay was without one of its principal objects. It was not, however, without much regret that I quitted the coast; both from its numerous harbours and better soil, and its greater proximity to our Indian possessions having made it become daily more interesting; and also, after struggling three months against foul winds, from their now being fair as could be wished for prosecuting the further examination. The accomplishment of the survey was, in fact, an object so near to my heart, that could I have foreseen the train of ills that were to follow the decay of the Investigator and prevent the survey being resumed--and had my existence depended upon the expression of a wish, I do not know that it would have received utterance; but Infinite Wisdom has, in infinite mercy, reserved the knowledge of futurity to itself.

[NORTH COAST. TOWARDS TIMOR.]
(Atlas Plate I.)

On quitting Wessel's Islands, we steered a north-west course all night, under easy sail; having a warrant officer placed at the look-out, and the lead hove every quarter of an hour. The soundings increased very gradually till daylight [MONDAY 7 MARCH 1803], when we had 30 fathoms; and no land being distinguishable, the course was then altered to W. by S. Our latitude at noon was 10° 56' 40", longitude by timekeeper 135° 10'; and I judged that part of the coast seen by lieutenant McCluer, in 1791, to lie about fifty miles to the southward. This was the first land seen by him in his course from New Guinea; and according to the comparison afterwards made of his longitude, it should not lie more than twelve leagues from the western part of Point Dale.

Mr. McCluer saw some islands near the coast, and amongst others an outer one called New Year's Isle, in latitude 10° 52' south and 133° 12' east, which I purposed to visit in the hope of procuring turtle. But our friendly trade wind gradually died away, and was succeeded by light airs from the N. W. and S. W., by calms, and afterwards by light winds from the north-eastward; so that it was not until daylight of the 12th [SATURDAY 12 MARCH 1803], that the island was seen. At eleven o'clock, lieutenant Fowler went on shore to examine the beach for traces of turtle; but finding none recent, he returned before two, and we again made sail to the westward.

New Year's Isle is a bed of sand mixed with broken coral, thrown up on a coral reef. It is four or five miles in circumference, and the higher parts are thickly covered with shrubs and brush wood; but much of it is over-run with mangroves, and laid under water by the tide. Fresh prints of feet on the sand showed that the natives had either visited it very lately, or were then upon the island; turtle also had been there, but their traces were of an old date. The reef extends about a mile off, all round; we had 22 fathoms very near the outer edge, and saw no other danger. Broken land was perceived to the southward, probably the inner isles marked by lieutenant McCluer; and six or seven leagues to the S. W. was a part of the main, somewhat higher but equally sandy, which we traced above half a degree to the westward. I made the *latitude* of the island to be 10° 55' south, and *longitude* by time keeper corrected 133° 4' east; being 3' more south and 8' less east than Mr. McCluer's position. The *variation* of the compass, from azimuths taken twenty leagues to the east of New Year's Isle, was 1° 55' east, with the ship's head W. N. W.; and at thirteen leagues on the west side, 1° 20' with the head N. W.; these being corrected to the meridian, will be 0° 23' and 0° 12' east. The *tide* ran strong to the N. W. whilst it was ebbing by the shore, so that the flood would seem to come from the westward; whereas in the neighbourhood of Cape Arnhem the flood came mostly from the opposite direction: whether this change were a general one, or arose from some opening to the S. E. of New Year's Isle, our knowledge of the coast was too imperfect to determine.

We had continued to have soundings, generally on a muddy bottom, from the time of quitting Wessel's Islands; nor did they vary much, being rarely less than 25, and never more than 35 fathoms. On the 13th [SUNDAY 13 MARCH 1803] at noon we had 34 fathoms, being then in 10° 41' south and 132° 40' east, and the coast still in sight to the southward. The winds then hung in the southern quarter, being sometimes S. W., and at others S. E., but always light; and I steered further off the land, in the hope of getting them more steady. Our soundings gradually increased until the 18th, when the depth was 150 fathoms in latitude 9° 47' and longitude 130° 17'; at midnight we had no ground at 160, but next morning [SATURDAY 19 MARCH 1803] the coral bottom was seen under the ship, and we tacked until a boat was sent ahead; from 7 fathoms on the bank, the soundings in steering after the boat increased to 9, 10, 13, and suddenly to 92 fathoms.

This small bank appeared to be nearly circular, and about four miles round; it lies in latitude 9° 56', longitude 129° 28' and as I judge, about twenty-five leagues from the western extremity of the northern Van Diemen's Land. In some of the old charts there are shoals marked to a considerable distance from that cape; and it seems not improbable, that a chain of reefs may extend as far out as the situation of this bank. We afterwards had soundings at irregular depths, from 30 to 100 fathoms, until the evening of the 26th [SATURDAY 26 MARCH 1803], in 10° 38' south and 126° 30' east; in which situation they were lost. (Atlas, Plate XVI.)

The winds had hung so much in the south-west, and retarded our passage as well as driven us near to the island Timor, that I judged it advisable to obtain refreshments there for my ship's company; under the apprehension that, as the winter season was fast advancing on the south coast of Terra Australis, the bad state of the ship might cause more labour at the pumps than our present strength was capable of exerting. Some of the smaller articles of sea provision., such as peas, rice, and sugar, which formed a principal part of our little comforts, were also become deficient, in consequence of losses sustained from the heat and moisture of the climate, and leakiness of the ship's upper works; and these I was anxious to replenish.

Coepang is a Dutch settlement at the south-west end of Timor and the determination to put in there being made, I revolved in my mind the possibility of afterwards returning to the examination of the north and north-west coasts of Terra Australis, during the winter six months, and taking the following summer to pass the higher latitudes and return to Port Jackson. There was little chance of obtaining salt provisions at Coepang, but there might be a ship or ships there, capable of furnishing a supply, and by which an officer might be conveyed to England; for it was a necessary part of my project to despatch lieutenant Fowler to the Admiralty, with an account of our proceedings, and a request that he might return as speedily as possible, with a vessel fit to accomplish all the objects of the voyage; and I calculated that six months employed upon the North and North-west Coasts, and the subsequent passage to Port Jackson, would not leave much more than the requisite time for refreshing the ship's company before his arrival might be expected. It is to be observed, that the ship had leaked very little in her sides since the caulking done at the head of the Gulph; and the carpenter being now directed to bore into some of the timbers then examined, did not find them to have become perceptibly worse; so that I was led to hope and believe that the ship might go through this service, without much more than common risk, provided we remained in fine-weather climates, as was intended.

MONDAY 28 MARCH 1803

On the 28th, being then in 10° 36' south, and 125° 47' east, the high land of Timor was seen bearing N. 61° W., at the distance of thirty, or perhaps more leagues; but no soundings could be obtained with 90, nor in the evening with 160 fathoms. Next day [TUESDAY 29 MARCH 1803], the light south-west wind suddenly veered to S. E., and blew fresh; and from its dying away at sunset was evidently a sea breeze attracted by the land, which, however, was forty miles off in its nearest part. Our latitude on the 30th [WEDNESDAY 30 MARCH 1803] was 10° 37' 13", longitude 124° 18½', and the land, mostly high mountains, extended from N. N. E. ½ E. to W. N. W., the nearest part was distant seven or eight leagues, but we still had no soundings. The island Rottee is reckoned tolerably high land, but must be greatly inferior to Timor; since the round hill at its eastern end was not seen from the mast head till four this afternoon, when its distance was little more than fifteen leagues. We carried all sail for the strait between the two islands till midnight, and then had soundings in 120 fathoms, muddy ground; an hour and a half afterwards the land was close, and the depth no more than 10 fathoms, upon which we hauled off till morning.

THURSDAY 31 MARCH 1803

At daylight, the north-east point of Rottee was distant two miles, and we steered along the shore, looking for boats and people to obtain intelligence, and if possible some refreshments; but none were seen, although we passed close to a deep and well-sheltered cove. At ten o'clock, when the sandy north point of Rottee was distant one mile and a half, we hauled up north-eastward, across the passage of about six miles wide, between it and the northern lands; for the purpose of entering Samow Strait, which was then open, and of which Mr. Westall took the view given in the Atlas (Plate XVIII, last View). The south-west point of Timor is surrounded by a reef, which extends from half a mile to a mile off, and runs some distance up the strait; both sides of the entrance are low land, yet at eleven o'clock we had no ground between them with 75 fathoms. The width of the entrance is three miles and a half, and continues nearly the same upwards, with a depth of 36 or more fathoms, and no dangers in it, other than the reef before mentioned. From the observations at noon, the extreme south-west point of Timor lies in 10° 22' south, and longitude by survey back from Coepang, 123° 29' east; captain Cook places it in 10° 23' and 123° 55', and calls it the south point, but there is a sloping projection, three leagues to the eastward, which I set in a line with it at E. 2° S.

[NORTH COAST. COEPANG BAY.]

Two vessels were lying under the north-east end of Samow; and on our ensign and pendant being hoisted, the one showed American, and the other Dutch colours. An officer was sent to them for information, as well of the propriety of going into Coepang Bay at this season, as of the political state of Europe; for although the intelligence of peace had arrived before we left Port Jackson, it seemed to be doubtful how long it might last. On his return with favourable intelligence, I steered through the northern outlet of the strait, which is not more than a mile and a half wide, but so deep that 65 fathoms did not reach the bottom; and at four o'clock the anchor was let go in 17 fathoms, muddy ground, half a mile from the shore, with the flag staff of Fort Concordia bearing S. S. E.

I sent the second lieutenant to present my respects to the Dutch governor, and inform him of our arrival and wants, with an offer of saluting the fort provided an equal number of guns should be returned; and the offer being accepted, mutual salutes of thirteen guns passed, and the same evening we received a boat load of refreshments. Next day [FRIDAY 1 APRIL 1803], I went with three officers and gentlemen to wait upon *Mynheer Giesler*, the governor, who sent the commandant of the fort and surgeon of the colony to receive us at the water side. The governor did not speak English, nor I any Dutch; and our communications would have been embarrassed but for the presence of captain Johnson, commander of the Dutch brig, who interpreted with much polite attention.

Coepang is dependant on Batavia for a variety of articles, and amongst others, for arrack, rice, sugar, etc. Mr. Johnson had arrived not long before with the annual supply, yet I found some difficulty in obtaining from the governor the comparatively small quantities of which we stood in need; and I had no resource but in his kindness, for there were no merchants in Coepang, nor any other who would receive bills in payment. Having made an agreement for the provisions, I requested permission for our botanists and painters to range the country, which was readily granted; with a caution not to extend their walks far from the town, as they might be there liable to insults from the natives, over whom the governor had no power.

We were occupied nearly a week in completing our water, which was brought on board in Malay boats, and in obtaining and stowing away the provisions. [SUNDAY 3 APRIL 1803] The governor, with captain Johnson and two other gentlemen were entertained on board the Investigator, and received under a salute; and the day before we proposed to sail [THURSDAY 7 APRIL 1803], I went with some of my principal officers and gentlemen to dine with the governor, the fort firing a salute on our landing; and it is but justice to Mr. Giesler and the orders under which he acted, to say, that he conducted himself throughout with that polite and respectful attention, which the representative of one friendly nation owes to that of another.

A part of the ship's company was permitted to go on shore so soon as our work was completed; and two men, my Malay cook and a youth from Port Jackson, being absent in the evening, the town was searched for them, but in vain. We got under way early next morning [FRIDAY 8 APRIL 1803], before the sea breeze set in, and stood off and on until lieutenant Fowler again went after the men. On his return without success, we stretched out of the bay; but the wind being light, and the governor having promised to send off the men, if found before the ship was out of sight, I still entertained a hope of receiving my deserters.

Timor is well known to be one of the southernmost and largest of the Molucca Islands. Its extent is more considerable than the charts usually represent it, being little less than 250 miles in a north-eastern direction, by from thirty to sixty in breadth. The interior part is a chain of mountains, some of which nearly equal the peak of Teneriffe in elevation; whilst the shores on the south-east side are represented to be exceedingly low, and over-run with mangroves. Gold is said to be contained in the mountains, and to be washed down the streams; but the natives are so jealous of Europeans gaining any knowledge of it, that at a former period, when forty men were sent by the Dutch to make search, they were cut off. In the vicinity of Coepang, the upper stone is mostly calcareous; but the basis is very different, and appeared to me to be argillaceous.

The original inhabitants of Timor, who are black but whose hair is not woolly, inhabit the mountainous parts, to which they appear to have been driven by the Malays, who are mostly in possession of the sea coast. There were formerly several Portuguese establishments on the north side of the island, of which Diely and Lefflow still remained; but these have all gradually declined, and the governor of Diely was now said to be the sole white Portuguese resident on the island. The Dutch territory at Coepang did not extend beyond four or five miles round Fort Concordia; and the settlement affording no other advantage to the Company than that of keeping out other nations, it seemed to be following, with accelerated steps, the ruin of their affairs. During the war which terminated in 1801, the communication with Batavia was interrupted, and the town taken by the English forces; an insurrection was raised by the half-cast people, and some of the troops left as a garrison were massacred, and the rest abandoned the island. During these troubles the town had been set on fire; and at this time, all the best houses were in ruins. The few troops kept by the Dutch were mostly Malays, some of the officers even, being mulattos; and the sole person amongst them, who had any claim to respectability, was a Swiss who had the command of Fort Concordia, but with no higher rank that that of serjeant-major. Besides the governor and two or three soldiers, I saw only two European residents at Coepang; one was the surgeon of whom captain Bligh speaks so handsomely in his narrative, the other a young gentleman named Viertzen, who had lately arrived.

Coepang has little other trade than with Batavia. Sandel wood, bees-wax, honey, and slaves, are exported; and rice, arrack, sugar, tea, coffee, beetel nut, and the manufactures of China, with some from India and Europe, received in return; and the duties upon these were said to suffice the expense of keeping up the establishment. A vessel laden with ammunition, clothing, and other supplies for the troops, is annually sent from Batavia; but what may be called the trade of Coepang, is mostly carried on by the Chinese, some of whom are settled in the town, and have intermixed with the Malays.

Coepang Bay is exposed to the westward; but from the beginning of May to the end of October, the anchorage is secure; and there is little to apprehend from north-west winds after the middle of March, or before the middle of November; but the standing regulations of the Dutch company were, that until the first of May their vessels should lie under the north-east end of Pulo Samow, about five miles from Coepang; although Babao Road on the north side of the bay, of which Dampier speaks, was said to be a more secure and convenient anchorage. The commander of the American ship Hunter had gone under Samow, because he found the Dutch brig there; and although assured there was almost nothing to be apprehended in the bay, he feared to come up till encouraged by our example.

This ship was upon a trading speculation, and the commander was buying here sandel wood and bees-wax. For the best kind of wood he paid twenty dollars per picol, for the inferior sort thirteen, and seven dollars for the refuse; and bees-wax cost him twenty-five dollars. Upon all these he expected to make three hundred per cent. at Canton, besides the advantage of paying for them with cutlasses, axes, and other iron tools, at an equally great advance; he reported, however, that iron was still more valuable at Solor, Flores, and the neighbouring islands; and that supplies of fresh provisions were more plentiful. The usual profits of trade here, seemed to be cent. per cent. upon every exchange; and this the commander of the Hunter proposed to make many times over, during his voyage. At Solor he had bought some slaves for two muskets each, which muskets he had purchased at the rate of 18s. in Holland, at the conclusion of the war; these slaves were expected to be sold at Batavia, for eighty, or more probably for a hundred dollars individually, making about thirty capitals of the first price of his muskets. If such advantages attend this traffic, humanity must expect no weak struggle to accomplish its suppression; but what was the result of this trading voyage? That the commander and his crew contracted a fever at Diely, and nearly the whole died before they reached Batavia.

Spanish dollars were rated at 5s. 4d. according to the Dutch company's regulations, but their currency at Coepang was sixty stivers or pence; whence it arose that to a stranger receiving dollars, they would be reckoned at 5s. 4d. each, but if he paid them it was at 5s. Besides dollars, the current coins were ducatoons, rupees, and doits, with some few gold rupees of Batavia; but the money accounts were usually kept in rix dollars, an imaginary coin of 4s.

I made many inquiries concerning the Malay trepang fishers, whom we had met at the entrance of the Gulph of Carpentaria, and learned the following particulars. The natives of Macassar had been long accustomed to fish for the trepang amongst the islands in the vicinity of Java, and upon a dry shoal lying to the south of Rottee; but about twenty years before, one of their prows was driven by the north-west monsoon to the coast of New Holland, and finding the trepang to be abundant, they afterwards returned; and had continued to fish there since that time. The governor was of opinion, that the Chinese did not meet them at Timor-laoet, but at Macassar itself, where they are accustomed to trade for birds nests, trepang, sharks fins, etc.; and it therefore seems probable that the prows rendezvous only at Timor-laoet, on quitting Carpentaria, and then return in a fleet, with their cargoes.

The value of the common trepang at Canton, was said to be forty dollars the picol, and for the best, or black kind, sixty; which agrees with what I had been told in Malay Road, allowing to the Chinese the usual profit of cent. per cent. from Macassar to their own country.

About ten days before our arrival, a homeward-bound ship from India had touched at Coepang; and had we been so fortunate as to meet with her, it might have enabled me to put in execution the plan I had formed of sending an officer to England, and returning to the examination of the north and north-west coasts of Terra Australis. This plan was now frustrated; and the sole opportunity of writing to Europe was by captain Johnson, who expected to sail for Batavia in May, and promised to forward our letters from thence. I committed to his care an account of our examinations and discoveries upon the East and North Coasts, for the Admiralty; with the report of the master and carpenter upon the state of the ship, and the information I had obtained of the trepang fishery.

Our supplies for the ship, procured at Coepang, were rice, arrack, sugar, and the palm syrup called *gulah*; with fresh meat, fruit, and vegetables during our stay, and for ten days afterwards. The animal food consisted of young *karabow*, a species of buffalo, and of small pigs and kids; the karabow being charged at eight, the pigs at five, and kids at two rix dollars each. Vegetables were dear and not good, and for many of the fruits we were too early in the season; but cocoa-nuts, oranges, limes, bananas, and shaddocks were tolerably plentiful. Tea, sugar candy, and some other articles for our messes, were purchased at the little shops kept by the Chinese-Malays; and poultry was obtained along-side by barter.

To judge from the appearance of those who had resided any length of time at Coepang, the climate is not good; for even in comparison with us, who had suffered considerably, they were sickly looking people. Yet they did not themselves consider the colony as unhealthy, probably from making their comparison with Batavia; but they spoke of Diely, the Portuguese settlement, as very bad in this respect. Captain Baudin had lost twelve men from dysentery, during his stay at Coepang, and I found a monument which he had erected to his principal gardener; but it was even then beginning to decay.

The *latitude* of our anchorage, three-fifths of a mile to the north of Fort Concordia, was 10° 8' 2" from seven meridian altitudes of the sun; but these being all taken to the north, I consider it to be more correctly, 10° 8½' S.

Longitude of the anchorage and fort, from fifty four sets of lunar distances, of which the particulars are given in Table VII. of the Appendix No. I., 123° 35' 46" E.

Lieutenant Flinders took altitudes from the sea horizon, between April 1 p.m. and 8 a.m., for the rates of the time keepers; the mean of which, with the errors from mean Greenwich time at noon there on the last day of observation, were as under:

Earnshaw's No. 543, slow 2h 57' 14.56", and losing 16.73", per day, Earnshaw's No. 520, fast 1h 57' 19.28", and losing 33.99", per day;

the rate of No. 543 differing only 0.2" from that with which we had left Caledon Bay. The longitude given by this time keeper on April 1, p.m., with the Caledon rate, was 123° 39' 8.4" east, or 3' 22" more than the lunars; and when the Caledon rate is accelerated, the difference is only 2' 3½" east. This quantity, if the longitudes of Caledon and Coepang Bays be correct, is the sum of the irregularities of No. 543, during the fifty-one days between one station and the other. The time keeper No. 520 had been let down on the passage, and its rate being now more than 3" greater than at Caledon Bay, its longitude was not attended to at this time.

In laying down the coasts and islands of Arnhem's Land, the bearings and observed latitudes were used, with very little reference to the time keepers; but No. 543, when corrected, did not differ so much from the survey as 1' in twenty-five days. The rest of the track, from Wessel's Islands to Coepang, is laid down by this time keeper with the accelerated rate, and the application of a proportional part of 2' 3½", its irregularity during fifty-one days.

Variation of the surveying compass, 0° 46' west, observed when the ship's head was E. S. E., or corrected to the meridian, 0° 37' east; but this variation seems to apply only to Coepang Bay; for about two degrees to the eastward it was 1° 4' west, corrected, and one degree to the south-west it was 1° 41' west.

The flood *tide* comes from the southward, through Samow Strait, and rises from three to nine or ten feet; high water usually took place as the moon passed under and over the meridian, but the winds make a great difference both in the time and rise of the tide.

CHAPTER X.

Departure from Timor.
Search made for the Trial Rocks.
Anchorage in Goose-Island Bay.
Interment of the boatswain, and sickly state of the ship's company.
Escape from the bay, and passage through Bass' Strait.
Arrival at Port Jackson.
Losses in men.
Survey and condemnation of the ship.
Plans for continuing the survey;
but preparation finally made for returning to England.
State of the colony at Port Jackson.

[FROM TIMOR. TOWARDS CAPE LEEUWIN.]
FRIDAY 8 APRIL 1803
(Atlas, Plate XVI.)

When we stretched out of Coepang Bay on the 8th of April, the wind was light from the westward; in the afternoon we tacked towards Pulo Samow, hoping that a canoe seen under the land might have the two deserters on board; but this not being the case, they were given up. At six in the evening, when we stood off, the town of Coepang bore S. 60° E., six or seven miles, and the north point of Samow distant one mile, with the north-west extremity behind it, S. 70° W. In this situation the depth was 74 fathoms, and soon afterwards 130 did not reach the bottom.

During the night the breeze veered to the south and eastward, and in the morning [SATURDAY 9 APRIL 1803] to north-east, and we coasted along the west side of Samow, four or five miles off, without getting soundings; it is woody, hilly land, but not mountainous, and toward the south end is quite low. A woody islet, called Tios in the charts, lies off the south-west point, which is the sole thing like danger on the west side of Samow; but the tides run strong here, and make ripplings which at first alarm, from their great resemblance to breakers.

SUNDAY 10 APRIL 1803

It was evening on the 10th before we had any regular wind; it then sprung up from the southward, and at six, when we made sail,

Samow, north-west point, bore   N. 48° E. Tios, dist. 5 miles, the south extreme,   S. 60 E. Rottee, furthest visible parts,   S. 51½° E. to 18 W.

The island Sauw, or Savu came in sight to the westward next morning [MONDAY 11 APRIL 1803], and also a small isle called Douw or Dowa, lying off the west end of Rottee; at noon, when our latitude was 10° 37' 22" and longitude 122° 35½',

Savu bore from the mast head,   N. 76° to 88° W. Rottee, furthest visible parts, S. 84 to 45 E. Dowa, distant ten miles,   S. 35 to 20 E.

We tried for soundings with 230 fathoms of line, without finding ground; and it should appear that there is no bottom amongst these islands at any reasonable depth, unless very near the shores.

The wind was still light; and on the following day [TUESDAY 12 APRIL 1803] we had rain, thunder, and lightning. Savu was seen in a clear interval towards evening, bearing N. 3° W., and another piece of land, apparently Benjoar, was perceived from the mast head to the N. N. W.; this was the last sight we had of these islands, for the breeze freshened up from the eastward, and at noon next day [WEDNESDAY 13 APRIL 1803] our latitude was 12° 20' south.

Having been disappointed in procuring salt provisions and the means of sending an officer to the Admiralty from Coepang, I had necessarily given up the project of going back to the north coast of Terra Australis; but since the decay of the ship did not appear to have advanced so rapidly as was expected, I judged there would not be much hazard in taking this opportunity of executing the article of my instructions, which directed me "to examine as particularly as circumstances would allow, the bank which extends itself from the Trial Rocks towards Timor." (Atlas, Plate I.) Upon what authority the bank was thus described, I had no information; but that it did not reach so far as either Timor or Rottee, was proved by our having passed the west end of the latter island and sounded with more than 200 fathoms

118

without finding bottom. It seemed to me probable, that if such a bank existed and had any connexion to the north-east, it was more likely to be with the Sahul Shoal than with Timor; and I therefore steered a course to get upon the line between the two; proposing afterwards to run westward, across the line of direction from the Rocks to Timor, so as in either case to fall in upon the bank.

We sounded every two hours, and hove to three times a day, to get a greater depth; and in this way ran S. W. until the 16th [SATURDAY 16 APRIL 1803] at noon, to latitude 16° 15' and longitude 116° 45', without finding bottom with from 100 to 240 fathoms of line. Our course was then W. by S., sounding in the same manner, until the 21st [THURSDAY 21 APRIL 1803] in the morning, to latitude 17° 45' and longitude 107° 58', but equally without success as to the bank; and I then hauled to the wind at S. E,. in order to make the rocks themselves.

The Trial Rocks obtained their name from the English ship Trial, which was lost upon them in 1622; but their exact situation seemed not to be well known. Mr. Dalrymple had published a sketch of them upon the authority of a Dutch sloop, apparently sent from Batavia expressly for their examination; and in this they are described to lie in 19° 30' south, eighty leagues from the coast of New Holland; but Arrowsmith in his large chart of the South Sea, laid the Trial Rocks down in 20° 40' south, and 104° 30' east, or near double the distance from the coast. The soundings of two East-Indiamen near the rocks, given in the South-Sea chart, stamped this last position with an authority which decided my opinion in its favour, and I accordingly steered for it.

Dull weather, with frequent heavy rain, thunder, and lightning, had prevailed from the time of leaving Coepang, and it produced the same effect upon the health of the ship's company as similar weather had before done in the Gulph of Carpentaria; for we had at this time ten men in the sick list with diarrhoea, and many others were slightly affected. It seemed possible that the change of food, from salt provisions to the fresh meat, fruit, and vegetables of Timor--a change by which I hoped to banish every appearance of scurvy, might have had an influence in producing the disease; and if so, it was avoiding Scylla to fall upon Charybdis, and was truly unfortunate.

SATURDAY 23 APRIL 1803

At noon of the 23rd, we had reached the latitude 20° 50', and were in longitude 105° 13' east, without having had soundings at 100 fathoms; I then steered a west course, lying to from eight in the evening till daylight; and at the following noon [SUNDAY 24 APRIL 1803] we observed in 20° 49' south, and the longitude was 103° 49' east. This was more than half a degree to the west of Mr. Arrowsmith's position, and we neither had soundings at 140 fathoms, nor any thing in sight to betoken the vicinity of land; I therefore ran N. W. to get somewhat to the north of the latitude 20° 40', and at dusk hauled up to the wind, as near to east as the ship could lie, to make further search in that direction.

On the 25th, some tropic birds were seen; and the next day [TUESDAY 26 APRIL 1803], when our latitude was 20° 36' and longitude 104° 55', there were several birds of the petrel kind about the ship; very vague signs of land, it is true, but still they gave us hopes; and once we were flattered with the appearance of breakers, and bore away for them, but it was a deception. We continued to stretch eastward all the next day [WEDNESDAY 27 APRIL 1803]; but the wind having veered from south to S. E., a good deal of northing was made with it; and having reached the latitude 19° 53' and longitude 106° 41', without finding bottom, or any more signs of land, I tacked to the S. S. W. and gave up the search.

It should appear from our examination, that the Trial Rocks do not lie in the space comprehended between the latitudes 20° 15' and 21° south, and the longitudes 103° 25' and 106° 30' east. That they exist, does not seem to admit of a doubt, and probably they will be found near the situation assigned to them by the Dutch sloop; but no bank can extend in a line from thence at all near to Timor. The variations of the compass observed during our search for the Trial Rocks, were 3° west with the head N. W., 5° 11' at E. by S., and 5° 38' at E. S.E.; and the mean, corrected to the meridian, will be 3° 43' west, in 20° 33' south and 104° 20' east longitude.

From the 27th of April we steered eight days to the S. S. W., mostly with south-eastern winds; they were sometimes light, but occasionally fresh, and at these times the ship made five inches of water in the hour. The diarrhoea on board was gaining ground, notwithstanding all the attention paid to keeping the ship dry and well aired, and the people clean and as comfortable as possible. Some of the officers began to feel its attack; and in order to relieve them and the people, now that we had no expectation of meeting danger, I directed the ship's company to be divided into three watches, and put the officers to four; giving Mr. Denis Lacy, master's mate, the charge of acting lieutenant in the fourth watch.

THURSDAY 5 MAY 1803

On May 5, in latitude 26° 24' and longitude 103° 21', the south-east wind died away, and a breeze sprung up from the opposite quarter, which veered afterwards to the S. W., blowing fresh with squally, moist weather. Our course was then directed for Cape Leeuwin, with the wind usually a-beam; the sea being too high for the ship to make good way any nearer. In this passage we were accompanied by several petrels, and amongst them by the albatross, the first of which had been seen in the latitude 23°

FRIDAY 13 MAY 1803

On the 13th, we had reached the parallel of Cape Leeuwin, and were steering E. by S., to make it. At six in the evening, tried for soundings with 180 fathoms, without finding ground; but after running S. 67° E. twenty-six miles, we had 75 fathoms, fine white sand; and at daylight [SATURDAY 14 MAY 1803] the land was seen, bearing N. 23° to 52° E. about eight leagues. (Atlas, Plate II.) The soundings should therefore seem not to extend more than ten or twelve leagues to the west, or but little further than the land will be visible in fine weather.

Our latitude at noon was 34° 43', and the land of Cape Leeuwin bore from N. 2° to 22° E.; the uncorrected longitude of the time keepers from Timor made the cape four or five leagues to the east of the position before ascertained, but when corrected, the difference was too small to be perceptible. At six in the evening we had 40 fathoms, coral bottom, at seven leagues from Point D'Entrecasteaux; but the weather was too thick to take any bearings which might improve my former survey. We steered along the coast at the distance of seven or eight leagues, with a fresh breeze and a strong current in our favour; and on the next day [SUNDAY 15 MAY 1803] at noon I set land, which had the appearance of Bald Head, at N. 31° W., distant about five leagues. Mount Gardner and Bald Island were distinguished in the afternoon; but the land was visible at times only, from the haziness of the weather.

[FROM TIMOR. ARCHIPELAGO OF THE RECHERCHE.]

My intention in coming so near the South Coast, was to skirt along the outer parts of the Archipelago of the Recherche, which had before been seen imperfectly; and to stop a day or two in Goose-Island Bay, for the purposes of procuring geese for our sick people, seal oil for our lamps, and a few casks of salt from the lake on Middle Island. It was night [MONDAY 16 MAY 1803] when we approached the archipelago, and I therefore steered to make Termination Island, which is the outermost part; at four in the morning of the 17th [TUESDAY 17 MAY 1803], it was seen about two leagues to the N. E, and we had 62 fathoms on a bottom of white sand. Mondrain Island was set at daylight, and the positions of many other places were either verified or corrected, during the run to noon; at that time we had 45 fathoms, and a reef was seen which may probably be that marked *Vigie*, in the French chart, and is the more dangerous from the sea breaking upon it only at times. No observation was obtained for the latitude, but it should be 34° 13' south, from the following bearings then taken.

Western Twin,   N. 5° W. A nearer isle, surrounded with breakers, N. 3 E. Cape Arid, top of the mount on it,   N. 53 E. Middle I., highest top of the mount,   N. 66½ E. Douglas's Isles, two appearing in one,   N. 80 E. High breakers, distant 6 miles,   S. 42 E.

At one o'clock in steering for Douglas's Isles, a single breaker was seen right ahead of the ship, lying six miles N. E. ½ N. of the former dangerous reef, and about eight from the isles, in a W. by ½ S. direction. We passed to the northward of it, having no ground at 25 fathoms; and as we approached to do the same by the isles, Mr. Charles Douglas, the boatswain, breathed his last; and I affixed his name to the two lumps of land, which seemed to offer themselves as a monument to his memory. We hauled up close along the east side of Middle Island with the wind at west; and at six in the evening anchored in Goose-Island Bay, in 12 fathoms, fine sand, one-third of a mile from the middle rock. and nearly in a line between it and the north-east point of Middle Island.

WEDNESDAY 18 MAY 1803

In the morning, a party of men was sent to kill geese and seals upon the rocky islets to the eastward, and another upon Middle Island to cut wood and brooms. There was now so much more surf upon the shores of the bay than in January of the former year, that we could not land at the eastern beach, behind which lies the salt lake; I therefore went with the master to the middle beach, and being scarcely able to get out of the boat from scorbutic sores, sent him to examine the lake and make choice of a convenient place for filling some casks; but to my surprise he reported that no good salt could be procured, although it had been so abundant before, that according to the testimony of all those who saw the lake, it would have furnished almost any quantity: this alteration had doubtless been produced by the heavy rains which appeared to have lately fallen. I caused a hole to be dug in a sandy gully, in order to fill a few casks of water, thinking it possible that what we had taken in at Timor might have been injurious; but the water was too salt to be drinkable, although draining from land much above the level of the sea. This may afford some insight into the formation of salt in the lake; and it seems not improbable, that rock salt may be contained in some part of Middle Island.

We remained here three days, cutting wood, boiling down seal oil, and killing geese; but our success in this last occupation was very inferior to what it had been in January 1802, no more than twelve geese being now shot, whereas sixty-five had then been procured. Mr. Douglas was interred upon Middle Island, and an inscription upon copper placed over his grave; William Hillier, one of my best men, also died of dysentery and fever before quitting the bay, and the surgeon had fourteen others in his list, unable to do any duty. At his well-judged suggestion, I ordered the cables, which the small size of the ship had made it necessary to coil between decks, to be put into the holds, our present light state permitting this to be done on clearing away the empty casks; by this arrangement more room was made for the messing and sleeping places; and almost every morning they were washed with boiling water, aired with stoves, and sprinkled with vinegar, for the surgeon considered the dysentery on board to be approaching that state when it becomes contagious.

SATURDAY 21 MAY 1803

At daylight of the 21st, having a fresh breeze at N. W., we prepared to depart, and hove short; but the ship driving before the sails were loosed, and there being little room astern, a second bower was dropped and a kedge anchor carried out. This last not holding after the bowers were weighed, a stream anchor was let go; and before the ship brought up, it was again necessary to drop the best bower. At this time we were not more than a cable's length from the rocks of Middle Island; and the ship being exposed to great danger with the least increase of wind, we got a spring on the stream cable and began to heave on the best bower. In the mean time the ship drove with both anchors ahead, which obliged me, on the instant, to cut both cables, heave upon the spring, and run up the jib and stay-sails; and my orders being obeyed with an alacrity not to be exceeded, we happily cleared the rocks by a few fathoms, and at noon made sail to the eastward.

This example proved the anchorage in the eastern part of Goose-Island Bay to be very bad, the sand being so loose as not to hold the ship with two anchors, though the water was smooth and the wind not more than a double-reefed-top-sail breeze; yet further westward, between Goose Island and the west beach, our anchor had held very well before. The most secure situation should seem to be off the east end of the middle beach, between it and the rock, in 4 or 5 fathoms; but I cannot answer for the ground there being good, though to all appearance it should be the best in the bay.

The *latitude* observed from an artificial horizon on the middle beach was 34° 5' 23" south; and the *longitude* of the place of observation, a little east of that before fixed by the time keepers from King George's Sound, (Vol. I.), will be 123° 9' 37.6" east. Mr. Flinders took three sets of altitudes between the 18th p.m. and 21st a.m., from which the rates of the time keepers, and their errors from Greenwich time at noon there of the 21st, were found to be as under;

Earnshaw's No. 543, slow 3h 10' 59.53" and losing 19.63" per day. Earnshaw's No. 520, fast 1h 31' 54.28" and losing 34.07" per day.

At the first observation, the longitudes deduced from the Coepang rates were, by No. 543--123° 33' 37.5" east, No. 520--123 25 22.5 east;

the mean of which is 19' 52.4" more than what I consider to be the true longitude, but on using rates equally accelerated from those at Coepang to what were found above, the error becomes reduced to 12' 11.6" east; which is the sum of the apparent irregularity of the time keepers from April 8 to May 18, or in 40.2 days. The corrections applied to the longitude during the last passage, are therefore what arise from the equal acceleration of the rates, and from the proportional part of the 12' 11.6" of irregularity; and when thus corrected, the time keepers did not appear to differ at Cape Leeuwin and Mount Gardner more than 1' from the longitude of the former year.

[SOUTH COAST. TOWARDS PORT JACKSON]
SATURDAY 21 MAY 1803

On clearing Goose-Island Bay we steered eastward, with cloudy weather and a fresh breeze which veered to S. S. W. A small round island, with two rocks on its north side, was discovered in the south-eastern part of the archipelago, and also a reef; neither of which I had before seen, nor are they noticed by admiral D'Entrecasteaux. At 3h 40' the following bearings were taken:

Cape Arid, top of the mount, N. 74½° W. Cape Pasley, N. 26 W. Two south-east isles, S. 19 W. Reef, distant 4 or 5 miles, S. 16 E. Small round isle, dist. 4 or 5 leagues, N. 88 E.

We passed within three miles of the round isle at dusk, and saw no other danger near it than the two rocks, which are very distinguishable; the weather was squally, but as I did not expect to meet with any more dangers, we kept on, steering seven points from the wind all night, with the precaution of having a warrant officer at the lookout. In the way to Bass' Strait I wished to have completed the examination of Kangaroo Island, and also to run along the space of main coast, from Cape Northumberland to Cape Otway, of which the bad weather had prevented a survey in the former year; but the sickly state of my people from dysentery and fever, as also of myself, did not admit of doing any thing to cause delay in our arrival at Port Jackson.

MONDAY 23 MAY 1803
(Atlas, Plate III.)

In the afternoon of the 23rd, being in latitude 35° 10' and longitude 128° 54', the variation was observed with three compasses to be 4° 58' west, when the ship's head was at magnetic east; this corrected, will be 1° 46' west, agreeing with the observations on each side of this longitude in sight of the coast. On the 26th [THURSDAY 26 MAY 1803], in 37° 53' south and 135° 48' east, with the head S. E. by E., the variation was 1° 33' west, or 1° 17' east corrected; and in the same longitude at the head of Port Lincoln, we had found 1° 39' east. This day James Greenhalgh, sergeant of marines, died of the dysentery; a man whom I sincerely regretted, from the zeal and fidelity with which he had constantly fulfilled the duties of his situation.

The winds continued to blow strong, usually between South and W. S. W.; but the ship did not at any time leak more than five inches an hour. On the 29th [SUNDAY 29 MAY 1803], when approaching Bass' Strait, the breeze died away, and after some hours calm sprung up from the northward; next day at noon [MONDAY 30 MAY 1803], our latitude was 40° 25 1/3', longitude 143° 8', and we sounded with 98 fathoms, no ground (Atlas, Plate VI). At two o'clock the south end of King's Island was in sight; and at 4h 40', when it bore N. 5° to 35° E, a small island was seen from the mast head, bearing E. by S., which I at first judged must be Albatross Island; but as no other could be seen more southward, it was probably the Black Pyramid of Hunter's Isles, discovered in the Norfolk sloop. I much wished to fix its relative situation to King's Island; but night coming on, the bearing of S. 5° W., in which this pyramidal lump was set at ten o'clock with the assistance of a night glass, was the best point of connexion to be obtained. The southern extremity of King's Island lies nearly in 40° 7' south and 143° 53' east; and by our run from 4h 40' to ten o'clock, corrected for a tide setting to the south-westward, this lump of land, which I believe to have been the

Black Pyramid, will be 29' or 30' of longitude more east: its latitude made in the Norfolk was 40° 32' south.

The wind blew fresh at north, and the ship could barely lie a course to clear Albatross Island, yet we passed without seeing it, though there was moonlight; so that supposing it was the Black Pyramid we had set at ten o'clock, the tide, which I calculated to turn about that time, must have run strong to the N. E. Our least sounding between King's Island and Hunter's Isles was 28 fathoms, on red coral sand, nine or ten miles to the south, as I judge, of Reid's Rocks; but they were not seen, nor have I any certain knowledge of their position. They are laid down in the chart partly from the journal of lieutenant Murray, who saw them in going from the Bay of Seals to Three-hummock Island; but principally from a rough sketch of Mr. Bass, then commander of the brig Venus, who appears to have seen King's Island, Reid's Rocks, and the Black Pyramid, all at the same time.

It was a great mortification to be thus obliged to pass Hunter's Isles and the north coast of Van Diemen's Land, without correcting their positions in longitude from the errors which the want of a time keeper in the Norfolk had made unavoidable; but when I contemplated eighteen of my men below, several of whom were stretched in their hammocks almost without hope, and reflected that the lives of the rest depended upon our speedy arrival in port, every other consideration vanished; and I carried all possible sail, day and night, making such observations only as could be done without causing delay.

TUESDAY 31 MAY 1803

At day break, land was seen from the mast head bearing S. W. by S., probably Three-hummock Island; and at noon our

Latitude observed was   39° 5 1/3' Wilson's Promontory, the S. W. part, bore   N. 16 1/2 E. Curtis' largest Isle, the top,   N. 51 E.

Kent's Group came in sight in the evening; and a little before nine o'clock the centre of the larger isles was set at N. by E, when the Pyramid was distant four miles bearing S. ½ W. At eleven, we passed sufficiently near to the new rock, lying four leagues to the E. S. E. of the group, to hear the growling of the seals; and land, apparently the Sisters, was distinguished soon afterward in the S. E., but too imperfectly to be known. A set of bearings here would have been essentially useful in fixing the relative positions of these lands, which remained in some degree doubtful; but I dared not lose an hour's fair wind to obtain them.

THURSDAY 2 JUNE 1803

On the 2nd of June we lost John Draper, quarter master, one of the most orderly men in the ship; and it seemed to be a fatality, that the dysentery should fall heaviest on the most valuable part of the crew. The wind had then veered against us, to the N. E., as it had done the year before in nearly the same situation; and it should seem that the direction of the coast influences it to blow either from N. E. or S. W. The weather was so hazy, that the hills at the back of the Long Beach were not seen till the evening of the 3rd; and on the 4th [SATURDAY 4 JUNE 1803] they were still visible, about twenty leagues to the N. 31° W. A fair breeze sprung up in the night; and at noon next day, the land from Cape Howe northward extended from S. 65° to N. 72° W., and a hill which appeared to be the highest of those behind Two-fold Bay, bore W. 1° S.; our latitude was then 37° 13', and longitude by time keepers 150° 44' east.

We steered a due north course, closing a little in with the land; at sunset [MONDAY 6 JUNE 1803] Mount Dromedary bore N. 45° W., and at eight next morning it was seen bearing S. 30° W., at the distance of twenty leagues, although the weather was hazy (Atlas, Plate VIII). The shore was five miles off at noon, when the observed latitude was 35° 17'; the outer part of Cape George bearing N. 32° E., about eight miles, and the Pigeon House S. 77° W. We passed the cape at the distance of two miles, having then but light winds; and at dusk, Bowen's Isle in the entrance of Jervis' Bay was set at N. 51° W. Hat Hill was abreast of the ship at noon next day; but the wind had then veered to the northward, and we beat up until the following noon [WEDNESDAY 8 JUNE 1803] with little advantage, our situation being then in

Latitude observed.   34° 21 2/3' Longitude by time keepers corrected,
151 12 1/2 Hat Hill bore   S. 70½ W. Saddle Hill, on Red Point,   S. 53

W. Point Bass,　　　　　　　S. 33 W. North extreme, near C. Solander.,　 N. 3 W. Nearest shore, distant 8 or 9 miles, N. 72. W.

[EAST COAST. PORT JACKSON]

Whilst beating against this foul wind the dysentery carried off another seaman, Thomas Smith, one of those obtained from governor King; and had the wind continued long in the same quarter, many others must have followed. Happily it veered to the southward at midnight, we passed Botany Bay at three in the morning [THURSDAY 9 JUNE 1803], and at daybreak tacked between the heads of Port Jackson, to work up for Sydney Cove. I left the ship at noon, above Garden Island, and waited upon His Excellency governor King, to inform him of our arrival, and concert arrangements for the reception of the sick at the colonial hospital. On the following day [FRIDAY 10 JUNE 1803] they were placed under the care of Thomas Jamison, Esq., principal surgeon of the colony; from whom they received that kind attention and care which their situation demanded; but four were too much exhausted, and died in a few days. The first of them was Mr. Peter Good, botanical gardener, a zealous, worthy man, who was regretted by all.

Lieutenant Murray had arrived safely with the Lady Nelson, after a somewhat tedious passage from the Barrier Reefs; he made himself an anchor of heavy wood on the coast, for fear of accident to his sole remaining bower, but fortunately had no occasion to use it. Besides the Lady Nelson, we found lying in Sydney Cove H. M. armed vessel Porpoise, the Bridgewater extra-Indiaman, the ships Cato, Rolla, and Alexander, and brig Nautilus. The Géographe and Naturaliste had not sailed for the South Coast till some months after I left Port Jackson to go to the northward, and so late as the end of December, captain Baudin was lying at King's Island in Bass' Strait; it was therefore not very probable that he should reach the Gulph of Carpentaria by the middle of February, when I had finished its examination, nor even at the beginning of March, when the south-west monsoon would set in against him.

We found also at Port Jackson Mr. James Inman (the present professor of mathematics at the Royal Naval College, Portsmouth), whom the Board of Longitude had sent out to join the expedition as astronomer, in the place of Mr. Crosley who had left us at the Cape of Good Hope. To this gentleman's care I committed all the larger astronomical instruments, and also the time keepers, after observations had been taken to compare their longitudes with that of Cattle Point. The results obtained on the 10th a.m., with the Goose-island-Bay rates, were,

From No. 543, 151° 18' 41" east. From No. 520, 151 16 22 east.

Cattle Point having been settled in 151° 11' 49" (see Vol. I.), the mean error of the time keepers was 5' 42.5" to the east; and as I have no means to form an accelerating correction to the Goose-Island Bay rates, the 5' 42.5" of error has been equally apportioned throughout the twenty days between the two stations.

In order to re-establish the health of the ship's company, I contracted for a regular supply of vegetables and fresh meat; and such was the favourable change in the state of the colony in one year, that the meat, pork one day and mutton another, was obtained at the average price of 10d. per pound, which before, if it could have been obtained, would have cost nearly double the sum. On my application to the governor, the commissary was ordered to supply us with two pipes of port wine; and a pint was given daily to all those on board, as well as on shore, whose debilitated health was judged by the surgeon to require it.

The arrangements being made which concerned the health of the ship's company, I inclosed to the governor the report of the master and carpenter upon the state of the ship when in the Gulph of Carpentaria; and requested that he would appoint officers to make a survey of her condition. A plank was ripped off all round, a little above the water's edge; and on the 14th, the officers appointed by His Excellency made the survey, and their report was as follows:

Pursuant to an order from His Excellency Philip Gidley King, esquire, principal commander of His Majesty's ship Buffalo.

We whose names are hereunto subscribed, have been on board His Majesty's ship Investigator, and taken a strict, careful, and minute survey of her defects, the state of which we find to be as follows.

One plank immediately above the wales being ripped off all round the ship, we began the examination on the larbord side forward; and out of ninety-eight timbers we find eleven to be sound, so far as the ripping off of one plank enables us to see into them, ten of which are amongst the aftermost timbers. Sixty-three of the remaining timbers are so far rotten as to make it necessary to shift them; and the remaining twenty-four entirely rotten, and these are principally in the bow and the middle of the ship.

On the starbord side forward we have minutely examined eighty-nine timbers, out of which we find only five sound; fifty-six are so far decayed as to require shifting, and the remaining twenty-eight are entirely rotten. The sound timbers are in the after part of the ship, and those totally decayed lie principally in the bow.

The stemson is so far decayed, principally in its outer part, as to make it absolutely necessary to be shifted.

As far as we could examine under the counter, both plank and timbers are rotten, and consequently necessary to be shifted.

We find generally, that the plank on both sides is so far decayed as to require shifting, even had the timbers been sound.

The above being the state of the Investigator thus far, we think it altogether unnecessary to make any further examination; being unanimously of opinion that she is not worth repairing in any country, and that it is impossible in this country to put her in a state fit for going to sea.

And we do further declare, that we have taken this survey with such care and circumspection, that we are ready, if required, to make oath to the veracity and impartiality of our proceedings.

Given under our hands on board the said ship in Sydney Cove, this 14th June 1803.
(Signed) W. Scott, Commander of H. M. armed vessel Porpoise.
E. H. Palmer, Commander of the Hon. East-India-Company's extra ship Bridgewater.
Thomas Moore, Master builder to the Territory of New South Wales.

I went round the ship with the officers in their examination, and was excessively surprised to see the state of rottenness in which the timbers were found. In the starbord bow there were thirteen close together, through any one of which a cane might have been thrust; and it was on this side that the ship had made twelve inches of water in an hour, in Torres' Strait, before the first examination. In the passage along the South Coast, the strong breezes were from the southward, and the starbord bow being out of the water, the leaks did not exceed five inches; had the wind come from the northward, the little exertion we were then capable of making at the pumps could hardly have kept the ship up; and a hard gale from any quarter must have sent us to the bottom.

The Investigator being thus found incapable of further service, various plans were suggested, and discussed with the governor, for prosecuting the voyage; but that which alone could be adopted without incurring a heavy expense to government, was to employ the armed vessel Porpoise; and as this ship was too small to carry all my complement, with the necessary provisions, to put the remainder into the Lady Nelson, under the command of my second lieutenant. Both vessels were at this time required for a few weeks colonial service to Van Diemen's Land; and my people not being in a state to fit out a new ship immediately, our final arrangements were deferred until their return. I took this opportunity of making an excursion to the Hawkesbury settlement, near the foot of the back mountains; and the fresh air there, with a vegetable diet and medical care, soon made a great alteration in the scorbutic sores which had disabled me for four months; and in the beginning of July I returned to the ship, nearly recovered. The sick in the hospital were also convalescent, and some had quitted it; but one or two cases still remained doubtful.

4 JULY 1803

On the 4th, the Porpoise arrived from Van Diemen's Land, and I requested the governor would order her to be surveyed, that it might be duly known whether she were, or could be in a short time made, capable of executing the service which remained to be done. I had heard some reports of her being unsound; and it seemed worse than folly to be at the trouble and expense of fitting out a ship which, besides causing a repetition of the risk we had incurred in the Investigator, might still leave the voyage unfinished. His Excellency, with that prompt zeal for His Majesty's service which characterised him, and was eminently shown in every thing wherein my voyage was concerned, immediately ordered the survey to be made; and it appeared that, besides having lost part of the copper which could not be replaced, the repairs necessary to make her fit for completing what remained of the voyage, could not be done in less than twelve months; and even then this ship was, from her small size and sharp construction, very ill adapted to this service. Other arrangements were therefore suggested; and I received the following letter of propositions from the governor.

Government House, Sydney, July 10, 1803.

I inclose the report of the survey on the Porpoise, and am much concerned that the repairs and alterations of that ship will require so much time to complete her fit for the service you have to execute. This being the case, I can see no other alternatives than the following:

    1. To wait the Porpoise being repaired and refitted.
    2. To purchase the Rolla, and fit her.
    3. To take the Lady Nelson and colonial schooner Francis.
    4. Wait for the Buffalo's return from India, which will be about the next January; or
    5. Return to England and solicit another ship to complete what you have so successfully begun.

On the first point, you will be the best able to determine how far it would be advisable to wait so long a time for the Porpoise's repairs, nor do I think they can be completed in a less time here.

The builder and your carpenter report to me, that the Rolla cannot be put into the least convenient state to receive your establishment, stores, and provisions, in less than six months. It must also be considered that she grounded on the Brake with a full cargo; from which cause, some defects may appear to render her useless in a shorter period than you can finish your voyage. Added to which, I do not consider myself justified in assuming the responsibility of giving £11,550. for little more than the hull, masts, and rigging of that ship; nor will the master, as he informs me, take less.

If you think the Lady Nelson and Francis schooner equal to execute what you have to finish, they are at your service. The latter being absent getting coals and cedar, I cannot say what state she may be in; although she will require considerable repairs to make her fit for a long voyage.

The Buffalo is now inspecting the islands to the eastward of Java, to ascertain whether breeding stock can be procured among them. That service performed, she proceeds to Calcutta for a cargo of cows, and may be expected about January, when she may want some repairs, and of course fitting. It is my intention, if you do not fix on her, to profit by your discovery in stocking this colony with breeding animals, by the safe and expeditious channel you have opened through Torres' Strait.

If you do not consider waiting for the Porpoise's repairs advisable, it is my intention to send her to England by a summer's passage round Cape Horn; which it is thought she may perform in her present state. But should you conceive it may ultimately forward the service you are employed on, to go to England in her, leaving this port when you judge proper, and taking the route most conducive to perfectioning any part of the surveys you have commenced; I shall direct the commander of that ship to receive you and as many of your officers and people as can be accommodated, as passengers; and to follow your directions and give you every assistance in every circumstance connected with the execution of the orders you have received from my Lords Commissioners of the Admiralty.

You will, Sir, have the goodness to consider of the above and whatever the result of your deliberation may be, I will most cheerfully give my concurrence and assistance; knowing that your zealous perseverance in wishing to complete the service you have so beneficially commenced, could only be impeded by unforeseen and distressing circumstances; but which I hope, for the benefit of science and navigation, will only be a temporary delay.

    I am, etc.
    (Signed), Philip Gidley King.

Each of the plans proposed in the governor's letter were attended with one common disadvantage: a delay in the completion of the surveys. Against the last proposition there did not seem to be any other objection; but the four first included so many more inconveniences and difficulties, either to the voyage, or to the colony, that I saw the necessity of concurring with the governor's opinion; notwithstanding the reluctance I felt at returning to England without having accomplished the objects for which the Investigator was fitted out. My election was therefore made to embark as a passenger in the Porpoise; in order to lay my charts and journals before the Lords Commissioners of the Admiralty, and obtain, if such should be their pleasure, another ship to complete the examination of Terra Australis. The last service I could render to the colony with the Investigator and my people, was to lay down an additional pair of moorings in Sydney Cove; and that done, we left the ship as a storehouse hulk on the 21st, and prepared for our voyage to England.

The Porpoise was commanded by Mr. William Scott, a senior master in the navy; but he and the greater part of his people having expressed a wish to be discharged, it was complied with; and the command was given to Mr. Fowler, first lieutenant of the Investigator, and another crew of thirty-eight men selected from the ship's company. In disposing of the other officers and people their several inclinations were consulted. The surgeon took his passage in the Bridgewater to India, the gunner remained charged with the care of the Investigator's stores, and Mr. Evans, master's mate, was left sick at the hospital; Messrs. Brown, Bauer, and Allen stayed at Port Jackson to prosecute their researches in natural history, until my arrival with another ship, or until eighteen months should expire without their having received intimation that the voyage was to be continued; nine men were discharged at their own request, and the twenty-two remaining officers and men, including myself, embarked in the Porpoise as passengers.

Of the nine convicts who had been received into the Investigator, one had died; another had behaved himself so improperly, that I could not recommend him to the governor; and the remaining seven were fully emancipated by His Excellency from their sentence of transportation, their conduct having been such throughout, as to receive my approbation. Four of these were entered into the complement of the Porpoise; but I am sorry to add, that the subsequent behaviour of two was different to what it had been when their liberty was at stake, and that a third was condemned to the hulks not very long after he reached England.

Being about to take leave of Port Jackson, it might be expected that I should give some account of our colony there, and could this voyage have appeared in due time, a chapter would have been devoted to it; but a much later account being now before the public, dispenses me from speaking of it in other than a few general terms. In 1803, it was progressively advancing towards a state of independence on the mother country for food and clothing; both the wild and tame cattle had augmented in a proportion to make it probable that they would, before many years, be very abundant; and manufactures of woollen, linen, cordage, and leather, with breweries and a pottery, were commenced. The number of inhabitants was increasing rapidly; and that energetic spirit of enterprize which characterises Britain's children, seemed to be throwing out vigorous shoots in this new world. The seal fishery in Bass' Strait was carried on with ardour--many boats were employed in catching and preparing fish along the coast--sloops and schooners were upon the stocks--various detached settlements were in a course of establishment, and more in project. And all this, with the commerce carried on from Sydney to Parramatta and the villages at the head of the port, and to those on the rivers falling into Broken and Botany Bays, made the fine harbour of Port Jackson a lively scene of business, highly interesting to the contemplator of the rise of nations.

In Sydney and Parramatta, houses of stone or brick were taking place of wood and plaster; a neat church was built in the latter, and one commenced in the former place; wharfs were constructing or repairing--a stone bridge over the stream which runs through the town of Sydney was nearly finished--and the whiskey, chariot, and heavy-laden waggon were seen moving on commodious roads to different parts of the colony. In the interior the forests were giving way before the axe, and their places becoming every year more extensively occupied by wheat, barley, oats, maize, and the vegetables and fruits of southern Europe; but the following extract from the official returns in 1803, the fifteenth year after the establishment of the colony, will show its progress in a more ostensible manner.

Lands employed by government, or granted to individuals   125,476 acres. Quantity cleared of wood,   16,624 Ditto, sown with wheat,   7,118 Last ann. increase 2,165 Ditto, sown with barley, maize, etc. 5,279 Average produce of wheat lands throughout the colony,   18 bushels/acre. No. of horned cattle domesticated, 2,447 Last increase   594 No. of Sheep,   11,232   2,614 No. of Hogs,   7,890   3,872 No. of Horses,   352 65 The number of wild horned cattle was supposed to exceed that of the tame, and to increase faster. Europeans of every description, resident in New South Wales,   7,134 Of which were victualled by government,   3,026 Number of inhabitants at Norfolk Island, 1,200

Amongst the obstacles which opposed themselves to the more rapid advancement of the colony, the principal were, the vicious propensities of a large portion of the convicts, a want of more frequent communication with England, and the prohibition to trading with India and the western coasts of South America, in consequence of the East-India-Company's charter. As these difficulties become obviated and capital increases, the progress of the colonists will be more rapid; and if the resources from government be not withdrawn too early, there is little doubt of New South Wales being one day a flourishing country, and of considerable benefit to the commerce and navigation of the parent state.

CHAPTER XI.
Of the winds, currents, and navigation along the east coast of Terra Australis, both without and within the tropic; also on the north coast.

Directions for sailing from Port Jackson, through Torres' Strait, towards India or the Cape of Good Hope.

Advantages of this passage over that round New Guinea.

[EAST COAST. WINDS AND CURRENTS.]

On completing the first portion of the voyage, I entered into an explanation of the winds and currents which had been found to prevail upon the south coast of Terra Australis; and to obtain greater perspicuity and connection, I there anticipated upon the second portion so far as those subjects required. This plan of assembling at the end of each book such general observations upon the coast immediately before examined as could not enter conveniently into the narrative, seeming liable to no material objection, I shall follow it here; and conclude this second part of the voyage with a statement of the winds and currents which appear to prevail most generally along the East and North Coasts; adding thereto such remarks, more particularly on Torres' Strait, as may tend to the safety of navigation. This statement will include the information gained in a subsequent passage, for the reasons which influenced me in the former account; and the reader must not be surprised, should he remark hereafter that I did not, in that passage, follow very closely the directions here given; for besides that my information was then possessed only in part, the directions are intended, not for vessels seeking dangers, which was partly my object, but for those desirous only of navigating these distant shores with expedition and safety.

The East Coast, with respect to winds and currents, requires a division, the part beyond the tropic of Capricorn being placed under different, and almost opposite circumstances, to that within, or close to it. (Atlas, Plate I.)

From Cape Howe, where the South Coast terminates and the East commences, to Sandy Cape, within a degree of the tropic, the south-east trade most generally prevails in the summer season, from the beginning of October to the end of April; and produces sea and land breezes near the shore, with fine weather. There are however many occasional intermissions, especially in the southern parts, wherein gales from South or S. W., and strong breezes between North and N. E., bring heavy rain, with thunder and lightning; but these are usually of short duration. A sultry land wind from the N. W. in the summer, is almost certainly followed by a sudden gust from between S. E. and S. S. W., against which a ship near the coast should be particularly guarded; I have seen the thermometer descend at Port Jackson, on one of these occasions, from 100° to 64° in less than half an hour.

In the winter season, from May to September, the western winds are most prevalent, and generally accompanied with fine weather; the gales then blow from the eastward, between north-east and south, and bring rain with them; indeed there is no settled weather in the winter, with any winds from the sea, and even between north-west and north there is frequent rain, though the wind be usually light in those quarters. It is however to be understood, that the sea and land breezes in the summer are more regular near the tropic; and that the winter winds partake more of the south-east trade than they do from latitude 30° to Cape Howe.

It is a fact difficult to be reconciled, that whilst the most prevailing winds blow from S. E. in summer, and S. W. in winter, upon this extra-tropical part of the East Coast, the current should almost constantly set to the south; at a rate which sometimes reaches two miles an hour. Its greatest strength is exerted near to the points which project most beyond the general line of the coast; but the usual limits of its force may be reckoned at from four, to twenty leagues from the land. Further out, there seems to be no constancy in the current; and close in with the shore, especially in the bights, there is commonly an eddy setting to the northward, from a quarter, to one mile an hour. It is in the most southern parts that the current runs strongest, and towards Cape Howe it takes a direction to the eastward of south; whereas in other places, it usually follows the line of the coast.

This exposition of the winds and currents beyond the tropic, points out the advantage of keeping at not more than three or four leagues from the land, when sailing northward and intending to touch on the coast; but in the winter season this must be done with caution, because gales then often blow from the eastward. A marine barometer will here be of signal advantage. If the weather be tolerably fine, and the mercury do not stand above 30 inches, there is no probability of danger; but when the mercury much exceeds this elevation and the weather is becoming thick, a gale is to be apprehended; and a ship should immediately steer off, until it is seen how far the wind veers to blow dead on the coast. With respect to a rise and fall in the marine barometer, it may be taken as a general rule upon this East Coast, that a rise denotes either a fresher wind in the quarter where it then may be, or that it will veer more to seaward; and a fall denotes less wind or a breeze more off the land; moreover, the mercury rises highest with a south-east, and falls lowest with a north-west wind; and north-east and south-west are points of mean elevation.

The shelter for ships which may be caught so suddenly as not to be able to clear the land, are these: Two-fold Bay, for vessels of four-hundred tons and under; Jervis and Botany Bays, Port Jackson, and Broken Bay; Port Hunter for brigs and small craft; Port Stephens; Shoal Bay for vessels not exceeding fifty tons; Glass-house Bay; and lastly Hervey's Bay, by going round Break-sea Spit. All these places will be found in Plates VI, VIII, IX, and X. of the Atlas, with particular plans of the entrances to some of them. Directions for Port Jackson, and Botany and Broken Bays are given by captain Hunter in his voyage; and they may be found in Horsburgh's *East-India Directory*, Part II, p. 465-468. Two-fold Bay is described in the Introduction to this voyage, and mention made of Jervis, Shoal, Glass-house, and Hervey's Bays.

A ship sailing along this coast to the southward, should not, to have the advantage of the current, come nearer than five or six leagues unless to the projecting points; and if the distance were doubled, so as to have the land just in sight, an advantage would be found in it; and such an offing obviates the danger of the gales.

Whilst western winds prevail on the southern parts of the East Coast, the south-east trade blows with most regularity within, and close to the tropic, producing sea and land breezes near the shore, and serenity in the atmosphere; and the further we go northward the longer does this fine weather last, till, near Cape York, it commences with the month of April, probably even March, and extends to the middle or end of November. How the winds blow from November to April, I have no experience; but there is great reason to believe that they come from the northward, and make the wet season here, whilst dry weather prevails beyond the tropic. In Broad Sound and Shoal-water Bay we had more northern winds than any other, in the month of September; but these appeared to be altogether local, caused by the peculiar formation of the coast; for they did not bring any rain, though it was evidently near the end of the dry season, and we found the south-east trade wind before losing sight of the land.

[NORTH COAST. WINDS AND CURRENTS.]

The North Coast appears to have the same winds, with a little exception, as the tropical part of the East Coast. From March or April to November, the south-east trade prevails; often veering, however, to east, and even north-east, and producing fine weather, with sea and land breezes near the shore. At the head of the Gulph of Carpentaria, the north-west monsoon began to blow at the end of November; but further westward, at the northern Van Diemen's Land, I apprehend it will set in at the beginning of that month, and continue till near the end of March. This is the season of heavy rains, thunder, and lightning, and should seem, from our experience, to be the sickly time of the year.

It is thought to be a general rule, that a monsoon blowing directly in from the sea, produces rain, and from off the land, fine weather, with sea and land breezes; this I found exemplified on the west side of the Gulph of Carpentaria, where the rainy north-west monsoon, which then came off the land, brought fine weather: the rain came with eastern winds, which set in occasionally and blew strong for two or three days together. It seems even possible, that what may be the dry season on the North Coast in general, may be the most rainy on the west side of the Gulph; but of this I have doubts.

According to Dampier, the winds and seasons on the north-west coast of Terra Australis are nearly the same as above mentioned upon the North Coast; but he found the sea and land breezes, during the south-east monsoon, to blow with much greater strength.

In speaking of the currents, I return to the tropical part of the East Coast. Within the Barrier Reefs, it is not the current, for there is almost none, but the tides which demand attention; and these, so far as they came under my observation, have been already described, and are marked on the charts. At a distance from the barrier there is a current of some strength, at least during the prevalence of south-east winds; but instead of setting southward, as I have described it to do from Sandy Cape to Cape Howe, the current follows the direction of the trade wind, and sets to the north-west, with some variation on either side, at the rate of half a mile, and from thence to one mile an hour. This I found to continue amongst the reefs of Torres' Strait, nearly as far as Murray's Islands; but from thence onward through the strait, its direction in October was nearly west, something more than half a mile; and so continued across the Gulph of Carpentaria to Cape Arnhem, with a little inclination toward the south.

Along the north coast of Terra Australis, the current seems to run as the wind blows. In March, before the south-east monsoon was regularly set in, I found no determinate current until the end of the month, when Timor was in sight, and it then set westward, three quarters of a mile an hour; but in the November following, I carried it all the way from Cape Arnhem, as captain Bligh had done from Torres' Strait in September 1792; the rate being from half a mile to one mile and a quarter in the hour.

The navigation along the tropical part of the East Coast, within the Barrier Reefs, is not likely to be soon followed, any more than that round the shores of the Gulph of Carpentaria; nor does much remain to be said upon them, beyond what will be found in this Book II, and in the charts; and in speaking of the outer navigation, my remarks will be more perspicuous and useful if I accompany a ship from Port Jackson, through Torres' Strait; pointing out the courses to be steered, and the precautions to be taken for avoiding the dangers. It is supposed that the ship has a time keeper, whose rate of going and error from mean Greenwich time have been found at Sydney Cove, taking its longitude at 151° 11' 49" east; and that the commander is not one who feels alarm at the mere sight of breakers: without a time keeper I scarcely dare recommend a ship to go through Torres' Strait; and from timidity in the commander, perhaps more danger is to be anticipated than from rashness. The best season for sailing is June or July; and it must not be earlier than March, nor later than the end of September.

[NORTH COAST. SAILING DIRECTIONS.]

On quitting Port Jackson, the course to be steered is N. E. by E. by compass, to longitude about 155½°, when the land will be fifty leagues off; then North, also by compass, as far as latitude 24°. Thus far no danger lies in the way; but there is then the *Cato's Bank*, a dry sand frequented by birds and surrounded with a reef (Atlas, Plate X), and further northward is *Wreck Reef*, both discovered in the future part of this voyage. Wreck Reef consists of six distinct patches of coral, extending twenty miles east and west; upon four of them there are dry banks, also frequented by birds, and the easternmost bank is covered with wiry grass and some shrubs, and is called*Bird Islet*. Their situations are these:

Cato's Bank 23° 6' south, 155° 23' east Bird Islet 22 11½   155 27

The bearing and distance of these dangers must be successively worked, and a course steered so as to leave them half a degree to the westward; but for fear of an error in the time keeper the latitude 23° 20' should not be passed in the night. It is better to make short tacks till daylight, than to heave to; and allowance should be made for a probable current of one mile an hour to the north-west. A good lookout must be constantly kept; and a confidential officer should now go to the masthead every two hours in the day and to the fore yard at night, to listen as well as look; for in dark nights the breakers may often be heard before they can be seen. It will not be amiss, if the time of the day be favourable, to make Bird Islet, which is well settled, in order to see how the longitude by time keeper agrees; and should it err, the difference, or more, must be added to, or subtracted from its future longitudes; for it is most probable that the error will continue to augment the same way, more especially if the time keeper be a good one.

[TORRES STRAIT. SAILING DIRECTIONS.]
(Atlas, Plate I.)

Having passed Wreck Reef, there are no other *known* dangers near the route for Torres' Strait, till we come to *Diana's Bank*; but as others may exist, it will be prudent to lie to, or preferably to make short tacks in the night, during the rest of the passage to the Strait. In light nights, however, and moderate weather, there would be not much risk in closely following the Cumberland's track, carrying no more sail than will allow of the ship being conveniently hauled to the wind; but if an unusual number of boobies and gannets be seen in the evening, there is strong suspicion of a bank and reef being near; and the direction which the birds take, if they all go one way as is usual in an evening, will nearly show its bearing. The longitude of Diana's Bank, according to M. de Bougainville, is 151° 19' from Greenwich; but his longitude at the New Hebrides, some days before, was 54' too far east, according to captain Cook; and it is therefore most probable, that Diana's Bank lies in 15° 41' south, 150° 25' east.

I should steer, after passing Wreck Reef, so as to go a full degree to the east of this position; and having so done, the next object of attention is the Eastern Fields, reefs which lie a degree from those where Torres' Strait may be said to commence. The position to be worked is, Eastern Fields (Atlas, Plate XIII), north-east end, 10° 2' south, 145° 45' east; and from this I would pass half a degree to the eastward. But if the Strait should be attempted without a time keeper, it will be advisable for a ship to make that part of New Guinea lying in about 10° south and 147¾° east, which may be seen as far as twelve or fifteen leagues in clear weather; and having corrected the dead-reckoning longitude by this land, to allow afterwards eighteen miles a day for a current setting to the W. N. W. The best latitude for passing the Eastern Fields, is 9° 45' to 50', steering a W. by S. course, by compass; and it will afterwards be proper, so long as there is daylight and no reefs seen, to carry all sail for the Pandora's Entrance, which is the best opening yet known to the Strait. It is formed by reefs, and is eleven or twelve miles wide, and lies, Pandora's Entrance, the middle, in 9° 54' S., 144° 42' E. and it is very possible, if the Eastern Fields be passed in the morning, to get through without seeing the breakers, and obtain a sight of Murray's Islands before dark. But it is most probable that reefs will be first met with; and should the latitude of the ship be then uncertain, even to 5', the wind must be hauled until an observation can be had, for it is by the latitude alone that the first reefs can be distinguished one from the other.

The reefs being in sight and the latitude known, a ship will steer for the Pandora's Entrance, if she can fetch it; but if too much to the north, she may pass round the north end of Portlock's Reef, and haul up S. W. for Murray's Islands, which are visible eight or ten leagues from the deck in fine weather. (See View No. 10 in Plate XVIII. of the Atlas.) It is best to approach these islands from the N. E. by N., following the Investigator's track, and to anchor the first night on the north side of the largest island, or otherwise under the reefs which lie to the north-east; but if neither can be reached before dark, haul to the wind and make short trips till daylight, in the space between these reefs and Portlock's Reef.

Murray's Islands should not be passed, or quitted if the ship have anchored there, later than ten or eleven o'clock in the morning; because the sun will be getting ahead and obscure the sight before another good anchorage can be secured. On passing the islands, keep the reef which lies five miles to the north about a mile on the starbord hand, steering W. ½ S. by compass, with a boat ahead; for in this part there are many tide ripplings scarcely to be distinguished from the reefs. Having passed the ripplings, haul a point more to the southward; and after having run eight or ten miles, from the time that the largest island bore south, there will be very few reefs to the northward, and Darnley's Island will be seen. On the larbord hand there will be a great mass of reefs: and these it is necessary to follow at the distance of two or three miles, steering mostly W. S. W., and gradually more southward as they are found to trend. Some small patches will occasionally be met with; but having the boat to go ahead, and the commander, or a careful officer looking out aloft, the Investigator's track between them may be safely followed. The leading mark in all this part of the course, is the line of the great south-eastern reefs; and the situation of the ship may be known at any time, by laying down cross bearings of Murray's and Darnley's Islands on the chart, allowing, if the ship's head be westward and the compass on the top of the binnacle, 5° of east variation.

Several low, woody isles will come in sight ahead, or on the starbord bow; and before reaching the end of the south-eastern reefs, *Hay-way Island*, which is the southernmost of them, will be seen to the southwest; and here I would recommend the ship to anchor for the night. If this island can be passed, however, before three in the afternoon, and the sun do not obscure the sight, she may push on south-westward till an hour before sunset; and anchor under the lee of any of those sand banks which lie in the route, the ground being better here than in the eastern part of the Strait.

From Half-way Island, continue to follow the Investigator's track, steering S. W. to S. W. by W. by compass, as the small reefs and banks will allow; and here there is no necessity for a boat to be kept ahead. The flat top of one of the York Isles, called Mount Adolphus by captain Bligh, will be the first high land seen, and afterwards Mount Ernest; the cross bearings of which will show the situation on the chart, until the Double Isle, which makes as two small hummocks, comes in sight. Steer then for Double Isle, pass on the north side, and haul south-westward for Wednesday Island, which will be three leagues distant. Pass it also on the north side, about one mile, and the same by Hammond's Island, which lies next to it. There will be an extensive reef on the starbord hand, but the smallest distance between it and the islands is above two miles; and a W. S. W. course by compass, will lead fair through the passage, with soundings from 9 to 6 fathoms. Booby Isle will presently be seen a-head, appearing at first like a white sand bank; it may be passed within a mile or two on either side, and is the last of the dangers, if it can be classed under them, of Torres' Strait. A ship should afterwards steer, by compass, W. by S. thirty or forty miles; and the course may then be directed for any part of the world.

In case the approach of night, or any other circumstance should make it desirable, shelter may be had under the Prince of Wales' Islands, or under Booby Isle; and if a boat be sent on shore at dusk to Booby Isle, many birds, and perhaps some turtle' may be procured.

This passage through Torres' Strait will occupy from three to five days, according to the freshness of the south-east trade, and the degree of caution which a commander may see necessary to employ.* He will, of course, sound continually, though it have not been specified; and keep a boat ahead with sounding signals, from the time of passing Murray's Isles till Half-way Island is in sight, and wherever else there appears to him a necessity. Should he miss the Investigator's track in any part, which is very possible, there is no occasion for alarm; most, if not all the inner reefs have deep channels through them at every four or five miles, and by these he may regain the track, with the assistance of his boat.

[* The most expeditious passage known to have been made through the Strait, previously to the Investigator, was that of captains Bligh and Portlock, in nineteen days; the account of which, as also, that of Messrs. Bampton and Alt in the Introduction, a commander should previously read with the chart before him; and if he do the same with the passage of the Investigator, in Chapter V. of this Book II., and that of the Cumberland in Chapter III. following, he will have a tolerably correct notion of the dangers in Torres' Strait, and of the advantage in pursuing the route above described.]

The following precautions must not be neglected: a strict and constant look-out at the mast head, by the commander or his most confidential officer, all the time that the ship is amongst the reefs--not to pass Murray's Islands without seeing them, since they are the leading mark for getting into the proper track--and on anchoring there, or at any other inhabited island, a strict watch must be kept on the natives, who will come off in canoes to barter a few cocoa-nuts, plantains, and their arms, for hatchets and other iron ware. No boat should be sent to an island where there are inhabitants; but if distress make it necessary, two or three should go together, well armed; for they will certainly be attacked, if the Indians have been able to lay a plan and collect their strength. A British seaman will, at the same time, studiously avoid all cause of quarrel with these poor misguided people, and not fire upon them but where self-defence makes it indispensable.

Most of the dry sands and the uninhabited islands in the Strait appear to be frequented by turtle; and in the month of August, September, or later, it is probable some might be taken by landing a party of men, who should silently watch for their coming on shore at dusk. I do not know the kind of turtle most common in the Strait; at Booby Isle they were hawkes-bill, which furnish the finest tortoise shell, but are small and not the best for food.

The advantage in point of time, which this route presents to a ship bound from the Great Ocean to India, or to the Cape of Good Hope, will be best seen by a statement of two passages made at the same season; the one by Torres' Strait, the other round New Guinea.

I sailed from Port Jackson in company with the Bridgewater, an extra East-Indiaman; and we made Wreck Reef in eight days. From thence the Bridgewater steered round Louisiade, through Bougainville's Strait, Dampier's Strait, Pitt's Passage, and the Strait of Salayer; and arrived at Batavia in *eighty-eight days*. I left Wreck Reef some time afterward, in a small schooner of twenty-nine tons; took ten days to reach Torres' Strait, three to pass through it, seventeen to reach Coepang Bay, and ten days to pass the longitude of Java Head. Adding to these the eight days to Wreck Reef, the passage from Port Jackson to Java Head was *forty-eight days*, including various deviations and stoppages for surveying; and it was principally made in a vessel which sailed no more than four or five knots, when the Bridgewater would have gone six or eight. The difference, nevertheless, in favour of Torres' Strait, was forty days; so that it seems within bounds to say, that in going from Port Jackson to India or the Cape of Good Hope, it offers an advantage over the northern route of six weeks; and of four weeks in going from the more eastern parts of the Great Ocean. In point of safety, I know not whether Torres' Strait have not also the advantage; for although it be certainly more dangerous than any one of the eastern passages, it is doubtful whether it be more so than a four or six weeks extra navigation amongst the straits and islands to the east and north of New Guinea, where some new shoal, bank, or island is discovered by every vessel going that way. For myself, I should not hesitate to prefer Torres' Strait, were it only on this account; considering the long continuance of the danger in one case, as being more than a counterbalance to the superior degree of it in the other.

With respect to a passage through Torres' Strait in the opposite direction--from the Indian Sea to the Great Ocean--it has not, to my knowledge, been attempted; and I have some doubt of its practicability. A ship would have an advantage in entering the strait by its least dangerous side; but as the passage could be made only in December, January, or February, the rainy squally weather which probably will then prevail, would augment the danger from the reefs ten fold. The experiment is therefore too hazardous for any except a ship on discovery; whose business it is to encounter, and even to seek danger, when it may produce any important benefit to geography and navigation.

BOOK III.
OCCURRENCES FROM THE TIME OF QUITTING PORT JACKSON, IN 1803, ARRIVING IN ENGLAND IN 1810.
CHAPTER I.

Departure from Port Jackson in the Porpoise,
accompanied by the Bridgewater and Cato.
The Cato's Bank.
Shipwreck of the Porpoise and Cato in the night.
The crews get on a sand bank; where they are left by the Bridgewater.
Provisions saved.
Regulations on the bank.
Measures adopted for getting back to Port Jackson.
Description of Wreck-Reef Bank.
Remarks on the loss of M. de La Pérouse.

[EAST COAST. PORT JACKSON]
1803

The third volume of my log book and journal having been lost in the events which succeeded the decay of the Investigator, I have had recourse to a memorandum book and to officers journals to supply the dates and leading facts contained in the first three chapters following; fortunately, my bearings and the astronomical observations taken by lieutenant Flinders and myself were preserved, as also were the rough charts, with one exception; so that there are few cases where this department of the voyage will have materially suffered. There are, however, many circumstances related in these chapters, which either do not enter at all, or are slightly mentioned in the officers journals; for these, my public papers and copies of letters have principally furnished materials, and a tolerably faithful memory has supplied the rest. It seemed necessary to explain this, that the reader may know to what the deficiencies and abridgments in some parts of these chapters are to be attributed; and this being premised, I resume the narrative of our preparations for returning to England.

20 JULY 1803

On July 20, lieutenant Fowler quitted the Investigator, with the crew selected for him, and took the command of His Majesty's armed vessel *Porpoise*; and on the following day I went on board with the rest of my officers and people, to go with him as passengers. Amongst other preparations for the voyage, a green house was set up on the quarter deck of that ship; and the plants collected in the Investigator from the south, the east, and north coasts of Terra Australis were deposited in it, to be conveyed to His Majesty's botanical garden at Kew; and as we had had the misfortune to lose the gardener of the expedition, and Mr. Brown, the naturalist, remained behind, a man from Port Jackson was engaged to take care of the plants during the passage.

The examination of Torres' Strait was one of the most important articles of my instructions which had been executed only in part; and although I could not pretend to make any regular survey in the Porpoise, it was yet desirable to pass again through the strait, and lay down as many more of its dangers as circumstances would admit; and this being represented to governor King, the following paragraph was made an article in lieutenant Fowler's orders.

"The objects which captain Flinders will have to finish in his route through Torres' Strait, requires that he should be assisted with boats, people, and have the entire direction of the ship as to the courses she is to steer, making and shortening sail, anchoring, and every other prompt attention to his directions as connected with his survey. You are therefore further required to comply with every direction he may give you, to enable him to execute the orders of my Lords Commissioners of the Admiralty; and as it will be necessary that the most expeditious route should be followed, for the purpose of ascertaining the length of time it will take to make the voyage from hence to England, by Torres' Strait, and to enable captain Flinders to be in England as early as possible, you will take especial care to lose no time in getting to England by the route captain Flinders may indicate."

AUGUST 1803

In the beginning of August, the Porpoise was nearly ready to sail; and two ships then lying in Sydney Cove, bound to Batavia, desired leave to accompany us through the Strait. These were the Hon. East-India-Company's extra-ship Bridgewater, of about 750 tons, commanded by E. H. Palmer, Esq., and the ship Cato of London, of about 450 tons, commanded by Mr. John Park. The company of these ships gave me pleasure; for if we should be able to make a safe and expeditious passage through the strait with them, of which I had but little doubt, it would be a manifest proof of the advantage of the route discovered in the Investigator, and tend to bring it into general use. On the 10th [WEDNESDAY 10 AUGUST 1803] I took leave of my respected friend the governor of New South Wales, and received his despatches for England; and lieutenant Fowler having given a small code of signals to the Bridgewater and Cato, we sailed out of Port Jackson together, at eleven o'clock of the same morning, and steered north-eastward for Torres' Strait.

Mr. Inman had re-delivered to me the two time-keepers, with a table of their rates deduced from equal altitudes, but the No. 543 had gone so very irregularly, as not to be entitled to any confidence; the error of No. 520 from mean Greenwich time at noon there on the 2nd, and its rate of going during the twenty-five preceding days were as under:

Earnshaw's No. 520, fast, 0h 49' 54.85" and losing 33.38" per day.

[EAST COAST. STEERING NORTHWARD.]

(Atlas, Plate I.)

The winds were light, and mostly from the eastward during the first two days of our quitting Port Jackson; and not being able to get far enough from the land to avoid the southern current, it had retarded us 35' on the 12th at noon [FRIDAY 12 AUGUST 1803], when the islands of Port Stephens were in sight. On the following day the wind became more steady in the south-western quarter, and as our distance from the land increased, the current abated; and on the 15th, when the latitude was 27° 27', longitude 156° 22', and distance from the coast about five leagues, the set was something in our favour. The wind was then at south, and our course steered was north for twenty-four hours, then N. by W.; and on the 17th at noon [WEDNESDAY 17 AUGUST 1803] we were in latitude 23° 22', longitude 155° 34', and had the wind at S. E. by S. (Atlas, Plate X.)

Soon after two o'clock, the Cato being some distance on our larbord quarter made the signal for seeing land. This proved to be a dry sand bank, which bore S. S. W. about three leagues; and the Porpoise sailing faster than the other ships, they were directed to keep on their course whilst we hauled up to take a nearer view of the bank. At three o'clock, when it bore S. by E. five or six miles, we hove to and sounded but had no bottom at 80 fathoms. The *Cato's Bank*, for so it was named, is small and seemed to be destitute of vegetation; there was an innumerable quantity of birds hovering about, and it was surrounded with breakers; but their extent seemed very little to exceed that of the bank, nor could any other reef near it be discovered. The situation was ascertained to be nearly 23° 6' south, and 155° 23' east; and we then made sail after the Bridgewater and Cato, to take our station ahead of them as before.

Some apprehensions were excited for the following night by meeting with this bank but as it was more than two degrees to the eastward of the great Barrier Reefs, we thought it unconnected with any other, like the two discovered by captain Ball and Mr. Bampton, further towards the north end of New Caledonia. I had, besides, steered for Torres' Strait in the Investigator, from reefs several degrees to the westward, without meeting with any other danger than what lay near the Barrier or belonged to the Strait; and by the time we had rejoined the ships in the evening, the distance run from the bank was thirty-five miles, and no other danger had been descried. It did not therefore seem necessary to lose a good night's run by heaving to; and I agreed with lieutenant Fowler, that it would be sufficient to make the signal for the ships to run under easy, working sail during the night--to take our usual station ahead--and to charge one of the Investigator's warrant officers with the look-out on the fore castle. These precautions being taken, and the top sails double reefed, our course was pursued to the N. by W., with a fresh breeze and cloudy weather; and at eight o'clock the lead was cast, but no bottom found at 85 fathoms. The Bridgewater was then about half a mile on the starbord, and the Cato a mile on the larbord quarter; and their distance seeming to increase at nine, when our rate of going was eight knots, the fore sail was hauled up to keep them in sight: wind then at S. E. by E.

[EAST COAST. WRECK REEF.]

In half an hour, and almost at the same instant by the Investigator's carpenter on the fore castle, and the master who had charge of the watch on the quarter deck--breakers were seen ahead. The helm was immediately put down, with the intention of tacking from them;

but the Porpoise having only three double-reefed top sails set, scarcely came up to the wind. Lieutenant Fowler sprang upon deck, on hearing the noise; but supposing it to be occasioned by carrying away the tiller rope, a circumstance which had often occurred in the Investigator, and having no orders to give, I remained some minutes longer, conversing with the gentlemen in the gun room. On going up, I found the sails shaking in the wind, and the ship in the act of paying off; at the same time there were very high breakers at not a quarter of a cable's length to leeward. In about a minute, the ship was carried amongst the breakers; and striking upon a coral reef, took a fearful heel over on her larbord beam ends, her head being north-eastward. A gun was attempted to be fired, to warn the other vessels of the danger; but owing to the violent motion and the heavy surfs flying over, this could not be done immediately; and before lights were brought up, the Bridgewater and Cato had hauled to the wind across each other.

Our fore mast was carried away at the second or third shock; and the bottom was presently reported to be stove in, and the hold full of water. When the surfs permitted us to look to windward, the Bridgewater and Cato were perceived at not more than a cable's length distance; and approaching each other so closely, that their running aboard seemed to us inevitable. This was an awful moment; the utmost silence prevailed; and when the bows of the two ships went to meet, even respiration seemed to be suspended. The ships advanced, and we expected to hear the dreadful crash; but presently they opened off from each other, having passed side by side without touching; the Cato steering to the north-east, and the Bridgewater to the southward. Our own safety seemed to have no other dependence than upon the two ships, and the exultation we felt at seeing this most imminent danger passed, was great, but of short duration; the Cato struck upon the reef about two cables length from the Porpoise, we saw her fall over on her broad side, and the masts almost instantly disappeared; but the darkness of the night did not admit of distinguishing, at that distance, what further might have happened.

Turning our eyes toward the Bridgewater, a light was perceived at her mast head, by which we knew she had cleared the reef; and our first sensations were, that the commander would certainly tack, and send boats to our assistance; but when a little reflexion had enabled us to put ourselves in his place, it became evident that he would not choose to come so near the reef in the night, blowing fresh as it did; and still less to send his boats and people into the breakers, to their certain destruction.

The Porpoise had very fortunately heeled towards the reef so that the surfs which struck against her turned-up side, flew over without washing any thing off the decks; and the smooth appearance of the water under the lee, afforded a prospect of being able to get the boats out on that side. The experiment was tried with a small four-oared gig, and succeeded; but a six-oared cutter was jerked against the sheet anchor by the violence of the shocks, and being stove, was filled with water.

It was by no means certain how long the ship, being slightly built and not in a sound state, might hold together; it was therefore deemed expedient to lighten her, that she might drive further up the coral bank and lie more easily. On sounding, the depth was found to be 17 fathoms on the windward side, but no more than a few feet on the reef; and Mr. Fowler ordered the main and mizen masts, and the starbord anchor to be cut away; but on my suggesting to him the possibility of driving over the reef, with the rise of tide, and sinking in deep water as the Pandora had done, the lightening of the ship was not prosecuted further.

Beyond the smooth water close under the lee, there was a line of breakers, and further on the sea appeared to be tranquil; it therefore seemed probable that boats might approach the ship on that side, and if this information could be conveyed to captain Palmer of the Bridgewater, that something might be speedily done towards saving the crew; and as it was likely that my influence with him might be greatest, and being a passenger in the Porpoise no charge made my presence on board immediately necessary, I proposed to make the attempt in the gig, to which Mr. Fowler assented. The boat being obliged to lie at a little distance from the ship, to prevent being stove, I jumped over-board and swam to her; and we pushed through the breakers to the smooth water, receiving two or three surfs by the way, from which we hardly escaped sinking. On examining into the condition of the boat, I found nothing to bale out the water, and only two oars which did not belong to it; and instead of the proper crew of four men, there were only three; but under the thwarts were stowed away three others, the armourer, a cook, and a marine, who did not know how to handle an oar. These last were set to baling with their hats and shoes, and we rowed towards the Bridgewater's light, keeping under the lee of the breakers. That ship was standing from us, and I saw that any attempt to get nearer before she tacked would be fruitless; and even afterwards, it was much to be doubted whether, with two awkward oars and an overloaded boat, we could make any way against the sea on the windward side of the reef; I therefore determined to remain under the lee of the breakers until she should approach, and to lie near the Porpoise; that in case of her going to pieces before morning, we might save some of the people. In rowing back we met the cutter, which the men in her, having got the leak partly stopped, had pushed off without an officer, and were going they scarcely knew whither; they furnished us with a third oar, and I desired them to keep close to the gig, near the wreck, until morning. We found the bottom here to be coral rock, and the water so shallow, that a man might stand up in many places without being over head.

    I wished to have got on board the ship, to let them know of the boats being safe and what we had discovered of the reef; but the breakers between us, and the darkness of the night cut off all hope of communication before morning. They burned blue lights every half hour, as a guide to the Bridgewater; but her light was lost to us in the boats at eleven o'clock, and after two in the morning [THURSDAY 18 AUGUST 1803] it was no longer seen from the Porpoise. At that time it appeared to be low water, and the ship lay so much more quiet than before, that the apprehension of her going to pieces before daylight had much subsided; to be prepared, however, for the next flood, Mr. Fowler employed his people during the night in making a raft of the spare top masts, yards, etc., with short ropes all round it, by which the people might hold on; and a cask of water, with a chest containing some provisions, a sextant, and the Investigator's log books, were secured upon the raft.

    In the small gig we were quite drenched, the south-east wind blew fresh and cold., and the reflexions excited by the great change so suddenly made in our situation. with the uncertainty of what had befallen the Cato and even the Bridgewater, did not tend to make this long night pass more agreeably. My thoughts were principally occupied in devising plans for saving ourselves, under the apprehension that we might see no more of the Bridgewater; but not to discourage the people, I spoke of every body getting on board that ship in the morning, and of continuing our voyage to England, as not at all doubtful.

    Of the poor Cato, we could neither see nor hear any thing. It appeared that captain Park, when meeting the Bridgewater on opposite tacks, stopped setting his main sail and bore away to leeward had he persevered, both ships must have come upon the reef together; but by his presence of mind on this occasion, the Bridgewater weathered the breakers and escaped the impending danger. When the Cato struck the reef, it was upon the point of a rock, under the larbord chess tree; and she fell over to windward, with her decks exposed to the waves. In a short time the decks and holds were torn up, and every thing washed away; and the sole place left, where the unfortunate people could hope to avoid the fury of the sea, was in the larbord fore channel, where they all crowded together, the greater part with no other covering than their shirts. Every time the sea struck the Cato, it twisted her about upon the rock with such violent jerks, that they expected the stern, which was down in the water, would part every moment. In this situation, some lashing themselves to the timber heads, others clinging to the chain plates and dead eyes, and to each other, captain Park and his crew passed the night; their hope being, that the fore castle of the ship might hold upon the rock till morning, and that the Bridgewater would then send her boats to save them. From the Porpoise they entertained no hope; and until the signal lights were seen, they thought her gone to pieces.

    At the first dawning of day, I got on board the Porpoise by the help of the fallen masts. Every body was in good spirits at seeing the ship hold together so well, and finding the boats safe; for the gig, with all in her, had been given up for lost, some one having thought he saw her sink in the breakers. With the daylight appeared a dry sand bank, not more than half a mile distant, sufficiently large to receive us all with what provisions might be got out of the ship; and the satisfaction arising from this discovery was increased by the Bridgewater being perceived under sail, and though distant, that she was standing towards the reef. On the other side, the appearance of the poor Cato, with the people waving to us from the bowsprit and fore castle, the only parts above water, was truly distressing.

The reef seemed to be a mile in breadth, and it extended in an east and west direction to a distance beyond what could be distinguished from the Porpoise's deck; but there were in it several wide, and apparently deep openings, by which the Bridgewater might run to leeward, and there anchor or lie to, whilst sending her boats to our assistance. Having made these remarks, I left Mr. Fowler and his people getting up water and provisions; and went to the bank for the purpose of being ready to go off in the gig so soon as that ship should be near enough, and pointing out to captain Palmer the means by which he might take on board the two crews and what else might be saved; but he went upon the other tack soon afterward, and no more was seen of him during the day.

A number of sea-birds eggs scattered over the bank, showed that it was above high-water mark, and I sent the gig back with this intelligence to lieutenant Fowler. Seeing that the Bridgewater did not approach, he ordered the boat to lie opposite to the Cato; and captain Park and his men, throwing themselves into the water with any pieces of spar or plank they could find, swam to her through the breakers; and were then taken to the Porpoise where they received food and some clothing. Several were bruised against the coral rocks, and three young lads were drowned. One of these poor boys, who, in the three or four voyages he had made to sea, had been each time shipwrecked, had bewailed himself through the night as the persecuted Jonas who carried misfortune wherever he went. He launched himself upon a broken spar with his captain; but having lost his hold in the breakers, was not seen afterwards.

At low water, which happened about two o'clock, the reef was dry very near to the Porpoise, and both officers and men were assiduously employed in getting upon it provisions and their clothes; they were brought from thence by the boats, for the depth was several feet at a distance round the bank. Before dark, five half hogsheads of water, some flour, salt meat, rice, and spirits were landed, with such of the pigs and sheep as had escaped drowning; and every man from both ships had got on shore. Some of the Cato's sailors appeared in officers uniforms, given to them in the Porpoise; and I was pleased to see that our situation was not thought so bad by the people, as to hinder all pleasantry upon these promotions. Those who had saved great coats or blankets shared with the less fortunate, and we laid down to sleep on the sand in tolerable tranquillity, being much oppressed with fatigue; and except from those of the Cato's men who had been bruised or cut by the rocks, there was not a complaining voice heard on the bank.

The Porpoise's two cutters and the gig were hauled up to high-water mark; but the latter not having been well secured, and the night tide rising higher than was expected, it was carried away, to our great loss. In the morning [FRIDAY 19 AUGUST 1803], we had the satisfaction to see the ship still entire, and thrown higher up the reef; the Cato had gone to pieces, and all that remained was one of the quarters, which had floated over the front ledge of the reef, and lodged near our bank. Of the Bridgewater nothing could be seen; and many fears were entertained for her safety.

For the better preservation of discipline, and of that union between the crews of the Porpoise and Cato and passengers of the Investigator, so necessary in our circumstances, it was highly expedient that they should be put on the same footing and united under one head. The Porpoise was lost beyond a possibility of hope, and the situation of the commander and crew thereby rendered similar to that of their passengers; I therefore considered myself authorised and called upon, as the senior officer, to take the command of the whole; and my intention being communicated to lieutenant Fowler, he assented without hesitation to its expediency and propriety, and I owe to captain Park a similar acknowledgement. The people were then assembled upon the top of the bank; and I informed the seamen of the Cato, one or two of whom had shown signs of discontent at being ordered to work, that as they doubtless expected to be fed from our provisions, so they must exert themselves to save as much as possible;* and although they were not in the King's pay, yet as a magistrate acting within the jurisdiction of the Admiralty, I would punish all deviations from obedience and good conduct in them, the same as amongst our own seamen. I ordered the Cato's men, who had saved nothing, to be quartered in the messes of our people, in the proportion of one to three; and directed lieutenant Fowler, who had charge of the provisions, to victual all alike. The surgeon of the Porpoise was ordered to examine the wounded, and give in a list of those really incapable of duty; and a large party, consisting of as many men as the two cutters could contain, went off to the wreck under the command of Mr. Fowler, to disembark provisions and stores.

[* When a merchant ship is lost, the seamen not only cease to be in pay, but lose all wages due to them after the last delivery of the cargo; and the sole interest they have to save the stores, even of their own ship, is for the preservation of themselves, or the prospect of being rewarded by the owners or insurers.]

A top-sail yard was set up and secured as a flag staff on the highest part of the bank, and a large blue ensign hoisted to it with the union downward, as a signal to the Bridgewater. We expected, if no accident had happened, that she would come to relieve us from our critical situation so soon as the wind should be perfectly moderate; but I judged it most prudent to act as if we had no such resource, and this was justified by the event. Captain Palmer had even then abandoned us to our fate, and was, at the moment, steering away for Batavia, without having made any effort to give us assistance. He saw the wrecks, as also the sand bank, on the morning after our disaster, and must have known that the reef was not all connected, since it is spoken of by him as lying in patches; but he did not seek to ascertain whether any of the openings were passable for the Bridgewater, and might enable him to take those on board who had escaped drowning. He bore away round all; and whilst the two hapless vessels were still visible from the mast head, passed the leeward extremity of the reef, and hove to for the night. The apprehension of danger to himself must then have ceased; but he neither attempted to work up in the smooth water, nor sent any of his boats to see whether some unfortunate individuals were not clinging to the wrecks, whom he might snatch from the sharks or save from a more lingering death; it was safer, in his estimation, to continue on his voyage and publish that we were all lost, as he did not fail to do on his arrival in India.*

>[* Against a British seaman filling a respectable situation, these are heavy charges; but Mr. Palmer is himself the authority. The following extracts from his account are taken from a Calcutta paper, the *Orphan* of Feb. 3, 1804.

The Bridgewater, he says, "was just beginning to draw off, when the Porpoise was scarcely a ship's length to leeward, settling with her head towards us, and her broadside upon the reef; her foremast was gone and the sea breaking over her. At this moment we perceived the Cato within half a cable's length, standing stem on for us. I hailed to put their helm a-starboard, by which means she just cleared us, and luffed up under our stern; had she fallen on board of us the consequences must have been dreadful indeed." On the 18th, "When the day was broke, we had the mortification to perceive the Cato had shared the fate of the Porpoise; the bow and bow sprit of the latter only at intervals appearing through the surf. (The Porpoise and Cato were mistaken for each other.) The latter lay with her bottom exposed to the sea, which broke with tremendous fury over her; not a mast standing. Finding we could not weather the reef, and that *it was too late had it been in our power to give any assistance*; and still fearing that we might be embayed or entangled by the supposed chain or patches; all therefore that remained for us to do was either by dint of carrying sail to weather the reef to the southward, (meaning the Cato's Bank,) or, if failing in that, to push to leeward and endeavour to find a passage through the *patches of reef* to the northward. At ten a.m., we found by chronometer we had got considerably to the westward; and that it would be impossible, with the wind as it was then blowing strong from the S. E. with a heavy sea, to weather the southern reef; we therefore determined, while we had the day before us, to run to the westward of the northern reef."

"At two p.m. we got sight of the reef bearing N. N. E. At five p.m. *we could perceive the wrecks, and ascertained the westernmost extent of the reef* to lay in 155° 42' 30" east longitude."

"*After passing the reef we lay too for the night*; and in the morning we lost sight cc of it, having drifted to the northward."

Such is the substantial part of Mr. Palmer's account, omitting his own fears and congratulations, and his "most painful reflexions on the sufferings of the shipwrecked."

Nothing is said of the sand bank; but I have been favoured with a copy of the journal of Mr. Williams, third mate of the Bridgewater, and the following passages are taken from it.

"At half past seven a.m. (Aug. 18.) saw the reef on our weather bow, and from the mast head we saw the two ships, and to leeward of them a *sand bank*. The weather abated much, we set all our sails, and every man rejoiced that they should have it in their power to assist their unfortunate companions; as there was every probability of our going within two miles of the reef. The morning threatened; but before the wind increased we had time to satisfy ourselves if there were any still in existence; we had nothing to apprehend but what could be seen before we approached so near. The ships were very distinctly to be seen from aloft, and also from the deck; but instead of rendering them any succour, the captain ordered the ship to be put on the other tack, and said it was impossible to render them any relief. What must be the sensations of each man at that instant? Instead of proceeding to the support of our unfortunate companions, to leave them to the mercy of the waves, without knowing whether they were in existence, or had perished! From the appearance of the wrecks, there was every probability of their existing; and if any survived at the time we were within sight, what must have been their sensations on seeing all their anxious expectations of relief blasted."

"Until our arrival at Bombay, nothing particular occurred, except my being sent on shore at Tillicherry with the account of the loss of the Porpoise and Cato; an account that served for the moment to blind the people. In executing this service, I did, for the first time to my knowledge, neglect my duty, and gave a contrary account; but for this reason--I was convinced that the crews of those ships were on the reefs, and that this was an erroneous account made by captain Palmer to excuse his own conduct. I left it on shore for the perusal of the inhabitants, after relating the story as contrary as possible. This was the cause of many words; and at length ended with my quitting the ship, and forfeiting my wages and a part of my clothes."

Such was the conduct of Mr. Palmer towards His Majesty's ship Porpoise, and towards the Cato which had given way in the moment of danger that he might be saved. But the officers and crews of the Porpoise and Cato reached England in safety; whilst captain Palmer and the Bridgewater, who left Bombay for Europe, have not been heard of, now for many years. How dreadful must have been his reflexions at the time his ship was going down! Lieutenant Tucker of the navy, who was first officer of the Bridgewater, and several others as well as Mr. Williams, had happily quitted the ship in India.]

The wind blew fresh from the south-eastward on the 18th, and 19th, but on the two following days it was moderate with fine weather; we worked hard on board the Porpoise, and by the 22nd [MONDAY 22 AUGUST 1803] had got most of the water and provisions secured in a large tent made with spars and sails; each mess of officers and men had also their private tent; and our manner of living and working had assumed the same regularity as before the shipwreck. One of the men whose liberty governor King had granted at my request, being guilty of disorderly conduct, the articles of war were publicly read, and the man punished at the flag staff. This example served to correct any evil disposition, if such existed; the men worked cordially together, and in all respects we preserved the same discipline and order as on board His Majesty's ships.

Our prospects of receiving succour from the Bridgewater having become very feeble, after two days of moderate weather had elapsed, I called a council of all the officers, to deliberate upon the best means of relieving ourselves from the precarious situation in which our misfortune, and captain Palmer's want of energy and humanity had left us exposed; and it was finally determined, that an officer and crew in the largest of the two six-oared cutters, should endeavour to get to Sandy Cape, sixty-three leagues distant, and from thence along the coast to Port Jackson; and pray His Excellency, the governor, to send vessels to carry us either back to that port or on towards England. But as the safe arrival of the cutter at that season of the year, when strong winds usually prevail from the southward, was a subject of much apprehension; it was resolved that two decked boats, capable of transporting every person remaining on the bank, except one officer and boat's crew, should be immediately laid down by the carpenters, to be built from what was already and might be still further saved from the wreck; and that, if the officer in the cutter did not return with assistance in two months, the boats should then, or as soon after as they could be ready to sail, proceed to Port Jackson. The first and principal means, however, through which our deliverance was to be expected, being the safe arrival of the cutter, the choice of an officer to conduct her was next considered. Lieutenant Fowler proposed, and it seemed to be the general wish, that I should undertake the execution of the task; and being satisfied that the preservation of order on the bank, and the saving of the stores would be left in good hands, the hope of being instrumental to the general safety induced me readily to comply. But to provide against sickness and the various accidents which might arise from the natives of the coast or otherwise, it was necessary that two officers should be in the boat; and captain Park of the Cato being desirous of returning to Port Jackson, to make the necessary statements relative to the loss of his ship, he was appointed my second with the general approbation.

The smaller cutter with an officer, his second, and a boat's crew, I proposed should remain with the stores, and in charge of my charts and books for a few weeks longer than the two months; and then go to Port Jackson also, should no vessel arrive before that time. This precaution was necessary, lest any unforeseen occurrence should delay my return to the bank beyond two months, though not prevent it altogether; that the charts, journals, and papers might still be found there, to be taken on to England if wanted. I designed my brother, lieutenant Flinders, for this service; but Mr. Fowler claiming it as the post of honour, I too much respected the principle that influenced him not to accede to his request; and therefore ordered, that the former officer and Mr. John Aken, master of the Investigator, should take charge of the decked boats, with a master's mate in each capable of conducting them to Port Jackson, should illness or any accident happen to either of the officers.

TUESDAY 23 AUGUST 1803

By the evening of the 23rd, the Porpoise was well nigh emptied of all the most essential things; and on a survey being made, there was found sufficient water and provisions on the bank to serve ninety-four men, which was our number, for three months, even at full allowance; although many casks were stove in the hold by the bulging of the larbord side, and much dry provisions spoiled by the salt water. The principal contents of the warrant officers store rooms, as well as the sails., rigging, and spars, were also on shore. My books, charts, and papers had suffered much damage, from the top of the cabin being displaced when the mizen mast fell; all such papers as chanced to be loose on the night of the shipwreck were then washed away by the surfs, and amongst them a chart of the west side of the Gulph of Carpentaria and part of the North Coast, upon which I had been occupied in the afternoon. Part of my small library shared the same fate; but the rest of the charts, with my log and bearing books and astronomical observations were all saved, though some of them in a wet and shattered state. The rare plants collected on different parts of the south, the east, and north coasts of Terra Australis, for His Majesty's botanic garden at Kew, and which were in a flourishing g state before the shipwreck., were totally destroyed by the salt water; as were the dried specimens of plants. Fortunately, the naturalist and natural-history painter, who remained at Port Jackson, had put on board only a small part of their collection of specimens; the great mass, with the preserved birds, quadrupeds, and insects being kept for a future opportunity. Mr. Westall. the landscape painter, had his sketches and drawings wetted and partly destroyed in his cabin; and my little collection in mineralogy and conchology was much defaced, and one-half lost.

THURSDAY 25 AUGUST 1803

The carpenters were employed until the evening of the 25th, in preparing the cutter for her intended expedition; and the rest of the people in adding to the stores on the bank. As the Porpoise became lighter, the sea threw her higher up on the reef, and she was much shaken; but we hoped the timbers and beams would hold together, at least until the next spring tides, and that every thing would be got out. Of the Cato, nothing but a few scattered fragments had remained for several days before.

Before leaving Wreck Reef, it will be proper to say something of the sand bank to which we were all indebted for our lives; and where the greater part of the officers and people were to remain in expectation of my return from Port Jackson. In the annexed view of it, Mr. Westall has represented the corals above water, to give a better notion of their forms and the way they are seen on the reefs; but in reality, the tide never leaves any considerable part of them uncovered. The length of the bank is about one hundred and fifty fathoms, by fifty in breadth, and the general elevation three or four feet above the common level of high water; it consists of sand and pieces of coral, thrown up by the waves and eddy tides on a patch of reef five or six miles in circuit; and being nearly in the middle of the patch, the sea does no more, even in a gale, than send a light spray over the bank, sufficient, however, to prevent the growth of any other than a few diminutive salt plants. On its north and north-west sides, and at one or two cables length from the reef, there is from 18 to 25 fathoms on a bottom of coral sand; where the Bridgewater might have anchored in safety, so long as the wind remained between S. W. and E. S. E., and received every person from the wrecks, with provisions for their subsistence. The latitude of the bank was found to be 22° 11' south, and longitude by the time keeper No. 520, reduced up from an observation on the afternoon preceding the shipwreck, 155° 3'; but this was afterwards found to require correction. This excellent time keeper did not seem to have been affected by the violent motion of the ship; but No. 513 stopped, and Arnold's watch No. 1736 was spoiled by the salt water.

View of Wreck-Reef Bank, taken at low water.

In searching for something wherewith to make a fire on the first night of our landing, a spar and a piece of timber, worm eaten and almost rotten, were found and burnt. The timber was seen by the master of the Porpoise, who judged it to have been part of the stern post of a ship of about four hundred tons; and I have thought it might, not improbably, have belonged to *La Boussole* or *L'Astrolabe*. Monsieur de la Pérouse, on quitting Botany Bay, intended to visit the south-west coast of New Caledonia; and he might have encountered in the night, as we did, some one of the several reefs which lie scattered in this sea.* (Atlas, Plate I.) Less fortunate than we were, he probably had no friendly sand bank near him, upon which his people might be collected together and the means of existence saved out of the ships; or perhaps his two vessels both took the unlucky direction of the Cato after striking, and the seas which broke into them carried away all his boats and provisions; nor would La Pérouse, his vessels, or crews be able, in such a case, to resist the impetuosity of the waves more than twenty-four hours. If such were the end of the regretted French navigator, as there is now but too much reason to fear, it is the counterpart of what would have befallen all on board the Porpoise and Cato, had the former ship, like the Cato, fallen over towards the sea instead of heeling to the reef.

[* La Pérouse says, in his letter to M. de Fleurieu, dated Feb. 7, 1789 from Botany Bay, "You will doubtless be glad to learn, that I have not allowed this misfortune (the massacre of captain De l'Angle and eleven others at the Navigator's Isles) to derange the plan of the remaining part of my voyage." This plan, as expressed in a preceding letter of Sept. 7, 1787, at Avatscha, was to "employ six months in visiting the Friendly Islands to procure refreshments, *the south-west coast of New Caledonia*, the island of Santa Cruz of Mendana, the southern coast of the land of the Arsacides, with that of Louisiade as far as New Guinea." *Voyage of La Pérouse*, Translation, London, 1799, VOL. II. p. 494-5, 502-3. As La Pe/rouse did not reach the Friendly Isles, it is probable that he began with New Caledonia; and that upon the south-west coast, or in the way to it, disaster befel him.]

An opinion that La Pérouse had been lost in this neighbourhood, induced me when examining the main coast to seek carefully at every place, amongst the refuse thrown upon the shores, for indications of shipwreck to windward; and could the search have been then prosecuted to the 15th, or 12th degree of latitude, I am persuaded it would not have been in vain. Besides the extensive reefs which skirt the western side of New Caledonia, and the Barrier Reefs on the opposite coast of New South Wales, we are now acquainted with the six or eight following distinct banks of coral in the sea between them, exclusive of Wreck Reef and the Cato's Bank.

Two reefs discovered by Bougainville. Bâture de Diane, by the same. Two reefs further westward, by the Investigator. Booby Shoal, towards New Caledonia, by captain H. L. Ball. Bellona's Shoal, by the ship of that name. Bampton's Shoal, an extensive reef with two small islands.

There are also the islets and shoals seen by the ship Sovereign, which are probably a part of those that extend so far from the northwest end of New Caledonia; and all these, with some others further northward, lie in the space comprehended between Louisiade and New Guinea on the north--New Caledonia to the east--New South Wales to the west--and a line drawn from Sandy Cape to the Isle of Pines on the south. Few ships have passed through this sea without making the discovery of some new bank of coral; and it is probable that several other patches of reef, yet unknown, will be found in it, especially on the Caledonian side. This space might be very appropriately called the *Corallian Sea*.

CHAPTER II.

Departure from Wreck-Reef Bank in a boat.
Boisterous weather.
The Coast of New South Wales reached, and followed.
Natives at Point Look-out.
Landing near Smoky Cape; and again near Port Hunter.
Arrival at Port Jackson on the thirteenth day.
Return to Wreck Reef with a ship and two schooners.
Arrangements at the Bank.
Account of the reef, with nautical and other remarks.

[EAST COAST. IN THE BOAT.]

FRIDAY 26 AUGUST 1803

(Atlas, Plate X.)

On August 26, the largest cutter being ready for her expedition, was launched and named the *Hope*. The morning was fine, and wind light from the southward; and notwithstanding the day, which in the seaman's calendar is the most unfortunate of the whole week to commence a voyage, I embarked for Port Jackson with the commander of the Cato. We had a double set of rowers, making in all fourteen persons, with three weeks provisions and two half hogsheads of water; so that the Hope was loaded rather too deeply. At eight in the morning, we pushed off amidst the cheers and good wishes of those for whom we were going to seek relief; an ensign with the union downward, had hitherto been kept hoisted as a signal to captain Palmer of our distress; but in this moment of enthusiasm a seaman quitted the crowd, and having obtained permission, ran to the flag staff, hauled down the ensign, and rehoisted it with the union in the upper canton. This symbolical expression of contempt for the Bridgewater and of confidence in the success of our voyage, I did not see without lively emotions.

We made sail to the westward under the lee of the reef, and passed two openings in it of nearly a mile wide. The second league brought us abreast of a dry sand bank, smaller than that quitted; and at noon we came to a third, lying ten miles west of Wreck-Reef Bank. Having then lost the breeze, we stopped to cook our dinner on shore; and in the mean time I shot as many noddies as would give all the boat's crew a meal. On quitting this third bank, which is near the western extremity of Wreck Reef, we crossed into the open sea; and a breeze springing up at south-east, made sail towards Sandy Cape. Many hump-backed whales were playing about the boat during the whole time we remained under the lee of the reef, but they did not follow us further.

Nothing but clear water was visible at sunset, nevertheless we ran cautiously in the dark, looking out for breakers; the night was fine, and we made good progress by means of the oars, at which the twelve men took watch and watch, as Mr. Park and myself did at the helm: it was for this purpose, and to guard against accidents, that I had taken so many men in the boat.

SATURDAY 27 AUGUST 1803

At day break the wind was E. S. E., and no land in sight; the boat was going four knots, and at noon our latitude by log was 23° 6' and the distance made from Wreck-Reef Bank, ninety miles. The wind freshened in the afternoon, and a cross sea rose which obliged us to reef the sails, and made the boat very wet. At four we close reefed and hauled to the wind, but this was not enough; the increased hollowness of the waves caused the boat to labour so much, that every plunge raised an apprehension that some of the planks would start from the timbers. Having no other resource, we emptied one of the two casks of water, threw over-board the stones of our fire place and wood for cooking, as also a bag of pease and whatever else could be best spared; the boat was then somewhat more easy; and before dark, the hollow swell had so far subsided that we kept two points from the wind, and again went along in tolerable tranquillity.

This hollow sea was probably caused by a weather tide setting out of some passage between the reefs to the north-westward; and the succeeding smooth water by the tide having turned to leeward, or otherwise from the boat having passed across the stream; it is at least certain, that the southern part of the Barrier Reefs, seen by captain Swain of the ship Eliza, was somewhere to the north-west of our situation at that time. To avoid all these reefs, and to counteract the effect of a north-western current, I kept a S. S. W. course all the following night.

SUNDAY 28 AUGUST 1803

We had fine weather next morning, with a moderate breeze at north-east; and at noon, the distance run in the preceding twenty-four hours was ninety-one miles by the log, and the observed latitude 24° 53' south: the lead was put over-board., but no bottom found at 50 fathoms. Our situation being to the south of Sandy Cape, we steered a point more west, in the hope of seeing the land before night; it being my intention to keep near the coast from thence to Port Jackson, that by landing, or running the boat on shore, we might escape foundering at sea should a gale of wind come on. At sunset, the land was visible to the westward at the distance of four or five leagues, and we then hauled up south, parallel to the coast; the night was fine, the wind light and fair, and at daylight [MONDAY 29 AUGUST 1803] the tops of the hills were seen in the west, at the same distance as before. Our latitude at noon was 26° 22', and a high hummock upon the land, somewhere between Double-island Point and Glass-house Bay, bore W. ¾ N.

(Atlas, Plate IX.)

Our favourable breeze died away in the afternoon, and we took to the oars; it however sprung up again from the northward, and brought us within sight of Cape Moreton at sunset. Towards midnight the weather became squally with heavy rain, and gave us all a thorough drenching; but the wind not being very strong in these squalls, our course was still pursued to the southward. After the rain ceased the wind came at S. S. W.; and the weather remaining unsettled, we tacked at daylight [TUESDAY 30 AUGUST 1803] to get close in with the land, and at noon anchored under Point Look-out. This was only the fourth day of our departure from Wreck Reef, and I considered the voyage to be half accomplished, since we had got firm hold of the main coast; for the probability of being lost is greater in making three hundred miles in an open boat at sea, than in running even six hundred along shore. It would have added much to our satisfaction, could we have conveyed the intelligence of this fortunate progress to our shipmates on the bank.

The necessity for a supply of fresh water was becoming urgent, for our remaining half hogshead was much reduced. There were about twenty Indians upon the side of a hill near the shore, who seemed to be peaceably disposed, amusing us with dances in imitation of the kangaroo; we made signs of wanting water, which they understood, and pointed to a small rill falling into the sea. Two of the sailors leaped over-board, with some trifles for the natives and one end of the lead line; with the other end we slung the empty cask, which they hauled on shore and filled without molestation. A shark had followed them to the beach; and fearing they might be attacked in returning, we got up the anchor and went to a place where the surf, though too much to allow of the boat landing, permitted us to lie closer. The cask of water, a bundle of wood, and the two men were received on board without accident; the natives keeping aloof during the whole time, and even retiring when our people approached, though they were without arms and naked. It is probable that the Indians were astonished at the comparison between the moderately white skins of the sailors and their own, and perhaps had heard of my expedition to Glass-house Bay in 1799, in which I had been provoked to make one of them feel the effect of our arms; and had they attempted any thing against my two men, we were prepared to have given them a volley from the boat which would probably have been a fearful confirmation of the truth of the report; but happily for both parties, we were not reduced to the necessity.

On rowing to Point Look-out, to continue the voyage, I found the wind so fresh from the southward that the greatest fatigue at the oars could advance us little; we therefore ran to leeward of two rocks, lying a mile and a half north-west from the extremity of the point; and having anchored there, arranged the boat so as that every person might take a better night's rest than we had hitherto been able to enjoy.

WEDNESDAY 31 AUGUST 1803

At daylight, the wind being light and variable, we proceeded along the coast by using both sails and oars. The weather was dull, and prevented an observation at noon for the latitude; but a sight of Mount Warning at dusk showed that our progress was equal to expectation. We then had a gentle breeze from the north-eastward; and at ten o'clock, passed close to a projection of land which I supposed to be Point Danger, without seeing any breakers; it is therefore probable, that the reef laid down by captain Cook does not join to the land, for we kept a good look out, and the night was tolerably fine.

THURSDAY 1 SEPTEMBER 1803

At five on the following morning we passed Cape Byron, with a breeze at north-west, and at noon had made a hundred miles by our reckoning from Point Look-out; the observed latitude was then 29° 16', and the land near Shoal Bay was three leagues distant. We continued steering to the southward, in high spirits at being so favoured by the northern winds, which there was so little reason to expect; and at eight in the evening reached abreast of the Solitary Isles. Smoky Cape was in sight next morning [FRIDAY 2 SEPTEMBER 1803]; but the wind coming round to south, and blowing fresh with thick weather, we tacked towards the shore; and at noon landed behind a small ledge of rocks, about three leagues short of the Cape. The distance run these twenty-four hours was eighty five miles, and the southwardly current had moreover given its assistance.

This ledge of rocks lies on the north side of a point upon which there are some hummocks; and on ascending the highest, I saw a lagoon into which the tide flowed by a narrow passage on the inner side of the point. The *pandanus* grows here; and as it was a tree unknown to Bongaree, this latitude (about 30° 45') is probably near its southern limit. We took in a supply of fuel and gathered some fine oysters, and the wind dying away to a calm in the afternoon, rowed out for Smoky Cape; but on reaching abreast of it the wind again rose ahead; and at one in the morning we anchored in a small bight at the extremity of the Cape, and remained until daylight.

SATURDAY 3 SEPTEMBER 1803

The wind was still contrary on the 3rd, nevertheless we stood out and beat to the southward until four in the afternoon; when the sea having become too high for the boat, we anchored under the lee of a small projecting point, eight or ten leagues to the south of Smoky Cape; which distance had been gained in about ten hours, principally by means of the current.

SUNDAY 4 SEPTEMBER 1803

On the 4th, we again attempted to beat to the southward; but the wind being light as well as foul, and the sea running high, not much was gained; at noon the weather threatened so much, that it became necessary to look out for a place of shelter, and we steered into a bight with rocks in it, which I judge to have been on the north side of Tacking Point. At the head of the bight is a lagoon; but the entrance proving to be very shallow, and finding no security, we continued on our voyage; trusting that some place of shelter would present itself, if obliged to seek it by necessity. Towards evening the wind and weather became more favourable; in the morning [MONDAY 5 SEPTEMBER 1803] the Three Brothers were in sight; and at noon I observed the latitude 31° 57', when the middlemost of these hills bore N. N. W. and our distance off shore was two or three leagues.

(Atlas, Plate VIII.)

At this time the wind blew a moderate sea breeze at E. S. E, Cape Hawke was seen soon afterward, and at eight in the evening we steered between Sugar-loaf Point and the two rocks lying from it three or four miles to the south-east. At four next morning [TUESDAY 6 SEPTEMBER 1803], passed the islands at the entrance of Port Stephens, and at noon the Coal Island in the mouth of Port Hunter bore N. W. by N.; the wind then shifted more to the southward, with squally weather, and both prevented the boat from lying along the coast and made it unsafe to be at sea. After struggling till four in the afternoon, with little advantage, we bore up to look for shelter behind some of the small projecting points; and almost immediately found it in a shallow cove, exposed only to the north-eastward. This was the eleventh day of our departure from Wreck Reef, and the distance of Port Jackson did not now exceed fifty miles.

At this place we slept on shore for the first time; but the weather being squally, rainy, and cold, and the boat's sails our best shelter, it was not with any great share of comfort; a good watch was kept during the night, but no molestation was received from the natives. Notwithstanding our cramped-up position in the boat, and exposure to all kinds of weather, we enjoyed excellent health; one man excepted, upon whom the dysentery, which had made such ravages in the Investigator, now returned with some violence.

[EAST COAST. PORT JACKSON.]
WEDNESDAY 7 SEPTEMBER 1803

A cask of water was filled on the morning of the 7th, and our biscuit being all expended or spoiled, some cakes were baked in the ashes for our future subsistence. At eleven o'clock, the rain having cleared away, we stood out to the offing with light baffling winds, and towards evening were enabled to lie along the coast; but the breeze at south-east not giving much assistance, we took to the oars and laboured hard all the following night, being animated with the prospect of a speedy termination to our voyage. The north head of Broken Bay was in sight next morning [THURSDAY 8 SEPTEMBER 1803], and at noon the south head was abreast of the boat; a sea breeze then setting in at E. N. E., we crowded all sail for Port Jackson, and soon after two o'clock had the happiness to enter between the heads.

The reader has perhaps never gone 250 leagues at sea in an open boat, or along a strange coast inhabited by savages; but if he recollect the eighty officers and men upon Wreck-Reef Bank, and how important was our arrival to their safety, and to the saving of the charts, journals, and papers of the Investigator's voyage, he may have some idea of the pleasure we felt, but particularly myself, at entering our destined port.

I proceeded immediately to the town of Sydney, and went with captain Park to wait upon His Excellency governor King, whom we found at dinner with his family. A razor had not passed over our faces from the time of the shipwreck, and the surprise of the governor was not little at seeing two persons thus appear whom he supposed to be many hundred leagues on their way to England; but so soon as he was convinced of the truth of the vision before him, and learned the melancholy cause, an involuntary tear started from the eye of friendship and compassion, and we were received in the most affectionate manner.

His Excellency lost no time in engaging the ship Rolla, then lying in port, bound to China, to go to the rescue of the officers and crews of the Porpoise and Cato; I accompanied the governor on board the Rolla a day or two afterwards, and articles were signed by which the commander, Mr. Robert Cumming, engaged to call at Wreck Reef, take every person on board and carry them to Canton, upon terms which showed him to take the interest in our misfortune which might be expected from a British seaman. The governor ordered two colonial schooners to accompany the Rolla, to bring back those who preferred returning to Port Jackson, with such stores of the Porpoise as could be procured; and every thing was done that an anxious desire to forward His Majesty's service and alleviate misfortune could devise; even private individuals put wine, live stock, and vegetables, unasked, on board the Rolla for the officers upon the reef.

My anxiety to get back to Wreck Reef, and from thence to England with the greatest despatch, induced the governor to offer me one of the schooners to go through Torres' Strait and by the most expeditious passage to Europe; rather than take the long route by China in the Rolla. This schooner was something less than a Gravesend passage boat, being only of twenty-nine tons burthen; and therefore it required some consideration before acceding to the proposal. Her small size, when compared with the distance from Port Jackson to England, was not my greatest objection to the little Cumberland; it was the quickness of her motion and the want of convenience, which would prevent the charts and journal of my voyage from being prepared on the passage, and render the whole so much time lost to this important object. On the other hand, the advantage of again passing through, and collecting more information of Torres' Strait, and of arriving in England three or four months sooner to commence the outfit of another ship, were important considerations; and joined to some ambition of being the first to undertake so long a voyage in such a small vessel, and a desire to put an early stop to the account which captain Palmer would probably give of our total loss, they proved sufficient inducements to accept the governor's offer, on finding his vessel had the character of being a strong, good little sea boat.

The Cumberland was at that time absent up the river Hawkesbury, and the Francis, the other schooner, was lying on shore and could not be got off before the following spring tides; on these accounts, and from the Rolla not being quite fitted, it was thirteen days after my arrival in the boat before the whole could be ready to sail. This delay caused me much uneasiness, under the apprehension that we might not arrive before our friends at the reef, despairing of assistance, should have made some unsuccessful attempt to save themselves; and this idea pursued me so much, that every day seemed to be a week until I got out of the harbour with the three vessels.

Governor King's answer to my communication respecting the shipwreck of the Porpoise and Cato, and the orders under which I acted in embarking in the Cumberland, are contained in the following letter.

Sydney, New South Wales., Sept. 17, 1803.
Sir,

In acknowledging the receipt of yours with its inclosure of the 9th instant, whilst I lament the misfortune that has befallen the Porpoise and Cato, I am thankful that no more lives have been lost than the three you mention. I have every reason to be assured that no precaution was omitted by lieutenant Fowler and yourself to avoid the accident, and I am equally satisfied with your account of the exertions of the officers and men after the loss of the ships, both for the preservation of the stores and maintaining order in their present situation; nor can I sufficiently commend your voluntary services and those who came with you, in undertaking a voyage of 700 miles in an open boat, to procure relief for our friends now on the bank; and I hope for the honour of humanity, that if the Bridgewater be safe, the commander may be able to give some possible reason for his not ascertaining whether any had survived the shipwreck, as there appears too much reason to believe he has persuaded himself all perished.

No time has been lost in prevailing upon the master of the Rolla, bound to China, to take on board the officers and seamen now on the reef, belonging to the Porpoise and Investigator, and carrying them to Canton whither he is bound; on the conditions expressed in the agreement entered into with him by me, and which you have witnessed. For that purpose I have caused a proportion of all species of provisions to be put on board at full allowance, for seventy men for ten weeks from the reef; I shall also give to lieutenant Fowler the instructions for his conduct which I have communicated to you, and direct him to consult with you on the measures to be adopted by him for executing those instructions, as far as situation and events may render them practicable.

And as you agree with me that the Cumberland, colonial schooner of twenty-nine tons, built here, is capable of performing the voyage to England by way of Torres' Strait, and it being essential to the furthering His Majesty's service that you should reach England by the most prompt conveyance with your charts and journals, I have directed the commissary to make that vessel over to you, with her present furniture, sails, etc; and to complete her from the stores of the Investigator with such other articles as you may require, together with a proportion of provisions for six months, for ten officers and men. And on your arrival at Wreck Reef you will select such officers and men as you may judge necessary, lieutenant Fowler having my orders on that head.

After having given every assistance to get the people and as many stores as can be taken on board the Rolla, and given the commander of the Francis schooner such orders as circumstances may require, for bringing those who may choose to be discharged from the service and as many stores as she can bring, you will then proceed to England by the route you may judge most advisable and beneficial for His Majesty's service. On your arrival in

London you will deliver my letters to the Admiralty and the principal secretary of state for the colonies.

In case any unforeseen circumstances should prevent the accomplishment of the voyage in the Cumberland, you will take such measures as may appear most conducive to the interest of His Majesty's service, either by selling the vessel, or letting her for freight at the Cape or elsewhere, if any merchants choose to send proper officers and men to conduct her back; and in the event of your being obliged to dispose of her, you will account with His Majesty's principal secretary of state for the colonies for the proceeds.

I am, etc.,

(Signed) Philip Gidley King.

[EAST COAST. TOWARDS WRECK REEF.]

The small size of the Cumberland made it necessary to stop at every convenient place on the way to England, for water and refreshment; and I proposed Coepang Bay in Timor, Mauritius, the Cape of Good Hope, St. Helena, and some one of the Western Isles; but governor King objected to Mauritius, from not wishing to encourage any communication between the French colonies and Port Jackson; and also because he had understood that hurricanes often prevailed in the neighbourhood of that island, about the time of year when I should be passing; he left this matter, however, to be decided by necessity and my judgment, and gave me two letters for the governor of Mauritius, to be forwarded from the Cape, or by the best opportunity. At those places in the Indian Seas where I might stop, he requested me to make inquires into the facility of obtaining cattle for his colony, with the price and the traffic with which they might be best procured; and to send this information by any ship bound to Port Jackson.

WEDNESDAY 21 SEPTEMBER 1803

Every thing being prepared for our departure, I sailed out of the harbour in the Cumberland on the 21st at daylight, with the Rolla and Francis in company. Mr. Inman, the astronomer, had taken a passage in the Rolla with his instruments; and of the thirteen persons who came with me in the boat, captain Park and his second mate were on board that ship, and the boatswain of the Investigator with the ten seamen composed my crew in the schooner. We had a fresh breeze at south-east, and the Cumberland appeared to sail as well as could be expected; but the wind becoming stronger towards night, she lay over so much upon the broad side that little sail could be carried; and instead of being tight, as had been represented, her upper works then admitted a great deal of water. Next morning [THURSDAY 22 SEPTEMBER 1803], the wind having rather increased than diminished, I found we should soon be obliged to lie to altogether, and that if we passed Port Stephens there was no place of shelter for a long distance where the schooner could be saved from drifting on shore; the signal was therefore made to tack, and at dusk the Rolla and Francis ran into Port Stephens. Not being able to reach so far, I anchored in a small bight under Point Stephens, in very bad plight; the pumps proving to be so nearly useless, that we could not prevent the water from half filling the hold; and two hours longer would have reduced us to baling with buckets, and perhaps have been fatal. This essay did not lead me to think favourably of the vessel, in which I had undertaken a voyage half round the globe.

FRIDAY 23 SEPTEMBER 1803

Next morning I joined the Rolla and Francis; and it being then calm, we did not quit Port Stephens until the afternoon. At night the wind again blew strong from the south-east; but the desire to arrive at Wreck Reef overcoming my apprehensions, the schooner was made snug and we persevered. Our inability to carry sail was so much the more provoking, that this wind was as fair as could be wished; but whilst the Cumberland could scarcely bear a close-reefed main sail and jib without danger of oversetting, the Rolla went along under double-reefed top sails in great tranquillity; and to avoid parting company was obliged to keep her courses up, and to back a top sail from time to time.

SATURDAY 24 SEPTEMBER 1803

(Atlas, Plate X.)

The wind moderated next day, and allowed us to make better progress. It afterwards veered round to the north-east, and prevented us from fetching more than ten miles to the east of the reef by Mr. Inman's time keeper, when we came into the proper latitude. We bore away for it, however, on Oct. 1 [SATURDAY 1 OCTOBER 1803], and ran more than a degree to the west; when finding no reef or bank, it appeared that we must have been something to the west of Wreck Reef when the time keeper showed ten miles to the eastward. This obliged us to work back again, and it was not till the 7th [FRIDAY 7 OCTOBER 1803] that we got sight of the ensign upon the top of the bank.*

[* The want of my journal has prevented me from stating any particulars of this passage very correctly; but I have lately obtained a sight of Mr. Inman's observations, and it appears from them that his time keeper (Kendal's No. 45) erred 31' to the east on Oct. 1, and that on the 2nd a.m. our corrected longitude was 153° 52'. We ran westward till that evening, and must therefore have gone to about 153° 25', or 1° 54' west of Wreck-Reef Bank; and as no dangers were seen, this shows how completely the Reef is separated from the great Barrier of the coast; a point which it is of some importance to have ascertained.]

[EAST COAST. WRECK REEF.]

It was six weeks on this day that I had quitted the reef in the boat, for the purpose of seeking the means to relieve my officers and people. The bank was first seen from the Rolla's mast head, and soon afterward two boats were perceived under sail; and advancing nearer, we saw one boat make for the Rolla and the other returning to the bank. The Porpoise had not yet gone to pieces; but was still lying on her beam ends, high up on the reef, a frail, but impressive monument of our misfortune.

In the afternoon I anchored under the lee of the bank, in 18 fathoms coral sand, and a salute of eleven guns from it was immediately fired, the carronades of the Porpoise having been transported from the wreck. On landing, I was greeted with three hearty cheers, and the utmost joy by my officers and people; and the pleasure of rejoining my companions so amply provided with the means of relieving their distress, made this one of the happiest moments of my life.

The two boats we had seen, were the Porpoise's remaining cutter and a new boat constructed during my absence; it was just completed, and lieutenant Fowler had this morning gone out to try its sailing against the cutter. My safe arrival at Port Jackson became a subject of much doubt after the first month; and they had begun to reconcile their minds to making the best use of the means they possessed to reach some frequented port. The Rolla's top-gallant sail was first seen in the horizon by a man in the new boat, and was taken for a bird; but regarding it more steadfastly, he started up and exclaimed, d--n my bl--d what's that! It was soon recognised to be a sail, and caused a general acclamation of joy, for they doubted not it was a ship coming to their succour. Lieutenant Flinders, then commanding officer on the bank, was in his tent calculating some lunar distances, when one of the young gentlemen ran to him, calling, "Sir, Sir! A ship and two schooners in sight!" After a little consideration, Mr. Flinders said he supposed it was his brother come back, and asked if the vessels were near? He was answered, not yet; upon which he desired to be informed when they should reach the anchorage, and very calmly resumed his calculations: such are the varied effects produced by the same circumstance upon different minds. When the desired report was made, he ordered the salute to be fired, and took part in the general satisfaction.

My plan of proceeding at the reef having been arranged on the passage, I immediately began to put it in execution. The people were assembled on the bank, and informed that such as chose to be discharged from the service might return to Port Jackson in the Francis schooner; and that the rest would be taken on board the Rolla and carried to China, with the exception of ten officers and men whom I named, to go to England with me in the Cumberland, if they would risk themselves in so small a vessel; for notwithstanding what had been discovered of the bad qualities of the schooner, I determined to proceed, at least so far as to reach some port where a passage might be procured in a better vessel without losing time. The determinations of all were required to be given on the following day; and in the mean time we began to take on board the few stores necessary to complete the Cumberland for our voyage, and especially to fill the holds with water, of which there was yet a good quantity remaining on the bank.

MONDAY 10 OCTOBER 1803

On the 10th, three days after our arrival, the Rolla had received the people destined for her, with part of the provisions and stores; and the Cumberland was ready to sail. All those whom I had named, with the exception of my clerk, volunteered to go in the schooner; viz., Mr. John Aken, master, and Mr. Edward Charrington, boatswain of the Investigator, my servant, and seven chosen seamen. A cask containing what had been saved of my specimens of mineralogy and conchology was taken on board, as also the charts, books, and papers of every kind, with the instruments received from the Navy Board and the sole time keeper which had not stopped.

Mr. Denis Lacy, master's mate of the Investigator, desiring to return to Port Jackson, he was charged with my letter to His Excellency governor King; and I gave him an order to command the new boat. It was about the size of the Cumberland, had a deck, and was called the *Resource*; and we manned her with a part of those people whose choice led them back to Port Jackson. I ordered Mr. James Aikin, commander of the Francis, and Mr. Lacy, to take on board for the colony as much of the stores as they should be able; and on their arrival, to make a statement to the governor of the condition in which they might leave the Porpoise, and what remained on the bank.

The officers journals, which were to be sent to the Admiralty at the conclusion of the voyage, had not been demanded at the time of our shipwreck; lieutenant Fowler was therefore directed to take all that were saved belonging to the officers embarked with him in the Rolla; and lest any accident should happen to the Cumberland, I committed to his charge a copy of four charts, being all of the East and North Coasts which there had been time to get ready; with these he took a short letter to the secretary of the Admiralty, and one to the Victualling Board inclosing such vouchers as had been saved from the wreck. To Mr. Inman I gave the remaining instruments belonging to the Board of Longitude, reserving only a time keeper and a telescope; the large and most valuable instruments had very fortunately been delivered to him before we had sailed from Port Jackson in the Porpoise.

These matters being arranged, I pressed captain Cumming to depart, fearing that a change of wind might expose the Rolla to danger; but finding him desirous to take off more provisions and stores, I made sail for a bank or rather islet seven miles distant at the eastern extremity of Wreck Reef, for the purpose of collecting seabirds eggs, and if possible taking a turtle. The Rolla joined on the following day [TUESDAY 11 OCTOBER 1803], and I went on board to take leave of Messrs. Fowler and Flinders and the other officers and gentlemen; at noon we parted company with three cheers, the Rolla steering north-eastward for China, whilst my course was directed for Torres' Strait.

With the time keeper, Earnshaw's No. 520, I had received from lieutenant Flinders an account of its error from mean Greenwich time at noon there Oct. 6, and its rate of going during the fourteen preceding days, which were as under.

No. 520, slow 0h 9' 49.35" and losing 34.13" per day.

The *latitude* of Wreck-Reef Bank was ascertained from eight meridian observations from the sea, and four from an artificial horizon: the mean of the latter, which are considered the best, is 22° 11' 23" S.

Longitude from sixty sets of lunar distances, of which the individual results are given in Table VIII. of the Appendix No. I. to this volume, 155° 18' 50.5" E.

The longitude of the bank, as given by Earnshaw's No. 520 on Aug. 28, eleven days after the shipwreck, was 155° 4' 14.6" with the Port Jackson rate, or 14' 35.9" less than the lunar observations. In laying down the Porpoise's track on the chart, this error has been corrected by an equal proportion, according to the time of each observation for the longitude.

Mr. Flinders deduced the *variation* of the compass from observing the sun's magnetic azimuth a. m. and p. m., when equal altitudes were taken, and comparing the mean azimuth at corresponding altitudes with the true meridian; this method is probably not the best, and the results from two compasses differed considerably; Walker's compass, marked No. 1, giving 9° 17' east from ten observations, and that marked No. 2, 13° 54' from five observations. The first is undoubtedly the best, though possibly not very correct.

There are here two regular *tides* daily, and it was high water on the day of full moon at 8h 50' in the morning; the rise was six feet two inches, but the night tide will probably reach to eight, or perhaps nine feet at the height of the springs.

Some account was given of Wreck-Reef Bank before quitting it in the boat, but I had not then acquired a knowledge of the whole extent of the reef. It is about twenty miles long, and from a quarter, to one mile and a half in breadth; and consists of many distinct patches of different magnitudes, the six principal of which are from four to eight or ten miles in circuit. They are separated by channels of one mile to near a league in width; and in the two easternmost I found from 8 to 10 fathoms, and nothing to prevent a ship passing through in a case of necessity. Four of the six larger patches have each a sand bank near the middle, which do not appear to have been lately covered by the tide; and they are now more or less frequented by sea birds, such as noddies, boobies, tropic, and man-of-war birds, gannets, and perhaps some others. Of these four banks, two lie to the west and one to the east of that near which our ships struck; but the eastern bank is the most considerable, and most frequented by birds; turtle also land there occasionally, and this bank was not improperly called *Bird Islet*, being now covered with coarse grass, some shrubs, and a soil to which the birds are every day making an increase.

Bird Islet being to windward of, and only seven miles distant from our bank, it was frequently visited by the gentlemen during my absence. Besides sea birds of the species already mentioned, they procured many thousand eggs; and also four turtle, of which one weighed 459 pounds, and contained so many eggs, that lieutenant Fowler's journal says no less than 1940, large and small, were counted. These supplies, with shell fish gathered from the reef, and fish, were a great resource, and admitted of a saving in the salt provisions; as the occasional rains, from which several casks were filled, did of their fresh water.

The *trepang* was found on Wreck Reef, and soup was attempted to be made of it; but whether our cooks had not the method of stewing it down, or that the trepang is suited only to the vitiated taste of the Chinese, nothing good was produced

Oats, maize, and pumpkin seeds were planted upon Wreck-Reef Bank, as also upon Bird Islet; and the young plants had come up, and were in a tolerably flourishing state; some of these may possibly succeed upon the islet, but upon the bank it is scarcely to be hoped. The cocoa nut is capable of resisting the light sprays of the sea which frequently pass over these banks, and it is to be regretted that we had none to plant upon them. A cluster of these majestic and useful palms would have been an excellent beacon to warn mariners of their danger; and in the case where darkness might render them unavailing in this respect, their fruit would at least afford some salutary nourishment to the shipwrecked seamen. The navigator who should distribute ten thousand cocoa nuts amongst the numerous sand banks of the Great Ocean and Indian Sea, would be entitled to the gratitude of all maritime nations, and of every friend to humanity. I may be thought to attribute too much importance to this object in saying, that such a distribution ought to be a leading article in the instructions for any succeeding voyage of discovery or investigation to these parts; but it is from having suffered ourselves that we learn to appreciate the misfortunes and wants of others. and become doubly interested in preventing or relieving them. "The human heart," as an elegant author observes, "resembles certain medicinal trees. which yield not their healing balm until they have themselves been wounded."*

[* Le coeur est comme ces sortes d'arbres, qui ne donnent leur baume pour les blessures des hommes que lorsque le fer les a blessés eux-mêmes. Chateaubriant's *Génie de Christianisme, Episode d' Attala.*]

CHAPTER III.
Passage in the Cumberland to Torres' Strait.
Eastern Fields and Pandora's Entrance.
New channels amongst the reefs.
Anchorage at Half-way Island, and under the York Isles.
Prince of Wales's Islands further examined.
Booby Isle.
Passage across the Gulph of Carpentaria.
Anchorage at Wessel's Islands.

Passage to Coepang Bay, in Timor; and to Mauritius, where the leakiness of the Cumberland makes it necessary to stop. Anchorage at the Baye du Cap, and departure for Port Louis.

[EAST COAST. TOWARDS TORRES' STRAIT]
TUESDAY 11 OCTOBER 1803
(Atlas, Plate I.)

On parting from the Rolla, at noon Oct. 11, off Bird Islet, our course was steered N. N. W. by compass for Torres' Strait. At eight in the evening we had run thirteen leagues from Wreck Reef, without seeing any danger; but I thought it advisable to lie to in the night, until the distance was further increased. We made sail again at five in the morning [WEDNESDAY 12 OCTOBER 1803], and at noon were in 20° 46' south and 155° 2' east. During the two following days and nights, our course by compass was N. W. by N., and afterwards N. W.; and on the 15th [SATURDAY 15 OCTOBER 1803] at noon we had reached the latitude 15° 29' and longitude 151° 24', the current having set, upon the average of four days, ¾ of a mile an hour to the W. N. W. This situation was a little to the north, and about one degree to the east of Bougainville's Bank of Diana, and the tropic birds, petrels, and boobies seen every day were this evening more numerous, especially the boobies; they most probably belonged to Diana's Bank, but lest some other might lie in our way, we hauled to the wind at eight o'clock. The little Cumberland was still very leaky at such times as the wind came more on the side and caused her to lie over; and the pumps were so bad that a fourth part of the day was frequently required at them to keep her free, and they were becoming worse from such constant use.

SUNDAY 16 OCTOBER 1803

Our north-west course was resumed at five in the morning, and continued without interruption, or sight of any danger, to the 19th [WEDNESDAY 19 OCTOBER 1803] at noon, when the latitude was 10° 53' south, and longitude by time keeper 147° 6' east; the current had set above ¾ of a mile an hour to the N. 60° W., and we had every day seen boobies, noddies, tropic birds, and some gulls. At four in the afternoon the course was altered one point more west, in order to make the Eastern Fields (Atlas, Plate XIII), whose extent to the southward, not having been seen in the Investigator, I wished now to ascertain. The breakers came in sight at eight next morning [THURSDAY 20 OCTOBER 1803], and we hauled up to pass round their south end; but the wind being scant for going to windward of all, and the small gap before seen in the middle appearing to be passable for the Cumberland, we bore up for it. The depth at less than a quarter of a mile off was 40 fathoms, then 6, 7, 4 in the centre of the opening, 8, and no ground with the hand line; this front reef seeming to be a mere ledge of coral, which extended N. N. E. and S. S. W.; and that part of the opening in it where the sea did not break, is about one mile wide. Immediately on getting through, altitudes were taken for the time keeper; and the longitude, reduced to the north-east extremity of the Eastern Fields, was 145° 44½' east, or about 1' less than what had been found in the Investigator from Broad Sound. In steering W. N. W., two small patches of reef were left to the south and one to the north, about five miles from the opening; other reefs then came in sight ahead and on each bow; and after sounding in 34 fathoms coral sand, and observing the latitude 10° 2 1/3', we passed through a narrow channel between them, having no ground at 7 fathoms. At one o'clock, the western extremity of these reefs bore S. 16° E. two miles, and others were seen in the horizon extending from N. W. to W. S. W.; we passed close round the north end of these; but the single breaker laid down the year before, and which should lie about five miles to the N. N. E., was not perceived. At three o'clock, in steering westward, the last reefs were out of sight astern; and nothing more had been seen at seven, when we hauled to the wind for the night. An amplitude observed at sunset, with the schooner's head W. by S., gave 6° 2' east variation.

FRIDAY 21 OCTOBER 1803

We tacked every two or three hours, until daylight; and then bore away W. S. W. by compass, to make the south side of the Pandora's Entrance, which I had not seen in the Investigator. Soon after eight o'clock, breakers came in sight; and we stood off and on till noon, to fix their latitude and longitude, and ascertain our position with respect to Murray's

Islands before entering the Strait. The sun was vertical and therefore difficult to be observed; but in taking Mr. Aken's observation on one side and mine on the other, which differed only 3½', the mean latitude 10° 0½', could not be far wrong. The reef in sight was shown by this observation to be on the south side of the Pandora's Entrance, as I wished; and its north end will lie in 10° 59' south, and longitude by the time keeper 144° 40' east. We bore away so soon as the observation was obtained, and in passing close round the north end, got soundings at two casts, in 7 and 5 fathoms.

This reef lies N. N. E. and S. S. W., and is about seven miles long with a breadth from one to three miles; its form is nearly that of a boot, and the outer edges are probably dry at low tide; but there was a considerable space within, where the water looked blue, as if very deep. The origin of that class of islands which abound in the Great Ocean, under the names of Bow, Lagoon, etc., may here be traced. The exterior bank of coral will, in the course of years, become land, as in them; whilst the interior water will preserve its depth to a longer period, and form a lagoon, with no other outlet than perhaps one or two little openings for canoes or boats. In Mr. Dalrymple's chart of the Pandora's track, there is a dry bank marked on the north-west part of the reef; but this commencement of the metamorphosis was not visible to us, probably from its being covered by the tide, for it was then near high water. In some future age, when Boot Island shall be visited, this little remark, it it live so long, may be of some interest to the geographer.

[NORTH COAST. TORRES' STRAIT.]

I hauled up under the lee side of the reef, intending to anchor and go in a boat to sound the deep water within; but not finding any ground with 70 fathoms at a mile off, we bore away at two o'clock to make Murray's Islands. At three, breakers were seen four or five miles to the southward, and others, perhaps on the same reef, about three miles W. S. W. from them; in half an hour the largest of Murray's Islands came in sight to the W. by N.; and our course being continued to six o'clock, the centre then bore N. 78° W. nearly four leagues, but the front reefs, which could not be more than half that distance in the same direction, were not visible. We then hauled to the wind, and stood off and on till daylight [SATURDAY 22 OCTOBER 1803], when the largest island bore W. by S.

Murray's Islands may be considered as the key to the best passage yet known through Torres' Strait, and my route to them in the Investigator being circuitous, I wished to ascertain whether a more direct track might not be found; we therefore steered to make the north-eastern reefs, and on coming in with the breakers, ran along their south side at the distance of one or two miles. At half past seven, the termination of these reefs bore N. N. W.; but another reef, which extended far to the south, had for some time been in sight, and a dry sand on its north end now bore S. W. by W. one mile. In the opening between them was a small patch of coral, and several green spots in the water round it; but there appearing to be room for the Cumberland to pass on the north side, I ventured through, sounding in 20 and 23 fathoms without finding bottom.

This opening is a mile wide, and lies five or six miles, nearly E. N. E., from the largest of Murray's Islands; it would consequently be more direct to pass through it than to follow the Investigator's track round the north-eastern reefs; but from the narrowness of the opening and the many green spots where the depth is unknown to me, I dare not recommend it to a ship, though very practicable for small vessels in fine weather. The dry bank on the south side of the opening will probably be covered at three-quarters flood.

After clearing the passage, I steered W. N. W. to avoid going near Murray's Islands, lest the small size of the Cumberland should tempt the Indians to make an attack; this they were likely to do if the opportunity offered, and many were standing on the shore with their canoes seemingly in readiness. At 8h 50' the large island bore S. 6° E. to 13° W., three or four miles; and our position in longitude being very nearly the same with that of my former anchorage, altitudes were taken for the time keeper. The result, when corrected, was 144° 2' 0" east, and in the Investigator it had been 144° 2' 58", being a difference scarcely worth notice. When it is considered that Wreck Reef, whence the Cumberland's departure was taken, and Coepang in Timor, by which the longitude is corrected, are laid down from observations wholly distinct from those at Upper Head and Sweers' Island, which regulated the Investigator's longitude, this near coincidence will be thought remarkable; and it must also be allowed to show, that an equally accelerated rate and supplemental correction are improvements on the ordinary management of time keepers.

At this time, the large reef to the north of Murray's Islands was distant one or two miles, and we steered westward along it, to get into my former track; but the man at the mast head saying that the water was discoloured, and that he did not think there was any passage in the direction we steered, I thought myself deceived in the distance of the island; and the schooner was hauled up two points to the southward, where the appearance was better. It became evident, however, that the discoloured water was in the same ripplings of tide through which the Investigator had passed without finding bottom at 30 fathoms; and no doubt it was from these ripplings that the discolouring arose.

At ten o'clock, the top of the largest island bore S. 74° E. five or six miles, we had reefs at the distance of half a mile to a mile on each beam, and I then found that we were to the south of the Investigator's track; but the channel being clear ahead, and taking a direction nearly straight for Cape York, I steered onward, being rather pleased than sorry at having thus got by accident into a new route. Darnley's Island was seen from the mast head before eleven; and when the top of Murray's Island bore E. 1° S. it was set at N. N. W., the depth being then 52 fathoms on a bottom of small stones, coral, and shells. The great line of reefs which had been kept on the larbord beam of the Investigator, was now on the starbord beam of the schooner; but we had also a great mass of reefs on the other side, forming between them a kind of channel from two to four miles broad, leading south-westward. We ran on at the rate of five knots until noon, when the depth was 25 fathoms, soft sand, and our situation as under,

Latitude observed to the south, 9° 58½' Longitude brought on, 143 45
Murray's I., top of the largest, N. 78 E. Murray's I., south-westernmost, N. 82 E.

The channel was now five or six miles wide, and no interruption yet appeared; but breakers were seen a-head before two o'clock, and seemed to connect the reefs to leeward with those on the weather side; and there being a small opening on the starbord beam, we bore away north-west through it, towards the Investigator's track. Other reefs, however, obstructed the way, upon one of which was a dry bank; and seeing a sort of middle channel within them, we hauled up W. by S. into it, and afterwards S. W. The sea did not break upon these reefs, and the sun being on the starbord bow, prevented us from knowing how they lay to leeward. At four, the coral bottom was seen under the schooner, and the depth was no more than 2 fathoms; we tacked immediately, and in ten minutes were able to weather the end of the reef at the outlet of the middle channel, where no obstruction appeared; but a bank, probably not of coral, was found to run across, and in passing over it we had 3, 1½, 2, 3, 8 fathoms, and in five minutes 22 on a soft bottom. A swell was then perceived coming from E. S. E., which showed that the weather reefs also there terminated; it even implied that the waves had no obstruction for many miles, probably as far as the great outer reef seen by the Pandora.

Half-way Island came in sight as soon as the middle channel was cleared, and we steered west, carrying all sail to reach it before dark. In passing round the north end of its reef at sunset, we had 18 fathoms, and presently anchored in 20, with the centre of the island bearing S. by E. ½ E. one mile, and the reef from E. ½ S. to S. W. by S. Next morning at daylight [SUNDAY 23 OCTOBER 1803], Mr. Aken went on shore to bring off some shells of the large cockle (*chama gigas*), which the Indians place under the pandanus trees to catch water, and on his return at eight o'clock, we resumed our course to the south-westward, passing between some dry sands before seen in the Investigator. I then kept up more southward to fetch the York Isles, and this took us between two other sands surrounded with small reefs. There were many birds, and a pole was standing up on the northern bank; and the wind becoming very light, an anchor was dropped in 14 fathoms under the west side, and I went on shore.

This bank or key was very little above high water; but a young pandanus had been planted on the top and surrounded with a circle of stones, apparently to protect it from the turtle, whose tracks were fresh on the sand. It appeared from thence, that the Indians come here at times; and this tree had been planted with a view, most probably, to obtain fresh water by the same means as at Half-way Island. The latitude of the bank, according to Mr.

Aken's meridian observation, is 10° 18' south, longitude by the time keeper 143° 6' east, and there is a similar bank lying two or three miles to the southward.

On my return the south-east trade had freshened up, and we steered S. W. by compass, in soundings from 13 to 11 fathoms, soft ground. Some of the small woody isles before laid down, were seen to the north-westward, but nothing else till four o'clock; the high flat-topped York Isle then came in sight, and at six the following bearings were set.

Mount Adolphus, the flat top, S. 33° W. Two rocks on its south side, S. 17 W. Western York Isle, the north end, S. 69 W. A low distant isle (from the mast head), S ½ E.

I purposed anchoring between the flat-topped island and the western isle; but several rocks being seen there, and the night coming on, we bore away to leeward of the rocks and came to in 13 fathoms, soon after seven o'clock. The tide was setting to the westward, and so continued till half past nine, when it turned to the east, and ran till half past three in the morning [MONDAY 24 OCTOBER 1803]; if the rise by the shore corresponded with the stream, it was high water *three hours and a half after* the moon's passage; which would be five hours later than at Murray's Islands, and one hour earlier than it had appeared to be at those of the Prince of Wales (see Ch. V, 1 November). A fresh breeze from south-east raised a swell here, but the anchor held all night; and before getting under way next morning, I set the following bearings of the land.

Flat-topped I., distant three miles S. 42° to 2° E. Flat-topped I., centre of Mount Adolphus, S. 32 E. C. York, outer of three islets near the E. extreme, S. 2 E. Western York I., distant 1½ miles S. 18 to 88 W. Northern double I., imperfectly from aloft, N. W. by W.½ W.

On passing the north end of the western isle at seven o'clock, I took altitudes for the time keeper, and from thence deduced the longitude of Mount Adolphus to be 142° 40' east; we then hauled up for Cape York, with soundings between 14 and 10 fathoms, leaving on the starbord hand a rock which lies S. 78° W. five miles from the north end of the western isle. At half past eight, two rocks close to the northern extremity of the Cape were distant four or five miles, the Prince of Wales's Islands were coming in sight, and the following bearings were taken.

Western York Isle, north end, N. 70° E. C. York, north extreme, S. 58 E. C. York, hill at the north-west extreme, S. 11 W. Possession Isle, apparently, of capt. Cook, S. 26° to 33 W. Northern double Isle, centre, North.

On the largest of the Prince of Wales' Islands was a hill forming something like two horns at the top; we steered a direct course for this hill, and perceived a bight or opening two miles to the south of it, by which the sea may probably have a communication with the water before observed within the great island. From abreast of Horned Hill we followed the line of the shore northward, in soundings from 4 to 7 fathoms at one or two miles off; and soon after ten o'clock hauled west into the opening between this land and Wednesday Island, to pass through the middle of the group. Our soundings were variable between 5 and 3 fathoms, until approaching Hammond's Island; when there not appearing to be depth enough on its south side, I steered out northward, leaving a rock on the starbord hand within which there was only 2 fathoms.

This rock seems to be the small, dark-coloured island described by Mr. Hamilton as being near the centre of Sandwich Sound (see Introduction); and if so, Wolf's Bay, in which he says there is from 5 to 7 fathoms and commodious anchorage for shipping, should be that inclosed piece of water seen from the top of Good's Island; but to me at this time, there did not appear to be any ship passage into it from the northward. An island lies at the entrance, and on its west side the depth may probably be more considerable.

On getting out from between Wednesday and Hammond's Islands, we steered along the south side of the great north-western reef; and at noon our observation and bearings were as under.

Latitude observed to the north, 10° 31' Hammond's I., the north rock dist. 2 miles, N. 73 E. Good's I., former station on the S. W. hill, S. 23 W. Hawkesbury I., the highest part, N. 14 W.

Booby Isle was in sight from the mast head at one o'clock, bearing nearly W. S. W.; and soon after three we anchored one mile to leeward of it, in 7 fathoms, soft sand. A boat was sent on shore, which presently came back loaded with boobies; and fresh turtle tracks having been perceived, the crew returned to watch, and at midnight we received five turtle. These appeared to be of the species called hawkes-bill; the shells and skins, as also their fat, were of a red tinge, and they had longer necks than the turtle procured at Wellesley's Islands, to which they were much inferior, both in size and quality.

When entering the Gulph of Carpentaria in the Investigator, I had remarked what appeared to be a considerable error in the relative positions of Booby Isle and the flat-topped York Island, as they are laid down by captain Cook; and to obtain more certainty, the longitude of the flat top had been observed this morning from the time keeper, and I anchored here this afternoon to do the same by Booby Isle. The result showed the difference of longitude between them to be 43½', differing less than 1' from what had been deduced in the Investigator, whereas, by captain Cook, they are placed 63' asunder. The high respect to which the labours of that great man are entitled, had caused me to entertain some doubt of the reality of this error until the present verification. It is to be wholly ascribed to the circumstance of his not having had a time keeper in his *first* voyage; and a more eminent proof of the utility of this valuable instrument cannot be given, than that so able a navigator could not always avoid making errors so considerable as this, when deprived of its assistance.

A meridian altitude of the moon placed Booby Isle in latitude 10° 36' south; and the longitude from a medium of the Investigator's and Cumberland's time keepers, was 141° 56½' east. A morning's amplitude taken after quitting the isle when the schooner's head was W. by S., gave the uncorrected variation 5° 38' east.

TUESDAY 25 OCTOBER 1803

At daybreak next morning, having a fresh trade wind, we steered W. by S. by compass, the soundings increasing gradually from 7 fathoms to 13 at noon, when our latitude was 10° 38' and longitude 141° 17'. No reefs or other dangers had been seen to the west of Booby Isle; nor were any met with in steering across the Gulph of Carpentaria towards Cape Wilberforce (Atlas, Plate XIV), though many birds, principally boobies, were seen every day. We ran in the night, with the precaution of heaving to every four hours, to sound; the depth was from 30 to 36 fathoms on a muddy bottom, nearly all across the Gulph.

FRIDAY 28 OCTOBER 1803

(Atlas, Plate XV.)

On 28th at two in the morning, Cape Wilberforce being seen directly ahead, we hove to in 18 fathoms till daylight; the south-east extreme of the cape then bore S. 54° W, and the largest of Bromby's Isles was two miles distant to the northward. After making some short tacks, we passed through between the two outer isles, with soundings from 6 to 11 fathoms; and at ten o'clock, when clear of the passage, the bearings of the nearest lands were as under:

Bromby's I., the largest, cliffy S. E. end, S. 34° W. Bromby's I., outermost, highest part, dist. 1¼ m., S. 50 E. Truant Isle, centre, N. 37 E. Two islets, dist. 5 miles, centres, N. 24° and 32 W. Wigram's Island, extremes, N. 55 to S. 87 W.

The longitude of our situation according to the positions laid down in the Investigator, would be 136° 41' 10", and the time keeper now gave 136° 42' 12". It was principally for the sake of comparing the two longitudes, that I made the land near Cape Wilberforce.

[NORTH COAST. WESSEL'S ISLANDS.]

We steered northward for the two islets, and at noon, when the latitude from an observation to the south was 11° 43', but from bearings 11° 42', they were distant three quarters of a mile to the W. by S.; these islets had been set from the south-east head of Cotton's Island at N. 42° 35' to 45° 5' E., and that head was now seen bearing S. 45¼° W. At one o'clock the Wessel's Islands came in sight, and I hauled more up, wishing to ascertain their extent to the northward; but the wind being at E. N. E, we could not pass to windward before dark, and therefore steered for an opening between the two outer islands. There were strong ripplings and whirlpools of tide at the entrance of the opening, with very variable soundings between 5 and 16 fathoms; and finding we could not get through in time, the sun being then near the horizon, an anchor was dropped near a small beach on the north side, in 4 fathoms, out of the set of the tides.

SATURDAY 29 OCTOBER 1803

Next morning I landed on the northern island, to take bearings and search for water, and the boat's crew had axes to cut some fire wood. Four or five Indians made their appearance, but as we advanced they retired; and I therefore left them to themselves, having usually found that to bring on an interview with the Australians, it was best to seem careless about it. A Malay prow had been thrown on the beach, and whilst the boat's crew was busied in cutting up the wreck for fuel, the Indians approached gradually, and a friendly intercourse took place; but as no water could be found, and time was more precious than the company of these people, they were presented with our axes after the work was done, and we got under way soon after ten o'clock.

This island appears to be the outermost of the chain called Wessel's Islands, which extend thirteen leagues in a north-east direction from the main land near Point Dale. It seemed to be eight or nine miles in length, by about five in breadth; the southern part is sandy and sterile, but some trees are produced; and I saw kangaroos of a small kind, too lean to be worth the pursuit their shyness required. The natives are of the same colour and appearance as in other parts of Terra Australis, and go equally naked; their presence here showed the south end of the island to be not wholly destitute of fresh water; but in the limited search we had time to make, none could be found, though traces of torrents denoted the falling of heavy rains in some part of the year. The island to the south-west, which is of somewhat greater extent, though less in elevation, had much the same appearance.

A distance of two miles between the islands seems to present a fair opening; but there is a reef of low rocks on the west side, and the ripplings and whirlpools caused by the meeting of the tides take away the command of a vessel in light winds; so that, although I went through safely in the Cumberland, the passage can be recommended to a *ship* only in a case of necessity. The latitude of our anchorage under the northern island, from a supplement of the moon's meridian altitude, was 11° 24 2/3' south; and the longitude by time keeper, from altitudes of the star *Altair*, 136° 28½' east, but it is placed in 1' less, conformably to the positions fixed in the Investigator. A head land seen in latitude 11° 18', was probably the northern extremity of this island, and of the whole chain; at least nothing beyond it could be perceived.

[NORTH COAST. TOWARDS TIMOR.]

In steering out of the channel we were carried near the western rocks by the tide; but the water was deep, and a breeze soon took the schooner out of its influence. At noon our observed latitude was 11° 21', the northern island bore N. 67° to S. 48° E, and the furthest part of the southern land S. 5° W.; the wind was light at north-east, and until midnight we steered north-west to get off the coast; our course was then more westward towards Timor, where I proposed to stop for a supply of water and provisions. (Atlas, Plate I.)

NOVEMBER 1803

A moderate trade wind, coming generally from S. E. in the first part, and E. N. E. in the latter part of the day, carried us to the longitude of the northern Cape Van Diemen; beyond that, the winds were light and variable, and frequently at south-west, which alarmed me lest the unfavourable monsoon should set in before we could get far enough to be out of its influence. Nov. 6 at noon [SUNDAY 6 NOVEMBER 1803], our latitude was 9° 28' south, longitude 127° 12' east (Atlas, Plate XVI), and I was surprised to see already the high land of Timor extending from N. ½ W. to W. N. W.; the first was probably the north-east extremity of the island, and distant about twenty-three leagues, but the high land in the latter bearing could scarcely be nearer than thirty-five leagues. This distance, with ten feet elevation of the eye on the schooner's deck, would give the height to be more than 9000 feet, had it been seen in the horizon, but it was perceptibly above, and this land is therefore probably not much inferior to the peak of Teneriffe. I did not measure its altitude above the horizon with a sextant, or the elevation might have been more nearly ascertained.

The westward current had hitherto not exceeded half a mile an hour; but the next day it was one mile, and on the day following [TUESDAY 8 NOVEMBER 1803] one and a quarter to the W. S. W. We had then regained the trade wind, and our situation at noon was 10° 3½' south and 125° 15' east; the northern part of Timor was obscured by haze, the nearest land visible bore N. 75° W. about eight leagues, and the southern extreme W. 5° S. On the 9th [WEDNESDAY 9 NOVEMBER 1803], the round hill upon Rottee came in sight, and bore S. 78° W. at noon, when our latitude was 10° 32¼' south and longitude 124° 0' east. We carried all sail to gain Samow Strait before dark; but it was eight o'clock when we hauled round the low south-west point of Timor, in soundings from 6 to 14 fathoms, within a quarter of a mile of the reef. There were lights on both shores, which were useful in directing our course up the strait; but having unfavourable winds, the northern outlet was not quite reached at noon next day [THURSDAY 10 NOVEMBER 1803]; and it was near five in the evening before we anchored abreast of Fort Concordia. This was the thirtieth day of our departure from Wreck Reef, and two days might be deducted from them for the deviations and stoppages made for surveying; the indifferent sailing of the schooner was also against making a quick passage, for with all the sail we could set, so much as six knots was not marked on the log board; yet notwithstanding these hindrances, and the much greater of my six-weeks voyage in the boat to Port Jackson and twelve days stay at Wreck Reef, the Bridgewater had arrived at Batavia only four days before we anchored in Coepang Bay. Had not the unfortunate accident happened to the Porpoise, I have little doubt that we could, with the superior sailing of that ship, have reached the longitude of Java Head on the fortieth, perhaps on the thirty-fifth day of our departure from Port Jackson.

[AT TIMOR. COEPANG BAY.]

Mynheer Geisler, the former governor of Coepang, died a month before our arrival, and Mr. Viertzen at this time commanded. He supplied us with almost every thing our situation required, and endeavoured to make my time pass as pleasantly as was in his power, furnishing me with a house near the fort to which I took the time keeper and instruments to ascertain a new rate and error; but my anxious desire to reach England, and the apprehension of being met by the north-west monsoon before passing Java, induced me to leave him as soon as we could be ready to sail, which was on the fourth day. The schooner had continued to be very leaky whenever the wind caused her to lie over on the side, and one of the pumps had nearly become useless; I should have risked staying two or three days longer, had Coepang furnished the means of fresh boring and fitting the pumps, or if pitch could have been procured to pay the seams in the upper works after they were caulked; but no assistance in this way could be obtained; we however got a leak stopped in the bow, and the vessel was afterwards tight so long as she remained at anchor.

Mr. Viertzen informed me that captain Baudin had arrived at Coepang near a month after I had left it in the Investigator, and had sailed early in June for the Gulph of Carpentaria; and I afterwards learned, that being delayed by calms and opposed by south-east winds, he had not reached Cape Arnhem when his people and himself began to be sickly; and fearing that the north-west monsoon might return before his examination was finished, and keep him in the Gulph beyond the extent of his provisions, he abandoned the voyage and steered for Mauritius in his way to Europe.

The situation of Fort Concordia is considered to be 10° 9¼' south and 123' 35' 46" east, according to the observations made in the Investigator (see Ch. IX). I took altitudes with a sextant and artificial horizon on the 11th, 12th, 13th, and 14th, for the rate of the time keeper, which, with its error from mean Greenwich time at noon there on the last day of observation, was found to be as under:

Earnshaw's No. 520, slow 0h 32' 59.91" and losing 36.74" per day.

From the first observation on the 11th p.m., the longitude given with the rate from Wreck Reef, was 123° 48' 34", or 12' 48" too far east; but on using a rate equally accelerated from that found at Wreck Reef to this at Coepang, the time keeper will differ only 0' 40" to the east, which is the presumable amount of its irregularities between Oct. 6 at noon and Nov. 11 p.m., or in 36.2 days. The longitudes of my track from Wreck Reef to Timor have been corrected agreeably to the accelerated rate, with the further allowance of a part of the supplemental error 0' 40", proportionate to the time of each observation; but in Torres' Strait, the situations are fixed from a medium of the longitudes so obtained and of those of the Investigator with the corrections specified in Ch. VI., preceding; the difference between them no where exceeding 1½' of longitude.

[FROM TIMOR. TOWARDS MAURITIUS.]

MONDAY 14 NOVEMBER 1803

On the evening of the 14th we sailed from Coepang, and having passed round the north end of Pulo Samow, steered south-westward with a fair breeze; but the wind being light, and afterwards veering to S. S. W., our progress was slow. At sunset on the 16th [WEDNESDAY 16 NOVEMBER 1803], the island Savu was seen to the N. W. by N., and next morning [THURSDAY 17 NOVEMBER 1803] at six o'clock, the following bearings were taken.

Savu., the highest part,   N. 39° E. Benjoar, a round hill on it,   N. 22 E. A rocky islet, distant 3 leagues, N. 48 W.

At noon, the rocky islet bore N. 63° E., and its position was ascertained to be 10° 49½' south and 122° 49' east. A small low island is laid down by admiral D'Entrecasteaux, about three leagues to the north-west of this position, and had been previously seen by captain Cook in 1770; it seems possible that these may be one and the same island, for the situation in D'Entrecasteaux's chart is marked *doubtful*; but they are both laid down in Plate XVI., and such additions made to what little could be distinguished of Savu and Benjoar, as D'Entrecasteaux, Cook, Bligh. and Dalrymple could furnish.

It was my intention on quitting Timor, if the leaky condition of the schooner and the north-west monsoon did not oppose it, to pass southward of all the Sunda Islands and direct for the Cape of Good Hope; but if impeded, to run through some one of the eastern straits, get into the north-east monsoon, and make for Batavia, or any port where the vessel could be repaired. The veering of the wind to the westward of south, accompanied by a swell and the occasional appearance of lightning in the north-western quarter, made me apprehensive of being forced to this latter plan; and we prepared a boarding netting to defend us against the Malay pirates, with which the straits between Java and Timor were said to be infested; the wind however came back to the eastward, although the south-west swell continued, and we had frequent rain with sometimes thunder and lightning.

FRIDAY 25 NOVEMBER 1803

On the 25th, our latitude was 12° 48' and longitude 103° 6', which was past the meridian of Java Head, and beyond the ordinary limits of the north-west monsoon. The schooner was leaky, more so than before, and the pumps were getting worse; but hoping to reach the Cape of Good Hope, I had wholly given up the idea of Batavia as lying too far out of the track; Mauritius besides was in the way, should the vessel become incapable of doubling the Cape without repairs.

Our course by compass was W. by S. for three days, and afterwards W. S. W., with fresh south-eastern breezes and cloudy weather; but in the upper regions of the atmosphere the wind was unsettled, showers of rain were frequent, and it appeared that we were only just in time to save our passage. On the 4th of December, in 19° 2' south and 83° 50' east, we had a good deal of following sea from the eastward, whilst the ground swell came from the south-west; and the jumble caused by these different movements in the water made the vessel labour exceedingly. I varied the course a point on either side, to keep the wind in the easiest direction; but during this and the following day the leaks augmented so much, that the starbord pump, which was alone effective, was obliged to be worked almost continually, day and night; and had the wind been on the starbord side, it is doubtful whether the schooner could have been kept above water.

This state of things made it necessary to take into serious consideration the propriety of attempting the passage round the Cape of Good Hope, without first having the vessel caulked and the pumps fresh bored and fitted. Should a western wind meet the current setting round the Cape, and it was to be expected, there would be much more sea running than we had yet encountered; and with a fresh wind on the starbord side, which might probably occur, the remaining pump would not touch the water until the hold was half full; there was moreover cause to fear, that it also would soon become ineffective from constant use. After turning these circumstances over in my mind for a day or two, and considering what else might be urged both for and against the measure, I determined to put in at

Mauritius; and on the 6th in the evening [TUESDAY 6 DECEMBER 1803], altered the course half a point for that island, to the satisfaction of the people.

[AT MAURITIUS. BAYE DU CAP.]

In the orders from governor King, the ports to be touched at on the way to England were left to my own choice; but when Mauritius had been mentioned amongst others in conversation, the governor had objected to it, both on account of the hurricanes in that neighbourhood, and from not wishing to encourage a communication between a French colony and a settlement composed as is that of Port Jackson. It was these considerations which had made me hesitate to take the step, though the necessity for it was pressing; and as, in the case of accident happening to the schooner, I might be called to answer before a court martial for going in opposition to the wish of a superior officer, it seemed proper to state in my journal all the reasons which had any influence on my decision. This journal is not in my possession; but notes of the statement were made whilst the recollection of it was strong, and the following was the substance and not far from the words.

1. The necessity of caulking the schooner and refitting the pumps before attempting to double the Cape, were stated nearly as above; to which was added a hope of obtaining a passage in a ship where my defaced charts and journals, which remained untouched from the time of the shipwreck, might be put into a state to be laid before the Admiralty on arriving in England. In the case of meeting with such a passage, I intended to let the Cumberland for freight back to Port Jackson, or to sell her, agreeably to the authority given me in governor King's orders.

2. Considering the proximity of Mauritius to the western coasts of Terra Australis, which remained to be examined, I was desirous to see in what state it had been left by the revolution, and to gain a practical knowledge of the port and periodical winds; with a view to its being used in the future part of my voyage as a place of refitting and refreshment, for which Port Jackson was at an inconvenient distance. It was also desirable to know how far Mauritius, and its dependencies in Madagascar which I knew to abound in cattle, could be useful to Port Jackson in supplying it with breeding stock; an object concerning which the governor had expressed anxiety for information from any place on the east side of the Cape of Good Hope.

3. The two letters from governor King to general Magallon, governor of Mauritius, instead of being forwarded from the Cape might be delivered in person.

4. I was a stranger to what had passed in Europe for nearly twelve months, and there was consequently a possibility that war might again have broken out; my passport from the French government would be good at Mauritius, but in going to the Cape, it was uncertain what attention the Dutch governor might pay to the orders of the first consul of France; and as promoters and encouragers of science, the character of the nation was not so high as to give me great expectation on that head. Mauritius was therefore much more certain than the Cape, since the necessary succour would be there obtained even in case of war; whereas at the Cape there might be a risk of losing my charts and journals and of being made a prisoner.

These reasons for stopping at Mauritius as we passed by it, in addition to the necessity arising from the state of the schooner, were written in my rough journal for reference, without any idea of their being criticised, or even seen by any other than myself; and I have been particular in detailing them, on account of the unexpected occurrences with which they became connected.

FRIDAY 9 DECEMBER 1803

On the evening of the 9th, a ship was seen to the northward, and we sought to speak her for information; but night coming on the sight of her was lost, and we resumed our western course. I had no chart of Mauritius, nor other description than what is contained in the third edition of the Encyclopedia Britannica; this informed me that Port Louis was on the north-west side of the island, but not of the route usually taken to reach it; and the prevailing wind being south-east, it seemed to be a matter of indifference; I therefore steered to make the middle of the island, intending to go by the north or south sides as the wind might happen to favour most. On the 15th [THURSDAY 15 DECEMBER 1803] before daylight, the land was seen, and the wind being E. by S. we hauled to the northward. When the day broke the island was seven or eight miles off, and bore from S. 42° to N. 51° W.; but there was a distant round lump, whether connected with it did not appear, which bore N. by W.; and finding the schooner could not clear it, from the sea running high and current setting to leeward, we veered round and steered southward along the edge of a reef which extends four or five miles from this part of the island. Soon after eight o'clock we passed three flat rocks within the reef, lying, as I now suppose, at the entrance of Port Bourbon; the extremes of the island then bore N. 1° to S. 69° W., and a steep point N. 39° W. five or six miles.

In steering westward along the shore, looking out for boats or vessels to gain information, a flag was seen upon one of the hills; our colours were then hoisted, and afterwards a French jack at the fore-top-mast head, as a signal for a pilot. At noon, the observed latitude was 20° 34' south, and the extremes of the island bore N. 54° E. to 61° W. There was a small town bearing N. by E. two or three miles, from whence a schooner had come out, and being ahead we made sail to speak her; but she hauled in towards the shore until we had passed, and then stood after us. On our heaving to, the schooner again steered for a place where some vessels were seen at anchor, and I began to take her movements as an intimation that we should go in there for a pilot; accordingly we followed her through a narrow pass in the reefs, and anchored in 2½ fathoms, in a small reef harbour which I afterwards understood was called the *Baye du Cap*.

If the schooner's actions were strange before, those of the people were now more so; for no sooner was their anchor dropped, than without furling the sails they went hastily on shore in a canoe, and made the best of their way up a steep hill, one of them with a trunk on his shoulder. They were met by a person who, from the plume in his hat, appeared to be an officer, and presently we saw several men with muskets on the top of the hill; this gave another view of the schooner's movements, and caused me to apprehend that England and France were either at war or very near it. To induce some person to come on board, I held up the letters for general Magallon, the governor; but this being to no purpose, Mr. Aken went on shore in our little boat, taking with him the letters and French passport; in a short time he returned with the officer and two others, and I learned to my great regret that war was actually declared.

The officer, whose name was *Dunienville*, spoke a little English; he asked if I were the captain Flinders mentioned in the passport, whether we had been shipwrecked, and to see my commission. Having perused it, he politely offered his services, inquired what were our immediate wants, and invited me to go on shore and dine with him, it being then near three o'clock. I explained my wish to have a pilot for Port North-West (the name at that time for Port Louis), since it appeared no reparations could be done in the little bay, and requested to have a cask or two of water. The pilot was promised for the next day, and Mons. Dunienville sent a canoe for our empty casks and the master of the French schooner to moor the Cumberland in a secure place.

My passport was in French, and being a stranger to the language, I had had its general purport explained on first receiving it from the Admiralty; but from that time, and more especially after the preliminaries of peace had reached Port Jackson, the passport had scarcely been looked at, and my knowledge of its contents was very imperfect. When the officer was gone, I set myself to consider it attentively; and so far as I could make out, it seemed to be solely for the Investigator, and without provision for any other vessel in which the loss of the ship, or her incapacity to pursue the voyage might oblige me to embark. The intention, no doubt, was to protect the voyage generally, and not the Investigator in particular; but it appeared that if the governor of Mauritius should adhere to the letter of the passport and disregard the intention, he might seize the Cumberland as a prize; and the idea of being detained even a week more than necessary was intolerable. I inquired of the pilot whether the Cape of Good Hope belonged to the Dutch or English; almost determining, should it not have been given up before the war commenced, to attempt the passage at all risks, rather than incur the hazard of being stopped; but the Cape was in the hands of the Dutch.

An hour after M. Dunienville had been gone, we saw him returning with another officer who proved to be his superior in rank; and they had with them a gentleman who spoke English intelligibly. My passport and commission were demanded in a rough manner, and after the officer had examined them with the assistance of his interpreter, he observed that the passport was not for the Cumberland, and required an explanation; having received it, he said it was necessary that both commission and passport should be sent to the governor, and that I should remain with the vessel till an answer was returned. To this arrangement I objected, alleging that since war was declared, these papers were my sole protection and could not be given up; but if copies would do they might be taken. It was at length settled, that I should go over land to Port Louis with the passport and commission, and that Mr. Aken should be furnished with a pilot and bring the schooner round after me.

I was conducted to the house of M. Dunienville, about a mile distant, to be ready to set off on horseback early next morning. The gentleman who interpreted informed me on the way, that general Magallon was at Bourbon, having been lately superseded by general De Caen, an officer of the French revolution. M. Dunienville had been a lieutenant of the navy and knight of St. Louis under the old government, and was then major of the district of *La Savanne*; but the other officer, M. Etienne Bolger, had lately been appointed commandant over his head, by the new governor.

My reception at the major's house was polite and hospitable; and at dawn of day [FRIDAY 16 DECEMBER 1803] I rose to set off with my host for Port Louis, according to the plan settled over night. It appeared, however, that he first expected some orders from the commandant; and at ten o'clock becoming impatient of the delay, I requested to know whether it were, or were not intended to go overland? Major Dunienville seemed to be hurt that the agreement had not been kept; but the direction was taken out of his hands, and not having received final orders he could do nothing. I then returned to the Cumberland, with the intention of sailing either with or without a pilot; but a wind favourable for quitting the bay being not expected before four o'clock it induced me to accept the major's pressing invitation to dine at his house, where four or five strangers were assembled. Before dinner was over, an order came to him from the commandant *to permit the departure of the schooner he had stopped*; and at five o'clock the pilot being on board, we stood out from the reefs in one of those squalls which come off the land at that hour in the summer season.

This little Baye du Cap lies about four miles east from Cape Brabant, a headland at the south-west extremity of the island. The shelter is formed by coral reefs, through which a small river falling into the bay has kept open a passage of about a cable's length wide, with a depth of 3 fathoms close to the eastern breakers; within side there appeared to be anchorage for six or eight small vessels, in from 2 to 3 fathoms; but on account of the flurries of wind which come down the gullies and off the precipices, it is necessary to moor head and stern. Mr. Aken found the latitude from an indifferent observation to be 20° 29½' south.

At seven in the evening we passed round Cape Brabant, and the pilot then kept north-eastward, close along the reefs under the high land; although by so doing we were frequently becalmed, and sometimes had strong flurries which made it necessary to take in all sail; but it appeared that he was afraid of being driven off the island. At eight in the morning [SATURDAY 17 DECEMBER 1803], the mast heads of the vessels in Port Louis were in sight, and there was a large ship lying without side which I hoped might be *Le Géographe*. Major Dunienville had informed me that this ship had been some time at Mauritius, and so far as he knew, was still at the port, though upon the eve of sailing for Europe. Captain Baudin died soon after his arrival, and Mons. Melius, who had been first lieutenant of Le Naturaliste when at Port Jackson, then commanded.

During this passage to Port Louis, my mind was occupied in turning over all the circumstances of my situation, and the mode of proceeding likely to be adopted by the new governor. The breaking out of the war, the neglect of providing in the passport for any such case as that in which I stood, and the ungracious conduct of the commandant at the Baye du Cap, gave me some apprehensions; but on the other hand, the intention of the passport to protect the persons employed in the expedition, with their charts and journals, must be evident; and the conduct of a governor appointed by the first consul Bonaparte, who was a professed patron of science, would hardly be less liberal than that of two preceding French governments to captain Cook in the American, and captain Vancouver in the last war; for both of whom protection and assistance had been ordered, though neither carried passports or had suffered shipwreck. These circumstances, with the testimony which the commanders of the Géographe and Naturaliste had doubtless given of their treatment at Port Jackson, seemed to insure for me the kindest reception; and I determined to rest confident in this assurance, and to banish all apprehension as derogatory to the governor of Mauritius and to the character of the French nation.

CHAPTER IV.

Arrival at Port Louis (or North-West) in Mauritius.
Interview with the French governor.
Seizure of the Cumberland, with the charts and journals of the
Investigator's voyage; and imprisonment of the commander and people.
Letters to the governor, with his answer.
Restitution of some books and charts.
Friendly act of the English interpreter.
Propositions made to the governor.
Humane conduct of captain Bergeret.
Reflections on a voyage of discovery.
Removal to the Maison Despeaux or Garden Prison.

[AT MAURITIUS. PORT LOUIS.]
SATURDAY 17 DECEMBER 1803

At four in the afternoon of Dec. 17, we got to an anchor at the entrance of Port Louis, near the ship which I had hoped might be Le Géographe; but captain Melius had sailed for France on the preceding day, and this proved to be L'Atalante frigate.

The peculiarity of my situation, arising from the renewal of war and neglect in the passport to provide for any accident happening to the Investigator, rendered great precaution necessary in my proceedings; and to remove as much possible, any doubts or misconceptions, I determined to go immediately with my passport and commission to the French governor, and request his leave to get the necessary reparations made to the schooner; but learning from the pilot that it was a regulation of the port for no person to land before the vessel had been visited by the officer of health, it was complied with. At five the boat came along-side; and having answered some general questions proposed in good English, I went into the boat in my frock uniform, and was conducted to the government house by an officer of the port and an interpreter. These gentlemen, after speaking with an aide-de-camp, told me that the captain-general was at dinner, and we must return in an hour or two; and they took me to a shady place which seemed to be the common lounge for the officers connected with the port. There were some who spoke English, and by way of passing the time, they asked if I had really come from Botany Bay in that little vessel; whether a corvette, sent out the night before to observe my motions, had been seen; and if I had not sent a boat on shore in the night? Others asked questions of monsieur Baudin's conduct at Port Jackson, and of the English colony there; and also concerning the voyage of monsieur Flinedare, of which, to their surprise, I knew nothing, but afterwards found it to be my own name which they so pronounced.

In two hours we again went to the government house, and the officers entered to render their account, leaving me at the door for half an hour longer. At length the interpreter desired me to follow him, and I was shown into a room where two officers were standing at a table; the one a shortish thick man in a laced round jacket, the other a genteel-looking man whose blood seemed to circulate more tranquilly. The first, which was the captain-general De Caen, fixed his eyes sternly upon me, and without salutation or preface demanded my passport, my commission! Having glanced over them, he asked in an impetuous manner, the reason for coming to the Isle of France in a small-schooner with a passport for the Investigator? I answered in a few words, that the Investigator having become rotten, the governor of New South Wales had given me the schooner to return to England; and that I had stopped at the island to repair my vessel and procure water and refreshments. He then demanded the order for embarking in the schooner and coming to the Isle of France; to which my answer was, that for coming to the island I had no order, necessity had obliged me to stop in passing--my order for embarking in the Cumberland was on board. At this answer, the general lost the small share of patience of which he seemed to be possessed, and said with much gesture and an elevated voice--"You are imposing on me, sir! (*Vous m'en imposez, monsieur!*) It is not probable that the governor of New South Wales should send away the commander of an expedition on discovery in so small a vessel!--" He then gave back my passport and commission, and I made a motion to follow the interpreter out, but was desired to stop a little. In a few minutes the interpreter returned with a military officer, to whom some orders not explained to me were given, and I was desired to follow them; when going out the captain-general said in a softer tone something about my being well treated, which I could not comprehend.

In the way to the wharf, I inquired of the interpreter where they were taking me? He said, on board the schooner, and that they had orders to bring my books and papers on shore; in effect, they took all the charts, papers, and journals relating to my voyage, as also the Port-Jackson letters and packets, both public and private; and having put them into a trunk which was sealed by me at their desire, they made out a report (*procès verbal*) of their proceedings, and requested me to sign it with them. The preamble of this report set forth something upon the suspicions excited by my appearance at the Isle of France, with the captain-general's opinion thereon; I therefore refused to sign it, but certified at the bottom, that all the charts, journals, and papers of the voyage, together with all the letters on board the schooner had been taken.

The conduct of these gentlemen being polite, I expressed to them my sentiments of general De Caen's manner of receiving me, and the injustice of taking away the papers of a voyage protected by a passport from the French government; and added, that the captain-general's conduct must alter very much before I should pay him a second visit, or even set my foot on shore again. The interpreter hoped I would go on shore with them, for the general had ordered a lodging to be provided for me; and that, in fact, they had orders to take me there. I looked at him and at the officer, who was one of the aides-de-camp--What! I exclaimed in the first transports of surprise and indignation--I am then a prisoner! They acknowledged it to be true; but said they hoped it would last only a few days, until my papers were examined; and that in the mean time, directions had been given that I should want for nothing.

Mr. Aken was also to go on shore; and whilst we put a few clothes together in a trunk, several black men, under the direction of another pilot, were warping the schooner up into the port. At one in the morning [SUNDAY 18 DECEMBER 1803] the officers took us into their boat, leaving the Cumberland, with Mr. Charrington and the crew, under a guard of soldiers.

We were conducted to a large house in the middle of the town, and through a long dark entry, up a dirty stair case, into the room destined for us; the aide-de-camp and interpreter then wished us a good night, and we afterwards heard nothing save the measured steps of a sentinel, walking in the gallery before our door. The chamber contained two truckle beds, a small table and two rush-bottomed chairs; and from the dirty appearance of the room I judged the lodging provided for us by the general to be one of the better apartments of a common prison; there were, however, no iron bars behind the lattice windows, and the frame of a looking-glass in the room had formerly been gilt. It seemed to me a wiser plan to leave the circumstances to develop themselves, rather than to fatigue ourselves with uncertain conjectures; therefore, telling Mr. Aken we should probably know the truth soon enough, I stripped and got into bed; but between the musketoes above and bugs below, and the novelty of our situation, it was near daybreak before either of us dropped asleep.

At six o'clock, I was awakened by two armed grenadiers entering the room. The one said some words to the other, pointing to us at the same time, and then went out; and he that remained began walking backward and forward between our beds, as a sentinel on his post, without seeming to pay great attention to us. Had there been curtains, I should have tried to regain my slumber; but not being able to sleep in such company, I rose and awoke my companion, who seeing the grenadier and not at first recollecting our situation, answered in a manner that would have diverted me at any other time. The sentinel did not prevent us speaking together; and on looking out at the window, we found that it was in reality a tavern where they had placed us, though a very dirty one; it bore the name of *Café Marengo*. A breakfast was brought at eight, and dinner at twelve, and we eat heartily; good bread, fresh meat, fruit, and vegetables being great rarities.

At one o'clock, the aide-de-camp, whom I learned to be lieut. colonel Monistrol, came to the tavern and desired me to accompany him to the general; and being shown into an office, a German secretary, who spoke some English, put various questions to me from a paper, in substance nearly as follows. How it was that I appeared at the Isle of France in so small a vessel, when my passport was for the Investigator? What was become of the officers and men of science who made part of the expedition? Whether I had any knowledge of the war before arriving? Why cartel colours had been hoisted, and a vessel chased in sight of the island? What were my objects for putting into Port North-West, and by what authority? The orders from governor King, relating to the Cumberland, were also demanded, and carried to the captain-general with my answers to the above questions; and soon afterward to my surprise, an invitation was brought me to go to the general's table, his dinner being then served up. This invitation was so contrary to all that had hitherto passed, and being unaccompanied with any explanation, that I at first thought it could not be serious, and answered that I had already dined; but on being pressed to go at least to the table, my reply was, that "under my present situation and treatment it was impossible; when they should be changed, when I should be set at liberty, if His Excellency thought proper to invite me, I should be flattered by it, and accept his invitation with pleasure." It had indeed the air of an experiment, to ascertain whether I were really a commander in the British navy; and had the invitation been accepted without explanation or a change of treatment, an inference might have been drawn that the charge of imposture was well founded; but in any case, having been grossly insulted both in my public and private character, I could not debase the situation I had the honour to hold by a tacit submission. When the aide-de-camp returned from carrying the above reply, he said that the general would invite me when set at liberty; but nothing was offered in the way of explanation.

A paper containing the questions of the German secretary with my answers, was required to be signed, but this being in French, I objected as not understanding it; a translation was therefore to be made, and the letter of governor King respecting the Cumberland was to be put into French for the captain-general. Extracts from my journal, showing the necessity of quitting the Investigator, were moreover desired, and also my reasons at full length for stopping at the Isle of France, instead of going to the Cape of Good Hope; it being necessary, they said, for the general to transmit these to the French government, to justify himself for granting that assistance to the Cumberland which had been ordered for the Investigator. It was already night, and the excessive heat, with being kept six hours answering questions, was very fatiguing; I therefore took the third volume of my rough log book, which contained the whole of what they desired to know, and pointing out the parts in question to the secretary, told him to make such extracts as should be thought requisite. I then requested to be shown back to the tavern, also that the sentinel might be taken out of our room, and Mr. Aken be permitted to return on board the schooner to keep order; to which the aide-de-camp brought for answer, that it was then too late to make new arrangements, but His Excellency would see me in the morning. All the books and papers, the third volume of my rough log book excepted, were then returned into the trunk and sealed as before; and I was reconducted to my confinement between eight and nine o'clock.

MONDAY 19 DECEMBER 1803

Next morning, the sentinel in our chamber was ordered to take his station without side; and in the afternoon M. Bonnefoy, the interpreter, came to say that business prevented the captain-general from seeing me before the following day. Mr. Aken had permission to go on board the schooner under the conduct of an officer; but not being allowed to remain, he brought away the time keeper, with my sextant and artificial horizon; and we commenced a series of observations for a new error and rate, ready against the day of our departure.

TUESDAY 20 DECEMBER 1803

Mr. Charrington came from the schooner on the 20th to inform me, that the seamen were committing many irregularities, taking spirits out of my cabin and going on shore as they pleased; the French guard seeming to take little or no cognisance of their actions. At one o'clock the interpreter and a military officer took me to the government house, and I expected to have an interview with the general and a termination put to our confinement. They showed me into the secretary's office, and requested a copy of my passport and commission; and having made out one myself and signed them both, the interpreter then said the general was busy and could not see me that day; and I was taken back without learning when he would be at liberty, or what was intended to be done.

As yet I was unable to comprehend any thing of the captain-general's conduct; but however great my indignation at seeing my liberty and time thus trifled with, it was to be feared that in writing to him for an explanation, before seeing what turn the affair would take, might be productive of more harm than good. The disorders on board the schooner, however, requiring immediate correction, I wrote a note to inform him of them; requesting at the same time, that Mr. Aken might remain in the Cumberland, and that the caulking of the vessel's upper works and fresh boring of the pumps might be commenced, these being the principal objects for which I had stopped at the island. In the evening the interpreter called to say, that the corporal of the guard on board the schooner had been punished for neglecting his orders; that one of the sailors, a Prussian, being found on shore had been put into the guard house, and that an answer would be given to my note in the morning [WEDNESDAY 21 DECEMBER 1803]. In effect, the interpreter then came with lieutenant-colonel Monistrol, and explained to me a paper to the following purport.

That the captain-general being convinced from the examination of my journal, that I had absolutely changed the nature of the mission for which the First Consul had granted a passport, wherein I was certainly not authorised to stop at the Isle of France to make myself acquainted with the *periodical winds, the port, present state Of the colony, etc.* That such conduct being a violation of neutrality, he ordered colonel Monistrol to go on board the Cumberland, and in my presence to collect into one or more trunks all other papers which might add to the proofs already acquired; and after sealing the trunks, I was to be taken back to the house where my suspicious conduct had made it necessary to confine me from the instant of arriving in the port. It was further ordered, that the crew of the schooner should be kept on board the prison ship; and that an inventory should be taken of every thing in the Cumberland, and the stores put under seal and guarded conformably to the regulations.*

[* The following is a copy of the order, as given to me by the interpreter and certified by colonel Monistrol (In French, not included here. Ebook editor.)]

Such was the answer given to my request for the repairs of the schooner to be commenced. In compliance with their order the officers took me on board, and the remaining books and papers, whether relating in any way to the Investigator's voyage or not, even to letters received from my family and friends during several years, were all taken away, locked up in a trunk, and sealed. Mr. Aken and myself were allowed to take our clothes, but the officers dared not venture to let me have any printed books; I must however do colonel Monistrol and M. Bonnefoy the justice to say, that they acted throughout with much politeness, apologizing for what they were obliged by their orders to execute; and the colonel said he would make a representation to the captain-general, who doubtless lay under some mistake.

This turn to my affairs surprised, and at first stunned me. The single circumstance about which I had entertained the least apprehension, was the neglect in my passport of providing for any other vessel than the Investigator; but from this order of the captain-general, I found myself considered in the light of a spy; my desire to know how far Mauritius could be useful as a place of refitment in the future part of my voyage--a desire formed and expressed in the belief of its being a time of peace, was made a plea for depriving me of liberty and the result of more than two years of risk and labour. The sensations raised by this violation of justice, of humanity, and of the faith of his own government, need not be described; they will be readily felt by every Englishman who has been subjected, were it only for a day, to French revolutionary power. On returning to my place of confinement, I immediately wrote and sent the following letter, addressed to His Excellency the captain-general De Caen, governor in chief, etc. etc. etc. Isle of France.

Sir,

From your order, which was explained to me this morning, I find that the plea for detaining me is not now that I do not appear with the Investigator, according to *the letter* of my passport from the first consul of France; but that I have violated the neutrality therein required by having given in my journal, as an additional reason for putting into this port, that "it would enable me to acquire a knowledge of the periodical winds, and of the present state of the French colony; how far it or its dependencies in Madagascar might be useful to Port Jackson, and how far it would be a convenient place for me to touch at in my future expected voyage:" I quote from memory only, my journal being in your possession. How this remark, made upon the supposition of our two nations being at peace, can be a breach of neutrality, I acknowledge myself unable to discover. Nothing can, in my opinion, add to the propriety of the intentions with which I put into this port, but I shall justify it by the example of your own nation; and to do so, it is only necessary for me to refer to the instructions which preface the published voyage of the unfortunate La Pérouse, by the judicious Fleurieu. Your Excellency will there see, that the much lamented navigator was ordered to make particular observations upon the trade, manufactures, strength, situation, etc. of every port where he might touch; so that, if the example of your own nation be taken as a standard of propriety, the plea for making me a prisoner is altogether untenable. Upon the supposition even of its being war, and that I knew it and still intended to make the observations expressed in my journal; upon this incorrect and worst supposition I have, I think, an example of similar conduct in your own nation; unless you can assure me that the captains Baudin and Hamelin made no such remarks upon Port Jackson, for it was a declared war at the time they lay in that port. But were they forbidden to make such remarks and notes upon the state of that English colony? Upon its progress, its strength, the possibility of its being attacked with advantage, and the utility it might afford to the French nation? I tell you, general De Caen, No. The governor in chief at Port Jackson knew too well the dignity of his own nation, either to lay any prohibition upon these commanders, or to demand to see what their journals might contain.

I shall next appeal to you as being the representative in this place of a great nation, which has hitherto shown itself forward to protect and encourage those sciences by which the knowledge of mankind is extended or their condition ameliorated. Understand then, Sir, that I was chosen by that patron of science sir Joseph Banks, president of the Royal Society of London, and one well known by all the literati throughout the world, to retrace part of the track of the immortal captain Cook--to complete what in New Holland and its neighbourhood he had left unfinished--and to perfect the discovery of that extensive country. This employment, Sir, as it was congenial to my own inclinations, so I pursued it with avidity; upon it, as from a convex lens, all the rays of knowledge and science which my opportunities have enabled me to collect, were thrown. I was unfortunate in that my ship decayed before the voyage was completed; but the captain-general at Port Jackson, who is also the senior naval officer there, was so sensible of the importance of the voyage and of the zeal with which I had pursued it (for the truth of which I appeal to his letters now in your possession), that he gave me a colonial ship of war to transport me with my officers, charts, etc. to England, that I might obtain another ship in which the voyage might be completed. In this second ship I was a passenger; and in her, shipwreck and the loss of charts which had cost me much labour and many risks to make perfect, were added to my first misfortune; but my zeal suffered no abatement. I returned to Port Jackson (734 miles) in an open boat, and got a merchant ship which was bound to China, hired to carry my officers and people to England by that circuitous route; but desirous of losing no time, I took a small schooner of twenty-nine tons, a mere boat, in order to reach England by a nearer passage, and thus gain two or three mouths of time in the outfit of my future expected ship; making my own case and safety to stand in no competition with the great object of forwarding my voyage. Necessity, and not inclination, obliged me to put in at the Isle of France in my route.

Now, Sir, I would beg to ask you whether it becomes the French nation, independently of all passport, to stop the progress of such a voyage, and of which the whole maritime world are to receive the benefit? How contrary to this was her conduct some years since towards captain Cook! But the world highly applauded her conduct then; and possibly we may sometime see what the general sentiment will be in the present case.

I sought protection and assistance in your port, and I have found a prison! Judge for me as a man, Sir--judge, for me as a British officer employed in a neutral occupation--judge for me as a zealous philanthropist, what I must feel at being thus treated.

At present I quit the subject with the following requests: that I may be permitted to have my printed books on shore; and that my servant may be allowed to attend me in my apartment.

With all the respect due from my situation to the captain-general,

I am From my confinement, Your Excellency's obedient servant, Dec. 21, 1803. Matthew Flinders.

The lapse of several years has enabled me to consider the transactions of this period under different views, to regard them with almost the coolness of an uninterested observer; and I see the possibility that a dispassionate reader may accuse me of taking too high a position, and using too warm a style--in rather giving way to the dictates of feeling than dwelling upon the proofs of my innocence; perhaps also, he may accuse me of vanity, in seeking to enhance my own zeal and claims. Without attempting to controvert these censures, I beg him to consider all the circumstances of my situation: my voyage, shipwreck, and anxiety to pursue the steps of our celebrated navigators. Let him suppose himself to have executed so much of the same task, escaped the same dangers; and under the influence of powerful motives to reach England with expedition, to be arrested on the way, his misfortunes either not heeded or converted into proofs of delinquency, and himself treated as a spy; and this is done by the representative of a government which had promised assistance and protection, and moreover owed him a return for the kind treatment recently experienced by Frenchmen in the port from whence he came. Let him suppose himself writing to his oppressor with these various recollections crowding on his imagination; and the allowances he would then desire for himself, I request of him to make for me.

THURSDAY 22 DECEMBER 1803

On the day following the transmission of the letter, my servant was brought on shore from the prison ship, where he left Mr. Charrington and the seamen closely confined; but no answer was returned either on the 22nd or 23rd, nor did we hear any thing that could give an insight into what further was intended to be done. We suffered much from the heat of the weather and want of fresh air; for the town of Port Louis is wholly exposed to the rays of the sun, whilst the mountains which form a semicircle round it to the east and south, not only prevent the trade wind from reaching it, but reflect the heat in such a manner, that from November to April it is almost insupportable. During this season, the inhabitants whose affairs do not oblige them to remain, fly to the higher and windward parts of the island; and the others take the air and their exercise very early in the morning and late in the evening. We who were shut up in the middle of the town, and from having been three months confined to a vessel of twenty-nine tons were much in need of exercise, could not but feel the personal inconveniences of such a situation in their full rigour; and the perturbation of mind, excited by such unworthy treatment, did not tend to alleviate their effects on our health. But the heat and want of fresh air were not the worst evils. Our undefended pallet beds were besieged by swarms of bugs and musketoes, and the bites of these noxious insects upon bodies ready to break out with scurvy, produced effects more than usually painful and disagreeable. Being almost covered with inflamed spots, some of which had become ulcers on my legs and feet, I wrote to the captain-general, requesting the assistance of a surgeon; and also to know under what limitations he would allow me to write to the Admiralty of Great Britain, and to my family and friends; but the main subject was left untouched, in expectation of an answer to the former letter.

In the afternoon, one of the aides-de-camp said that His Excellency did not prevent me from writing to whom I pleased; but that my letters must be sent open to the town major, who would forward them to their address. The same evening a surgeon, who did not speak English, came to our room; next morning [SATURDAY 24 DECEMBER 1803] he returned with the interpreter, and finding the ulcers to be scorbutic, ordered me, in addition to his dressings, to drink plentifully of lemonade and live upon fruit and vegetables. Their visit was repeated on the following day [SUNDAY 25 DECEMBER 1803]; but nothing transpired relative to the general's intentions, nor to any answer proposed to be given to my letter of the 21st; and I therefore wrote another in the following terms.

Sir,

From whatever cause it may be that I have received no answer to my letter of the 21st last, I shall yet continue to do my duty to my government and the cause of discovery, by pointing out every circumstance that may have a probability of inducing you to liberate my people, my vessel, and myself.

A former letter showed, that upon the principles adopted in voyages of discovery by your own nation, the plea for detaining me a prisoner was untenable; and also that independently of any passport, it ill became the French nation to stop the prosecution of a voyage of discovery, especially one carried on with the zeal that mine has hitherto been. In this letter I shall endeavour to point out another circumstance, at least as important as the former, so far as regards the injustice of my detainer. In this point of view then, Sir, I shall admit, that to make any remarks upon a port which might enable either myself or others to come into it again with more facility, or which might give information concerning the refreshments and articles of commerce to be procured at it, is, although made in time of peace, a crime; and consequently, that if La Pérouse executed his instructions, he was no better than a spy at the different ports where he put in. Let this, Sir, for the moment be admitted; and I ask what proofs you have that I have made such remarks? You will probably say, I *intended* to make them. True, but intention is not action. I might have altered my intentions on coming into the port, and finding our two nations to be at war: you cannot know what alteration a knowledge of the war might have made in my sentiments. We do indeed judge much of the merit or demerit of an action by the intention with which it is performed; but in all cases there must be an action performed to constitute any certain merit or demerit amongst men. Now in my case there appears to have been intention only; and even this intention I have before shown to be consistent with the practice of your own nation, and I believe of all nations.

As it appears that Your Excellency had formed a determination to stop the Cumberland, previously even to seeing me, if a specious pretext were wanting for it, it would have been more like wisdom to have let me alone until the eve of sailing, and then to have seized my journal; where it is possible something better than *intention* might have been fixed upon as a cause for making me a prisoner. This would have been a mean action, and altogether unworthy of you or your nation; but it might have answered your purpose better than the step now taken. I say there appears to have been a previous determination to stop the Cumberland, and from this cause; that on the first evening of my arrival, and before any examination was made into my papers (my commission and passport excepted), you told me impetuously that I was *imposing upon you*. Now I cannot think that an officer of your rank and judgment could act either so ungentlemanlike, or so unguardedly, as to make such a declaration without proof; unless his reason had been blinded by passion, or a previous determination that it should be so, *nolens volens*. In your order of the 21st last it is indeed said, that the captain-general has acquired conviction that I am the person I pretend to be, and the same for whom a passport was obtained by the English government from the First Consul; it follows then, as I am willing to explain it, that I *am not* and *was not* an impostor. This plea was given up when a more plausible one was thought to be found; but I cannot compliment Your Excellency upon this alteration in your position, for the first, although false, is the most tenable post of the two.

Trusting that upon a due consideration of all the circumstances, you will be pleased to fulfil the intention for which the passport was given, I have the honour to be,

From my confinement, Your Excellency's obedient servant, Dec. 25, 1803. Matthew Flinders.

In the evening, a letter was brought me by a soldier from general De Caen, and the haste with which it had been sent inspired favourable hopes; I did not expect the visit of the interpreter until the following day, and therefore attempted to decipher the letter by the help of a French dictionary, with a degree of anxiety which its contents were but little calculated to satisfy: it was as follows.

I did not answer your letter of the 21st December, Sir, because it was useless to commence a debate here between you and me, upon the motives well or ill founded from which I took upon myself to stop the Cumberland until further orders. On the other hand, I should have had too much advantage in refuting your assertions, notwithstanding the reasonings and quotations with which you have adorned them.

I was still willing to attribute the unreserved tone you had used in that letter, to the ill humour produced by your present situation. I was far from thinking that after having seriously reflected upon the causes and circumstances, you should take occasion from a silence so delicate to go still further; but your last letter no longer leaves me an alternative.

Your undertaking, as extraordinary as it was inconsiderate, to depart from Port Jackson in the Cumberland, more to give proof of an officious zeal, more for the private interests of Great Britain than for what had induced the French government to give you a passport, which I shall unfold at a proper opportunity, had already given me an idea of your character; but this letter overstepping all the bounds of civility, obliges me to tell you, until *the general opinion judges of your faults or of mine*, to cease all correspondence tending to demonstrate the justice of your cause; since you know so little how to preserve the rules of decorum.*

[The text of the letter, in French, was set out in the book, but is not set out in this ebook.]

The accusation of not preserving the rules of decorum, seemed not a little extraordinary from one who had kept me above two hours in the street when I had gone to wait upon him, and who had qualified me with the title of impostor without examination; but it seemed that any act of aggression on the part of the general was to meet only with submission and respect. Embarrassment sheltering itself under despotic power, was evident in this letter; but it gave no further insight into the reasons for making me a prisoner, and consequently no opportunity of vindicating my innocence. It therefore seemed wisest, seeing the kind of man with whom I had to deal, to follow his directions and leave the main subject to the operation of time; but to take off my mind from dwelling too intensely upon the circumstance of being arrested at such a conjuncture, I determined to employ it in forwarding my voyage, if an application for the necessary papers should be attended with success.

MONDAY 26 DECEMBER 1803

Having obtained a translation of the general's letter from the interpreter, who came next morning in company with the surgeon, I wrote to request,

1st. My printed books from the schooner.

2nd. My private letters and papers out of the secretary's office.

3rd. To have two or three charts and three or four manuscript books, for the purpose of finishing the chart of the Gulph of Carpentaria; adding in explanation, that the parts wanting were mostly lost in the shipwreck, and I wished to replace them from my memory and remaining materials before it were too late. For these a receipt was offered, and my word that nothing in the books should be erased or destroyed; but I wished to make additions to one or two of the books as well as to the charts, and would afterwards be ready to give up the whole.

4th. I represented a complaint from my seamen, of being shut up at night in a place where not a breath of air could come to them; which, in a climate like this, must be not only uncomfortable in the last degree, but very destructive to European constitutions. Also, that the people with whom they were placed were affected with that disagreeable and contagious disorder the itch; and that their provisions were too scanty, except in the article of bread, the proportion of which was large, but of a bad quality.

An answer was given on the same day by one of the general's aides-de-camp, who said that orders had been given for the delivery of the books and papers; that the place where the seamen were kept was very wholesome; and as to the provisions, that orders had been given on my arrival for the people of the Cumberland to be treated as French seamen in actual service; that he would inquire whether any thing contrary had been done, which he did not think, but in that case it should be set right.

TUESDAY 27 DECEMBER 1803

At noon next day colonel Monistrol and M. Bonnefoy called, and a trunk was brought from on board the schooner, containing a part of my printed books. The colonel seemed to be sorry that my letters to the general had been couched in a style so far from humble, and to think that they might rather tend to protract than terminate my confinement; on which I observed, believing him to be in the general's confidence, that as my demand was to obtain common justice, an adulatory style did not seem proper, more especially when addressed to a republican who must despise it: my rights had been invaded, and I used the language natural to a man so circumstanced. Had favours been wanted, or there had been any thing to conceal, my language would probably have been different; but of all things I desired that the strictest scrutiny should be made into my papers, and that it should be confronted with any examination they might choose to make of myself or people. The colonel and interpreter, either from politeness or conviction, did not disagree with these sentiments, but repeated that a different mode of writing might have answered better; it appeared indeed, from their conversation, that French republicanism involved any thing rather than liberty, justice, and equality, of which it had so much boasted.

So soon as the two gentlemen were gone, I took out my naval signal book from the trunk and tore it to pieces; the private signals had been lost in the shipwreck, so that my mind was now freed from apprehensions which had given much inquietude.

WEDNESDAY 28 DECEMBER 1803

On the 28th, M. Chapotin, the surgeon, called as usual with the interpreter. He said that air and exercise were necessary to the re-establishment of my health, and that so soon as I should be able to walk out, it would be proper to apply to the general for a permission; and on my objecting to ask any thing like a personal favour, he promised with some degree of feeling to take the application on himself.

No mention was made this day of the books and papers, to be delivered from the sealed trunks; but next morning [THURSDAY 29 DECEMBER 1803] I was conducted to the government house, and took out all my private letters and papers, the journals of bearings and astronomical observations, two log books, and such charts as were necessary to completing the Gulph of Carpentaria; for which a receipt was required, without any obligation to return them. The third log book, containing transactions and remarks in different vessels during the preceding six months, was important to me on many accounts, and especially for the observations it contained upon Torres' Strait and the Gulph; but it was said to be in the hands of the general, who could not be disturbed, and two boxes of despatches from governor King and colonel Paterson had been taken away. All the other books and papers, including my passport, commission, etc., with some accounts from the commissary of New South Wales and many private letters from individuals in that colony, were locked up in a trunk and sealed as before.

SATURDAY 31 DECEMBER 1803

On the 31st. I sent to the town major's office an open letter addressed to the secretary of the Admiralty, giving a short account of my embarkation and shipwreck in the Porpoise, voyage in the Cumberland, and situation in Mauritius; with two private letters, and a request that they might be forwarded by the first opportunity. Next day [SUNDAY 1 JANUARY 1804] the receipt of them was acknowledged, and a promise given to inform me of the means by which they should be sent, and it was done accordingly; but not one of the letters, or of their duplicates, was ever received.

Having calculated with Mr. Aken the observations previously taken for the rate of the time keeper,* I now worked earnestly upon the chart of the Gulph of Carpentaria; and this employment served to divert my chagrin, and the indignation which, however useless it might be, I could not but feel at the author of our imprisonment. The want of my log book, however, was a great obstacle to laying down the parts seen in the Cumberland; and nothing more having been said of it, a short letter was written to general De Caen on the 5th, reminding him that the log was necessary to the construction of my charts, and that only a small part of the printed books had yet been delivered. A verbal answer was brought by the interpreter, and two days afterward the books came from the schooner; but respecting the log no answer was made.

[* The rate from December 19 to 25, was 36.9" losing, or only 0.16" more than that previously found at Coepang in Timor; but the longitude deduced from the first observation with the Coepang rate, was 57° 40' 40.5", or 10' 43.5" greater than afterwards obtained from twenty-seven sets of lunar distances. In laying down the track from Timor, this error has been equally distributed throughout the thirty five days between November 14 and December 19, 1803.]

The sentinel placed at the door of our chambers (for we had a few days before obtained a second, with musketo curtains to our beds), became unusually strict at this time, scarcely allowing the master of the tavern, or even the interpreter or surgeon to see us; and one day, hearing me inquire the name of some dish in French from the slave who waited at dinner, the sentinel burst into the room and drove away the poor affrighted black, saying that we were not to speak to any person. Previously to this, a Dutch, a Swiss, a Norwegian, and two American gentlemen had called; but except the Swiss, who found means to bid us good day occasionally without being noticed, not one came a second time, for fear of being held in a suspicious light by the government; and now, the surgeon and interpreter were not admitted without a written order. Two applications had been made by the surgeon in my behalf, to walk in the fields near the town; the last was personally to the captain-general, but although he might have caused a sentinel to follow, or a whole guard if thought necessary, an unqualified refusal was given to M. Chapotin's humane request.

We were lodged and supplied with meals in the tavern at the public expense; but having lost part of our clothes in the shipwreck, and distributed some to those of our companions who had saved nothing, both Mr. Aken and myself were much in want of linen and other necessaries; and after the few dollars I chanced to have about me were gone, we knew not how to pay for our washing. All strangers being refused admittance took away the chance of negotiating bills, for the surgeon spoke no English and the interpreter always avoided the subject; one morning however, having previously ascertained that it would not give umbrage, the interpreter offered to attempt the negotiation of a bill drawn upon the commissioners of the navy; but the sentinel, seeing him take a paper, gave information, and M. Bonnefoy was scarcely out of the room when a file of soldiers made him prisoner; nor, although a public officer, was he liberated until it was ascertained that he acted with permission, and had received no other paper than the bill. In the evening he brought the full sum, at a time when bills upon England could obtain cash with difficulty at a discount of thirty per cent. It was the chevalier Pelgrom, who filled the offices of Danish and Imperial consul, that had acted thus liberally; and he caused me to be informed, that the fear of incurring the general's displeasure had alone prevented him from offering his assistance sooner.

Although Mr. Aken and myself were strictly confined and closely watched, my servant was left at liberty to go upon my commissions; and once a week I sent him on board the prison ship, to take Mr. Charrington and the seamen a basket of fruit and vegetables from the market. They had always been permitted to walk upon deck in the day time, and latterly been sometimes allowed to go into the town, accompanied by a soldier; and since from all we could learn, the final decision of the captain-general was yet in suspense, I augured favourably of the result from this relaxation towards the men. My hopes became strengthened on the 14th, by learning from M. Bonnefoy that it was believed we should be permitted to walk out, and perhaps depart altogether, so soon as three Dutch ships commanded by rear-admiral Dekker should have sailed. These ships were loaded with pepper from Batavia, and bound to Europe; and it seemed possible that one reason of our detention might be to prevent English ships gaining intelligence of them by our means; but this could be no excuse for close imprisonment and taking away my charts and journals, whatever it might be made for delaying our departure.

Finding it impossible to obtain the third volume of my log book, the charts of Torres' Strait and the Gulph of Carpentaria were finished without it; fortunately the journal kept by Mr. Aken in the Cumberland had not been taken away, and it proved of great assistance. Our time passed on in this manner, hoping that the Dutch ships would sail, and that general De Caen would then suffer us to depart, either in the Cumberland or some other way; the surgeon came almost daily, on account of my scorbutic sores, and the interpreter called frequently. I was careful not to send out my servant often, for it appeared that he was dogged by spies, and that people were afraid of speaking to him; the surgeon and interpreter were almost equally cautious with me, so that although in the midst of a town where news arrived continually from some part of the world, every thing to us was wrapped in mystery; and M. Bonnefoy afterwards acknowledged, in answer to a direct question put to him, that an order had been given to prevent us receiving any intelligence.

On the 29th, admiral Dekker sailed with his three ships; and whilst anxiously expecting some communication, the interpreter called to inform me that an order had been given for the schooner to be moved up the harbour, and the stores to be taken out; and he wished to know if Mr. Aken should be present at making the inventory. I asked what was to be done with us--with my books and papers? To which he answered by a shrug of the shoulders: he had come only for the purpose of executing his order. On each of the two following days Mr. Aken was taken down to the schooner; for he accepted the proposition to accompany the officers for the sake of the walk, and in the hope of obtaining some intelligence. He found the poor Cumberland covered with blue mold within side, and many of the stores in a decaying state, no precautions having been taken to preserve her from the heat or the rains; the French inventory was afterwards brought to him to be signed, but he refused it with my approbation.

FEBRUARY 1804

This new proceeding seemed to bespeak the captain-general to have finally taken his resolution to keep us prisoners; and my disappointment at seeing it, instead of receiving back my books and papers and permission to depart, was extreme. In the hope to obtain some information I wrote a note on the 3rd, to solicit of His Excellency the honour of an audience; and five days having elapsed without an answer, the interpreter was requested to deliver a message to the same effect. He presently returned with the concise answer, *No*; but afterwards told me in conversation that the general had said, "captain Flinders might have known that I did not wish to see him, by not giving an answer to his note. It is needless for me to see him, for the conversation will probably be such as to oblige me to send him to the tower."

My intention in requesting the audience was to have offered certain proposals to the general's consideration, and if possible to obtain some explanation of the reasons for a detention so extraordinary, and now protracted beyond six weeks; and being disappointed in this, a letter was written on the 12th, containing the following propositions.

1st. If your Excellency will permit me to depart with my vessel, papers, etc., I will pledge my honour not to give any information of the Isle of France or any thing belonging to it, for a limited time, if it be thought that I can have gained any information; or if judged necessary, any other restrictions can be laid upon me. If this will not be complied with, I request,

2nd, to be sent to France.

3rd. But if it be indispensable to detain me here, I request that my officer and people may be permitted to depart in the schooner; as well for the purpose of informing the British Admiralty where I am, as to relieve our families and friends from the report which will be spread of the total loss of the Porpoise and Cato, with all on board. Mr. Aken can be laid under what restrictions may be deemed requisite; and my honour shall be a security that nothing shall be transmitted by me, but what passes under the inspection of the officer who may be appointed for that purpose.

In case of refusing to adopt any of these modes, by which my voyage might proceed without possibility of injury to the Isle of France, I then reminded His Excellency that since the shipwreck of the Porpoise, six months before, my people as well as myself had been mostly confined either upon a small sand bank in the open sea, or in a boat, or otherwise on board the Cumberland where there was no room to walk, or been kept prisoners as at that time; and that I had not previously recovered from a scorbutic and very debilitated state, arising from eleven months exposure to great fatigue, bad climate, and salt provisions. After noticing my scorbutic sores, and his refusal of the surgeon's application for me to walk out, it was added--The captain-general best knows whether my conduct has deserved, or the exigencies of his government require, that I should continue to be closely confined in this sickly town and cut off from society; but of no part of this letter was any notice taken.

Two days before, I had been favoured with a visit from captain Bergeret of the French navy, who had commanded *La Virginie* frigate when taken by Sir Edward Pellew, and of whose honourable conduct in the affair of Sir W. Sydney Smith's imprisonment, public mention had been made in England. This gentleman sat some time conversing upon my situation, which he seemed desirous to ameliorate; he said that "the general did not consider me to be a prisoner of war, and that my confinement did not arise from any thing I had done." From what then did it arise? At this question he was silent. He regretted not to have been in town on my arrival, believing it would have been in his power to have turned the tide of consequences; and obligingly offered to supply me with money, if in want.

During a fortnight from this time, no incident occurred worth notice. My scorbutic sores being much better, the surgeon came but seldom; and the visits of the interpreter being less frequent than before, our solitude was rarely interrupted. The Gulph of Carpentaria and Torres' Strait being finished, my time had since been employed in writing an explanatory memoir upon the latter chart; Mr. Aken was occupied in copying the journal of bearings for the Admiralty, and my servant in transcribing the two first volumes of the log, which had been torn and defaced in the shipwreck; so that our time did not pass wholly in vain. It was the completion of the charts, however, that I had most at heart; and although the success of an application for more materials were very doubtful, an essay to obtain them was made on the 27th, in the following letter to the captain-general.

Sir,

The term of my imprisonment being lengthened out much beyond my expectation, puts me under the necessity of making another application to Your Excellency for more books and charts, that I may still proceed in completing the account of my observations and discoveries. If the whole were put into my possession it would be of much service to my labour, and save Your Excellency from being troubled with any further application on this head; but if this will not be complied with, I beg to make a small selection from them, which will principally consist of a roll of charts. I am not however to deceive Your Excellency--this roll contains the greater part of my original fair charts, and I am desirous to have them principally for the purpose of making an abridgment of my discoveries upon a single sheet. With all due consideration, I am

Your Excellency's prisoner,

Matthew Flinders.

This letter was no more fortunate than the last, and it seemed that general De Caen had determined upon giving me no answer to any thing.

The Admiral Aplin, an extra-indiaman outward bound, on board of which were several officers of the army and four ladies, had been brought in as a prize; the ladies with their husbands were suffered to remain at a tavern in the town, at the instance of captain Bergeret, by whose privateer, La Psyché, they had been taken; the others were sent to a house at a little distance in the country, where all the English officers had been a short time confined. I ventured to send my servant to the tavern, to inquire after my countrymen and women; and they obligingly furnished me with magazines, newspapers, and a Steele's list of the navy, up to August 1803, which in such a place, and after so long an ignorance of what was passing in England, were highly acceptable.

MARCH 1804

On March 1, the interpreter made a personal application to general De Caen concerning the books and charts mentioned in my last letter; to which he received for answer, that so soon as the governor was a little freed from business he would attend to this request. I asked M. Bonnefoy to give me his opinion of what was likely to be done with us? He replied that we should probably be kept prisoners so long as the war lasted, but might perhaps have permission to live in some interior part of the island, and liberty to take exercise within certain limits. This opinion surprised me; but I considered it to be that of a man unacquainted with the nature of a voyage of discovery, and the interest it excites in every nation of the civilised world, and not the least in France. To be liberated in an honourable manner by an order of the French government, so soon as it should be informed of my detention, appeared to be certain; for whatever colour general De Caen might give to his proceedings, it could not be disguised that he had arrested the commander of a voyage bearing a French passport, and had taken from him his charts, journals, and vessel; but as yet I could not be persuaded that the general would risk the displeasure of his government, and particularly of the first consul Bonaparte, by whose order my passport had been given, and who had professed himself to be a patron of science. A voyage of discovery undertaken upon liberal principles, and carried on with zeal, tempered with humanity towards the inhabitants of the countries visited, seemed to me an object to interest every person, of whatever nation or profession. The philosopher, or man of general science would see his knowledge of the globe, and of man, its principal inhabitant, so much the object of such a voyage, that he might consider it as undertaken for his gratification; and he who professed a particular branch, whether of natural philosophy or natural history, would expect so many new observations and discoveries in his favourite pursuit, that the voyagers could not fail to have his best wishes for their success. A professor of the fine arts might expect new and striking subjects to be brought to light, upon which to exercise his genius and display his powers; the merchant and manufacturer would anticipate fresh aids to their industry, and new markets for its produce; and the seaman, from such a voyage, would expect the discovery of new passages and harbours, to which he might have recourse either for convenience or safety; and he would also see in it the adoption of the best means for advancing his art to perfection. The philanthropist and zealous Christian would have delight in observing the blessings of civilization thus continually extending themselves, and in seeing new fields opened in which to sow the seeds of righteousness; and even the man without profession, science, or zeal, the perfectly idle, could not be without interest in a voyage of discovery, since the gratification of curiosity is an object of at least as much concern with them as with any other class of men. Considering, thus, a voyage for the investigation of new countries as of extensive interest and importance, it was with difficulty I could be convinced that there were people who thought it of none; or of so little, that the putting a stop to it, imprisoning the commander and seizing his charts and papers, required no more consideration than if it were a common voyage. To be kept a prisoner so long as the war should last, did not therefore enter into my conception as within the bounds of probability, but it is the failing of men of all professions to over-rate the importance of that which they have themselves adopted, and into this error it will probably be thought I had fallen with respect to voyages of discovery.

We had a second visit on the 6th from captain Bergeret, to whom the passengers of the Aplin, and particularly the married gentlemen, were indebted for much attention and indulgence. He seemed to think that nothing could at this time be able to procure our release, but that we might perhaps be permitted to live in the country; and he promised to interest himself in it, so soon as a proper time and opportunity could be found for speaking to the captain-general.

The season was arrived in which, should we be set at liberty, it would be too late to attempt a passage round the Cape of Good Hope in the schooner, and before the return of another year, the stores, and perhaps the vessel itself might be rotten; and having no hope to obtain an answer to a letter, I requested M. Bonnefoy to make an application to the general for permission to sell the Cumberland. Ten days afterward the interpreter informed me, that general De Caen had spoken to him of my wish to live in the country, which had been made known to him by captain Bergeret; and he desired him to tell me, "to have a little patience, he should soon come to some determination upon my affair;" being spoken to upon the sale of the Cumberland, his reply was, "a little patience, it is time enough yet;" and when the charts and books for which I had applied on Feb. 27 were mentioned, he still gave the same answer.

My people were brought on shore on the 23rd, with other British subjects from the prison ship, in order to be sent to a district called Flacq, on the east side of the island; and this circumstance confirmed my suspicion that it was not intended to liberate us until orders were received from France. Mr. Charrington, the boatswain, was permitted to speak to me in the presence of an officer before their departure; and after learning the condition of the poor prisoners, I recommended him to keep our people as clean in their persons and regular in their conduct as circumstances would permit; and not to attempt any escape, since we must be liberated in six or eight months by order of the French government. One of them, the Prussian who had behaved so ill, had gone away in the Spanish frigate Fama, by permission of the French; the others had been kept strictly on board the prison ship after the departure of the three Dutch men of war. Although several prizes had been brought in, the number of English prisoners was inconsiderable; owing to some of the vessels being manned with lascars who were not confined and in part to the sailors having been induced to enter on board the French privateers, for the sake of obtaining more provisions and to avoid being kept in irons.

I had hitherto forborne to write any letters to England, whether public or private, but what passed open through the office of the town major, that no plea, even what arbitrary power could construe into such, might be taken for continuing our imprisonment; but the arrival of letters thus sent being exceedingly problematical, and my hope of liberation from general De Caen having disappeared, the motive for this forbearance had ceased to exist. An account was therefore written to the secretary of the Admiralty of my arrival, reception, and treatment in Mauritius, inclosing copies of all the letters written or received; that my Lords Commissioners might be enabled to take proper measures for obtaining our liberty and the restitution of my charts and journals; especial care was taken at the same time, to avoid the mention of any thing which could be thought to infringe on the passport, as much as if it had remained inviolate on the part of general De Caen. This letter was inclosed to a friend in London, and sent by the way of America; and I afterwards learned from the public papers that it was received in the August following.

The end of March had arrived, and nothing more was said of our permission to reside in the country; and being most heartily weary of close confinement, I requested to be removed to the same place with the British officers, prisoners of war; the house where they were kept being described to be large, and surrounded with a wall inclosing about two acres of ground, within which the prisoners were allowed to take exercise. On the 30th colonel Monistrol came to confer on the subject, and next day conducted me to the house for the purpose of choosing two rooms. He said on the way that the house was originally built by a surgeon named Despeaux, and now hired by the government at twenty-five dollars per month to accommodate the English gentlemen; that it was very spacious, and had formerly lodged the ambassadors sent by Tippoo Sultaun to this island; I found it to be situate about a mile north-east from our tavern in the middle of the town, and enjoying a fresh air which, in comparison with our place of confinement, made me think it a paradise. After the unpleasant task of selecting two rooms, which colonel Monistrol, ordered to be vacated by the officers who were in possession, he returned with me to the town; and promised at parting to speak again to the captain-general concerning my charts and books.

This little walk of a mile showed how debilitating is the want of exercise and fresh air, for it was not without the assistance of colonel Monistrol's arm, that I was able to get through it. Conveyances were sent in the evening for our trunks, and we took possession of our new prison with a considerable degree of pleasure; this change of situation and surrounding objects producing an exhilaration of spirits to which we had long been strangers.

CHAPTER V.
Prisoners in the Maison Despeaux or Garden Prison.
Application to admiral Linois.
Spy-glasses and swords taken.
Some papers restored.
Opinions upon the detention of the Cumberland.
Letter of captain Baudin.
An English squadron arrives off Mauritius: its consequences.
Arrival of a French officer with despatches, and observations thereon.
Passages in the Moniteur, with remarks.
Mr. Aken liberated.
Arrival of cartels from India.
Application made by the marquis Wellesley.

Different treatment of English and French prisoners.
Prizes brought to Mauritius in sixteen months.
Departure of all prisoners of war.
Permission to quit the Garden Prison.
Astronomical observations.

[AT MAURITIUS. GARDEN PRISON.]
APRIL 1804

We lost no time in exploring our new place of confinement, and in making acquaintance with our fellow prisoners. These were major Shippard and Mr. W. H. Robertson, who had come from India during the peace on account of their health, and been detained; the captains Mathews, Dansey, and Loane, and Mr. McCrae of the Indian army, taken in the Admiral Aplin; and Messrs. Dale and Seymour of H. M. frigate La DéDaigneuse, who having been sent with a prize to Bombay had fallen in with the corvette Le Bélier, and been brought to Mauritius. The officers of merchant ships, at first confined in the Garden Prison, had a few days before been sent out to Flacq; and the four remaining officers of the army taken in the Aplin, were allowed, at the intercession of captain Bergeret, to dwell with their wives at a plantation in the quarter of Pamplemousses, about six miles from the port.

M. Bonnefoy, the interpreter, continued to visit us occasionally; and gave some useful assistance in forming our little establishment, by procuring the restitution of a part of my private property left in the Cumberland, and obtaining a permanent permission for my servant to pass the sentinel at the gate. Our lodging and table in the Café Marengo had been defrayed by the government; and during the first month, six dollars per day, being two for each person, had been charged; but the *préfet*, thinking this too much, had fixed the allowance at 116 dollars per month, for which the tavern keeper agreed to supply us nearly as before. On being removed to the Garden Prison, the interpreter informed me with some degree of shame, that a further reduction of eleven dollars per month had been ordered, to go towards paying the rent of the house; which is perhaps the first instance of men being charged for the accommodation of a prison.

Towards the middle of the month, rear-admiral Linois came into port after his unsuccessful attempt upon our China fleet, the same in which my officers and people were passengers. As I believed the want of nautical information, and especially upon the usages adopted towards voyages of discovery, had materially contributed to the extraordinary proceedings of general De Caen, it seemed probable that an examination of my conduct and papers by the rear-admiral might clear up the affair; and this hope, with the character of the admiral as an upright and humane man, induced me to write to him. I described the leading circumstances of my voyage, and situation at that time; and said, "I should willingly undergo an examination by the captains of your squadron, and my papers would either prove or disprove my assertions. If it be found that I have committed any act of hostility against the French nation or its allies, my passport will become forfeited, and I expect no favour; but if my conduct hath been altogether consistent with the passport, I hope to be set at liberty, or at least to be sent to France for the decision of the government." Admiral Linois had the politeness to return an immediate answer; but said, that not being in the port at the time of my arrival, it belonged to the captain-general to appreciate the motives of my stopping at the Isle of France, and to determine the time of my momentary detention. "Nevertheless Sir," he added, "believe, that taking an interest in your situation, I shall have the honour to speak to the captain-general concerning it; and shall be flattered in contributing to your being set at liberty." Unfortunately a difference arose between the admiral and general De Caen; and the answer given to the application was, that my case having been submitted to the French government, his request could not be complied with.

Captain Halgan of the French corvette Le Berceau, having been in England during the short peace and heard my voyage there mentioned, as well as by the officers of Le Géographe, did me the favour of a visit more than once. He testified a lively interest in my situation, and offered pecuniary assistance if wanted; and being afterwards ordered to France, applied for me to be sent on board his ship; which being refused, he obligingly took a letter to captain Melius of Le Géographe, and two others for England which were punctually sent. In May [MAY 1804] I addressed a letter to His Excellency the marquis Wellesley, governor-general of British India, giving an account of my imprisonment. The character of general De Caen permitted but little hope to be entertained from the interference of His Lordship, but it seemed proper to acquaint him with the circumstances; and it was possible that some unforeseen occurrence might put it in the power of the marquis to demand my liberty in a way not to be refused: in all these letters I continued to adhere most scrupulously to the line of perfect neutrality indicated by the passport.

A detention of some months longer, until orders should arrive from France, appeared now to be inevitable, and the captain-general, by withholding the charts, papers, and log book, seemed to desire that nothing should take off my attention from feeling the weight of his power; but both Mr. Aken and myself contrived to pass some months neither uselessly nor disagreeably. We associated at table with Mr. Robertson and the two young gentlemen of the Dédaigneuse, by which our society was enlivened; and between the employments of copying my bearing book and defaced journals, making some astronomical observations, reading, and the amusements of music, walking in the inclosure, and an old billiard table left in the house, the days passed along rather lightly than otherwise. A prisoner or two were occasionally added to our number from the prizes brought in; but when amounting to six or eight, they were marched off to join the other merchant officers at Flacq. The seamen there were kept closely confined; but the officers enjoyed some share of liberty, and were as happy as they could make themselves upon fourteen dollars a month, in a place where the necessaries of life were exorbitantly dear; the hospitality of the French families in the neighbourhood, however, aided them considerably, and they spoke of the kindness and attention received in high terms.

JUNE 1804

On June 1, captain Neufville, the officer commanding the guard over the Prison, demanded all the spy-glasses in our possession; at the same time promising that each should be returned when the owner had permission to quit the island, and threatening those with close confinement in the tower, by whom any glass should be concealed. There was no cause to doubt the authority captain Neufville had to make the threat, but it should seem he had none to promise the restitution of the glasses; for I saw all the officers depart, and to the best of my knowledge not one of them could obtain their own. When Mr. Robertson quitted the island, and he was one of the first, his spy-glass was not to be found. The French gentleman to whom he delegated his claim, wrote to the town major upon the subject; and the answer was, that all arms and instruments taken from prisoners of war were the lawful property of the captors, as a reward for their courage; that for himself, he had not taken advantage of this right, but had given the glass in question to an officer of La Semillante, to be used against the enemies of his country. This answer not appearing satisfactory, the gentleman replied that he did not understand how a spy-glass, belonging to a surgeon, as Mr. Robertson was, could be construed into arms or instruments of war. The owner had come to the island on account of his health, previously to the war, and been detained, therefore no extraordinary courage had been displayed in his case; and as these circumstances must have been forgotten by the major, he hoped the glass would be restored according to promise. To this no answer was returned; and whether all the glasses were given away, or how disposed of I did not learn, but had to regret the loss of two.

To the measure of taking away our spy-glasses was added that of nailing up the door leading to the flat roof of the house. At sunset the sentinel was accustomed to quit the outer gate, and to be posted before the door of the prison to prevent any person going into the inclosure after that time; then it was that a walk upon the roof, after the heat of the day was passed, became a real pleasure; but of this we were now deprived.* On the following day a demand was made by a serjeant of invalids, who lived in the house as police officer, of the swords and all other arms in possession of the prisoners, and of mine amongst the rest; but not choosing to deliver up my sword in this manner, I addressed a short letter to the captain-general, representing that it was inconsistent with my situation in His Britannic Majesty's service to do so; I was ready to deliver it to an officer bearing His Excellency's order, but requested that officer might be of equal rank to myself. In a week captain Neufville called to say, that it was altogether a mistake of the serjeant that my arms had been asked for, and he was sorry it had taken place; had the captain-general meant to demand my sword, it would have been done by an officer of equal rank; but he had no intention to make me a prisoner until he should receive orders to that effect. The explanation attending this apology seemed to be strange; and the next time captain Neufville came to the house I observed to him, that it appeared singular, after having been confined six months, to be told I was not a prisoner, and asked him to explain it. He said, no certainly, I was not a prisoner--my sword had not been taken away; that I was simply detained for reasons which he did not pretend to penetrate, and put under *surveillance* for a short period.

[* It being afterward suspected, and not without reason, that some of the gentlemen had forced the door, we were officially informed that the sentinels had received orders to shoot any one who might be seen on the roof; this produced greater circumspection, but the pleasure of the walk and having a view of the sea was such, that it did not wholly remedy the evil.]

In this affair of the sword I thought myself rather handsomely treated; but about three months afterward, one of the lower officers of the staff came to demand it in the name of the town major, by order of the captain-general. When told the circumstances which had occurred upon the same subject, he said the general had consented to my wish at that time, but had since altered his mind; and upon the promise of sending an officer of equal rank, he said there was no officer of the same rank at that time in readiness--that colonel D'Arsonval (the town major) would himself have come had he not been engaged. I might, by a refusal, have given the officer the trouble of searching my trunks, and perhaps have received some further degradation; but since the order had come from the general, who had broken his word, my sword was delivered, with the observation that I should not forget the manner of its being taken. The officer described himself as *lieutenant-adjutant de place*; he conducted himself with politeness, and did not ask if I or Mr. Aken had any other weapons.

A seaman of the Cumberland and another prisoner from Flacq made their appearance one morning behind the wall of our inclosure. They had come to make a complaint of the scantiness of their provisions; for besides bread, they had only six ounces of meat or fish in the day, without salt or vegetables, which afforded them but a poor dinner and was their only meal in twenty-four hours. Several petitions and complaints had been made to the officer who had charge of them, but without effect; and they at length resolved that two of their number should escape out of the prison, and go to the *préfet* to make their complaint. It was to be feared that they would be considered as prisoners attempting to escape, if found openly in the town; and therefore, after giving them money to satisfy their immediate hunger, my servant was sent with them and a note to the interpreter, requesting he would be good enough to take them to the town major's office, where they might tell their story; and the result was, that they were put on board the prison ship, and kept in irons for several weeks. Mr. Charrington, my boatswain, had hitherto been treated as a common seaman; but through the obliging mediation of M. Bonnefoy, the allowance and portion of liberty granted to mates of merchant ships were obtained for him; and by two or three opportunities I sent tea and a few dollars to the seamen, on finding they were so miserably fed.

In the middle of this month, two of the officers who had resided with their wives at Pamplemousses, obtained permission to go on their parole to India, through the interest of captain Bergeret. This worthy man had frequently come to the Garden Prison, and at this time undertook to apply to the captain-general for my books and papers, and for Mr. Aken and myself to be removed to Pamplemousses.

JULY 1804

On the 2nd of July he called early with information of having succeeded in both applications; he had even ventured to propose my being sent to France, but to this it was answered, that the affair being submitted to the decision of the government, I must remain until its orders were received.

In a few days M. Bonnefoy conducted me to the secretary's office, and I took out of the sealed trunk all the books, charts, and papers which required any additions, or were necessary to the finishing of others; as also a bundle of papers containing my passport commission, etc., and the shattered accounts of the Investigator's stores. For these a receipt was required, the same as before; but the third volume of my log book, for which so many applications had been made, was still refused. Word had been sent me privately, that *the trunk had been opened and copies taken of the charts*, but to judge from appearances this was not true; and on putting the question to colonel Monistrol, whether the trunk or papers had been disturbed, he answered by an unqualified negative. In regard to our living in the country, the general had said to captain Bergeret, "he should think further upon it;" and this we were given to understand must be considered as a retraction of his promise: a second example of how little general De Caen respected his own word.

Charles Lambert, Esq., owner of the Althaea indiaman, brought in some time before as a prize, having obtained permission to go to England by the way of America, and no restriction being laid upon him as to taking letters, had the goodness to receive a packet for the Admiralty, containing copies of the charts constructed here and several other papers.

AUGUST 1804

In August I found means of sending to India, for Port Jackson, a letter addressed to governor King; describing my second passage through Torres' Strait, and the bad state of the Cumberland which had obliged me to stop at Mauritius, with the particulars of my imprisonment and the fate of his despatches. This letter was received in the April following, and extracts from it were published in the Sydney gazette; wherein was made a comparison between my treatment in Mauritius and that of captain Baudin at Port Jackson, as described by himself and captain Melius. This account was copied into the *Times* of Oct. 19, 1805, whence it afterwards came to my knowledge.

One advantage of being confined in the Garden Prison rather than at the Café Marengo, was in the frequency of visitors to one or other of the prisoners; permissions were required to be obtained from the town major, but these were seldom refused to people of respectability. In this manner we became acquainted with all the public news, and also with the opinions entertained in the island upon the subject of my imprisonment. Those who knew that I had a passport, and was confined upon suspicion only, thought the conduct of the captain-general severe, impolitic, and unjust; and some who pretended to have information from near the fountain head, hinted that if his invitation to dinner had been accepted, a few days would have been the whole of my detention. Others understood my passport and papers to have been lost in the shipwreck, and that it was uncertain whether I were the commander of the expedition on discovery or not; whilst many, not conceiving that their governor could thus treat an officer employed in the service of science without his having given some very sufficient cause, naturally enough made a variety of unfavourable conjectures, and in due time, that is, when these conjectures had passed through several hands, reports were in circulation of my having chased a vessel on shore on the south side of the island--of soundings and surveys of the coast found upon me--and of having quarrelled with the governor of New South Wales, who had refused to certify on my passport the necessity of quitting the Investigator and embarking in the Cumberland; and this last seemed to have acquired credit. I will not pretend to say, that general De Caen had any part in propagating these reports, for the purpose of satisfying the curiosity of an inquisitive public and turning its attention from the truth, though far from thinking it improbable; be that as it may, the nature of my voyage, our shipwreck, the long passage made in the little Cumberland, and our severe imprisonment, had excited a considerable degree of interest; and I was told that this imprisonment had been mentioned in an anonymous letter to the captain-general, as one of the many tyrannical acts committed in the short time he had held the government of the island.

One of the persons who asked permission to see me, was M. Augustin Baudin, brother of the deceased commander of Le Géographe; he testified the grateful sense his brother had always entertained of the generous reception and great assistance received from governor King at Port Jackson, and expressed his own regret at not being able to do any thing for my release. On learning from him that a letter still existed, written by captain Baudin to a member of the tribunal of appeal in Mauritius, I succeeded in obtaining an extract, of which the following is an exact translation.

On board Le Geographe, New Holland,
Port Jackson, the 3rd December, 1802.

After having traversed the sea in different directions for nine months after leaving Timor, I came to Port Jackson to pass the winter. The scurvy had then made such rapid progress, that I had no more than twelve men fit for duty when I arrived in this colony. The succours which were lavishly bestowed, the affectionate and obliging cares of governor King, his unremitting conduct and proceedings beyond example, every thing in fine, has concurred to make the effects of this disorder less fatal than the first (a dysentery contracted at Timor), although the cause was not less serious. I cannot pass in silence an act of humanity to which our situation gave rise. These are the facts.

On our arrival at Port Jackson, to the number of a hundred and seventy persons, the resources in corn were far from abundant; a great inundation and the overflowing of the River Hawkesbury, having in part destroyed the harvest which was upon the eve of being got in, and the following one being distant and uncertain, was not a fortunate circumstance for us. Nevertheless we were made perfectly welcome, and so soon as our present and future wants were known, the ration given daily to the inhabitants and the garrison was reduced one-half. The governor and the civil and military officers set the example of this generosity, which was immediately followed by the others. We were not only strangers, but still at war, for the news of the peace was not yet known.

The original extract in my possession, is certified to be true by the gentleman to whom the letter was addressed. Its contents afford a contrast to the proceedings of the governor of Mauritius, too striking to require any comment.

Amongst the acquaintances formed whilst in the Garden Prison, the most agreeable, most useful, and at the same time durable, was that of a young French merchant; a man well informed, a friend to letters, to science, and the arts; who spoke and wrote English, and had read many of our best authors. To him I am principally indebted for having passed some agreeable days in prison, and his name therefore merits a place in this history of the misfortune which his friendship contributed to alleviate; nor am I the sole English prisoner who will mention the name of *Thomas Pitot* with eulogium.

On the 27th, an English squadron consisting of two ships of the line and two frigates, under the command of captain John Osborn, arrived to cruise off the island.

SEPTEMBER 1804

Some days afterward, my boatswain and six of the merchant officers, prisoners at Flacq, made their escape to one of the ships. The captain-general, in a paroxysm of rage, ordered the officer commanding at Flacq to be dismissed, and every Englishman in the island, without distinction, to be closely confined; neither paroles of honour, nor sureties, nor permissions previously given to depart, being respected. Six were brought to the Garden Prison, of whom the captains Moffat and Henry from Pamplemousses were two, and their wives followed them. The seamen and remaining officers from Flacq passed our gate under a strong guard, and were marched to an old hospital about one mile on the south-west side of the town; where the seamen were shut up in the lower, and the officers in the upper apartment, there being only two rooms.

The arrival of the squadron gave the prisoners a hope of being released, either from a general exchange, or for such Frenchmen as our ships might take whilst cruising off the island; even Mr. Aken and myself, since our swords had been taken away, conceived some hopes, for we were then prisoners according to the definition of M. Neufville. There was, however, no intercourse with the squadron until the 19th, on which, and the two following days, a frigate was lying off the port with a flag of truce hoisted, and boats passed and repassed between her and the shore. Our anxiety to know the result was not a little; and we soon learned that captain Cockburne of the Phaeton had come in for the purpose of seeing general De Caen; but on entering the port he had been met, blindfolded, and taken on board the prison ship, which was also the guard ship; that finding he could not see the general, and that no officer was sent to treat with him, he left a packet from captain Osborn and returned in disgust. His mission, we were told, was to negotiate an exchange of prisoners, particularly mine; but in the answer given by general De Caen it was said, that not being a prisoner of war, no exchange for me could be accepted; nor did any one obtain his liberty in consequence.

OCTOBER 1804

Few persons were admitted to the Garden Prison during the presence of the English squadron; but it did not prevent captain Bergeret and M. Bonnefoy from coming occasionally. In the end of October I learned with much regret, that the interpreter had been dismissed from his employment, in consequence of having carried only one copy of the same newspaper to general De Caen, when two had been found in an American vessel which he had boarded off the port, according to custom; the other had been communicated to some of his friends, which was deemed an irremissible offence. This obliging man, to whom I was under obligations for many acts of attention and some of real service, feared to ask any future permission to visit the Garden Prison.

Admiral Linois arrived from a cruise on the 31st, with three rich prizes, and got into Port Bourbon unimpeded by our ships, which were off another part of the island; and the same evening commodore Osborn quitted Mauritius. Mr. Robertson and Mr. Webb of the Aplin were now permitted to go to England by the way of America [NOVEMBER 1804]; and I took the good opportunity of sending by the first of these gentlemen a copy of the general chart of Terra Australis, comprehending the whole of my discoveries and examinations in abridgment, and a paper on the magnetism of ships addressed to the president of the Royal Society.* Four officers of the army also obtained permission to go to India, on condition of returning, should four French officers whose names were specified, be not sent back in exchange; and two other gentlemen left the Garden Prison, and the island soon afterward. In lieu of these, were sent in captain Turner and lieutenant Cartwright of the Indian army, and the officers of the Princess Charlotte indiaman.

[* This paper was read before the Society, and published in the Transactions of 1805, Part II.]

By information received from the Grande-Riviere prison, where the merchant officers and the seamen were confined, it appeared that my six remaining people, and no doubt many others, were very miserable and almost naked; having been hurried off suddenly from Flacq, and compelled to leave their few clothes behind. On this occasion I addressed the captain-general on the score of humanity, intreating him either to order their clothes to be restored, or that they should be furnished with others; and on the same day an answer was returned in the most polite manner by colonel D'Arsonval, saying that an order had been given for all the prisoners to be fresh clothed, and their wants supplied. Six weeks afterward, however, finding that the poor seamen remained in the same naked state as before, I wrote to remind the town major of what he had said; requesting at the same time, if it were not intended to give these unfortunate men any clothing, that Mr. Aken might be permitted to visit them, in order to relieve their urgent necessities from my own purse. No answer was returned to this letter, but it produced the desired effect.

DECEMBER 1804

My hopes of a speedy liberation by an order of the first consul became weakened in December, on seeing nothing arrive to confirm them after a whole year's imprisonment. On the 17th I wrote to remind the captain-general that one year had elapsed; and requested him to consider that the chance of war rendered the arrival of despatches uncertain--that I was suffering an irretrievable loss of time, and very severely in my health, advancement, and every thing that man holds dear; I begged him to reflect, that the rights of the most severe justice would be ensured by sending me to France, where the decision of my fate was remitted; and where, should the judgment of the French government be favourable, it could be immediately followed by a return to my country and family, and the resumption of my peaceable labours. No answer being given at the end of a week, a second letter was sent, inclosing a copy of the extract from captain Baudin; and His Excellency was requested to compare the treatment of the French commander at Port Jackson with what I had received at Mauritius, and at least to give Mr. Aken and myself the liberty of some district in the island where we might take exercise, and find the amusement necessary to the re-establishment of our health; but neither of these letters obtained any reply, or the least notice.

Mr. Aken had been removed to the hospital in September, and after a stay of six weeks had returned, more from finding himself so ill accommodated and fed than from the improvement in his health. He now declined rapidly; [JANUARY 1805] and my own health was impaired by a constitutional gravelly complaint to which confinement had given accelerated force, and by a bilious disorder arising partly from the same cause, from the return of hot weather, and discouraging reflections on our prospects. We were therefore visited by Dr. Laborde, principal physician of the medical staff, who judged the air and exercises of the country to be the most certain means of restoration; and in order to our procuring them, he gave a certificate which I sent to general De Caen through colonel Monistrol, then become town major. No answer was returned; but after some days it was told me that Dr. Laborde had received a message from the general, desiring him not to interfere with matters which did not concern him; and this was the sole mark of attention paid to his certificate or to our situation.*

[* The doctor had said in his certificate, "J'estime qu'il faut prévenir 'augmentation de ses maux; et en le secourant apropos, c'est assurer la conservation d'un homme dont les travaux doivent servir aux progrès des sciences, et a l'utilité de ses semblables."]

Being thus disappointed in every attempt to procure an amelioration for my companion and myself, I sought the means of dispensing with the captain-general's humanity. I rose very early, and took much exercise in our inclosure before the heat of the sun, became too powerful; and applied closely to the charts and accounts of my voyage, which ill health and a languid melancholy had for some time caused to be neglected. By perseverance in these means, my disorders were at least prevented from becoming worse; but more particularly I acquired a tranquil state of mind, and had even the happiness of forgetting general De Caen, sometimes for days together. The strength of my companion was too much exhausted for such a regimen; and he was obliged to return to the hospital, being so much reduced that there was reason to fear for his life.

Several military and merchant officers obtained permissions at this time to depart on parole, some to India, others to America; which furnished opportunities of writing many letters. I addressed one to admiral Rainier, the commander in chief of His Majesty's ships in India, upon the subject of my detention; and another to lord William Bentinck, governor of Madras, in favour of two relations of my friend Pitot, who were prisoners under his government; and it is with much gratitude to His Lordship that I add his more than compliance with the request: he not only set the two prisoners at liberty, but used his endeavours to procure my release from general De Caen.

On the 29th, an American vessel arrived from France with many passengers, and amongst them monsieur Barrois, the brother-in-law of the general. He was charged with despatches; and I was told upon good authorities that he had been sent to France in Le Géographe upon the same service, in December 1803. The knowledge of this fact gave an insight into various circumstances which took place at, and some time after my arrival at Mauritius. Le Géographe having an English passport, was equally bound with myself to observe a strict neutrality; and the conveyance of an officer with public despatches in time of war was therefore improper. Common report said, that captain Melius objected to it, as compromising the safety of his ship and results of the voyage; but on its being known from the signals that an English vessel was on the south side of the island, M. Barrois embarked secretly, and the ship was ordered off the same evening. Hence I missed seeing her, and was arrested on arriving at Port Louis without examination; and hence it appeared to have been, that an embargo was immediately laid on all foreign ships for ten days, that none of our cruisers might get information of the circumstance and stop Le Géographe; hence also the truth of what was told me in the Café Marengo, that *my confinement did not arise from any thing I had done.*

Such was the respect paid by general De Caen to the English passport; and how little sacred he held that given by his own government for the protection of the Investigator's voyage, will in part have already appeared. The conduct of the British government and its officers in these two cases was widely different. In consequence of the English passport, the Géographe and Naturaliste were received at Port Jackson as friends, and treated with the kindness due to their employment and distressed situation, as will satisfactorily appear from M. Peron's account of their voyage; and with regard to the French passport, it may be remembered that the Admiralty directed me, on leaving England, not even to take letters or packets other than such as might be received from that office, or that of the secretary of state; and the despatches sent from those offices were to governor King alone, and related solely to the Investigator's voyage. I was ordered to stop at Madeira and the Cape of Good Hope, but neither to the officers commanding His Majesty's land or sea forces at one, nor at the other place was any despatch sent; although no opportunity of writing to the Cape had for some time presented itself.

FEBRUARY 1805

The return of M. Barrois gave a reasonable hope that the captain-general might have received orders concerning me, and that some thing would be immediately determined; but a whole month passed in silence as so many others had before done. It was reported, however, as having come from the general, that the council of state had approved of the precautions he had taken; but whether it had decided upon my being set at liberty, sent to France, or continued a prisoner, was not said.

There were at this time only six officers in the Garden Prison, Mr. Aken being still at the hospital; lieutenant Manwaring of the Bombay marine, before commander of the Fly packet, with two of his officers had possession of one part of the house, and Messrs. Dale and Seymour, midshipmen of the Dédaigneuse, lived with me in the other. These two young gentlemen, the first in particular, aided me in making copies of charts and memoirs, in calculating astronomical observations, etc.; and I had much pleasure in furnishing them with books and assisting their studies.

MARCH 1805

In the beginning of March, I was surprised to see in the official gazette of the French government, the Moniteur of July 7, 1804, a long letter from Dunkirk addressed to the editor; containing many particulars of my voyage, praising the zeal with which it had been conducted, and describing my detention in Mauritius as a circumstance which had originated in a mistake and was understood to be terminated. In the succeeding Moniteur of the 11th, some observations were made upon this letter on the part of the government, which afforded some insight into what was alleged against me; and these being important to the elucidation of general De Caen's policy, a translation of them is here given.

MONITEUR, No. 292.

Wednesday 22 Messidor, year 12; or July 11, 1804.

In a letter from Dunkirk, addressed to the editor of the Moniteur, and inserted in the paper of the 18th of this month, No. 288, we read an account of the voyage of Mr. Flinders, an English navigator, who arrived at the Isle of France the 24 Frimaire last, in the schooner Cumberland. The author of the letter in the Moniteur says, that Mr. Flinders, *"not knowing of the war, stopped at the Isle of France which was in his route, to obtain water and refreshments: that some secret articles in his instructions gave rise to suspicions upon which the captain-general at first thought it his duty to detain him prisoner; but that, nevertheless, the passports he had obtained from the French government and all other nations, the nature even of his expedition which interested all civilized people, were not long in procuring his release."*

The fact is, that Mr. Flinders not knowing of, but suspecting the war, ventured to come to the Isle of France; where having learned its declaration, he doubted whether the passport granted him by the French government in the year 9, would serve him. In reality, the passport was exclusively for the sloop*Investigator, of which it contained the description*; and it is not in the Investigator that he has been arrested, but in the Cumberland.

The same passport did not permit Mr. Flinders to stop at French colonies but on condition that he should not deviate from his route to go there; and Mr. Flinders acknowledges in his journal that he deviated voluntarily, (for the Isle of France was not in his passage, as the author of the above cited letter says). In fine, the passport granted to Mr. Flinders did not admit of any equivocation upon the objects of the expedition for which it was given: but we read in one part of his journal, *that he suspected the war*, and in another, *that he had resolved to touch at the Isle of France, as well in the hope of selling his vessel advantageously, as from the desire of knowing the present state of that colony, and the utility of which it and its dependencies in Madagascar could be to Port Jackson.*

As the passport given by the French government to Mr. Flinders, an English navigator, was far from admitting an examination of that nature in a French colony; it is not

184

at all surprising that the captain-general of that colony has arrested him; and nothing announces as yet, that he has thought it necessary to release him.

An elaborate refutation of these trifling, and in part false and contradictory charges, will not, I should hope, be thought necessary. By turning to Chapter 3 (December), and comparing my reasons for putting in at Mauritius with what the Moniteur says, it will be seen that the necessity of the measure, arising from the bad state of the Cumberland, is kept wholly out of sight; and that in giving the subordinate reasons, there is much omission and misrepresentation. The charges, even as they stand in the Moniteur, amount to nothing, if my suspicion of the war be taken away; and it has no other foundation than that, being a stranger to what had passed in Europe for twelve months, I thought there was a possibility of war between England and France; and thence deduced an additional reason for stopping at Mauritius where my passport would be respected, in preference to going on to the Cape of Good Hope where it might not. This suspicion, which is twice brought forward, is moreover contradicted by inference, in the Moniteur itself. It says, "Mr. Flinders not knowing of, but suspecting the war, ventured to come to the Isle of France; where having learned its declaration, he doubted whether the passport would serve him." Now it is not credible, that with such a suspicion, and being aware, consequently, of the great importance of the passport, I should wait until arriving at the island before seeking to know its particular contents; but going to Mauritius under the belief of peace, and finding war declared, an examination of the passport was then natural. It is true that I did then entertain some apprehensions, from not finding any provision made for another vessel in case of shipwreck or other accident to the Investigator; but my confidence in the justice and liberality of the French government overcame them; and had general Magallon remained governor, this confidence would most probably have been justified by the event.

How my reasons for stopping at Mauritius were worded in the log book, I certainly do not remember correctly, nor how far they were accompanied with explanations; and particular care has been taken to prevent me giving the words themselves; but is it possible to suppose, that suspecting the war and entertaining inimical designs, I should have inserted this suspicion and these designs in my common journal? Or that, having done so, the book would have been put into the hands of general De Caen's secretary, and these very passages pointed out for him to copy? Yet the reasons alleged in the Moniteur, to be true, require no less.

The assertion that I acknowledge to have deviated *voluntarily* from my route, for the Isle of France was not in my passage--if voluntarily mean, *without necessity*, must be false altogether. I had intended to pass the island without stopping, and probably said so; but that the intention was altered voluntarily, could not have been said, for the *necessity* arising from the bad state of the schooner was alleged for it. Whether Mauritius be in the passage from Timor to the Cape of Good Hope, any seaman or geographer who knows the trade winds, can tell: it is as much in the passage as is the Cape in going from Europe to India. The above assertion induced me to examine captain Cook's track from Timor to the Cape, as it is traced upon Arrowsmith's general chart, and to measure the distance from a certain part of it to Port Louis, and from thence to regain the track really made; and I found that his distance would not have been increased so much as *one hundred miles*, or less than the half of what ships augment their distance by stopping at Table Bay, in their route to India. It may perhaps be said, that my *voluntary* deviation and the island not being in the passage, apply only to my intention of passing Mauritius and then changing it. If so, the assertion could only be made for superficial readers, and contains nothing; such, in fact, are all the charges when duly examined, not excepting the pretence that the passport was *exclusively for the Investigator*; and more has already been said upon them than is due to their real importance.

These Moniteurs, however, informed me of two material circumstances--that there was at least one person in France who viewed my detention in its true light, and that the government had either been deceived by the representations of general De Caen, or coincided with his views from some secret motive; consequently, that too much reliance ought not to be placed in an early liberation by its orders. I then determined to write to monsieur De Fleurieu, author of the instructions to La Pérouse, etc., and counsellor of state, who might be supposed to interest himself in my voyage; and annexed to the letter copies of papers showing the reception given to the French ships at Port Jackson, and the necessity which had forced me to stop at Mauritius; and begged him in the name of humanity and the sciences, to use his influence that I might either be permitted to continue the voyage, or otherwise be ordered to France for examination. My worthy friend Pitot wrote to the same effect, to M. De Bougainville, the navigator and counsellor of state--to M. De la Lande, the astronomer--to M. Chaptal, minister of the interior--and to M. Dupuis, counsellor of state; and admiral Linois had the goodness to write to M. De Fleurieu in favour of my request. At the same time I wrote to the secretary of the Admiralty, inclosing a copy of the first letter; and all these being sent away in duplicate, by opportunities which occurred soon afterward, every step seemed to have been taken that could afford any hope of liberty and the restitution of my books and papers.

APRIL 1805

The fate of my officers and people on board the Rolla had been a subject of some anxiety; but about this time I had the satisfaction to learn from the public papers, that they had arrived safely in England; that lieutenant Fowler and the officers and company of the Porpoise had been honourably acquitted of all blame for the loss of the ship, and that Mr. Fowler had much distinguished himself in the action between the China fleet and admiral Linois' squadron.

MAY 1805

Permissions being granted to several prisoners to go away on their parole in American vessels, Mr. Aken, who still remained at the hospital, conceived hopes that his might pass amongst the rest, if he applied. In this notion I encouraged him, since my own prospects were so obscure; and recommended that his plea should turn wholly upon his long-continued ill health, and to say nothing of his connexion with me. The application was made accordingly; and on the 7th, he came to the Garden Prison with the unexpected information of being then at liberty to depart, on giving his parole "not to serve against France or its allies, until after having been legally exchanged;" that is, as a *prisoner of war.*

It seemed doubtful whether this permission had been granted from motives of humanity, from forgetfulness, or from some new plan having been adopted; the general might possibly have received orders, permitting him to dispose of us as he should think proper, and have no objection to getting rid of me also, as a prisoner of war, provided an application gave him the opportunity. In this uncertainty of what might be his intentions, I wrote to colonel Monistrol, requesting him to state the length of my imprisonment and ill health; and to move His Excellency to let me depart on parole, or in any other way he should judge proper; but it appeared after waiting several days, that the colonel foreseeing the request could answer no purpose, had not laid it before the captain-general. I then resolved to make good use of the opportunity presented by Mr. Aken's departure, and from this time to that of his sailing, was fully occupied in making up my despatches; and Mr. Aken's health being improved, he took up his residence in the Garden Prison for the purpose of giving his assistance.

Besides a general chart of Terra Australis, showing the whole of my discoveries, examinations and tracks in abridgment, this packet for the Admiralty contained nine sheets upon a scale of four inches to a degree of longitude, and three sheets of particular parts in a larger size; also five chapters of a memoir explanatory of their construction, of the changes in the variation on shipboard, etc.; an enlarged copy of my log book, with remarks and astronomical observations from the commencement of the voyage to quitting the north coast of Terra Australis in March 1803; and a book containing all the bearings and angles which entered into the construction of the charts. The time keeper, with the mathematical and nautical instruments belonging to the Navy Board were also sent; and in fine, either the original or a copy of every thing in my possession which related either to the Investigator or the voyage.

Mr. Campbell, commander of the American ship James, bound to New York, liberally gave Mr. Aken and some other prisoners a passage free of expense;* and the paroles they were required to sign laying no other injunction than that of not serving until legally exchanged, the books. etc. above mentioned, with many letters both public and private, were safely embarked; and on the 20th in the evening, the ship got under sail, to my great satisfaction. Of the ten officers and men who had come with me to Mauritius, only four now remained; one was in the hospital with a broken leg, another with me in the Garden Prison, and two were shut up at the Grande Rivière. A seaman had been allowed to go with Mr. Aken in the James, and all our endeavours were used to obtain permission for the two in prison to embark also, but without effect; about a month afterwards, however, they were suffered to enter on board an American ship, at the request of the commander.

[* It gives me pleasure to say, that almost the whole of the American commanders were ready to accommodate the English prisoners who, from time to time, obtained leave to depart, and the greater number without any other expense than that of laying in provisions for themselves; some were received on board as officers for wages, and others had a table found for them without any specified duty being required. In most cases these were beneficent actions, for, as will readily be imagined, the greater part of the prisoners had no means of obtaining money in Mauritius; the military officers, however, and those who had money at their disposal, were required to pay for their passages, and in some cases, dear enough.]

JUNE 1805

On June 4, a fortnight after Mr. Aken had sailed, captain Osborn again came off the island, with His Majesty's ships Tremendous, Grampus, Pitt, and Terpsichore; and an embargo on all foreign vessels was, as usual, the immediate consequence. On the 23rd, the ship Thetis arrived from Bengal under cartel colours, having on board captain Bergeret, with such of his officers and people as had not been killed in the action he had sustained against our frigate the St. Fiorenzo. This arrival animated the spirits of all the prisoners in the island; and the return of my friend Bergeret even gave me some hopes, particularly after the reception of a note from him, promising to use his exertions to obtain a favourable change in my situation. Mr. Richardson, commander of the Thetis, informed us some days afterward [JULY 1805], that all the prisoners of war would be allowed to go to India in his ship, and that hopes were entertained of an application for me also being successful. Captain Bergeret did not call until the 3rd of July, after having used his promised endeavours in vain, as I had foreseen from the delay of his visit; for every good Frenchman has an invincible dislike to be the bearer of disagreeable intelligence.

On the 5th, a letter came from Mr. Lumsden, chief secretary of the government at Calcutta, acknowledging the receipt of mine addressed to the marquis Wellesley in May 1804; he said in reply, "that although the governor-general had felt the deepest regret at the circumstances of my detention and imprisonment, it had not been in His Excellency's power to remedy either before the present time. The ship Thetis," he added, "now proceeds to the Isle of France as a cartel; and I have the honour to transmit to you the annexed extract from the letter of the governor-general to His Excellency general De Caen, captain-general of the French establishments to the eastward of the Cape of Good Hope. The governor-general entertains no doubt that the captain-general of the Isle of France will release you immediately on receipt of that letter."

EXTRACT.--I avail myself of this opportunity to request your Excelleney's particular attention to the truly severe case of captain Flinders; and I earnestly request Your Excellency to release captain Flinders immediately, and to allow him either to take his passage to India in the Thetis, or to return to India in the first neutral ship.

Mr. Lumsden's letter and the above extract were inclosed to me by the secretary of general De Caen, who at the same time said, "I wish with all my heart that the captain-general could accede to the request of His Excellency the marquis Wellesley; but the motives of your detention having been of a nature to be submitted to the French government, the captain-general cannot, before he has received an answer, change any thing in the measures which have been adopted on your account." Thus whatever hope had been entertained of liberation from the side of India was done away, but I did not feel less gratitude to the noble marquis for his attempt; after eighteen months of indignities, this attention, and the previous arrival of the two relations of my friend Pitot, set at liberty by lord William Bentinck, were gratifying proofs that my situation was known and excited an interest in India.

An exchange of prisoners was soon afterwards agreed upon between commodore Osborn and colonel Monistrol, with the exception of post-captains and commanders in the navy and officers of similar rank in the army; it was not said that the exceptions had any reference to captain Bergeret or myself, the sole officers in Mauritius of the ranks specified, but it seemed probable.

On the 28th, the ship Prime arrived from Bombay with French prisoners, having on board lieutenant Blast of the Company's marine, as agent; admiral Linois had met the ship near Ceylon, and taken seventy-nine of the French seamen on board his squadron, notwithstanding the representation of Mr. Blast that no exchange had yet been settled. This proceeding was said to be disapproved by general De Caen; and afterwards to be the cause of the exchange being declared void by Sir Edward Pellew, then become commander in chief in the Indian seas.

AUGUST 1805

There was at this time an almost uncontrolled liberty to enter the Garden Prison, and I was favoured with frequent visits by Mr. Richardson of the Thetis, and by Messrs. Blast, Madegon, and Davies of the Prime; these gentlemen, finding they should be obliged to leave me behind and alone, rendered every service I could permit myself to receive at their hands, and made an impression by their kindness which will ever be retained. From their conversation I learned what was the treatment of French prisoners at Bengal and Bombay; and the contrast it formed with that of English officers and seamen in Mauritius, both in the degree of liberty and allowance for subsistence, was indeed striking. Something has already been said upon this subject, and much more might be said; but it is a more agreeable task to bestow praise where it can with truth be given. It is therefore with pleasure, and with gratitude on the part of my unfortunate countrymen to admiral Linois and the officers of his squadron, as also to the commanders of privateers, that I declare no one of the several prisoners I conversed with to have made any complaint of them; on the contrary, almost all acknowledged to have been treated with kindness *whilst on board*, and except sometimes a little pilfering by the sailors, to have lost nothing of what they had a right to keep by the received usages of war; the trunks of many were not searched, it being only required of the possessor to declare, that it was his private property and that no letters or journals were contained therein. When the Fly packet was taken by the privateer La Fortune, lieutenant Manwaring's table plate and time keeper were returned to him; and his treatment by M. Lamême was altogether so liberal, when compared with the usual conduct of privateers in Europe, as to merit being cited.

In order to give some notion of the mischief done to British commerce in India, by ships from Mauritius, an abstract of all the captures made in the first sixteen months of the war, so far as they came to our knowledge in the Garden Prison, is subjoined. There are probably several omissions; and the supposed values annexed to them are the least that can be estimated, perhaps not exceeding two-thirds of the prime cost.

By admiral Linois' squadron, three Indiamen and five country ships mostly large, £505,000 By La Psyché privateer, one Indiaman and two private ships, 95,000 La Henriette, six ships and small vessels, 150,000 La Fortune, one packet, three ships, four small vessels, 103,000 Cutter commanded by Surcouf, four vessels, 75,000 L'Alfred, one ship, 10,000 Le Pariah, one ship, 10,000 -------- Brought into Port Louis, 948,000 Ships known to have been sent to France or Batavia, run on shore, or sunk at sea, 200,000 Mischief done at Bencoolen by admiral Linois' squadron, 800,000 -------- Estimated loss to British commerce in 16 months, 1948,000

The sailing of the Thetis and Prime, and of a little brig named the Ariel which had brought prisoners from Ceylon, was delayed until the cruising squadron had left the island. On the 13th commodore Osborn took his departure, and my young friends Dale and Seymour quitted the Garden Prison; the first carrying for me a letter to Sir Edward Pellew, giving an account of my situation, and another to Mr. Lumsden, informing him of the little success attending the governor-general's request. In the evening of the same day the cartels sailed; and I remained with my servant, who refused to profit by the occasion of obtaining his liberty, and my lame seaman, the sole English prisoners at Mauritius.

Captain Bergeret informed me two days afterward, that the general was disposed to permit of my residence in the interior part of the island; and he advised a written application to be made, specifying the place of my choice. After consulting with M. Pitot, who had received several offers to accommodate me from different parts of the island, I wrote on the 17th, pointing out the plantation of Madame D'Arifat at Wilhems Plains; which being at some distance from the sea, seemed least liable to objection. On the 19th, a polite note from colonel Monistrol said that my request was granted; and he sent word next day, that I was at liberty to quit the Garden Prison, and pass two or three days in town previously to going into the country; and being importuned by my friend Pitot to spend the evening with him, immediate advantage was taken of the permission.

On taking leave of the old serjeant, who had behaved kindly to all the prisoners, and finding myself without side the iron gate, I felt that even a prison one has long inhabited is not quitted without some sentiment of regret, unless it be to receive liberty. Of the twenty months which my detention had now reached, more than sixteen had been passed in the Garden Prison, sometimes rather lightly, but the greater part in bitterness; and my strength and appearance were so changed, that I felt to be scarcely recognisable for the same person who had supported so much fatigue in exploring the coasts of Terra Australis.

Various observations had been taken in the Garden Prison, both by Mr. Aken and myself, principally for our amusement and to exercise Messrs. Dale and Seymour in the calculations. The corrected results of my observations were as follow:

Latitude from eight meridian altitudes of the sun, taken with a sextant and artificial horizon, 20° 9' 13.5" S.

Longitude from twenty-seven sets of lunar distances, the particulars of which are given in Table IX. of the first Appendix to this volume, 57° 30' 42" E.

Variation of the theodolite from azimuths a.m. and p.m. 11° 42' 30" W.

The middle of the town being nearly one mile south-west from the prison, its situation should be: Port Louis, latitude 20° 9' 56" south, longitude 57° 29' 57" east.

CHAPTER VI.
Parole given.
Journey into the interior of Mauritius.
The governor's country seat.
Residence at the Refuge, in that Part of Wilhems Plains called Vacouas.
Its situation and climate, with the mountains, rivers, cascades, and views near it.
The Mare aux Vacouas and Grand Bassin.
State of cultivation and produce of Vacouas; its black ebony, game, and wild fruits; and freedom from noxious insects.

[AT MAURITIUS. PORT LOUIS.]
AUGUST 1805

My first visit after being liberated from the Garden Prison, was to captain Bergeret, whose interposition I considered to have been the principal cause of this favourable change; he obligingly offered me the accommodation of his lodging whilst in town, but M. Pitot had previously engaged my residence with him. Next morning I accompanied captain Bergeret to the town major's office for the purpose of giving my parole, which colonel Monistrol proposed to take verbally; but to avoid all future misunderstanding, I desired that it might be taken in writing, and two days afterward it was made out as follows.

His Excellency the captain-general De Caen having given me permission to reside at Wilhems Plains, at the habitation of Madame D'Arifat, I do hereby promise, upon my parole of honour, not to go more than the distance of two leagues from the said habitation, without His Excellency's permission; and to conduct myself with that proper degree of reserve, becoming an officer residing in a country with which his nation is at war. I will also answer for the proper conduct of my two servants.

Town of Port North-west, Matthew Flinders. August 23, 1805

The habitation, for so plantations are here called, which was to be my residence, belonged to a respectable widow with a large family; and was represented to be five French leagues, or twelve miles from the town, in a S. S. W. direction. The permission to range two leagues all round I considered to be an approach towards liberality; and a proof that, if general De Caen had ever really believed me to be a spy, he had ceased to think so; it was not indeed consistent with the reason alleged for my imprisonment, to grant a parole at all, but this it was no part of my business to point out. On the other hand, by signing this parole I cut myself off from the possibility of an escape; but it seemed incredible, after the various letters written and representations made both in England and France, that a favourable order should not arrive in six or eight months. I moreover entertained some hopes of Mauritius being attacked, for it was not to be imagined that either the East-India company or the government should quietly submit to such losses as it caused to British commerce; and if attacked with judgment, it appeared to me that a moderate force would carry it; upon this subject, however, an absolute silence was preserved in my letters, for although the passport had been so violated by general De Caen, I was determined to adhere to it strictly.

During four days stay in the to town of Port Louis no restriction of any kind was imposed; I visited the theatre, and several families to whom my friends Pitot and Bergeret introduced me, and passed the time as pleasantly as any one who spoke no French could do in such a situation. A young Englishman, who under the name of an American expected to sail immediately for Europe, took charge of a box containing letters and papers for the Admiralty and president of the Royal Society, one of which was upon the effect produced on the marine barometer by sea and land winds;* and on the 24th in the afternoon I set off with M. Pitot's family for their country house, which was four miles on the way to my intended residence.

[* This paper appeared in the Society's Transactions of 1806, Part II.]
[AT MAURITIUS. WILHEMS PLAINS.]

On the following day we visited the country seat of the governor, called the *Reduit*, about seven miles from the town, and at the edge of my limit of two leagues from the habitation at Wilhems Plains. It stands upon an elevated point of land between the Rivière de Mocha, which comes from the east, and an equally large stream which collects the waters of Wilhems Plains from the southward; their junction at this place forms the Grande Rivière, and the Reduit commands a view of its windings in the low land to the north, until it is discharged into the sea about a mile on the west side of Port Louis. There was little water in the two rivers at this time; but the extraordinary depth of their channels, which seemed to be not less than a hundred feet, and to have been cut through the solid rock, bespoke that the current must be immense during the hurricanes and heavy summer rains; and the views which the different falls of water amongst the overhanging woods will then present, cannot be otherwise than highly picturesque. At the Reduit the sides of these ravines were planted with the waving bamboo, and the road leading up to the house, with the gardens around it, were shaded by the mango and various other fruit trees; but all was in great disorder, having suffered more than neglect during the turbulent period of the French revolution. The house was said to be capable of containing thirty-five beds, and was at this time in a state of preparation for general De Caen; and when completed, and the gardens, alleys, fish ponds, and roads put into order, it would be an elegant residence for the governor of the island. Our inspection was confined to the gardens and prospects, from the house being shut up; we afterwards made a rural dinner under the shade of a banian tree, and my friend Pitot, with M. Bayard, a judge in the court of appeal, then separated from their families to conduct me onward to my asylum.

Instead of taking the direct road, they pursued a winding route more to the eastward, to pay a visit to M. Plumet, a friend of the judge; and we reached his habitation not much before sunset, though still four or five miles short of our destination. Thus far I found the country to be stony and not very fertile, the roads bad and irregular, with several places in them which must be impracticable in the heavy rains; here and there, however, we were gratified with the view of country houses, surrounded with fruit trees and well watered gardens; and once turned out of the road to see a water fall made by a considerable stream down a precipice of at least a hundred feet. The cultivated fields seemed to be generally planted either with sugar cane, maize, or manioc, but we were often in the shade of the primitive woods.

M. Plumet had passed many years in India, in the service of Scindeah, the Mahratta chief, and spoke some English; he received us so kindly that we remained with him until the following afternoon, and his habitation being within my limits, he invited me to visit him afterwards. From the time of quitting the port we had been continually ascending; so that here the elevation was probably not less than a thousand feet, and the climate and productions were much altered. Coffee seemed to be a great object of attention, and there were some rising plantations of clove trees; I found also strawberries, and even a few young oaks of tolerable growth. A vast advantage, as well as ornament in this and many other parts of the island, is the abundance of never failing streams; by which the gardens are embellished with cascades and fish ponds, and their fruit trees and vegetables watered at little expense.

Quitting M. Plumet in the afternoon of the 26th, we rode in intricate paths and crossed various plantations to get into the direct road. In these, besides sugar cane, coffee, maize, and manioc, some fields were totally covered with a creeping plant bearing a heart-shaped leaf; this was the *patate*, or sweet potatoe, a root of great utility to the nourishment of the slaves; and in the higher parts of the island, where it succeeds best, is a favourite object of cultivation, being little subject to injury from the hurricanes. As we advanced the streams became smaller and more numerous, and the uncleared woods more extensive; the country was still partly covered with large stones; but I remarked with some surprise, that the productions of the stony land were generally the most vigorous.

Neither of my conductors were acquainted with the place of my retreat; they inquired of every black man on the road, as to the right path and the distance that yet remained; but often could get no answer--sometimes it was three-quarters, and sometimes two leagues; at length we found ourselves surrounded on all sides by wood, the road had diminished to a foot path, it was dark, and began to rain. It was then judged necessary to turn back and make for a light near the road, to obtain a guide; and it seemed odd that the person applied to should answer in English, that the plantation of Madame D'Arifat was just bye. He proved to be an Irishman named Druse, who had been settled more than twenty years in this distant island as a carpenter; he had known that an English officer was coming to reside here, and undertook to be our guide, seeming to be not a little pleased at again using his native language.

A black man who had charge of the plantation in the absence of the proprietor, had received orders to accommodate us; but not finding my servant and lame seaman who should have arrived the day before, we walked half a league to the habitation of M. de Chazal, a friend of M. Pitot who had the goodness to send out my baggage. Next morning we returned, and my abode was fixed in one of two little pavilions detached from the house, the other being appropriated to my two men; and M. Pitot having brought me acquainted with a family resident on an adjoining plantation, and made some inquiries and arrangements as to supplies of provisions, he and his companion M. Bayard then returned to the town.

SEPTEMBER 1805

My attention for the first several weeks was principally directed to acquiring a knowledge of the surrounding country, its natural curiosities and romantic views; and as these are well worth notice, a description of the most remarkable objects, with an account of the cultivation and produce of this secluded part of Mauritius, may probably be acceptable to some readers.

The district or quarter called Wilhems Plains, occupies a considerable portion of the interior of the island; its northern extremity borders on the sea by the side of the district of Port Louis, from which it is separated by the Grande Rivière; and it extends southward from thence, rising gradually in elevation and increasing in breadth. The body of the quarter is bounded to the N. E. by the district of Mocha--to the S. E. by that of Port Bourbon or the Grand Port--to the south by the quarter of La Savanne--and to the west by the Plains of St. Piérre. Its length from the sea to the Grand Bassin at its southern extremity, is about five geographic leagues in a straight line, and mean breadth nearly two leagues; whence the superficial extent of this district should not be much less than ninety square miles. In the upper part is a lake called the *Mare aux Vacouas*, apparently so named from the number of pandanus trees, called vacouas, on its borders; and that part of Wilhems Plains by which the lake is surrounded, at the distance of a league, more or less, bears the appellation of Vacouas; in this part my residence was situate, in a country overspread with thick woods, a few plantations excepted, which had been mostly cleared within a few years.

In consequence of the elevation of Vacouas, the climate is as much different from that of the low parts of the island as if it were several degrees without the tropic; June, July, and August are the driest months at Port Louis, but here they are most rainy, and the thermometer stands from 7° to 12° lower upon an average throughout the year.* In a west direction, across that part of the Plains of St. Pierre called Le Tamarin, the sea is not more distant than six miles; the descent is therefore rapid, and is rendered more so from three-fourths of the space being flat, low land; in comparison with Le Tamarin, Vacouas is in fact an irregular plain upon the top of the mountains, to which there is almost no other access than by making a circuit of four or five miles round by the lower part of Wilhems Plains. Three rugged peaks called the Trois Mamelles, and another, the Montagne du Rempart, all of them conspicuous at sea, are the highest points of a ridge somewhat elevated above this irregular plain, and bounding it to the westward; and the road forming the ordinary communication between the high and low land passes round them. My retreat, which very appropriately to the circumstances of my situation bore the name of *The Refuge*, lay two or three miles to the south-east of the Trois Mamelles.

[* The mean height of the thermometer in July 1805, which is the middle of winter, was 67¼°, and of the barometer in French inches and lines, 26.7¾; and during February 1806, the middle of summer. 76° and 26.5¾ were the mean heights. At M. Pitot's house in the town of Port Louis, the averages in the same February were 86° and 27.7¾. According to De Luc, the difference between the logarithms of the two heights of the barometer expresses very nearly the difference of elevation in thousand toises, when the thermometer stands at 70° in both places; and therefore the approximate elevation of Vacouas above M. Pitot's house, should be 187¼ toises, or in French feet, 1123 Correction for excess of thermometers above 70°, + 25 Supposed elevation of M. Pitot's house above the sea, + 40 ---- Elevation of Vacouas in French feet, 1188 The English foot being to the French, as 12 is to 12.816, the height of Vacouas above the level of the sea should be nearly 1269 English feet.]

The principal rivers in the neighbourhood are the R. du Tamarin and the R. du Rempart, each branching into two principal arms; these collect all the smaller streams in this portion of the island, and arriving by different routes at the same point, make their junction at the head of the Baye du Tamarin, where their waters are discharged into the sea. In wet weather these rivers run with great force, but in ordinary times they do not contain much water; and their smaller branches are mostly dried up in October and November. Both arms of the R. du Rempart take their rise between one and two miles to the S. by E. of the Refuge, and within half a mile of the Mare aux Vacouas, from which it is thought their sources are derived; the western arm bears the name of R. des Papayas, probably from the number of those trees found on its banks;* and taking its course northward, is the boundary between two series of plantations, until it joins the other branch at the foot of the Montagne du Rempart and its name is lost. The Refuge was one of these plantations bounded by the R. des Papayes, being situate on its eastern bank, and receiving from it an accession of value; for this arm does not dry up in the most unfavourable seasons, neither does it overflow in the hurricanes.

[* The papaye, papaya, or papaw, is a tree well known in the East and West Indies, and is common in Mauritius; the acrid milk of the green fruit, when softened with an equal quantity of honey, is considered to be the best remedy against worms, with which the negroes and young children, who live mostly on vegetable diet, are much troubled.]

The eastern arm bears the name of R. du Rempart throughout, from its source near the *mare* or lake to its embouchure. Its course is nearly parallel to that of the sister stream, the distance between them varying only from about half a mile to one hundred and twenty yards; and the Refuge, as also the greater number of plantations on the eastern, or right bank of the R. des Papayes, is divided by it into two unequal parts, and bridges are necessary to keep up a communication between them. Although the source of this arm be never dried up, yet much of its water is lost in the passage; and during five or six months of the year that nothing is received from the small branches, greater or less portions of its bed are left dry; there seems, however, to be springs in the bed, for at a distance from where the water disappears a stream is found running lower down, which is also lost and another appears further on. In the summer rains, more especially in the hurricanes, the R. du Rempart receives numberless re-enforcements, and its torrent then becomes impetuous, carrying away the bridges, loose rocks, and every moveable obstruction; its partial inundations do great damage to the coffee trees, which cannot bear the water, and in washing off the best of the vegetable soil. During these times, the communication between those parts of the plantations on different sides of the river is cut off, until the waters have in part subsided; and this occurred thrice in one year and a half.

At the western end of the Mare aux Vacouas is an outlet through which a constant stream flows, and this is the commencement of the principal branch of the R. du Tamarin; the other branch, called the R. des Aigrettes, is said to take its rise near a more distant lake, named the Grand Bassin; and their junction is made about one mile to the S. S. W. of the Refuge, near the boundary ridge of the high land, through which they have made a deep cut, and formed a valley of a very romantic character. A short distance above their junction, each branch takes a leap downward of about seventy feet; and when united, they do not run above a quarter of a mile northward before they descend with redoubled force a precipice of nearly one hundred and twenty feet; there are then one or two small cascades, and in a short distance another of eighty or a hundred feet; and from thence to the bottom of the valley, the descent is made by smaller cascades and numberless rapids. After the united stream has run about half a mile northward, and in that space descended near a thousand feet from the level of Vacouas, the river turns west; and passing through the deep cut or chasm in the boundary ridge, enters the plain of Le Tamarin and winds in a serpentine course to the sea.

The R. du Tamarin is at no time a trifling stream, and in rainy weather the quantity of water thrown down the cascades is considerable; by a calculation from the estimated width, depth, and rate of the current after a hurricane, the water then precipitated was 1500 tons in a minute. There are some points on the high land whence most of the cascades may be seen at one view, about a mile distant; from a nearer point some of them are perceived to the left, the Trois Mamelles tower over the woods to the right, and almost perpendicularly under foot is the impetuous stream of the river, driving its way amongst the rocks and woods at the bottom of the valley. In front is the steep gap, through which the river rushes to the low land of Le Tamarin; and there the eye quits it to survey the sugar plantations, the alleys of tamarinds and mangoes, the villages of huts, and all the party-coloured vegetation with which that district is adorned; but soon it passes on to the Baye du Tamarin, to the breakers on the coral reefs which skirt the shore, and to the sea expanded out to a very distant horizon. An elevation of ten or eleven hundred feet, and the distance of three or four miles which a spectator is placed from the plantations, gives a part of this view all the softness of a well-finished drawing; and when the sun sets in front of the gap, and vessels are seen passing before it along the coast, nothing seems wanting to complete this charming and romantic prospect.

Amongst the natural curiosities of Mauritius may be reckoned the *Mare aux Vacouas*, situate about two miles S. by E. of the Refuge. It is an irregular piece of fresh water of about one mile in length, surrounded with many hundred acres of swampy land, through which run four or five little streams from the back hills; in some places it is from 20 to 25 fathoms deep, as reported, and is well stocked with eels, prawns and a small red fish called *dame-ceré*, originally brought from China. The eels and prawns are indigenous, and reach to a large size; the latter are sometimes found of six inches long without the beard, and the eels commonly offered for sale ran from six to twenty, and some were said to attain the enormous weight of eighty pounds. This fish is delicate eating, and the largest are accounted the best; its form has more affinity to the conger than to our fresh-water eel, and much resembles, if it be not exactly the same species caught in the small streams of Norfolk Island in the Pacific Ocean. Whence it is that fresh-water fish should be found on small islands, frequently at several hundred leagues from other land, will probably long remain one of the secrets of nature; if it were granted that they might come by sea, the difficulty would scarcely be less to know how they should have mounted precipices of many hundred feet, to reach lakes at the tops of mountains where they are not uncommonly seen.

Five or six miles to the south of the Refuge lies another lake of fresh water, called the *Grand Bassin*; its situation is more elevated than Vacouas, and except the ridges and tops of mountains, it seemed to be in the highest part of the island. This basin is nearly half a mile in diameter, of a form not far from circular, and is certainly deep; but that it should be 84 fathoms as was said, is scarcely credible. The banks are rocky, and appear like a mound thrown up to keep the water from overflowing; and the surrounding land, particularly to the south, being lower than the surface of the water, gives the Grand Bassin an appearance of a cauldron three-quarters full. No perceptible stream runs into it, but several go out, draining through hollow parts of the rocky bank, and forming the commencement of so many rivers; the Rivières des Anguilles, Dragon, and du Poste fall into the sea on the south or south-east parts of the island; the R. des Aigrettes before mentioned, and the R. Noire which runs westward, rise not far off, but their asserted subterraneous communication with the basin is doubtful. No great difference takes place in the level of the water except after heavy rains; when the supply, which must principally come from springs in the bottom, so far exceeds the quantity thrown out, as to raise it sometimes as much as six feet.

On the western bank is a peaked hill, from which the Grand Bassin is not only seen to much advantage, but the view extends over great part of Mauritius, and in several places to the horizon of the sea. It was apparent from hence, that between the mountains behind Port Louis and those of La Savanne to the south, and from the R. Noire eastward to Port Bourbon, not one-half, probably not a third part of the primitive woods were cut down; and this space comprehends three-fifths of the island, but excludes great part of the shores, near which the plantations are most numerous.

The elevated bank round the Grand Bassin consists partly of stones thrown loosely together; though porous, the stone is heavy and hard, of a dark grey colour, and contains numerous specks of what seemed to be feldtspath, with sometimes particles of mica and olivine; it is more or less ferruginous, gives a bell-like sound when struck, and in some parts appeared to have run in the manner of lava. From this description, and the circular form and elevated position of this basin, the geologist will probably be induced to think it the crater of an ancient volcano; and since there are other large holes nearly similar to it, and many caverns and streams under ground in other parts, it may perhaps be concluded that if the island do not owe its origin to subterraneous fire, it has yet been subject to volcanic eruptions, and that the Grand Bassin was one of the vents.

Such were the rivers, lakes, and views which most excited my excursions to the north, the west, and south of the Refuge. To the east at a league distance, there was, according to my information, a lake called the Mare aux Joncs, from whence rises the R. du Menil; and taking its course northward, joins the R. de Wilhems and at length falls into the Grande Rivière. At a further distance several other streams were said to rise, some running northward to the same destination as the above, and others south-eastward towards Port Bourbon; but having never visited this part of my limits, I can speak of it only from report, corroborated by a view of the chart. The country was represented as less inhabited than Vacouas, owing to the want of roads and consequent difficulty of conveyance to the town, upon which the value of land very much depends: an uncleared *habitation** near the Mare aux Joncs was sold for 500 dollars, whilst the same quantity of land at Vacouas was worth six times that sum.

[* The original concessions of land in Mauritius were usually of 156½ *arpents*, of 40,000 French square feet each, making about 160½ acres English; this is called *un terrein d'habitation*, and in abridgment a *habitation*, although no house should be built, nor a tree cut down; by corruption however, the word is also used for any farm or plantation, though of much smaller extent.]

Upon the high land near the Grand Bassin and in some other central parts of Mauritius, a day seldom passes throughout the year without rain; even at Vacouas it falls more or less during six or eight months, whilst in the low lands there is very little except from December to March. This moisture creates an abundance of vegetation, and should have rendered the middle parts of the island extremely fertile; as they would be if the soil were not washed down to the low lands and into the sea, almost as soon as formed. Large timber, whose roots are not seen on the surface, and a black soil, are here the exterior marks of fertility; but near the Grand Bassin the trees are small, though thickly set, and the roots, unable to penetrate below, spread along the ground. The little soil which has accumulated seemed to be good, and it will increase, though slowly; for the decayed wood adds something to its quantity every year, whilst the trunks and roots of the trees save a part from being washed away. Both these advantages are lost in the cleared lands of Vacouas, which besides are made to produce from two to four crops every year; the soil is therefore soon exhausted, and manuring is scarcely known. A plantation covered with loose rocks is found to retain its fertility longest; apparently from the stones preserving the vegetable earth against the heavy rains, as the roots of the trees did before the ground was cleared.

Much of the lower part of Wilhems Plains has been long cleared and occupied, and this is one of the most agreeable portions of the island; but Vacouas is in its infancy of cultivation, three-fourths of it being still covered with wood. This neglect it owes to the coldness and moisture of the climate rendering it unfit for the produce of sugar and cotton, to its being remote from the sea side, and more than all to its distance from the town of Port Louis, the great mart for all kinds of productions. Mauritius is not laid out like the counties in England and other parts of Europe, with a city or market town at every ten or twenty miles; nor yet like the neighbouring isle Bourbon, where there are two or three towns and some villages; it has but one town, which is the seat of government and commerce for both islands. In other parts the plantations are scattered irregularly; and although half a dozen houses may sometimes be found near together, families within a mile of each other are considered as next door neighbours. There being few tradesmen except in the town, the more considerable planters have blacksmiths, carpenters, and one or more taylors and shoemakers amongst their slaves, with forges and workshops on their plantations; but every thing they have occasion to buy, even the bread for daily consumption, is generally brought from Port Louis.

The produce of the different districts in Mauritius varies according to the elevation and climate of each; and the temperature of Vacouas being better suited to European vegetables, the daily supply of the bazar or market with them, is a great object to the inhabitants. Owing to the bad roads and excessive price of beasts of burthen, the manner universally adopted of sending these supplies is upon the heads of slaves; and the distance being twelve heavy miles, this employment occupies nearly the whole time of two or more strong negroes, besides that of a trusty man in the town to make the necessary purchases and sales. The distance of a plantation from Port Louis therefore causes a material increase of expense and inconvenience for this object alone, and is one reason why Vacouas is less cultivated than many other districts; in proportion, however, as timber becomes more scarce in the neighbourhood of the town, the woods of Vacouas will rise in value and present a greater inducement to clear the lands. Timber and planks for ships, and also for building houses, with shingles to cover them, were fast increasing in demand; and the frequent presence of English cruisers, which prevented supplies being sent from La Savanne and other woody parts of the sea coast, tended powerfully to throw this lucrative branch of internal commerce more into the hands of the landholders at Vacouas, and to clear the district of its superfluous woods.

Besides various kinds of excellent timber for building, these woods contain the black ebony, the heart of which is sold by weight. The tree is tall and slender, having but few branches which are near the top; its exterior bark is blackish, the foliage thick, and the leaf, of a dark green above and pale below, is smooth, not very pointed, and larger than those of most forest trees. It produces clusters of an oblong fruit, of the size of a plum, and full of a viscous, sweetish juice, rather agreeable to the taste. The ordinary circumference of a good tree is three or four feet; when cut down, the head lopped off and exterior white wood chipped away, a black log remains of about six inches in diameter, and from twelve to fifteen feet in length, the weight of which is something above 300 pounds. In 1806 several inhabitants permitted a contractor to cut down their ebony, on condition of receiving half a Spanish dollar for each hundred pounds of the black wood; others cut it down themselves, trimmed and piled the logs together, and sold them on the spot for one dollar the hundred; but those who possessed means of transporting the wood to town, obtained from $1\frac{1}{2}$ to $2\frac{1}{2}$ dollars, the price depending upon the supply, and the number of American vessels in port, bound to China, whither it was principally carried. Many of the plantations in Vacouas were thus exhausted of their ebony; and the tree is of so slow a growth, that the occupiers could expect afterwards to cut those only which, being too small, they had before spared; these were very few, for the object of the planter being generally to realize a sum which should enable him to return to Europe, the future was mostly sacrificed to present convenience.

Such cleared parts of Vacouas as are not planted with maize, manioc, or sweet potatoes for the support of the slaves, or with vegetables and fruits for the bazar, are commonly laid out in coffee plantations, which were becoming more an object of attention, as they have long been at Bourbon; the great demand made for coffee by the Americans, and its consequent high price, had caused this object of commerce to flourish in both islands, notwithstanding the war. Indigo and the clove tree were also obtaining a footing at Vacouas; but the extensive plantations of sugar cane and cotton shrubs found in the low parts of the island, appeared not to have been attempted, and it is certain that the cotton would not succeed.

The portions of each habitation allotted to different objects of culture, are usually separated by a double row of some tree or shrub, either useful or ornamental, with a road or path running between the lines. Amongst the useful is the vacoua or pandanus; whose leaves being strongly fibrous, long, spreading, and armed with prickles, both form a tolerable fence and supply a good material for making sacks, bags, etc. It is only whilst young that the vacoua answers this double purpose; but the tree is twelve or fifteen years before it arrives at maturity, and the leaves may be annually cut: no other use is made of the fruit than to plant it for the production of other trees. A double row of the tall jamb-rosa, or rose apple, makes the principal divisions in some plantations, forming agreeable, shady walks; and from the shelter it affords is preferred for surrounding the coffee trees, which require the utmost care to protect them from hurricanes. A tree once violently shaken, dies five or six months afterward, as it does if water stand several days together round its foot; sloping situations, where the water may run off, are therefore preferred for it, and if rocky they are the more advantageous, from the firmness which the roots thereby acquire to resist the hurricanes. Rows of the banana, of which the island possesses a great variety of species, are also planted by the sides of the paths leading through the habitations, sometimes behind the vacoua, but often alone; the pine apple serves the same purpose in others, as do the peach and other fruit trees where the paths are more considerable. A long and strong grass, called *vitti-vert*, is occasionally preferred for the lines of division; this is cut twice or thrice in the year to be used as thatch, for which it is well adapted. Hedges of the ever-flowering China rose, and of the *netshouly*, a bushy shrub from India which prospers in every soil, are often used in place of the tall jamb-rosa to form alleys leading up to the house of the planter, and also the principal walks in his garden; the waving bamboo, whose numberless uses are well known, is planted by the sides of the rivers and canals.

A notion of the working and produce of a plantation at Vacouas will be most concisely given by a statement of the ordinary expenses and returns; and to render it more nearly applicable to the case of such persons in Europe as might form the project of becoming settlers, I will suppose a young man, with his wife and child, arrived at Mauritius with the intention of employing his time and means on a plantation in this district; and at the end of five years other affairs call him thence, and he sells every thing. He is supposed to possess 18,000 dollars in money or property, to be active, industrious, and frugal, and though unacquainted with the business of a planter, to be sufficiently intelligent to gain the necessary information in one year. With these requisites, I would examine whether he will have been able to subsist his family comfortably during the five years, and what will then be the state of his funds.

EXPENSES.   Dollars. In town the first year,   1,800
Price of an uncleared habitation,   3,000 Twenty negroes, some being mechanics,
4,000 Ten negresses,   1,500 Ten children of different ages,   1,000
Maize 500 lbs. (7½ D.), sweet potatoes 1250 lbs. (3¾ D.) to subsist each slave the first year,
450 Head tax for 5 years, at .1 D. each per an. 100 Maroon tax for ditto   100
Surgeon to attend the slaves,   200 Building and furnishing a house, magazine, etc.,
exclusive of wood and labourers from the plantation,   2,500 Agricultural utensils, hand mills, etc.   300 100 fowls and 50 ducks for a breed,   100 Ten goats,
60 Ten pigs,   100 A horse, saddle, etc.   250 A good ass,

side saddle, etc. 120 Seeds and fruit trees, 50 Coffee plants 30,000 for 20 acres, 450 Expenses at the plantation in 4 years, exclusive of domestic supplies, 3,600 Losses from two hurricanes, 2,000 ------ Total 21,680 RECEIPTS. Dollars. Of 60 acres cleared to raise provisions, 30 are necessary to support the slaves; from the rest may be sold 150,000 lbs. of maize in 4 years, for 2,250 Ebony, timber, planks and shingles, sold on the spot during 5 years, 3,000 Coffee reaped on the 5th year, 50 bales (100 lbs. each) at 15 D. per bale, 750 Vegetables and fruit sold at the bazar, aver age 2 D. per day, during four years, 2,920 Fowls and ducks 2000 at ½ D. 1,000 Thirty goats sold, 180 Thirty hogs, 600 At the end of 5 years, the plantation, buildings, etc., will probably bring, 7,000 Probable value of the slaves, 5,500 Pigs, goats, and poultry remaining, 260 Horse, ass, etc. probably not more than 200 ------ Whole receipts 23,660 Expenses and losses 21,680 ------ Increase 1,980

The taxes and price of provisions, coffee, etc. in the above calculation, are taken as they usually stood in time of war, under the government of general De Caen; and every thing is taken against, rather than in favour of the planter. In his expenses a sufficiency is allowed to live comfortably, to see his friends at times, and something for the pleasure of himself and wife; but if he choose to be very economical, 2000 dollars might be saved from the sums allotted.

In selling his plantation at the end of five years, he is in a great measure losing the fruit of his labour; for the coffee alone might be reasonably expected to produce annually one hundred bales for the following ten years, and make his revenue exceed 3000 dollars per annum; and if he continued to live economically upon the plantation, this, with the rising interest of his surplus money, would double his property in a short time. It is therefore better, supposing a man to possess the requisite knowledge, to purchase a habitation already established, than to commence upon a new one.

The same person going to Vaucouas with the intention of quitting it at the end of five years, would not plant coffee, but turn his attention to providing different kinds of wood and sending it to Port Louis. With this object principally in view, he would purchase two habitations instead of one; and as this and other expenses incident to the new arrangement would require a greater sum than he is supposed to possess, he must borrow, at high interest, what is necessary to make up the deficiency. The amount of his receipts and expenses for the five years. would then be nearly as follows.

EXPENSES. Dollars. As before, deducting coffee plants, 21,230 An additional habitation, 3,000 Twenty asses, at 90 D. each, 1,800 Harnesses for three teams, 300 Three waggons built on the plantation, 150 Three additional slaves, 600 Interest of 6,000 dollars borrowed for three years, at 18 per cent. per an. 3,240 ------ Total 30,320 Total receipts 41,922 ------ Increase 11,602 RECEIPTS. Dollars. As before, deducting wood, coffee, plantation and buildings, 12,910 Trimmed ebony sent to the town 375, 6000 lbs. at 2 D. per 100, 7,512 Timber sent to Port Louis in 4 years, 640 loads at 25 D. each, 16,000 Two habitations stripped of the best wood may sell for, with buildings, 4,000 Asses and additional slaves, 1,500 ------ Total 41,922

These statements will give a general idea of a plantation at Vacouas, the employments of the more considerable inhabitants, of the food of the slaves, etc., and will render unnecessary any further explanation on these heads.

It was considered a fair estimate, that a habitation should give yearly 20 per cent. on the capital employed, after allowance made for all common losses; and money placed on good security obtained from 9 to 18 per cent. in time of war, and 12 to 24 in the preceding peace. Had my planter put his 18,000 dollars out at interest, instead of employing them on a plantation at Vacouas, and been able to obtain 15 per cent, he would at the end of five years, after expending 150 dollars each month in the town of Port Louis, have increased his capital nearly 5,000 dollars; but it is more than probable that he would have fallen into the luxury of the place, and have rather diminished than increased his fortune.

The woods of Vacouas are exceedingly thick, and so interwoven with different kinds of climbing plants, that it is difficult to force a passage through; and to take a ride where no roads have been cut, is as impossible as to take a flight in the air. Except morasses and the borders of lakes, I did not see a space of five square yards in these woods, which was covered with grass and unencumbered with shrubs or trees; even the paths not much frequented, if not impassable, are rendered very embarrassing by the raspberries, wild tobacco, and other shrubs with which they are quickly overgrown. Cleared lands which have ceased to be cultivated, are usually clothed with a strong, coarse grass, called *chien-dent*, intermixed with ferns, wild tobacco, and other noxious weeds. In the low districts the grass is of a better kind, and supplies the cattle with tolerable food during three or four months that it is young and tender, and for most of the year in marshy places; at other times they are partly fed with maize straw, the refuse of the sugar mills, and the leaves and tender branches of some trees.

A few short-legged hares and some scattered partridges are found near the skirts of the plantations, and further in the woods there are some deer and wild hogs. Monkeys are more numerous, and when the maize is ripe they venture into the plantations to steal; which obliges the inhabitants to set a watch over the fields in the day, as the maroons and other thieves do at night. There are some wood pigeons and two species of doves, and the marshy places are frequented by a few water hens; but neither wild geese nor ducks are known in the island. Game of all kinds was at this time so little abundant in the woods of Vacouas, that even a creole, who is an intrepid hunter and a good shot, and can live where an European would starve, could not subsist himself and his dogs upon the produce of the chase. Before the revolution this was said to have been possible; but in that time of disorder the citizen mulattoes preferred hunting to work, and the woods were nearly depopulated of hares and deer.

Of indigenous fruits there are none worth notice, for that produced by the ebony scarcely deserves the name; a large, but almost tasteless raspberry is however now found every where by the road side, and citrons of two kinds grow in the woods. A small species of cabbage tree, called here *palmiste*, is not rare and is much esteemed; the undeveloped leaves at the head of the tree, when eaten raw, resemble in taste a walnut, and a cauliflower when boiled; dressed as a salad they are superior to perhaps any other, and make an excellent pickle. Upon the deserted plantations, peaches, guavas, pine apples, bananas, mulberries and strawberries are often left growing; these are considered to be the property of the first comer, and usually fall to the lot of the maroons, or to the slaves in the neighbourhood who watch their ripening; the wild bees also furnish them with an occasional regale of honey.

With respect to noxious insects, the scourge of most tropical countries, the wet and cold weather which renders Vacouas a disagreeable residence in the winter, is of singular advantage; the numerous musketoes and sand flies, the swarms of wasps, the ants, centipedes, scorpions, bugs and lizards, with which the lower parts of the island are more or less tormented, are almost unknown here; and fleas and cockroaches are less numerous. A serpent is not known to exist in Mauritius, though several have been found on some of the neighbouring islets; it is therefore not the climate which destroys them, nor has it been ascertained what is the cause.*

[* Mauritius is not singular in being free of serpents whilst they exist on lands within sight, or not far off; but a late account says that one of great size has been killed on that island near the Reduit, supposed to have escaped out of a ship from India, wrecked on the coast a few years before.]

From this account of the situation of my retreat, it will be perceived that it was a vast acquisition to exchange the Garden Prison for Vacouas; there, it had been too warm to take exercise, except in the mornings and evenings, had there been room and inducements; whilst at the Refuge I was obliged to clothe in woollen, had space to range in, and a variety of interesting objects, with the charm of novelty to keep me in continual motion. I bathed frequently in the R. du Rempart, walked out every fine day, and in a few weeks my former health was in a great measure recovered. Those who can receive gratification from opening

the door to an imprisoned bird, and remarking the joy with which it hops from spray to spray, tastes of every seed and sips from every rill, will readily conceive the sensations of a man during the first days of liberation from a long confinement.
CHAPTER VII.
Occupations at Vacouas.
Hospitality of the inhabitants.
Letters from England.
Refusal to be sent to France repeated.
Account of two hurricanes, of a subterraneous stream and circular pit.
Habitation of La Pérouse.
Letters to the French marine minister, National Institute, etc.
Letters from Sir Edward Pellew.
Caverns in the Plains of St. Piérre.
Visit to Port Louis.
Narrative transmitted to England.
Letter to captain Bergeret on his departure for France.
[AT MAURITIUS. WILHEMS PLAINS.]
SEPTEMBER 1805

The latter end of August and beginning of September appertain to the winter in the southern hemisphere, during which it rains frequently at Vacouas; in the first month after my arrival there were few days that continued fine throughout, and although all opportunities were taken to make excursions in the neighbourhood, a considerable part of the time was necessarily passed within doors. Having sent away my charts and instruments, and most of the books and papers, no object of my voyage could be prosecuted until a further supply should be obtained from the captain-general De Caen; and this being the time, should it ever arrive, to which I had looked for gaining some knowledge of the French language, the study of it was now made a serious employment.

Amongst the principal habitations near the Refuge, the proprietor of one only was resident in the country; and the introduction of my friend Pitot having produced an invitation, I profited by it to spend there several evenings, which, besides being passed agreeably, facilitated the study to which my attention was directed. There was living in the family an unemployed commander of a merchant ship, M. Murat, who had made the voyage with Etienne Marchand, the account of which is so ably written by M. de Fleurieu; he was obliging enough to accompany me in several excursions, and amongst them in a walk of five miles to the house of M. Giblot, commandant of the quarter of Wilhems Plains, to whom it seemed proper to show myself and pay a visit of ceremony. The commandant was unacquainted with my residence in his district, which was so far gratifying that it showed I was not an object of suspicion in the eye of the government.

OCTOBER 1805

M. Pitot came to pass a day with me at the end of a month, as did captain Bergeret; and on the 9th of October, the proprietor of the Refuge arrived with two of her sons and three daughters, to take up their residence on the plantation. On the following day I received a proposal from Madame D'Arifat, as liberal as the terms in which it was couched were obliging, to partake of her table with the family, which after some necessary stipulations, was accepted; and in a short time I had the happiness to enumerate amongst my friends one of the most worthy families in the island. The arrival of two other proprietors from the town increased the number of our neighbours, and of those who sought by their hospitable kindness to make my time pass agreeably. To M. de Chazal I was indebted for sending out my baggage, and in the sequel for many acts of civility and service; this gentleman had passed two years in England, during the tyranny of Robespiérre, and consequently my want of knowledge in the French language, at first an obstacle to communication with others, was none to reaping the advantage of his information.

On the 22nd, a packet of letters brought intelligence from my family and friends in England, of whom I had not heard for more than three years; Mr. Robertson, my former companion in the Garden Prison, had found means to forward it to M. Pitot, by whom it was immediately sent to Vacouas. A letter from the president of the Royal Society informed me that the misunderstanding between the French and British governments was so great, that no communication existed between them; but that the president himself, having obtained the approbation of the ministry, had made an application in my behalf to the National Institute, from which a favourable answer had been received; and there were strong hopes that so soon as the emperor Napoléon should return from Italy, an order for my liberation would be obtained. Our frigates, the Pitt and Terpsichore, came to cruise off Mauritius a short time afterward [NOVEMBER 1805], for which I was as sorry on one account as any of the inhabitants; every week might produce the arrival of the expected order, but it would probably be thrown overboard if the vessel should be chased, or have an engagement with our ships.

FEBRUARY 1806

Three months thus passed in fruitless expectation; at length an aide-de-camp of the general arrived, and gave a spur to my hopes; but after many days of anxiety to know the result, I learned from captain Bergeret that the despatches said nothing upon my imprisonment. This silence of the marine minister and the great events rising in Europe, admitted little hope of my situation being remembered; and I was thence led to entertain the project of once more requesting general De Caen to send me to France for trial; but the brother of the general and another officer being also expected, it was deferred at that time. In effect, M. De Caen arrived on the 25th, in the frigate La Canonnière from Cherbourg, and excited a renewal of hope only to be again disappointed; the news of victories gained by the French over the Austrians seemed to occupy every attention, and threw a dark shade over all expectation of present liberty. I learned, however, and a prisoner's mind would not fail to speculate thereon, that my detention was well known in Paris, and thought to be hard; but it was also said, that I was considered in the same light as those persons who were arrested in France, as hostages for the vessels and men said to have been stopped by our ships before the declaration of war.

MARCH 1806

My proposed letter to general De Caen was then sent; and after pointing out the uncertainty of orders arriving, or even that the marine minister should find time to think of a prisoner in a distant island, I repeated for the third time my request to be sent to France; where a speedy punishment would put an end to my anxieties, if found culpable, or in the contrary case, a few days would restore me to my country, my family, and occupations. Captain Bergeret had the goodness to deliver this letter, and to give it his support; but it was unsuccessful, the verbal answer being that nothing could be done until the orders of the government were received. To a proposal of taking my parole to deliver myself up in France, should the ship be taken on the passage, the general would not listen; though my friend said he had read the letter with attention, and promised to repeat his request to the minister for orders.

A hurricane had desolated the island on the 20th and 21st of February; and on the 10th of this month a second came on, causing a repetition of mischief in the port and upon the plantations. Several vessels were driven on shore or blown out to sea, and more than one lost; the fruit trees, sugar cane, maize, etc. were laid flat with the earth; the different streams swelled to an extraordinary size, carrying away the best of the vegetable soil from the higher habitations, mixed with all kinds of produce, branches and trunks of trees, and the wrecks of bridges torn away; and the huts of the slaves, magazines, and some houses were either unroofed or blown down. All communication with the port was cut off from the distant quarters, and the intercourse between adjoining plantations rendered difficult; yet this chaotic derangement was said to be trifling in comparison with what was suffered in the first hurricane at Bourbon, where the vessels have no better shelter than open roadsteds, and the plantations of cloves, coffee and maize are so much more extensive. Some American vessels were amongst the sufferers, but as domestic occurrences were not allowed to be published here, I learned only a very general account from the different reports: happily for our cruisers the last had quitted the island in January.

In the evening of Feb. 20, when the first hurricane came on, the swift-passing clouds were tinged at sunset with a deep copper colour; but the moon not being near the full, it excited little apprehension at the Refuge. The wind was fresh, and kept increasing until eleven o'clock, at which time it blew very hard; the rain fell in torrents, accompanied with loud claps of thunder and lightning, which at every instant imparted to one of the darkest nights the brightness of day. The course of the wind was from south-west to south, south-east, east, and north-east, where it blew hardest between one and three in the morning, giving me an apprehension that the house, pavilions, and all would be blown away together. At four o'clock the wind had got round to north and began to moderate, as did the rain which afterwards came only in squalls; at nine, the rain had nearly ceased, and the wind was no more than a common gale, and after passing round to N. N. W. it died away. At the time the wind moderated at Mauritius its fury was most exerted at Bourbon, which it was said to have attacked with a degree of violence that any thing less solid than a mountain was scarcely able to resist. The lowest to which the mercury descended in the barometer at Vacouas, was 5½ lines below the mean level of two days before and two days afterward; and this was at daybreak, when the wind and rain were subsiding.

Soon after the violence of the hurricane had abated, I went to the cascades of the R. du Tamarin, to enjoy the magnificent prospect which the fall of so considerable a body of water must afford; the path through the wood was strewed with the branches and trunks of trees, in the forest the grass and shrubs were so beaten down as to present the appearance of an army having passed that way, and the river was full up to its banks. Having seen the fall in the nearest of the two arms, I descended below their junction, to contemplate the cascade they formed when united, down the precipice of 120 feet; the noise of the fall was such that my own voice was scarcely audible, but a thick mist which rose up to the clouds from the abyss, admitted of a white foam only being distinguished.

During these hurricanes in Mauritius, the wind usually makes the whole tour of the compass; and as during this of February it made little more than half, the apprehension of a second hurricane was entertained, and became verified about a fortnight afterwards. The wind began at E. S. E. with rainy weather, and continued there twenty-four hours, with increasing force; it then shifted quickly to north-east, north, north-west, and on the third evening was at W. S. W., where it gradually subsided. This was not so violent as the first hurricane, but the rain fell in torrents, and did great mischief to the land, besides destroying such remaining part of the crops as were at all in an advanced state: at Bourbon it did not do much injury, the former, it was said, having left little to destroy. The wind had now completed the half of the compass which it wanted in the first hurricane; and the unfortunate planters were left to repair their losses without further dread for this year: maize and manioc, upon which the slaves are principally fed, rose two hundred per cent.

An opinion commonly entertained in Mauritius, that hurricanes are little to be apprehended except near the time of full moon, does not seem to be well founded. In 1805 indeed, there was a heavy gale on April 14 and 15, a few days after the full; but the first of the two hurricanes abovementioned took place a day or two before the new moon, and the middle of the second within twenty-four hours of the last quarter; whence it should appear that the hurricanes have no certain connexion with the state of this planet. January, February, and March are the months which excite the most dread, and December and April do not pass without apprehension; for several years, however, previously to 1805, no hurricane had been experienced; and the inhabitants began to hope, that if the clearing of the country caused a dearth of rain at some times of the year, it would also deliver them from these dreadful scourges; for it was to the destruction of the woods that the dryness of preceding years and the cessation of hurricanes were generally attributed.

On the 21st, His Majesty's ship Russel came off the island upon a cruise, and chased into Port Louis La Piémontaise, a French frigate which had sailed from Europe in December. By this opportunity a confirmation of some, and an account of other victories gained over the Austrians were received, as also of the great naval action off Cape Trafalgar; the bulletins of the former were inserted in the gazette of the island, but except a report from the officers of Le Redoubtable, not a word of the naval action; amidst such events as these, the misfortunes of an individual must be very striking to occupy even a thought.

In a visit to M. Plumet, and to M. Airolles, the proprietor of an extensive plantation called Ménil, in his neighbourhood, I had an opportunity of seeing a rivulet, which for some distance runs under ground. The bed of this stream resembled a work of art, seeming to have been nicely cut out of the solid rock; and close by the side of it was a cavern, containing layers of a ferruginous stone like lava; their combined appearance excited an idea that the canal might have been once occupied by a vein of iron ore, which being melted by subterraneous fire, found an exit, and left a place for the future passage of the waters. About one mile from hence, and in a more elevated situation, is a large and deep hole, of a form nearly approaching to a perfect circle, and its upper part occupying, according to M. Airolles, the place of seventeen arpents of land; I judged it to be two hundred feet deep, and that the loose stones in its bottom formed a flat of four or five acres, the angle of descent being nearly equal on all sides. The stones around, and at the bottom of this vast pit are more honeycombed than is usual in other parts, and much resemble those of the Grand Bassin, of whose nature they seemed to partake in other respects.

Ménil comprehends a smaller plantation, formerly occupied by the unfortunate La Pérouse, who was some time an inhabitant of this island. I surveyed it with mixed sensations of pleasure and melancholy; the ruins of his house, the garden he had laid out, the still blooming hedge-rows of China roses--emblems of his reputation, every thing was an object of interest and curiosity. This spot is nearly in the centre of the island, and upon the road from Port Louis to Port Bourbon. It was here that the man lamented by the good and well informed of all nations--whom science illumined, and humanity, joined to an honest ambition, conducted to the haunts of remote savages--in this spot he once dwelt, perhaps little known to the world, but happy; when he became celebrated he had ceased to exist. M. Airolles promised me to place three square blocks of stone, one upon the other, in the spot where the house of this lamented navigator had stood; and upon the uppermost stone facing the road, to engrave, LA PÉROUSE.

APRIL 1806

My lame seaman having recovered from the accident of his broken leg, colonel Monistrol granted a permission for his departure in the beginning of April; and he was shipped on board the Telemaque -- Clark, bound to Boston in America. His companion, the last of the Cumberland's crew, had the same means offered of recovering his liberty; but he still refused to leave me in Mauritius.

On the 15th I sent away two packets of letters, one for the Admiralty and my friends in England, the other to France; the last contained a second letter to M. de Fleurieu, and one to the French marine minister giving a short account of my voyage and detention; it inclosed the extract from captain Baudin (Chapter V., August.), and requested His Excellency would direct general De Caen either to set me at liberty, or send me to France with my books and papers for examination. These letters were accompanied by duplicates of those written by my friend Pitot in March 1805, to Messieurs De Bougainville, De la Lande, Chaptal, and Dupuis, and were sent away by two different conveyances. The Society of Emulation, formed in Mauritius the preceding year to promote literary and philosophical pursuits, but especially to advance the agriculture, navigation, and commerce of the two islands, wrote also to the National Institute in my favour; and as its sentiments may be supposed analogous to those of the most enlightened part of the inhabitants, I venture to give in the original French a copy of that letter in a note, to show what those sentiments were.*

[Not included in this ebook.]

MAY 1806

In May, my friend Pitot was accompanied in his monthly visit by M. Baudin, an officer of the frigate last arrived from France, who had made the voyage in Le Géographe with his name sake; and with liberality of sentiment, possessed that ardent spirit of enterprise by which the best navigators have been distinguished. He informed me that M. de Fleurieu was acquainted with most of the circumstances attending my arrival in this island, and took an interest in my situation, as did many others in Paris; but could not say what might be the opinion or intentions of the government.

On the 6th, colonel Monistrol sent me two open letters from rear-admiral sir Edward Pellew, commander in chief in the East Indies; in the first of which it was said, "The circumstances of your situation have impressed themselves most strongly on my attention; and I feel every disposition to alleviate your anxiety, without, I fear, the means of affording you any present relief from your very unpleasant situation. I have transmitted your letter to the Admiralty, that steps may forthwith be taken for your release at home, by effecting your exchange for an officer of equivalent rank; under an impression that at least it may insure your return to Europe on parole, if that should be a necessary preliminary to your final liberation." To give an officer of equivalent rank was probably the most certain mode of obtaining my speedy release, but was not altogether agreeable to justice. It seemed to me, that the liberation of an officer employed on discovery, and bearing a passport, ought to be granted as a matter of right, without any conditions; and accompanied with the restitution of every thing belonging to his mission and himself, if not with an atonement to the offended laws of good faith and humanity; but this was only the *just*, the views of sir Edward were directed to the *expedient*, and showed a better knowledge of mankind. His second letter, dated January 15, 1806, contained sentiments nearly similar to the first, without any new subject upon which to ground the hope of an early release; that my situation, however, should have excited the attention and interest of an officer of sir Edward Pellew's established character and merit, if it did not much increase the prospect of a speedy return to my country and occupations, was yet gratifying to the feelings, and a consolation under misfortune.

In compliance with an invitation from M. Curtat, a friend of our good family at the Refuge, I went to his plantation near the Baye du Tamarin, which was within my limits; and had an opportunity of seeing his sugar and cotton manufactories, as also the embouchure of the rivers du Tamarin and du Rempart. The bay into which they are discharged is no more than a sandy bight in the low land, partly filled up with coral; and it would soon be wholly so, did not the fresh stream from the rivers keep a channel open in the middle; it is however so shallow, that except in fine weather fishing boats even cannot enter without risk.

Upon a plantation in the Plains of St. Piérre, about one mile from the foot of the Montagne du Rempart, are some caverns which M. Curtat procured me the means of examining. In the entrance of one is a perpetual spring, from which a stream takes its course under ground, in a vaulted passage; M. Ducas, the proprietor of the plantation, said he had traced it upon a raft, by the light of flambeaux, more than half a mile without finding its issue; but he supposed it to be in a small lake near the sea side. The other caverns had evidently been connected with the first, until the roof gave way in two places and separated them. The middle portion has a lofty arch, and might be formed into two spacious apartments; its length is not many fathoms, but the third portion, though less spacious, runs in a winding course of several hundred yards. From being unprovided with torches we did not pass the whole length of this third cavern; but at the two extremities, and as far within as could be distinguished, the roof admitted of standing upright, and the breadth was eight or ten yards from side to side.

About thirty years before, this part of the Plains de St. Piérre had been covered with wood, and the caverns inhabited by a set of maroon negroes, whose depredations and murders spread consternation in the neighbourhood. Their main retreat in the third cavern was discovered by a man whom they had left for dead; but having watched them to their haunt, he gave information to the officers of justice, and troops were sent to take them. After securing the further outlet, the soldiers crept to the principal entrance, near which the maroons kept a sentinel with loaded musket in the top of a tree; he was found nodding on his post, and having shot him they rushed in a body to the mouth of the cavern. The poor wretches within started from their beds, for they slept in the day time, and flew to arms; a skirmish ensued, in which another of them was killed and two soldiers wounded; but at length, finding their retreat cut off, the sentinel, who happened to be their captain and chief instigator, killed, and the force opposed to them too great to be overcome, they yielded themselves prisoners to the number of fifty-one; and were marched off, with their hands tied, to head quarters, to the great joy of the district. Besides arms and a small quantity of ammunition, there was little else found in the cavern than a bag of dollars, a case of wine, some pieces of cloth, a slaughtered goat, and a small provision of maize not more than enough for one day. The skull of their captain, who was said to be possessed of much cunning and audacity, was at this time lying upon a stone at the entrance of the cavern; and for narrowness of front and large extent at the back part of the head, was the most singularly formed cranium I ever saw. Little oblong inclosures, formed with small stones by the sides of the cavern, once the sleeping places of these wretches, also existed, nearly in the state they had been left; owing apparently to the superstition of the black, and the policy and disgust of the white visitants to these excavations.

The stone here is mostly of an iron-grey colour, heavy, and porous; and there were marks upon the sides of the middle cavern which might have arisen either from a sulphureous substance yielded by the stone when in a state of ignition, or from an impregnated water draining through the roof during a succession of time; upon the whole, though it seemed probable that these caverns owe their origin to the same cause as the subterraneous canal at Ménil, the marks of fire in them were neither distinct nor unequivocal. The position of these long, winding excavations, in a country nearly level and of small elevation, appeared to be the most extraordinary circumstance attending them; but in this island they are commonly so situate, particularly that remarkable one, of which a detailed account is given in Grant's *History of Mauritius* from M. de St. Pierre.

Quitting Le Tamarin with M. Curtat, I went to the town of Port Louis, to take up my residence for a few days with my friend Pitot, the captain-general having granted a permission to that effect. One of the objects for which I had asked the permission, was to obtain a further one to visit La Poudre d'Or and Flacq, on the north-east side of the island; but my application was refused after two or three days consideration, and accompanied with an order to return immediately to Wilhems Plains. It appeared that general De Caen had received a letter of reproach from governor King of Port Jackson, inclosing, it was said, a copy of that I had written to the governor in August 1804, wherein my reception and treatment at Mauritius were described in colours not calculated to gratify the general's feelings; it was even considered, and perhaps was in him, a great act of forbearance that he did not order me to be closely confined in the tower.

During this short residence in town, the attentions of my friend Pitot, of captain Bergeret, and several other French inhabitants were such as bespoke a desire to indemnify me for the ill treatment of their governor, whose conduct seemed to be generally disapproved; my acquaintance with major Dunienville of La Savanne was renewed, as also with M. Boand, the good Swiss, whose anxiety to serve me when a prisoner in the Café Marengo, had not lost any thing of its ardour. At the Garden Prison, which I could not refrain from visiting, there was no one but the old serjeant, the six or eight Englishmen in the island being kept at the Grande Rivière. In returning to Wilhems Plains I made a tour by the district of Mocha, both to see that part of the island and to visit M. Huet de Froberville, with whom his intimacy with the good family at the Refuge had brought me acquainted; this gentleman was nephew of Huetius, the celebrated bishop of Avranches, and author of *Sidner, or the dangers of imagination*, a little work published in Mauritius.

JUNE 1806

The usual season of arrivals from France expired with the month of May, and the time elapsed since my first detention, without being otherwise noticed by the French government than giving general De Caen its temporary approbation, had exceedingly weakened my confidence in its justice; it appeared moreover, that not only had no public application been made by our government for my liberty and the restitution of my charts and journals, but that the advancement I had been led to expect in consequence of the voyage, was stopped. This could not be from inattention, and therefore probably arose either from a want of information, or from some misconceived opinions at the Admiralty; to remove which, it seemed necessary to transmit an account of all the circumstances attending my imprisonment, accompanied with the letters to and from the captain-general, and such other pieces as were proper to the authentication of the narrative.

JULY 1806

I was occupied in writing this account when the Warren Hastings, richly laden from China, was taken by La Piémontaise and brought to Mauritius; and captain Larkins having obtained permission to return to England, he offered by letter to take charge of any thing I desired to transmit. The narrative, completed to the time of leaving the Garden Prison, was therefore conveyed to him; and in an accompanying letter to the Admiralty, my hopes were expressed that their Lordships would not suffer an imprisonment, contrary to every principle of justice and humanity, to continue without notice--without such steps being taken to obtain my release and the restitution of my remaining charts and papers, as in their wisdom should seem meet. Captain Larkins had ineffectually sought to obtain a permission to come to Wilhems Plains, and my request to go to the town for a day or two was refused; he therefore sailed [AUGUST 1806] without my being able to see him or any of his officers; and his departure was preceded by that of my friend Pitot for Bourbon, and followed by the embarkation of captain Bergeret for France.

In consequence of the many kindnesses conferred by M. Pitot on several of our countrymen as well as myself, I had been induced to write some letters at his request to the commanders of His Majesty's ships; recommending to their favour, in case of being taken, such of his friends as had a claim to it, either from services rendered to prisoners or from their superior talents; and I did not let slip the occasion of his voyage to Bourbon, to testify in this manner my sense of his worth. To soften the rigour of confinement to deserving men, is a grateful task; I conceived that a war between two nations does not necessarily entrain personal enmity between each of their respective individuals, nor should prevent us from doing particular acts of kindness where merit and misfortune make the claim; and in the confidence that such were the general sentiments of officers in the navy, I had no hesitation in addressing myself to them. Possibly some would think these applications unadvisably made; but no--to distinguish merit and repay the debt of gratitude contracted by unfortunate brother officers or countrymen, are too congenial to the hearts of Britons; to those who produced either, or both of these titles an English seaman could not be deaf, and on no other account was my suffrage obtained.

Captain Bergeret's name was too well known to need any recommendation from me; but I wished to express my gratitude for his generous proceedings to many English prisoners, and to have the advantage of his influence in obtaining an order from his government for my liberty, or otherwise for being sent to France to be examined. The letter transmitted a short time before he sailed, expresses the state of a prisoner's mind when suffering under injustice and wearied with disappointment; on this account, the greater number of readers will be induced to excuse the insertion of the following passages, which otherwise are without importance, and perhaps without interest.

I need not at this time call to your recollection what my situation is in this place. I have been so long pressed under the hand of injustice, and my confidence in the French government is so much exhausted, that I am reduced to asking as a favour what ought to be demanded as a right. On your arrival in France then, my dear Sir, forget not that I am here--that my prayer is, to be examined, to be tried, to be condemned, if I have in action, intention, or thought, done any thing whilst employed in my voyage of discovery, against the French nation or its allies--if in any way I have infringed upon the line of conduct prescribed by the passport of the first consul of France. To have the best years of my life, the essence of my existence thus drained away without any examination into the affair; to have the fruits of my labours and risks thus ravished from me--my hopes of advancement and of reputation thus cruelly blasted, is almost beyond what I am able to support. Use then, I conjure you, Sir, your best endeavours with those men in France who have it in their power to forward my wish; with those men for whom a voyage of discovery, the preservation of national faith, and the exercise of humanity have still attractions. With such men, in spite of the neglect which my extraordinary situation here has undergone, now near three years, I will not believe but that the French empire abounds; a Fleurieu, a Bougainville, a Lalande, a Delambre, and numberless others--can such men be strangers to national honour and humanity? Has a man reduced to misfortune by his ardent zeal to advance geography and its kindred sciences, no claims upon men like these? It cannot be. However unworthy an instrument I am in the hands of our literary British worthies, my employment, if not my misfortunes, give me a claim upon their assistance in obtaining, at least, an examination into my crimes or my innocence; and this claim I now make. See these celebrated men, Sir, explain to them the circumstances of my situation, tell them the plain tale, and that it is towards them, though so distant, that my looks are directed; your own name will give you an introduction, and the cause you undertake will not disgrace it.

Adieu, worthy Sir, may the winds be propitious, and may you never be reduced to the bitterness of sighing after justice in vain.

CHAPTER VIII.

Effects of repeated disappointment on the mind.
Arrival of a cartel, and of letters from India.
Letter of the French marine minister.
Restitution of papers.
Applications for liberty evasively answered.
Attempted seizure of private letters.
Memorial to the minister.
Encroachments made at Paris on the Investigator's discoveries.
Expected attack on Mauritius produces an abridgment of Liberty.
Strict blockade.
Arrival of another cartel from India.
State of the public finances in Mauritius.
French cartel sails for the Cape of Good Hope.
[AT MAURITIUS. WILHEMS PLAINS]
SEPTEMBER 1806

News of negotiations at Paris for peace formed the principal topic of conversation at Mauritius in September, and no one more than myself could desire that the efforts of Lord Lauderdale might be crowned with success; a return to England in consequence of such an event was of all things what I most desired, but the hope of peace, before national animosity and the means of carrying on war became diminished, was too feeble to admit of indulging in the anticipation.

NOVEMBER 1806

The state of incertitude in which I remained after nearly three years of anxiety, joined to the absence of my friends Bergeret and Pitot, brought on a dejection of spirits which might have proved fatal, had I not sought by constant occupation to force my mind from a subject so destructive to its repose; such an end to my detention would have given too much pleasure to the captain-general, and from a sort of perversity in human nature, this conviction even brought its share of support. I reconstructed some of my charts on a larger scale, corrected and extended the explanatory memoir, and completed for the Admiralty an enlarged copy of the Investigator's log book, so far as the materials in my hands could admit; the study of the French language was pursued with increased application, and many books in it, particularly voyages and travels, were read. But what assisted most in dispelling this melancholy, was a packet of letters from England, bringing intelligence of my family and friends; and the satisfactory information that Mr. Aken had safely reached London, with all the charts, journals, letters and instruments committed to his charge.

JANUARY 1807

No occurrence more particular than the departure in January of a prisoner of war, which furnished an opportunity of writing to England, took place for several months. In April [APRIL 1807] the season for the arrival of ships from France was mostly passed, and the captain-general had still received no orders; being than at the town, I requested of him an audience through the intervention of M. Beckmann, who engaged, in case of refusal, to enter into an explanation with His Excellency and endeavour to learn his intentions. On his return, M. Beckmann said that the general had expressed himself sensible of the hardship of my situation, and that he every day expected to receive orders from France; but being unable to do any thing without these orders, it was useless to see me, and he recommended waiting with patience for their arrival.

MAY 1807

In acknowledgment for the letter written to the National Institute by the Society of Emulation, I sent to it a description of Wreck Reef, with my conjectures upon the place where the unfortunate La Pérouse had probably been lost; and this letter, as also a succeeding one upon the differences in the variation of the magnetic needle on ship-board, was transmitted by the Society to the Institute at Paris.

JUNE 1807

The effect of long protracted expectation, repeatedly changing its object and as often disappointed, became strongly marked in my faithful servant. This worthy man had refused to quit the island at the general exchange of prisoners in August 1805, and also in the following year when his companion, the lame seaman, went to America, because he would not abandon me in misfortune; but the despair of our being ever set at liberty had now wholly taken possession of his senses. He imagined that all the inhabitants of the island, even those who were most friendly, were leagued with the captain-general against us; the signals on the hills communicated my every step, the political articles in the gazettes related in a metaphorical manner the designs carrying on, the new laws at that time publishing showed the punishments we were doomed to suffer, persons seen in conversation, every thing in fine, had some connexion with this mysterious league; and the dread of some sudden and overwhelming blow left him no peace, either by day or night. This state of mind continued some months, his sleep and appetite had forsaken him, and he wasted daily; and finding no other means of cure than persuading him to return to England, where he might still render me service, a permission for his departure was requested and obtained; and in the beginning of July [JULY 1807] he embarked on board an American brig, for Baltimore. I gave into his charge some remaining charts and books, and many letters; and had the satisfaction to see him more easy, and almost convinced of the folly of his terrors on finding he was really allowed to go away, which till then, had appeared to him incredible.

On the 18th, arrived the Hon. Company's ship Marquis Wellesley, as a cartel from Madras, with French prisoners; and four days afterward colonel Monistrol transmitted me a letter from the secretary of sir Edward Pellew, containing the extract of a despatch to the captain-general, and two letters of a more recent date from the admiral himself. One of these, addressed upon His Majesty's service, was as follows.

H. M. ship Duncan, Madras Roads, 21st June, 1807.

Sir,

Two days ago I renewed my application to the captain-general De Caen in your favour, requesting that His Excellency would permit of your departure from the Isle of France, and suggesting the opportunity now offered by His Majesty's ship Greyhound.

I have since received despatches from England, containing the letter of which a copy is now inclosed, from Mr. Marsden, secretary of the Admiralty,* therewith transmitting instructions for your release under the authority of the French minister of marine, to the captain-general of the French establishments.

I congratulate you most sincerely on this long protracted event; and I trust, if your wishes induce you to proceed to India, that you may be enabled to embark with captain Troubridge, for the purpose of proceeding to England from hence by the first opportunity.

(Signed.) Edward Pellew.

[* COPY.

The accompanying letter is understood to contain a direction from the French government for the release of captain Flinders. It has already been transmitted to the Isle of France in triplicate; but as it may be hoped that the vessels have been all captured, you had better take an opportunity of sending this copy by a flag of truce, provided you have not heard in the mean time of Flinders being at liberty.

Admiralty, 30th Dec. 1806. (Signed) William Marsden.]

The admiral's second letter was a private one, inviting me to take up my residence in his house at Madras, until such time as the departure of a King's ship should furnish an opportunity of returning to England; and was accompanied by one from captain Troubridge, expressing the pleasure he should have in receiving me; but the Greyhound had already been sent away two days! and nothing announced any haste in the general to put the order into execution. I then wrote to request His Excellency would have the goodness to confirm the hopes produced by these letters; or that, if they were fallacious, he would be pleased to let me know it. It was seven days before an answer was given; colonel Monistrol then said, "His Excellency the captain-general has charged me to answer the letter which you addressed to him on the 24th of this month; and to tell you that, in effect, he has received through the medium of His Excellency sir Edward Pellew, a despatch from His Excellency the minister of the marine and the colonies of France, relative to you. I am also charged to send you the copy, herewith joined, of that letter; and to inform you that so soon as circumstances will permit, you will fully enjoy the favour which has been granted you by his Majesty the

Emperor and King." This long expected document from the marine minister was literally as follows.*

[* The document, in French, is not included in this ebook.]

It appeared from this letter, that so long before as July 1804, the council of state had come to a decision upon my case; which was, *to approve of the conduct of general De Caen, and from a pure sentiment of generosity, to grant my liberty and the restitution of the Cumberland*. This decision had lain over until March 1806, before it was made efficient by the approval of the French emperor; it had then been sent in triplicate by French vessels; and it seemed very extraordinary that in July 1807, the quadruplicate sent from England in December, round by India, should first arrive, when two or more vessels had come from France in the preceding twelve months.

Colonel Monistrol's letter gave me to understand that the order would be executed, but the time when, and the manner, were left in uncertainty; I therefore requested a permission to go to town for the arrangement of my affairs, hoping there to learn some further particulars; this however was refused, the answer being, "that when the time of my departure should be fixed," a permission would be granted for as many days as were necessary. Whence this delay in executing the minister's order could arise, I knew not; but having heard that the Cumberland had been removed from her usual place, and fearing that her reparation and refitment might be the cause, a letter was sent to inform colonel Monistrol, [AUGUST 1805] "that the impossibility of obtaining any better vessel for a direct passage to England could alone have induced me to undertake it in the Cumberland; and that unless His Excellency denied me any other means of quitting the Isle of France, it was not my intention to re-embark in her. If therefore it were His Excellency's desire that she should be restored to me, rather than her value, I hoped he would admit of her being sold; and allow me to take a passage on board some ship bound to America or India;" a request for the restitution of my books and papers was also made, that the intervening time might be employed in arranging them from the disorder into which they had been thrown at the shipwreck, four years before. At the end of three weeks, a letter from the colonel invited me to go to town, that he might restore the books and papers, with the other objects relating to my voyage of discovery; and on presenting myself at his office, the trunk into which they had been put was given up; my sword and spy-glasses were to be returned at the time of departure, as also the amount of the schooner and her stores, which had been valued soon after my arrival. On asking for the two boxes of despatches, the colonel said they had long been disposed of, and he believed that something in them had contributed to my imprisonment; and to an application for the remaining journal, he replied that it was wanted for the purpose of making extracts, at which I expressed surprise, seeing that it had been in the general's possession near four years, and the French government had made its decision. On requesting to know if it were intended to let me embark in the Wellesley cartel, then in port, it appeared that this had not been thought of; and the colonel hinted, that the order for my liberation had been given at a moment when England and France were in better intelligence than usual, and perhaps would not be granted to an application made at the present time; and it appeared from his conversation, that the restitution of my papers was not to be considered an assurance of a speedy departure.

After quitting colonel Monistrol, I examined the condition of the papers, and then sent him the following note and receipt.

I have the honour to inclose a receipt for the books and papers received yesterday. The rats have made great havock amongst them, and many papers are wholly destroyed; but so far as I have yet examined, those which are of the most importance seem to have wholly, or in part escaped their ravages. I shall return immediately within the limits of my parole, according to the directions of His Excellency the captain-general; to wait the time when he shall be pleased to execute the orders which his Imperial and Royal Majesty thought proper to give on March 11, 1806, for my liberation; and I have the honour to be, etc.

Received from colonel Monistrol, *chef de l'état-major-général* in the Isle of France, one trunk containing the remainder of the books, papers, etc. taken from me in Port North-West on Dec. 17, 1803, and Dec. 21 of the same year; which books and papers, with those received at two different times in 1804, make up the whole that were so taken, with the following exceptions.

1. Various letters and papers either wholly or in part destroyed by the rats, the remains of which are in the trunk.

2. The third volume of my rough log book, containing the journal of transactions and observations on board the Investigator, Porpoise, the Hope cutter, and Cumberland schooner, from sometime in June to Dec. 17, 1803, of which I have no duplicate.

3. Two boxes of despatches. The one from His Excellency governor King of New South Wales, addressed to His Majesty's principal secretary of state for the colonies; the other from colonel Paterson, lieutenant-governor of Port Jackson, the address of which I cannot remember.

In truth of which I hereunto sign my name, at Port Napoleon,* Isle of France., this 24th day of August 1807.

Matthew Flinders.
Late commander of H. M. sloop Investigator,
employed on discoveries to the South Seas with a French passport.

[* Port Louis, after having been changed to Port de la Montagne, Port North-West, and I believe borne one or two other names, was now called Port Napoleon; Port Bourbon and Isle Bourbon underwent similar changes: such was the inflexibility of French republicanism.]

Messrs Le Blanc and Stock, the commander and commissary of the Wellesley cartel, having a house in the town, I took this opportunity of seeing them; and it was agreed between us, that when the cartel was allowed to sail, Mr. Stock should make an official request for my embarkation with him. As, however, there was much reason to apprehend a refusal, I arranged a great part of the books and papers just received, with all the Port-Jackson letters, and sent them on board the Wellesley; writing at the same time [SEPTEMBER 1807] to Sir Edward Pellew my suspicion, that general De Caen would not execute the order he had received from the marine minister. This precaution was not useless, for in the beginning of October the Wellesly was sent away suddenly; and although she had been detained three months, not a prisoner was given in exchange for those brought from India. Mr. Stock left a copy of the letter he had written, as was agreed, and of the answer from the general's secretary; this said, "the captain-general is very sorry that he cannot allow captain Flinders to embark in the cartel Wellesley. So soon as circumstances will permit, that officer will be set at liberty, and to that effect be sent to London." The most direct means of conveyance to London in time of war, was assuredly by the way of France; but two vessels, the first of which was commanded by the brother of the captain-general, had sailed a short time before for that destination; so that this answer, if not false, was at least equivocal. My opinion of the general's unfair dealing had induced me to write by the last of these French vessels to the minister of the marine, representing the little probability there was of his order being executed; but this vessel was captured, and my letter most probably thrown overboard.

An attempt to gain some knowledge of what were the captain-general's intentions was made in the following letter, written on the 16th, to colonel Monistrol.

Sir,

You will do me a favour in transmitting the log book which was detained for the purpose of making extracts from it, as they have doubtless been made long since. At the same time, Sir, you would relieve me from much inquietude, if you could inform me of the time at which it is the intention of His Excellency the captain-general to grant me the liberty which His Imperial and Royal Majesty was pleased to accord in March 1806. BY your letter of July 27 last, I was led to hope from the expression, "vous jouirez pleinement de la faveur," etc., that this long desired period would soon arrive. What the circumstances are to which you allude in that letter, it is impossible for me to know; nor is it within my imagination to conceive the circumstances which permit vessels to sail for India or America, but which cannot allow of my departure.

The desire expressed by His Excellency to captain Bergeret and M. Beckmann, to receive orders relating to me, and to the latter that he was sensible of the hardship of my situation, led me to hope that he would have taken into consideration the length of time that my detention had continued, the misfortune which preceded it, and the time elapsed since the date of the marine minister's letter; and I still intreat him to take them into his consideration. I have suffered much, Sir, in the Isle of France, and the uncertainty in which I have ever been kept has been one of the bitterest ingredients in the cup; I thought it exhausted when you favoured me with the copy of the letter from His Excellency the minister; but the dregs remained, and it seems as if I must swallow them to the last drop.

If the means of my return to England cause any part of the delay, I beg to inform you of my readiness to embrace any means, or any route, in the Cumberland even, if it will save time, or in any other vessel of any nation. A passage on board the finest ship one month hence, would not indemnify me for one month longer of suffering, such as the last forty-six have been.

I am fully persuaded that no representation of mine can change the arrangements of the captain-general; if therefore the time and manner of my return be absolutely fixed, I have only to request that he will have so much charity as to impart them; or even the time only, when I may expect to see myself out of this fatal island; for the manner, when compared to the time, becomes almost indifferent. To know at what period this waste of the best years of my life was to end, would soften the anguish of my mind; and if you would favour me with the return of my log book, I should have an occupation which would still further tend to diminish it.

I request you to accept the assurances of consideration with which I have the honour to be, etc.

The answer received eight days afterward, said not a word of the log book; but simply that "so soon as a convenient opportunity for my departure presented itself, the captain-general would order it to be communicated;" which was evidently no more than an evasion, for vessels had gone to France, and others were at that very time sailing every week, either to India or America, in any one of which a passage might have been obtained. I was now induced to enter into the examination whether, in justice and honour, my parole ought to continue to be a restraint from quitting the island; it had been given to general De Caen as the representative of the French government--that government had ordered me to be set at liberty--and nothing was alleged for not putting the order into execution, other than the want of a convenient opportunity; had I not then a right to seek that opportunity for myself, since the captain-general had let pass so many without indicating any one of them? This question was debated a long time, and under every point of view, before deciding upon the line of conduct which duty to my country, my family and myself prescribed to be right.

Many letters for India, and a copy of my narrative for sir Edward Pellew had been confided to my Swiss friend, M. Boand, who was to have embarked in the Wellesley; but at the moment of sailing, the captain-general gave an order to prevent his going on board; the good man went immediately to ask an audience of His Excellency, and after discussing his own case, spoke of my imprisonment and tried to learn when it would cease. That he could obtain nothing decisive, was to be expected; but that the general should preserve his temper during this conversation, and even answer gaily, though equivocally, to several closely-put questions, was contrary to what usually happened when my name had been mentioned before him. M. Boand was permitted to embark in a Danish ship, which sailed early on the 24th; but late in the evening before, some police officers went on board, searched his trunk, and took away all the letters they could find, telling him he might then sail, they had got what they wanted. This transaction explained the general's views in preventing M. Boand's departure in the cartel, where a search could not decently have been made; also why the cartel had been sent off so suddenly that my letters could not be put on board, and the cause of his moderation when speaking of my imprisonment. He was not deceived in supposing this friend would be the bearer of many letters, though very much so if he hoped to find therein proofs of my having acted, or intending to act contrary to the passport; he however missed his aim altogether, as I learned some months afterward; the cautious Swiss had separated my letters from those he had received from other persons, and these last only were found; but it was not less evident, that general De Caen was seeking all means to fortify himself with pretexts to avoid setting me at liberty.

DECEMBER 1807

This year finished in the same manner as the preceding, without the least change in my situation; but if I had reason to complain of the want of justice, humanity, and good faith in the captain-general, there was, on the other hand, great cause to be satisfied with the sustained attentions of the inhabitants in my small circle, especially of those in the house where I still continued to dwell; and it was some consolation to see, that the interest generally taken in my liberation increased with every fresh act denoting perseverance in rigorous measures.

JULY 1808

Six other months had elapsed when two vessels came from France, and it was known that the captain-general's brother had safely reached Paris; he had sailed two months after the order for my liberty had arrived, and as the general had probably communicated his intentions to the marine minister, he might have received fresh directions; I therefore wrote to the chief of the staff, requesting to know whether the despatches contained any thing to give me hopes of early liberty, and repeating my readiness to embark in any vessel of any nation; but it was answered, that nothing in the despatches related to this subject.

SEPTEMBER 1808

Several ships being in preparation to depart for France in September, a memorial containing the circumstances previous to and attending my imprisonment was made out, with authenticating papers annexed, to be transmitted to the minister of the French marine; in this, I explained the late conduct of the captain-general, and earnestly entreated that His Excellency would direct him to send me to France, by an order couched in such terms as should leave no room for evasion; declaring at the same time, perhaps incautiously, that I considered his previous order to have released me from parole. Two copies of this memorial were confided to gentlemen who promised to deliver them in person to the minister; or in case of being taken, to the captain of the English man of war who would forward them to the Admiralty. There still remained La Semillante, an old frigate sold to the merchants, on board of which two officers of the French navy were to go as passengers. This afforded the most desirable opportunity of sending me to France, if such had been the general's intention; and to do away all after pretext of not knowing it to be my wish, another request was made to that effect [OCTOBER 1808]; with a proposition to engage, "in case La Semillante should not arrive at her destination, to take the most direct means that could be found of reaching France, and giving myself up into the hands of the government; should it be judged expedient to require from me such a parole." In answer to this letter, it was then said for the first time, fifteen months after receiving the order for my liberty, that the captain-general, "having communicated to His Excellency the marine minister the motives which had determined him to suspend my return to Europe, he could not authorise my departure before having received an answer upon the subject." Thus the frequently expressed desire of general De Caen to receive orders, and the promise, when they arrived, that I should be set at liberty so soon as circumstances would permit, were shown to be fallacious; and the so long expected order to be of none effect. The reasoning of the inhabitants upon this suspension was, that having been so long in the island, I had gained too much knowledge of it for my departure to be admitted with safety; but if this were so, the captain-general was punishing me for his own oversight, since without the detention forced by himself, the supposed dangerous knowledge could not have been acquired. In calling it an oversight I am probably wrong. When the general suffered me to quit the Garden Prison, he expected the order which afterwards arrived; and what appeared to be granted as an indulgence, was perhaps done with a view to this very pretext of my too extended knowledge of the island; a pretext which could scarcely have been alleged so long as I remained shut up in prison.

NOVEMBER 1808

One of the naval officers who embarked in La Semillante had served in the expedition of captain Baudin; he took charge of a triplicate of my memorial to the marine minister, and promised to use his efforts in obtaining for it a powerful support. This triplicate was accompanied by many letters, addressed to distinguished characters in the ministry, the senate, in the council of state and the national institute; as well from myself as from several worthy persons who interested themselves in the issue of my detention. By this and another opportunity, I stated to the Admiralty and the president of the Royal Society the circumstances attending the order which had arrived; and from these various steps united, my friends in Mauritius conceived the hope of a success almost certain; but from having been so often deceived I was less sanguine, and saw only that if this memorial and these letters failed, there was little hope of being restored to liberty before the uncertain epoch of peace.

1809

Constant occupation was, as usual, my resource to beguile the time until the effect of the memorial and letters could be known. Being furnished by some friends with several manuscript travels and journals in the interior, and along the coasts of Madagascar, I constructed a chart of the northern half of that extensive island, accompanied with an analytical account of my materials; and in this employment, reading various French authors, mathematical studies, and visiting occasionally some of the inhabitants within my circle, this time of anxious suspense passed not unprofitably. In the month of March [MARCH 1809] arrived the frigate La Venus, captain Hamelin, the same who had commanded Le Naturaliste at Port Jackson. His affairs, or some other cause, prevented him from seeing or writing to me; but he told M. Pitot that many persons took an interest in my situation, and that several officers of Le Géographe and Naturaliste had made applications to the marine minister. The answers they received had constantly been, that orders were sent out to Mauritius to set me at liberty and restore the Cumberland; yet it was known in France before captain Hamelin sailed, that these orders had not been executed, and the future intentions of the government were unknown. The publication of the French voyage of discovery, written by M. Peron, was in great forwardness; and the emperor Napoléon considering it to be a national work, had granted a considerable sum to render the publication complete. From a Moniteur of July 1808, it appeared that French names were given to all my discoveries and those of captain Grant on the south coast of Terra Australis; it was kept out of sight that I had ever been upon the coast; and in speaking of M. Peron's first volume the newspapers asserted, that no voyage *ever* made by the English nation could be compared with that of the Géographe and Naturaliste. It may be remembered, that after exploring the South Coast up to Kangaroo Island, with the two gulphs, I met captain Baudin, and gave him the first information of these places and of the advantages they offered him; and it was but an ill return to seek to deprive me of the little honour attending the discovery. No means were spared by the French government to enhance the merit of this voyage, and all the officers employed in it had received promotion; but the Investigator's voyage seemed to obtain as little public notice in England as in France, no one of my officers had been advanced on their arrival, and in addition to so many years of imprisonment my own promotion was suspended. It would ill become me to say that in one case there was an ostentatious munificence, or in the other, injustice and neglect; but the extreme difference made between the two voyages could not but add to the bitterness of my situation, and diminish the little remaining hope of being speedily and honourably liberated.

A vessel from St. Malo arrived in May, and gave information that one of the ships which carried a duplicate of my memorial to the marine minister, had reached France; and in a few days La Bellone, a frigate in which the brother of the captain-general was an officer, got into Port Louis; she had sailed in the end of January and brought despatches, but if the general received any new order by this or the former vessel, it was kept to himself. In June the English cruisers sent in a flag of truce with a French lady, taken in L'Agile from St. Malo; this lady brought many letters, in some of which the arrival in France of La Semillante was mentioned; also that Bonaparte was at Paris when L'Agile sailed, and that the naval officer who carried the last copy of my memorial had been promoted and made a member of the legion of honour. I did now certainly entertain hopes that general De Caen would have received an order to set me at liberty, and that no further pretext for prolonging my detention would be admitted; but week after week passed as before, without any intimation of this so much desired event.

JULY 1809

There was reason to believe that a direct application to know whether any order had arrived, would obtain no answer; therefore after waiting a month, I wrote to ask "whether His Excellency would permit my wife to come and join me, should she present herself before Port Napoléon." It was not in reality my intention that she should leave England, but I hoped to draw the desired information from the answer; and in six weeks [SEPTEMBER 1809], after another vessel had arrived from France, one was given to the following effect: "The captain-general will not oppose the residence of your wife in the colony; but with respect to a safe conduct, it is necessary that Mrs. Flinders should apply to the ministers of His Britannic Majesty, who should make the request to those of His Majesty the Emperor and King;" which was equivalent to saying, either that no fresh order to set me at liberty had been received, or that it would not be put into execution.

At this time there was much talk of an attack upon the island, said to be projected by the British government; and all the English officers, prisoners of war, were taken from their paroles and closely shut up. In the middle of the month our cruisers quitted the island unexpectedly, and a fortnight afterwards it was known that they gone to Bourbon, and made an attack upon the town of St. Paul; both the town and bay were then in their possession, as also La Coraline frigate and two Indiamen her prizes, upon which this government had counted for supplying its deficiency of revenue. During the attack, great disorders had been committed by the black slaves, and the humane care of commodore Rowley and his captains had alone prevented greater excesses; this intelligence put a stop to the raising of regiments of slaves for the defence of Mauritius, which the captain-general had commenced under the name of African battalions, much against the sense of the inhabitants. These various circumstances, with the distress of the government for money, caused much agitation in the public mind; and it was to be apprehended that general De Caen would scarcely suffer me to remain with the usual degree of liberty, whilst all the other prisoners were shut up. I endeavoured by great circumspection to give no umbrage, in order to avoid the numberless inconveniences of a close imprisonment; but in the beginning of October [OCTOBER 1809] a letter came from colonel Monistrol, saying that "His Excellency the captain-general having learned that I sometimes went to a considerable distance from the habitation of Madame D'Arifat, had thought proper to restrain my permission to reside in the interior of the colony on parole, to the lands composing that habitation." This order showed that the general had either no distinct idea of a parole of honour, or that his opinion of it differed widely from that commonly received; a parole is usually thought to be a convention, whereby, in order to obtain a certain portion of liberty, an officer promises not to take any greater; but general De Caen seemed to expect me to be bound by the convention, whilst he withdrew such portion of the advantages as he thought proper, and this without troubling himself about my consent. If any doubts remained that the order of the French government had in strict justice liberated me from parole, this infraction by the captain-general was sufficient to do them away; nevertheless the same reasons which had prevented me declaring this conviction long before, restrained the declaration at this time; and I returned the following answer to colonel Monistrol, written in French that no pretext of bad translation might afterwards be alleged.

Sir,

Yesterday at noon I had the honour of receiving your letter of the 1st. inst. It is true that I have sometimes profited by the permission contained in the parole which I had given (que j'avais donnée) on Aug 23, 1805, by which I was allowed to go as far as two leagues from the plantation of Madame D'Arifat; but since His Excellency the captain-general has thought good to make other regulations, I shall endeavour to conduct myself with so much prudence respecting the orders now given, that His Excellency will not have any just cause of complaint against me.

I have the honour to be, etc.

The two objects I had in view in giving this answer, were, to promise nothing in regard to my movements, and to avoid close imprisonment if it could be done without dishonour; had it been demanded whether I still considered the parole to be in force, my answer was perfectly ready and very short, but no such question was asked. Many circumstances had given room to suspect, that the captain-general secretly desired I should attempt an escape; and his view in it might either have been to some extraordinary severity, or in case his spies failed of giving timely information, to charging me with having broken parole and thus to throw a veil over his own injustice. Hence it might have been that he did not seek to know whether, being restricted to the plantation of Madame D'Arifat, I still admitted the obligatory part of the parole to be binding; and that the expression in my answer--*the parole which I had given*, implying that it existed no longer, passed without question. However this might be, I thenceforward declined accepting any invitations beyond the immediate neighbourhood of the plantation; and until the decisive moment should arrive, amused by solitude with instructing the two younger sons of our good family in the elements of mathematical science, with inventing problems and calculating tables that might be useful to navigation, and in reading the most esteemed French authors.

After the evacuation of the town and bay of St. Paul at Bourbon, the blockade of Mauritius was resumed by commodore Rowley with increased strictness. The frigate La Canonnière and the prize formerly H. M. ship Laurel, which the want of a few thousand dollars had induced the government to let for freight to the merchants, were thus prevented sailing; and a cartel fitted long before to carry the English prisoners to the Cape of Good Hope, and waiting only, as was generally supposed, for the departure of these two ships, was delayed in consequence. When captains Woolcombe and Lynne of the navy had been desired in August to keep themselves in readiness, I had committed to the obliging care of the latter many letters for England, and one for admiral Bertie at the Cape; but instead of being sent away, these officers with the others were put into close confinement, and their prospects retarded until the hurricane season, when it was expected the island would have a respite from our cruisers.

DECEMBER 1809

In the beginning of December, despatches were said to have arrived from France, and the marine minister having received my memorial in the early part of the year, full time had been given to send out a fresh order; but disappointment on such arrivals had been so constant during greater part of the six years to which my imprisonment was now prolonged, that I did not at this time think it worth asking a question on the subject. A British cartel, the Harriet, arrived from India on the 12th, with the officers of La Piémontaise and La Jena; the Harriet was commanded by Mr. John Ramsden, formerly confined with me in the Garden Prison, and the commissary of prisoners was Hugh Hope, Esq., whom Lord Minto had particularly sent to negotiate an exchange with general De Caen. The cartel had been stopped at the entrance of the port by the blockading squadron, and been permitted to come in only at the earnest request of Mr. Hope and the parole of the prisoners to go out again with him should the exchange be refused. In a few days I received an open letter from Mr. Stock, the former commissary; and having learned that Mr. Hope proposed to use his endeavours for my release, a copy of all the letters to and from colonel Monistrol, subsequent to the marine minister's order, was transmitted, that he might be better enabled to take his measures with effect; and towards the end of the month, a letter from the commissary informed me of the very favourable reception he had met with from the captain-general, of the subject of my liberty having been touched upon, and of his entertaining hopes of a final success. The flattering reception given to Mr. Hope had been remarked to me with surprise from several hands; but a long experience of general De Caen prevented any faith in the success of his application for my release: I feared that Mr. Hope's wishes had caused him to interpret favourably some softened expressions of the general, which he would in the end find to merit no sort of confidence.

JANUARY 1810

La Venus frigate, after her exploit at Tappanouli, got into the Black River on the first of January, notwithstanding the presence of our cruisers; she had on board a part of the 69th regiment, with the officers and passengers of the Windham, including five ladies, and announced the capture of two other ships belonging to the East-India Company; and two days afterward, the frigates La Manche and La Bellone entered Port Louis with the United Kingdom and Charleston, the Portuguese frigate Minerva, and His Majesty's sloop Victor (formerly La Jena). This was a most provoking sight to commodore Rowley, whom baffling winds and his position off the Black River prevented stopping them; whilst the joy it produced in the island, more especially amongst the officers of the government who had been many months without pay, was excessive. The ordinary sources of revenue and emolument were nearly dried up, and to have recourse to the merchants for a loan was impossible, the former bills upon the French treasury, drawn it was said for three millions of livres, remaining in great part unpaid; and to such distress was the captain-general reduced for ways and means, that he had submitted to ask a voluntary contribution in money, wheat, maize, or any kind of produce from the half-ruined colonists. Promises of great reform in the administration were made at that time; and it was even said to have been promised, that if pecuniary succour did not arrive in six months, the captain-general would retire and leave the inhabitants to govern themselves; and had the frigates not returned, or returned without prizes, it seemed probable that such must have been the case.*

[* According to information from various sources, the prizes brought to Mauritius were disposed of in this manner. The proceeds went first into the hands of the government, which took ten per cent. as a duty upon the sales, and afterwards one-third of the remainder as its proper right. Sixty per cent. remained for the captors, but the necessities of the state being generally urgent, it took thirty more, giving bills for the amount on the treasury of France; and for the remaining portion, it was parted with so reluctantly that the inferior officers and seamen were seldom able to obtain a dollar; but they were offered other bills, and these they were glad to sell for almost any thing to the inhabitants. This was the distribution to the frigates; the prizes brought in by privateers were not so profitable to the government, its claims being limited, I believe, to the ten per cent. duty and one-third of the remainder.]

The hurricane season was now arrived; and the Canonnière and Laurel having taken advantage of our cruisers being at a little distance to get out at night, the British squadron abandoned the island. Expecting then that the cartel for the Cape of Good Hope would be sent away, I augmented the number of letters for England and the Cape in the hands of captain Lynne; and transmitted to him the greater part of my books and clothes, which he had the goodness to send on board with his own. So many vessels had arrived from France, and amongst them two during this month of January, without producing any fresh information, that almost all hope from my memorial to the marine minister had ceased; and should the captain-general send me in this cartel, contrary to expectation, then my effects were already on board. She sailed on the 29th, with captains Woolcombe and Lynne and the commanders of the Company's ships Windham, Charleston and United Kingdom, and their officers; captain W. Owen of the Sea Flower and the remaining English officers were reserved for the Bengal cartel, commanded by Mr. Ramsden; and with respect to the seamen and soldiers, a part only of the crews of the Laurel and Sea Flower, and of the 69th regiment were left, many of them having been seduced from their allegiance to enlist in the French service.

CHAPTER IX.
A prospect of liberty, which is officially confirmed.
Occurrences during eleven weeks residence in the town of Port Louis and on board the Harriet cartel.
Parole and certificates.
Departure from Port Louis, and embarkation in the Otter.
Eulogium on the inhabitants of Mauritius.
Review of the conduct of general De Caen.
Passage to the Cape of Good Hope, and after seven weeks stay, from thence to England.
Conclusion.
[AT MAURITIUS. WILHEMS PLAINS.]
JANUARY 1810
The French cartel for the Cape of Good Hope had sailed two days when a packet boat arrived with despatches from Bayonne, and from the unusual degree of secrecy observed respecting them, some persons were willing to suppose that orders to set me at liberty formed part of their contents; of this, the most prudent mode to gain information was to wait patiently for the sailing of the English cartel for India, when my embarkation therein or being again left the sole British prisoner in the island, would afford a practical solution of the question. In the time of waiting for this event, I revised some notes upon the magnetism of the earth and of ships, and considered the experiments necessary to elucidate the opinions formed from observations made in the Investigator; and I was thus occupied

when, on March 13th [MARCH 1810], a letter came from Mr. Hope, the commissary of prisoners, to inform me that he had obtained the captain-general's promise for my liberty, and departure from the island with him in the Harriet. This unhoped for intelligence would have produced excessive joy, had not experience taught me to distrust even the promises of the general; and especially when, as in the present case, there was no cause assigned for this change in his conduct.

I dared not therefore allow my imagination to contemplate a meeting with my family and friends as likely to soon take place, nor to dwell upon any subject altogether English; the same preparation however was made for a departure, as if this promise were expected to be fulfilled. It was reported that the Harriet would sail within a fortnight after two frigates and a sloop should have gone out upon a cruise; and as these ships sailed on the 14th, the official information of my liberty, if really granted, might be expected daily.

It will be believed that I sought on all hands to learn whether any thing had transpired from the government to bespeak an intention of suffering me to go in the cartel; but it was without success, and every person endeavoured to discourage the hope, with a friendly design of softening another probable disappointment. They argued, that for general De Caen to let me go at this time, when I knew so much of the island and an attack upon it was expected, would be to contradict all the reasons hitherto given for my detention; and therefore, that unless he had received a new and positive order, he could not with any degree of consistency set me at liberty. This state of suspense, between hope and apprehension, continued until the 28th, when an express from the town, sent by M. Pitot, brought the following welcome information from colonel Monistrol.

His Excellency the captain-general charges me to have the honour of informing you, that he authorises you to return to your country in the cartel Harriet, on condition of not serving in a hostile manner against France or its allies during the course of the present war.

Receive, I pray you, Sir, the assurance of the pleasure I have in making you this communication, and of the sentiments of perfect consideration with which I have the honour to be, etc.

P. S. The cartel is to sail on Saturday next (31st.)

Being then satisfied of the intention to permit my return to England, though the cause of it was involved in mystery, I visited our immediate, and still almost incredulous neighbours, to take leave of them; and wrote letters to the principal of those more distant inhabitants, whose kindness demanded my gratitude. Early next morning a red flag with a pendant under it, showing one or more of our ships to be cruising before the port, was hoisted upon the signal hills; this was an unwelcome sight, for it had been an invariable rule to let no cartel or neutral vessel go out, so long as English ships were before the island. I however took leave of the benevolent and respectable family which had afforded me an asylum during four years and a half; and on arriving at my friend Pitot's in the town, was met by Messrs. Hope and Ramsden, neither of whom knew any other reason for setting me at liberty than that the captain-general had granted it to Mr. Hope's solicitations.

[AT MAURITIUS. PORT LOUIS.]

On waiting upon colonel Monistrol on the 30th, it appeared that nothing had been done relative to the Cumberland, or to returning what had been taken away, particularly the third volume of my log book so often before mentioned; he promised however to take the captain-general's pleasure upon these subjects, and to repeat my offer of making and signing any extracts from the book which His Excellency might desire to preserve. In the evening I had the pleasure to meet a large party of my countrymen and women, at a dinner given by M. Foisy, president of the Society of Emulation; and from the difficulty of speaking English after a cessation of four years, I then became convinced of the possibility of a man's forgetting his own language.

APRIL 1810

There were lying in port two Dutch and one American vessel, with a number of Frenchmen on board, whom marshal Daendels, governor of the remaining Dutch possessions in the East, had engaged to officer some new regiments of Malays; these vessels waited only for the absence of our cruisers to go to Batavia; and that we might not give information of them was the alleged cause for detaining the cartel all the month of April, our squadron keeping so close off the port that they dared not venture out.

MAY 1810

On May 2, captain Willoughby of the Néréide made a descent upon the south side of the island, at Port Jacotet; where he cut out L'Estafette packet boat, spiked the guns of the fort, carried off the officer with two field pieces, and M. Etienne Bolger, commandant of the quarter of La Savanne, the same who had acted so ungraciously on my arrival at the Baye du Cap. This *sullying of the French territory* produced a fulminating proclamation from general De Caen, nearly similar in terms to that of the emperor Napoléon after the descent at Walcheren; its effect on the inhabitants, however, was not much, for on asking some of them what they thought of this second-hand gasconade, the reply was, "Oh it is not to us, it is to Bonaparte that the proclamation is addressed;" meaning that it was a bait to catch his approbation. Three days afterwards a flag of truce was sent out to negotiate an exchange for M. Bolger and the officer who had commanded the fort, for whom twenty soldiers of the 69th regiment were given; we afterwards learned that a proposal had been made to let the cartel sail, provided the squadron would suffer her to pass without being visited; but to this arrangement captain Pym, the then senior officer, refused his consent.

An order was given on the 8th for all the British officers to embark in the cartel, and we hoped to sail immediately; but the merchants of the town presented a petition to the captain-general for a delay, lest we might give information of the expected arrival of some ships from France. Our cruisers were stationed purposely to stop every French vessel, whether going in or out, and this petition therefore seemed to be ridiculous; it appeared however to be complied with, for we not only were prevented sailing, but denied all communication with the inhabitants for several weeks; and the five ladies on board were as much subjected to these restrictions as the officers. The French cartel returned from the Cape of Good Hope on the 10th, with exchanged prisoners; and the former reports of a projected attack on Mauritius and Bourbon were so strongly revived that general De Caen made a tour of the island, in order, as was said, to have batteries erected at all the landing places without defence, and to strengthen the existing fortifications. On the 18th, an exchange was made with the squadron of sixteen soldiers and people out of the prison on shore, for the commander and some others of L'Estafette; but nothing transpired relative to the sailing of the cartel.

JUNE 1810

June 2, a salute of twenty-one guns was fired to celebrate the marriage of the French emperor with the princess Maria Louisa of Austria. This intelligence, accompanied with that of the capture of La Canonniere, was brought by a ship from Bourdeaux, which had succeeded in getting into the Black River, as had L'Atrée frigate some weeks before. The entrance of these vessels at the time that five or six of our ships were cruising round the island, affords additional proof of the impossibility of blockading it effectually, without a much more extensive force than so small a spot can be thought to deserve. Mauritius owes this advantage principally to its numerous hills; from whence vessels at sea are informed by signal of the situation of the cruisers, and are thus enabled to avoid them.

On the 7th, a parole made out by the English interpreter was brought on board for me to sign; and at daylight of the 18th a pilot came to take the cartel out of harbour, and we received forty-six seamen of the Sea Flower and soldiers of the 69th; my sword was then delivered back, and the following duplicate of the parole was given, with a certificate annexed from colonel Monistrol.

I undersigned, captain in His Britannic Majesty's navy, having obtained leave of His Excellency the captain-general to return in my country by the way of Bengal, promise on my word of honour not to act in any service which might be considered as directly or indirectly hostile to France or its allies, during the course of the present war.

Matthew Flinders.

Je soussigné certifie que monsieur Mathieu Flinders, capitaine des vaisseaux de Sa Majesté Britannique, a obtenu l'autorisation de Son Excellence le capitaine-général De Caen de retourner dans sa patrie, aux conditions énoncées ci-dessus, dont le double est resté entre mes mains.

Au Port Napoléon, Isle de France, le 7 Juin 1810.
L'adjutant commt., chef de l'état-major-gen.
(Signed) Monistrol.

I had much feared to be laid under the obligation of going to India, and of thus losing some months of time and incurring a considerable and useless expense; but although the parole expresses the "having obtained leave to return by the way of Bengal," neither the part containing my promise nor the certificate of colonel Monistrol specified any particular route; and the officer of the staff who delivered this duplicate, said he supposed I should not lose time in going to India, but proceed to the Cape in the first vessel sent in by the squadron.

Frequent mention has been made of attempts to procure back the third volume of my journal, the sole book remaining in the hands of the captain-general. Twice during my residence in the town these attempts had been renewed, but with no better effect than were my applications respecting the Cumberland; nor would certificates be given of the refusal either of these objects or of the Port-Jackson despatches. I therefore requested Mr. Hope to certify the steps which had been taken, that the Admiralty and Secretary of State might be satisfied of every thing in my power having been done; and this he did in the following terms.

This is to certify to whomsoever it may concern, that after having succeeded in executing that part of the instructions of His Excellency lord Minto, governor-general of British India, relating to the liberation of Matthew Flinders, Esq., late commander of His Majesty's ship Investigator, who had been detained more than six years in the Isle of France, I did, at the request of captain Flinders, make a personal application to His Excellency general De Caen for the third volume of the log book of his voyage of discovery, which that officer represented to be still kept from him by His Excellency. That the answer to this was a positive refusal, both of the book and of permission to take a copy of it; and the reason given for this refusal was, that captain F. *not being set at liberty in consequence of any orders from France*, every thing relating to this log book and to his little schooner Cumberland must remain to be settled between the French and British governments in Europe.

I do further certify that captain Flinders did, in my presence, apply to the chief of the staff in the Isle of France, for certificates of the above log book and schooner being refused to be given up; and also for a certificate of two boxes of despatches having been taken on his arrival in this island, in December 1803, and that I have since made a similar application to the same officer for the said certificates; but which have been refused for the same alleged reason as before given to me by His Excellency the captain-general De Caen.

Witness my hand on board the Harriet cartel, in Port Napoléon,
Isle of France, this 9th of June 1810.
(Signed) H. HOPE,
Commissary and agent of the British government in India
for the exchange of prisoners.

It may probably be asked, what could be general De Caen's object in refusing throughout to give up this log book, or to suffer any copy to be taken? I can see no other reasonable one, than that the statements from it, sent to the French government as reasons for detaining me a prisoner, might have been partial and mutilated extracts; and he did not choose to have his accusations disproved by the production either of the original or an authentic copy. Besides this book and the little schooner, I lost a cask containing pieces of rock collected from different parts of Terra Australis, the two spy-glasses taken in the Garden Prison, and various small articles belonging to myself; but I was too happy at the prospect of getting out of the island to make any difficulty upon these heads.

[OFF MAURITIUS.]

On the same morning that the pilot came on board, the anchors were weighed; but in swinging out, the ship touched the ground, and hung till past four in the afternoon. During this time we saw L'Estafette coming in with a flag of truce from the squadron; and the boat that went to meet her was returning when the cartel had floated off, and sail was made. We were a good deal alarmed at what might be the subject of L'Estafette's communication, and particularly anxious to get without side of the port before any counter order should come from the general; at sunset it was effected, the French pilot left us, and after a captivity of six years, five months and twenty-seven days, I at length had the inexpressible pleasure of being out of the reach of general De Caen.

Three frigates and a sloop of war composed the squadron cruising before the port; but instead of coming to speak us for information, as was expected, we observed them standing away to the southward; a proceeding which could be reconciled only upon the supposition, that commodore Rowley had sent in an offer not to communicate with the cartel. This was too important an affair to me to be let pass without due inquiry; my endeavours were therefore used with Mr. Ramsden, the commander, to induce him to run down to the ships; and this was done, on finding they persisted in stretching to the southward. At nine o'clock Mr. Ramsden went in a boat to the Boadicea, but was desired to keep off; a letter was handed to him for the commissary, containing a copy of one sent in by L'Estafette, wherein it was proposed, if general De Caen would suffer the cartel to sail, that she should not be visited by any ship under the commodore's orders. Mr. Hope replied that the cartel had not come out in consequence of this proposal, nor had the boat reached the shore at the time; and this point being clearly ascertained, a communication was opened, and I applied for a passage to the Cape of Good Hope. It happened fortunately, that the Otter sloop of war was required to go there immediately with despatches; and the commodore having satisfied himself that no engagement of the commissary opposed it, complied with my request. Next day I took leave of Mr. Hope, to whose zeal and address I owed so much, and wished my companions in the cartel, with her worthy commander, a good voyage; and after dining with commodore Rowley, embarked in the evening on board the Otter with captain Tomkinson.

On bidding adieu to Mauritius, it is but justice to declare that during my long residence in the island, as a marked object of suspicion to the government, the kind attention of the inhabitants who could have access to me was invariable; never, in any place, or amongst any people, have I seen more hospitality and attention to strangers--more sensibility to the misfortunes of others, of what ever nation, than here--than I have myself experienced in Mauritius. To the names of the two families whose unremitting kindness formed a great counterpoise to the protracted persecution of their governor, might be added a long list of others whose endeavours were used to soften my captivity; and who sought to alleviate the chagrin which perhaps the strongest minds cannot but sometimes feel in the course of years, when reflecting on their far-distant families and friends, on their prospects in life indefinitely suspended, and their hopes of liberty and justice followed by continual disappointment; and to the honour of the inhabitants in general be it spoken, that many who knew no more than my former employment and my misfortunes, sought to render me service by such ways as seemed open to them. The long continuation and notorious injustice of my imprisonment had raised a sensation more strong and widely extended than I could believe, before arriving at Port Louis to embark in the cartel; when the number of persons who sought to be introduced, for the purpose of offering their felicitations upon this unexpected event, confirmed what had been before said by my friends; and afforded a satisfactory proof that even arbitrary power, animated by strong national prejudice, though it may turn aside or depress for a time, cannot yet extinguish in a people the broad principles of justice and humanity generally prevalent in the human heart.

Some part of my desire to ascertain the motives which influenced general De Caen to act so contrary to the passport of the first consul, and to the usages adopted towards voyages of discovery, may perhaps be felt by the reader; and he may therefore not be displeased to see the leading points in his conduct brought into one view, in order to deducing therefrom some reasonable conclusion.

On arriving at Mauritius after the shipwreck, and producing my passport and commission, the captain-general accused me of being an impostor; took possession of the Cumberland with the charts and journals of my voyage, and made me a close prisoner. On the following day, without any previous change of conduct or offering an explanation, he invited me to his table.

All other books and papers were taken on the fourth day, and my imprisonment confirmed; the alleged cause for it being the expression in my journal of a desire to become acquainted with *the periodical winds, the port, and present state of the colony*, which it was asserted were contrary to the passport; though it was not said that I knew of the war when the desire was expressed.

After three months seclusion as a *spy*, I was admitted to join the prisoners of war, and in twenty months to go into the interior of the island, on *parole*; I there had liberty to range two leagues all round, and was unrestricted either from seeing any person within those limits or writing to any part of the world. It might be thought, that the most certain way of counteracting my desire to gain information alleged to be contrary to the passport, would have been *to send me from the island*; but general De Caen took the contrary method, and kept me there above six years.

His feeling for my situation, and desire to receive orders from the French marine minister had been more than once expressed, when at the end of three years and a half, he sent official information that the government granted my liberty and the restitution of the Cumberland; and this was accompanied with the promise, that I, so soon as circumstances would permit, I should fully enjoy the favour which had been granted me by His Majesty the Emperor and "King;" yet, after a delay of *fifteen months*, an application was answered by saying, "that having communicated to His Excellency the marine minister the motives which had determined him to suspend my return to Europe, he could not authorize my departure before having received an answer upon the subject;" in twenty months more, however, he let me go, and declared to Mr. commissary Hope that it was *not in consequence of any orders from France*.

When first imprisoned in 1803, for having expressed a wish to learn the present state of the colony, there was no suspicion of any projected attack upon it; in 1810, preparations of defence were making against an attack almost immediately expected, and there were few circumstances relating to the island in which I was not as well informed as the generality of the inhabitants; then it was, after giving me the opportunity of becoming acquainted with the town and harbour of Port Louis, that general De Caen suffered me to go away in a ship bound to the place whence the attack was expected, and without laying any restriction upon my communications.

Such are the leading characteristics of the conduct pursued by His Excellency general De Caen, and they will be admitted to be so far contradictory as to make the reconciling them with any uniform principle a difficult task; with the aid however of various collateral circumstances, of opinions entertained by well informed people, and of facts which transpired in the shape of opinions, I will endeavour to give some insight into his policy; requesting the reader to bear in mind that much of what is said must necessarily depend upon conjecture.

After the peace of Amiens, general De Caen went out to Pondicherry as captain-general of all the French possessions to the east of the Cape of Good Hope; he had a few troops and a number of extra officers, some of whom appear to have been intended for seapoy regiments proposed to be raised, and others for the service of the Mahrattas. The plan of operations in India was probably extensive, but the early declaration of war by England put a stop to them, and obliged His Excellency to abandon the brilliant prospect of making a figure in the annals of the East; he then came to Mauritius, exclaiming against the perfidy of the British government, and with a strong dislike, if not hatred to the whole nation. I arrived about three months subsequent to this period, and the day after M. Barrois had been sent on board Le Géographe with despatches for France; which transaction being contrary to the English passport, and subjecting the ship to capture, if known, it was resolved to detain me a short time, and an embargo was laid upon all neutral ships for ten days. It would appear that the report of the commandant at La Savanne gave some suspicion of my identity, which was eagerly adopted as a cause of detention; I was therefore accused at once of imposture, closely confined, and my books, papers, and vessel seized. Next day another report arrived from La Savanne, that of major Dunienville; from which, and the examination I had just undergone, it appeared that the accusation of imposture was untenable; an invitation to go to the general's table was then sent me, no suspicion being entertained that this condescension to an Englishman, and to an officer of inferior rank, might not be thought an equivalent for what had passed. My refusal of the intended honour until set at liberty, so much exasperated the captain-general that he determined to make me repent it; and a wish to be acquainted with the present state of Mauritius being found in my journal, it was fixed upon as a pretext for detaining me until orders should arrive from France, by which an imprisonment of at least twelve months was insured. The first motive for my detention therefore arose from the infraction previously made of the English passport, by sending despatches in Le Géographe; and the probable cause of its being prolonged beyond what seems to have been originally intended, was to punish me for refusing the invitation to dinner.

The marine minister's letter admits little doubt that general De Caen knew, on the return of his brother-in-law in January 1805, that the council of state at Paris, though approving of his conduct, proposed granting my liberty and the restitution of the Cumberland; and he must have expected by every vessel to receive orders to that effect; but punishment had not yet produced a sufficient degree of humiliation to make him execute such an order willingly. When the exchange was made with commodore Osborn in the following August, it became convenient to let me quit the Garden Prison, in order to take away the sentinels; captain Bergeret also, who as a prisoner in India had been treated with distinction, strongly pressed my going into the country; these circumstances alone might possibly have induced the captain-general to take the parole of one who had been detained as a spy; but his subsequent conduct leaves a strong suspicion that he proposed to make the portion of liberty, thus granted as a favour, subservient to evading the expected order from France, should such a measure be then desirable. At length the order arrived, and three years and a half of detention had not produced any very sensible effect on his prisoner; the execution of it was therefore suspended, until another reference should be made to the government and an answer returned. What was the subject of this reference could not be known, but there existed in the island only one conjecture; that from having had such a degree of liberty during near two years, I had acquired a knowledge of the colony which made it unsafe to permit my departure.

Extensive wars were at this time carrying on in Europe, the French arms were victorious, and general De Caen saw his former companions becoming counts, dukes, and marshals of the empire, whilst he remained an untitled general of division; he and his officers, as one of them told me, then felt themselves little better circumstanced than myself--than prisoners in an almost forgotten speck of the globe, with their promotion suspended. Rumours of a premeditated attack at length reached the island, which it was said the captain-general heard with pleasure; and it was attributed to the prospect of making military levies on the inhabitants, and increasing his authority by the proclamation of martial law; but if I mistake not, the general's pleasure arose from more extended views and a more permanent source. If the island were attacked and he could repulse the English forces, distinction would follow; if unsuccessful, a capitulation would restore him to France and the career of advancement. An attack was therefore desirable; and as the captain-general probably imagined that an officer who had been six years a prisoner, and whose liberty had been so often requested by the different authorities in India, would not only be anxious to forward it with all his might, but that his representations would be attended to, the pretexts before alleged for my imprisonment and the answer from France were waved; and after passing six weeks in the town of Port Louis and five on board a ship in the harbour, from which I had before been debarred, he suffered me to depart in a cartel bound to the place where the attack was publicly said to be in meditation. This is the sole motive which, upon a review of the general's conduct, I can assign for being set at liberty so unexpectedly, and without any restriction upon my communications; and if such a result to an attack upon Mauritius were foreseen by the present count De Caen, captain-general of Catalonia, events have proved that he was no mean calculator. But perhaps this, as well as the preceding conjectures on his motives may be erroneous; if so, possibly the count himself, or some one on the part of the French government may give a more correct statement--one which may not only reconcile the facts here brought together, but explain many lesser incidents which have been omitted from fear of tiring the patience of the reader.

[CAPE OF GOOD HOPE.]

I thought it a happy concurrence of circumstances, that on the same day we quitted Port Louis in the cartel, the arrival of a frigate from India should require commodore

Rowley to despatch the Otter to the Cape of Good Hope. Captain Tomkinson took his departure on the 14th at nine in the evening, from Cape Brabant, with a fresh trade wind and squally weather; at noon next day the island Bourbon was in sight, and the breakers on the south-east end distinguishable from the deck; but thick clouds obscured all the hills. The winds from south-east and north-east carried us to the latitude 27° and longitude 49°; they were afterwards variable, and sometimes foul for days together, and we did not make the coast of Africa until the 3rd of July [JULY 1810]. Being then in latitude 34° 52' and longitude 25½°, the hills were descried at the distance of twenty leagues to the northward; and the water being remarkably smooth, the lead was hove, but no bottom found at 200 fathoms. A continuance of western winds obliged us to work along the greater part of the coast, and Cape Agulhas was not seen before the 10th; we then had a strong breeze at S. E., and Cape Hanglip being distinguished at dusk, captain Tomkinson steered up False Bay, and anchored at eleven at night in 22 fathoms, sandy bottom. In this passage of twenty-six days from Mauritius, the error in dead reckoning amounted to 1° 18' south and 2° 21' west, which might be reasonably attributed to the current.

On the 11th we ran into Simon's Bay, and captain Tomkinson set off immediately for Cape Town with his despatches to vice-admiral Bertie and His Excellency the earl of Caledon; he took also a letter from me to the admiral, making application, conformably to my instructions, for the earliest passage to England; and requesting, if any circumstance should place general De Caen within his power, that he would be pleased to demand my journal from him, and cause it to be transmitted to the Admiralty. I went on shore next morning and waited upon colonel sir Edward Butler, the commanding officer at Simon's Town; and learning that an India packet had put into Table Bay, on her way to England, made preparation for going over on the following day. At noon, however, a telegraphic signal expressed the admiral's desire to see me immediately; and as the packet was expected to stop only a short time, I hoped it was for the purpose of embarking in her, and hastened over with horses and a dragoon guide furnished by the commandant; but to my mortification, the packet was standing out of Table Bay at the time I alighted at the admiral's door, and no other opportunity for England presented itself for more than six weeks afterward.

During the tedious time of waiting at Cape Town for a passage, I received much polite attention from His Excellency the earl of Caledon, and Mr. Alexander, secretary to the colony; as also from the Hon. general Grey, commander of the forces, commissioner Shield of the navy, and several other civil and military officers of the Cape establishment. I made little excursions to Constantia and in the neighbourhood of the town; but feared to go into the interior of the country lest an opportunity, such as that which the India packet had presented, might be lost. Towards the latter end of August [AUGUST 1810], captain Parkinson of the army and lieutenant Robb of the navy arrived from commodore Rowley's squadron, with intelligence of the island Bourbon being captured; and a cutter being ordered to convey them to England, I requested of the admiral and obtained a passage in her.

SEPTEMBER 1810

We sailed from Simon's Bay on the 28th August, in the Olympia, commanded by lieutenant Henry Taylor; and after a passage of fourteen days, anchored in St. Helena road on the afternoon of September 11; and having obtained water and a few supplies from the town, sailed again the same night. On the 16th, passed close to the north side of Ascension, in the hope of procuring a turtle should any vessel be lying there; but seeing none, steered onward and crossed the Line on the 19th, in longitude 19½° west. The trade wind shifted to the S. W. in latitude 5° north, and continued to blow until we had reached abreast of the Cape-Verde Islands, as it had done at the same time of year in 1801. At my recommendation lieutenant Taylor did not run so far west as ships usually do in returning to England, but passed the Cape-Verdes not further distant than sixty leagues; we there met the north-east trade, and on the 29th Mr. Taylor took the brig Atalante from Mauritius.

[IN ENGLAND]

OCTOBER 1810

On reaching the latitude 22¾° north and longitude 33° west, the north-east trade veered to east and south-eastward, which enabled us to make some easting; and being succeeded by north-west winds, we passed within the Azores, and took a fresh departure from St. Mary's on the 15th of October. Soundings in 75 fathoms were obtained on the 21st, at the entrance of the English Channel; but it then blew a gale of wind from the westward, and obliged us to lie to on this, as it did on the following night; and it was greatly feared that the cutter would be driven on the coast of France, near the Casket rocks. In the morning of the 23rd, the wind being more moderate, we made sail to the northward, and got sight of the Bill of Portland; and at five in the evening came to an anchor in Studland Bay, off the entrance of Pool Harbour, after a run from St. Helena of six weeks; which in an indifferent sailing vessel, very leaky, and excessively ill found, must be considered an excellent passage.

Captain Parkinson and lieutenant Robb went off the same night with their despatches; and next morning we ran through the Needles and came to at Spithead, where the prize brig, from which we had been long separated, had just before dropped her anchor. I went on shore to wait upon admiral sir Roger Curtis, and the same evening set off for London; having been absent from England nine years and three months, and nearly four years and a half without intelligence from any part of my connexions.

The account of the Investigator's voyage, and of the events resulting from it is concluded; but there is one or two circumstances which the naval reader may probably desire to see further explained.

A regulation adopted at the Admiralty forbids any officer to be promoted whilst a prisoner, upon the principle apparently, that officers in that situation have almost always to undergo a court martial, which cannot be done until they are set at liberty. My case was made subject to this regulation, although it required no court martial; and was moreover so different to that of prisoners in general, that nothing similar perhaps ever occurred. In consequence of my French passport, not only was the possibility of reaping any advantage from the war done away, but the liberation on parole or by exchange, granted to all others in Mauritius, was refused for years, the passport removing me from the class of prisoners of war; yet one of the greatest hardships to officers of a state of warfare was at the same time applied to me in England, and continued throughout this protracted detention. So soon as it was known that I had been released, and was arrived at the Cape of Good Hope, a commission for post rank was issued; and on my representations to the Right Hon. Charles Yorke, first lord commissioner of the Admiralty, by whom I had the honour to be received with the condescension and feeling natural to his character, he was pleased to direct that it should take date as near to that of general De Caen's permission to quit Mauritius, as the patent which constituted the existing Board of Admiralty would allow. A more retrospective date could be given to it only by an order of the King in council; unhappily His Majesty was then incapable of exercising his royal functions; and when the Regency was established, my proposed petition did not meet with that official encouragement which was necessary to obtain success. It was candidly acknowledged, that my services in the Investigator would have been deemed a sufficient title to advancement in 1804, had I then arrived in England and the Admiralty been composed of the same members; but no representation could overcome the reluctance to admitting an exception to the established rule; thus the injustice of the French governor of Mauritius, besides all its other consequences, was attended with the loss of six years post rank in His Majesty's naval service.

One of my first cares was to seek the means of relieving some relations of my Mauritius friends, prisoners of war in England; and in a few months, through the indulgence of the Admiralty and of the earl of Liverpool, secretary of state for the colonies, I had the gratification of sending five young men back to the island, to families who had shown kindness to English prisoners.

The Board of Admiralty was pleased to countenance the publication of the Investigator's voyage by providing for the charts and embellishments; and a strong representation was made by its directions to the French government, upon the subjects of my detained journal, the schooner Cumberland, and the parole exacted on quitting Mauritius. A release from the parole was transmitted in April 1812, after three applications; but upon the other points it was answered, that "the vessel of captain Flinders was at the Isle of France at the capitulation of that colony, and returned in consequence to the power of the English government. With respect to the journal of that navigator, as it did not make part of the papers brought from the Isle of France by the prefect of that colony, a demand has been made for it to the captain-general De Caen, who is with the army. In default of an answer he will be again written to, and so soon as it shall be remitted, my first object will be to send it." The Cumberland had been seized in 1803, and the capitulation was made in 1810; in the interval, both vessel and stores, if not used, would be in great part rotten; but I saw the Cumberland employed in the French service, and believe that the stores were also. General De Caen, it appeared, still kept the log book in his own hands; although, if considered to be private property, it was undoubtedly mine, and if as a public document it ought to have been given up at the capitulation, or at least to have been deposited in the office of the marine minister. But the captain-general had probably his reasons for not wishing even the minister to see it; and up to this time, the commencement of 1814, he has so far persevered against both public and private applications, that neither the original nor a copy has been obtained.

APPENDICES.
APPENDIX I.
ACCOUNT OF THE OBSERVATIONS BY WHICH THE LONGITUDES OF PLACES ON THE EAST AND NORTH COASTS OF TERRA AUSTRALIS HAVE BEEN SETTLED.

In the Appendix to Vol. I. a statement was made of the circumstances under which the observations for settling the longitudes of places on the South Coast were taken; as also of the method used in the calculations, and the corrections applied more than what is usual in the common practice at sea. That statement is equally applicable to the following tables for the East and North Coasts, and the explanation of their different columns is the same; a reference therefore to the former Appendix will render unnecessary any further remark on these heads.

The first observations on the East Coast were taken at Port Jackson, and the results would naturally form the first table of this Appendix; but these observations being so intimately connected with those on the South Coast that the time keepers could not receive their final corrections without them, the Port-Jackson table became an indispensable conclusion to the former series; and it is thought unnecessary to repeat it in this place.

APPENDIX II.
ON THE ERRORS OF THE COMPASS ARISING FROM ATTRACTIONS WITHIN THE SHIP, AND OTHERS FROM THE MAGNETISM OF LAND; WITH PRECAUTIONS FOR OBVIATING THEIR EFFECTS IN MARINE SURVEYING.

[Not included in this ebook.]

APPENDIX III.
GENERAL REMARKS, GEOGRAPHICAL AND SYSTEMATICAL, ON THE BOTANY OF TERRA AUSTRALIS. BY ROBERT BROWN, F. R. S. ACAD. REG. SCIENT. BEROLIN. CORRESP., NATURALIST TO THE VOYAGE.
A LIST OF PLANTS NATIVE BOTH OF TERRA AUSTRALIS AND OF EUROPE.

DESCRIPTION OF PLANTS FIGURED IN THE ATLAS.
[Appendix III. not included in this ebook.]
END OF VOLUME II

Detail from Plate 10

Detail from Plate XVIII.

Detail from Plate VII.

Printed in Great Britain
by Amazon

44084989R00129